T0334111

THEORIES OF VALUE FROM
ADAM SMITH TO PIERO SRAFFA

This book presents a comprehensive account of more than 200 years of controversy on the classical theories of value and distribution. The author focuses on four, perhaps the most critical classics — Adam Smith's *Wealth of Nations*, David Ricardo's *Principles of Political Economy*, Karl Marx's *Capital* and Piero Sraffa's *Production of Commodities by Means of Commodities*. The book highlights several significant differences in the widely celebrated theories of the four authors as it searches for the 'classical standpoint' that separates them from the 'moderns'. It also challenges canonical interpretations to analyse their flaws and weaknesses, in addition to the already obvious strengths, and critically engages with the major alternative interpretations and criticisms of the theories.

With a new Afterword that follows up on the debates and developments since the first edition, this book will appeal to scholars and academics of economic theory and philosophy, as well as to the general reader.

Ajit Sinha is Professor of Economics at Azim Premji University, Bengaluru, India. He has published extensively on the history of economic theory. He is also the author of *A Revolution in Economic Theory: The Economics of Piero Sraffa* (2016) and *Essays on Theories of Value in the Classical Tradition* (forthcoming).

"Ajit Sinha's *Theories of Value from Adam Smith to Piero Sraffa* exemplifies the best characteristics of proper scholarship. Sinha has combined critical yet sympathetic analysis of primary sources with keen understanding of the secondary literature. He has definite points of view which are always established by deep analytical arguments combined with careful attention to the relevant evidence. His book is a splendid example for all those interested in the best ways of understanding the relevant links between the past of our discipline and the present."

— **G.C. Harcourt**, *Emeritus Reader in the History of Economic Theory, University of Cambridge, Professor Emeritus, University of Adelaide, Emeritus Fellow, Jesus College, University of Cambridge*

"The excess confidence of contemporary economists in the strength of the existing body of their knowledge has been struck by the recent crisis. The same excess confidence had often fed the belief that the history of ideas did not matter. In fact, the understanding of the limits of any knowledge in the field of social sciences cannot be separated from the understanding of the conditions of its construction. The work of Ajit Sinha, as conveyed in the present book, provides a brilliant illustration of the fact that the history of economic thought, on the one hand, and economic analysis, on the other, are neither antagonistic, nor substitutes, but necessary complements."

— **Roger Guesnerie**, *Honorary Professor and Ex. Chair, Economic Theory and Social Organisation, Collège de France, Paris, Founding President, Paris School of Economics*

"This excellent book will be of interest to a wide range of scholars, especially historians of economic thought, and also heterodox economists in general. ... I learned a good deal from reading this book, especially about Sraffa's theory, and I recommend it highly despite my disagreements with some of its interpretations, especially about Marx's theory. The quality of scholarship is high throughout. Sinha states in the Preface that he hopes that his book will be particularly useful for graduate students and young scholars, and I think it will be."

— **Fred Moseley**, *Review of Political Economy*

"Readers of Ajit Sinha can look forward to a lively and engaging discourse that displays the author's meticulous scholarship and breadth of vision. Both graduate students and teachers of political economy will find in the book an excellent reader on the state of the art in classical and Marxian theories of prices. They are also themes that we may hope will shape the future course of economic science."

— **G. Omkarnath**, *Economic and Political Weekly*

THEORIES OF VALUE FROM ADAM SMITH TO PIERO SRAFFA

SECOND EDITION
With a new Afterword

Ajit Sinha

LONDON AND NEW YORK

First published 2010 by Routledge
Second edition published 2019 by Routledge

2 Park Square, Milton Park, Abingdon, Oxon, OX14 4RN
605 Third Avenue, New York, NY 10017

Routledge is an imprint of the Taylor & Francis Group, an informa business

First issued in paperback 2020

British Library Cataloguing-in-Publication Data
A catalogue record for this book is available from the British Library

Library of Congress Cataloging-in-Publication Data
A catalog record has been requested for this book

ISBN: 978-1-138-33801-2 (hbk)
ISBN: 978-0-367-78701-1 (pbk)

Typeset in Sabon
by Apex CoVantage, LLC

Dedicated to my parents
Satyabhama Sinha and the late *Dr B.P. Sinh*a
and also for
Anne and Alice

CONTENTS

PREFACE TO
THE SECOND EDITION

I am happy that Routledge has decided to bring out a second edition of the *Theories of Value from Adam Smith to Piero Sraffa*. It is a testimony not only to how well the book was received by the wider audience but more importantly to the fact that the intellectual community's interest in classical economic theory is alive and well. Though the book received a few positive and sympathetic reviews, many reviews, mostly coming from the 'Sraffian quarters', ranged from unsympathetic to hostile, particularly to my chapter on Sraffa. In the Afterword to this edition, I have responded to my critics in the hope of clarifying and furthering the understanding of intricate theoretical and interpretive issues involved. It has been eight years since the first edition was published and it is natural that my own ideas on various issues dealt with in the book have gone through further development and refinement. In this context, I would only mention a few later publications of mine that the reader may find useful to consult along with this book. On Smith: 'Centrality of "corn" in Adam Smith's Theory of Value' in *Essays on Theories of Value in the Classical Tradition*, 2018, Cham: Palgrave Macmillan; on Ricardo: 'A Comment on Sraffa's "Classical Economics"', *Cambridge Journal of Economics*, 2017, 41(2), pp. 661–677, also reprinted in the *Essays on Theories of Value in the Classical Tradition*; on Marx: 'On Marx's law of the falling rate of profit: disentangling some entangled variables', *Review of Radical Political Economics*, 2014, 46(2), pp. 184–89, also reprinted in the *Essays on Theories of Value*; and on Sraffa: *A Revolution in Economic Theory: The Economics of Piero Sraffa*, 2016, Cham: Palgrave Macmillan.

It is natural for an author to want to tinker with old publications but following the good advice of the publisher, I have refrained from fiddling with the text and have kept the changes only to minor typo corrections. I, however, must point out to one 'non-typo' mistake that had slipped through my fingers last time and remains in the text because of technical reasons related to reprinting. There is a widespread misunderstanding that Sraffa's Standard commodity solves Ricardo's problem of the 'invariable measure of value'. In the famous 'Introduction' to Ricardo's *Principles*, Sraffa (1951) argued that Ricardo was worried that the size of the pie appears to change with changes in how the pie is cut when it is measured by any arbitrary commodity as the Standard of measure. This happens because the measuring Standard itself gets affected with changes in how the pie is divided. Therefore, Ricardo looked for an 'invariable measure of value', which will ensure that the size of the pie remains constant while it is cut in different proportions: 'If measured in such a standard, the average price of all commodities, and their aggregate value, would remain unaffected by a rise or fall of wages' (Sraffa 1951, pp. xliv-xlv). The general misunderstanding is that Sraffa's Standard commodity developed in his book (Sraffa 1960) solves this problem, that is, when the Standard commodity is used to measure the prices and wages then the size of the net output of an economic system remains constant with respect to changes in the rate of profits or the wages. I had accepted this general misunderstanding without much reflection while I was writing this book and it shows up on page 101 in the footnote 24. Now I am convinced that this is a mistake. Sraffa's Standard commodity does not solve Ricardo's 'problem', if that was Ricardo's problem. What Sraffa's Standard commodity ensures is that the *ratio* of net output to capital remains constant with respect to changes in the rate of profits or wages and not the size of the net output itself. Sraffa himself clarifies this in para 32 of his book (Sraffa 1960, p. 23).

Bengaluru
April 2018

PREFACE TO
THE FIRST EDITION

In the 'Preface' to the *Production of Commodities*, Piero Sraffa wrote:

> The investigation [in the *Production of Commodities*] is con-
> cerned exclusively with such properties of an economic system
> as do not depend on changes in the scale of production or in
> proportions of 'factors'.

> This standpoint, which is that of old classical economists from
> Adam Smith to Ricardo, has been submerged and forgotten
> since the advent of the 'marginal' method (Sraffa 1960: v).

It was Sraffa's bold claim of a paradigm shift in the history of economics that inspired me to read these four classics closely. I found
two points in Sraffa's claim highly intriguing. First of all, any casual
reader of classics is struck by the preponderance of dynamic analysis
and concern for change in their treatises. So how could Sraffa ascribe
to them a standpoint that does not admit change? What is this standpoint, after all? Second, why Marx is absent from the list? This book
is a result of those preliminary questions.

In the modern version of what Sraffa has characterised as the
'marginal method' the values of commodities are determined by the
techniques of production in use. However, those techniques are determined by the factor prices (or the distribution of income) that are
themselves, in the last instance, determined by the subjective pattern
of our demand for consumption goods; for example, if demand shifts
in favour of relatively 'labour intensive' consumption goods then,
given total labour supply, it will raise the wage rate and cause *changes*
in techniques of production in the direction of 'capital intensity' and
hence changes in the prices of goods. Thus the question: 'do the classical economists determine the distribution of income within the context

of a theory of prices and resource allocation or do they take it as *given* from outside the system of price determination?' has become contentious among the historians of economic theory.

In the following pages, we keep this question in mind as we read the four classics. Though the book is inspired by Sraffa's *Production of Commodities*, it is neither designed to 'prove' Sraffa right nor someone wrong. It simply presents a close reading of the theories of value and distribution of, what I consider, the four most significant 'surplus approach' economists of the past, namely, Adam Smith, David Ricardo, Karl Marx and Piero Sraffa. The book is somewhat unique in its organisation, as it first presents in Part I my reading of the theories of value and distribution found in the four classics: the *Wealth of Nations*, the *Principles of Political Economy*, *Capital* and the *Production of Commodities*. In Part II, it critically engages with the major alternative interpretations and criticisms of their theories, starting from their contemporaries all the way to our contemporaries in almost chronological order. The attempt is to present a comprehensive account of more than 230 years of theoretical controversy on the subject. It is, however, not a work of encyclopaedic nature. Its aim is to throw new light on some old questions and introduce new and controversial interpretations in the literature on the subject.

The unconventional organisation of the book was chosen for two reasons. First of all, by separating my voice from several other contending voices as much as possible, I have tried to increase clarity in its presentation. Second, some readers may have only casual interest in the subject and not in the specific and intricate controversies among the historians of economic thought. Such readers could simply decide to read the first parts of the chapters and get a somewhat informed and coherent story without having to shift through the long controversies. I also hope that the separation of my critical survey of the literature from my reading of the classics would be particularly helpful to graduate students. In the end, I must warn my readers that in these pages my approach has been to read the classics and not the minds of their authors.

A substantial part of this book was written during my two years' visit to Collége de France, Paris, and I am really grateful to Professor Roger Guesnerie for giving me an opportunity to write a book of this nature. Roger has not only been highly encouraging but also very generous with his time whenever I needed to discuss certain theoretical issues or bounce off certain ideas. Professor Geoffrey Harcourt has been most supportive of me since the day we met in Australia more than a decade ago. It was his invitation to visit Cambridge University as a visiting scholar in 1998 that made it possible for me to read

Sraffa's unpublished notes, without which this book would not have been possible. Geoff has read every word of this book throughout its progress and has been extremely kind with his encouraging words. Professors Samuel Hollander and John King have also read most parts of the book during its progress. Sam's and John's long and penetrating reviews of my chapters have been most valuable to me. I am also thankful to Professor Pierangelo Garegnani, the literary executor of Sraffa's unpublished papers, for allowing me to quote from Sraffa's unpublished notes and to the very friendly and helpful staff of the Wren library at Trinity College, Cambridge, where Sraffa-Papers are housed.

Over the years several scholars have read some parts of the draft of the book or discussed one issue or the other with me. Though it would be difficult to mention all those who I have gained from, I will be starkly remiss in my duty if I don't express my sincere thanks to Richard Arena, Carlo Benetti, Christian Bidard, Jérôme de Boyer, Murray Brown, Paul Cockshott, Daniel Diatkine, Michel-Stéphane Dupertuis, Gilbert Faccarello, Duncan Foley, Pierangelo Garegnani, Steve Keen, Heinz Kurz, Catherine Martin, Stéphane Moulin, G. Omkarnath, Antoine Rebeyrol, Paul Samuelson, Paul Zarembka, and an anonymous reviewer for the Routledge Press. In this context, I would especially like to remember the late P.R. Brahmananda, with whom I had several long discussions and dozens of e-mail exchanges on the nature of Sraffa's work.

Jean Bernard, Maurice Bernard and Claude Henry have been very helpful in finding me the right contacts in France and I thank them for their help, without which this book might have remained just an idea. In the end, I thank my wife, Anne Maugier-Sinha, for the translations of some quotations from the original French texts and for putting up with me during these difficult years.

The reader will find that the book throughout engages critically with two leading contemporary combatants in the field of history of economic theory, namely, Pierangelo Garegnani and Samuel Hollander. It is because, apart from Sraffa, they are the two I have learnt most from.

Paris
March 2009

1

THE THEORY OF VALUE IN ADAM SMITH'S *WEALTH OF NATIONS*

Part I

Why Value?

In the 'Introduction and Plan of the Book' of the *Wealth of Nations*, Adam Smith does not mention anything pertaining to the question of value. The first four brief paragraphs explain the nature or the purpose of the book, which is to establish that the true nature of the wealth of a nation lies in its per capita real income and that it depends largely upon two things: (*i*) the productivity of its labour, and (*ii*) its division of total labour into productive employment and unproductive employment. Of the two, the first is much more important than the second. The rest of the five paragraphs are devoted to explaining the division of the work into five 'books'. The first book deals with the causes of improvement in labour productivity and the distribution of the total product among different classes. The second deals with the nature of capital and its investment in employing productive and unproductive labour. The third deals with the natural course of development of a nation and the various government policies that in one way or another favour one sector over others and thus interfere with the natural course of development. The fourth is a critique of two great economic doctrines: Mercantilism and Physiocracy. And the fifth and last book deals with the issues of public finance in great detail.

The problem of value or prices of commodities is nevertheless broached at the end of Chapter IV in Book I. The reader is entreated for 'patience and attention', for the 'subject' is 'in its own nature extremely abstracted' (p. 46, all the references to *WN* are from 1981 Library Fund edition). The topic occupies three full chapters from V to VII. His deliberation on the question of value is sandwiched between his deliberations on the causes that lead to increase in labour productivity and the distribution of total product among the three classes. It would

1

appear from the design of the scheme that the problem of value had to be resolved before an understanding of the distribution of income could be developed. However, the questions that Adam Smith poses to himself at the end of Chapter IV suggest something entirely different. The problems for Chapters VI and VII are stated as:

> ... what are the different parts of which this real price is composed or made up, ...

> And lastly, what are the different circumstances which sometimes raise some or all of these different parts of price above, and sometimes sink them below their natural or ordinary rate; or, what are the causes which sometimes hinder the market price, that is, the actual price of commodities, from coinciding exactly with what may be called their natural price (p. 46).

Here, the first statement seems to treat prices as a dependent variable made up of various parts. It would therefore appear that the discovery of those parts would be essential for the investigation of the principle that regulates the exchangeable values of commodities. The second statement apparently confirms the methodology indicated above; here the causes for market prices deviating from their natural prices are identified with the circumstances that raise or sink the levels of its parts from their natural levels. Thus, apparently, while the natural price is determined by the natural levels of its parts, the subject matter of the determination of the natural levels of those parts belongs to the investigation of the distribution of the total product. On the other hand, however, we frequently come across such statements as:

> In every society the price of every commodity finally resolves itself into some one or other, or all of those three parts; and in every improved society, all the three enter more or less, as component parts, into price of the far greater part of commodities (p. 68).

Here, price 'resolving' itself into three parts would imply that price is the independent variable while distribution is the dependent one. But reference to three parts as components of price implies that it is the other way round. Modern readers of Adam Smith are constantly faced with such 'contradictory' juxtapositions and it would be helpful for them to keep in mind that the epistemological foundation of Smith's theory is not necessarily the same as theirs. We will take up this issue at the end of our reading. At the end of Chapter IV, paragraph 12, Adam Smith writes: 'What are the rules which men naturally observe in exchanging them [commodities] either for money or for one another, I shall now proceed to examine. These rules determine what may be called the relative or exchangeable value of goods' (p. 44). By the phrase 'the rules which men naturally observe', Adam Smith could mean some kind of social convention that men naturally observe, such as the convention to drive on either the right or left side of the road. However, in paragraph 14, he goes on to say: 'In order to investigate the principles which regulate the exchangeable value of commodities, I shall en-deavour to shew ...' (p. 46). Here, the word 'principle' apparently points in the direction of some sort of a theory, i.e., the 'investigation of the principles' may amount to a discovery of the variables and their relations that regulate the exchangeable value of commodities.

Measure of Value

Be that as it may, the *problematique* of Chapter V is introduced as 'what is the real measure of this exchangeable value; or, wherein consists the real price of all commodities', and is entitled, 'Of the Real and Nominal Price of Commodities, or of their Price in Labour, and their Price in Money'. As is obvious from the title, from the very outset Smith declares that the real price of a commodity is in terms of labour, whereas its nominal price is in terms of money. The question is: What does Smith mean by 'real price' and 'labour'? Before we investigate this question, it is important to note that for Smith the problem of distinguishing the 'real price' from 'nominal price' arises only in the context of comparison of value over a period of time or across spaces. As he writes:

> At the same time and place the real and the nominal price of all commodities are exactly in proportion to one another. The more or less money you get for any commodity, in the London market, for example, the more or less labour it will at that time and place enable you to purchase or command. At the same time and place, therefore, money is the exact measure of the real exchangeable value of all commodities. It is so, however, at the same time and place only (p. 55).

Thus the *problematique* of the chapter is apparently not concerned with the determination of exchangeable value of commodities in a market at any given point in time; rather, it is concerned with the measure of changes in the value of a commodity over a period of time in a given market. Smith notes that though the exchangeable value of every commodity is frequently estimated by the quantity of money, like any other commodity the money commodity is itself exposed to variation in its price. Thus when it comes to an estimation of the changes in the value of a commodity over a period of time, the money commodity turns out to be an unsatisfactory measure:

> [A]s a measure of quantity, such as the natural foot, fathom, or handful, which is continually varying in its own quantity, can never be an accurate measure of the quantity of other things; so a commodity which is itself continually varying in its own value, can never be an accurate measure of the value of other commodities (p. 50).

It is in this context that he proposes *labour* as the 'real measure' of value or the price of a commodity estimated in terms of labour as its 'real price'.

Now let us see why Adam Smith considers the price of a commodity estimated in terms of labour as its 'real' price. He argues:

> The real price of every thing, what every thing really costs to the man who wants to acquire it, is the toil and trouble of acquiring it. What every thing is really worth to the man who has acquired it, and who wants to dispose of it or exchange it for something else, is the toil and trouble which it can save to himself, and which it can impose upon other people. What is bought with money or with goods is purchased by labour as much as what we acquire by the toil of our own body. That money or those goods indeed save us the toil. They contain the value of a certain quantity of labour which we exchange for what is supposed at the time to contain the value of an equal quantity. Labour was the first price, the original pur-chase-money that was paid for all things. It was not by gold or by silver, but by labour, that all the wealth of the world was originally purchased; and its value, to those who possess it and who want to exchange it for some new production, is precisely equal to the quantity of labour which it can enable them to purchase or command (pp. 47–48).

Clearly the reason for labour to be the real price lies in the fact that stripped of all social relations, production remains a relation between the labourer and nature. In this relationship the labourer is the *subject*. He pays a price through toil or sacrifice of his comfort to acquire a commodity. This is the original price and thus the real price of the commodity to the *labourer*. It should be, however, also noted that in this context Adam Smith maintains that:

> What is bought with money or with goods is purchased by labour as much as what we acquire by the toil of our own body. That money or those goods indeed save us the toil. They contain the value of a certain quantity of labour which we exchange for what is supposed at the time to contain the value of an equal quantity (ibid.).

This is a statement of a pure labour theory of value — a statement that will recur in the next chapter as well.

Now when one places the commodity within a social relation and asks what the real price of the commodity is, then it is not clear who is the subject of this question. Is it still the labourer who needs to acquire this commodity or the owner of the commodity who needs to exchange it for some other commodity or direct labour services? Usually the question is understood from the point of view of the owner of the commodity as the *subject*. If that is the case, then the switch in the position of the subject creates an apparent disconnect between Smith's reason for labour to be the real price and his insistence that the real price must be measured in terms of quantity of labour. Smith is thus guilty of switching his *subject* around on this question and thereby causing a great deal of confusion among his readers. For example, in the passage just quoted, his reference to 'those who possess it and who want to exchange it for some new production' switches the *subject* of the passage from labourer to the owner of the commodity. However, if the *subject* is the owner of a commodity who can exchange the commodity with any other commodity or money or services of labour, then it is not clear in what sense its exchange relation with labour can be privileged among all other exchange relations. Furthermore, for the commodity owner the value of labour is susceptible to as many variations as any other commodity. But Smith's real measure of value is supposed to remain constant over time and space. Confronted with this problem, Smith reverts back to his original position of positing the labourer as the *subject*:

> Equal quantities of labour, at all times and places, may be said to be of equal value to the labourer. In his ordinary state of

health, strength, and spirits; in the ordinary degree of his skill and dexterity, he must always lay down the same portion of his ease, his liberty, and his happiness.[1] The price which he pays must always be the same, whatever may be the quantity of goods which he receives in return for it. Of these indeed, it may sometimes purchase a greater and sometimes a smaller quantity; but it is their value which varies, not that of the labour which purchases them. At all times and places that is dear which it is difficult to come at, or which it costs much labour to acquire; and that cheap which is to be had easily, or with very little labour. Labour alone, therefore, never varying in its value, is alone the ultimate and real standard by which the value of all commodities can at all times and places be estimated and compared. It is their real price; money is their nominal price only (pp. 50–51).

From this position it is easy for Adam Smith to reject the argument that the value of labour is susceptible to as many variations as any other commodity:

But though equal quantities of labour are always of equal value to the labourer, yet to the person who employs him they appear sometimes to be of greater and sometimes of smaller

---

1 This, of course, is based on the obvious implicit assumption that the ordinary intensity of work remains constant over periods of time. It should be noted that Smith takes account of differences in hardship and skill of labours at any given point of time and homogenises them by multiplying them by wage differentials observed in the market: 'There may be more labour in an hour's hard work than in two hours easy business; or in an hours application to a trade which it cost ten years of labour to learn, than in a month's industry at an ordinary and obvious employment. But it is not easy to find any accurate measure either of hardship or ingenuity. ... It is adjusted, however, not by any accurate measure, but by the haggling and bargaining of the market, according to that sort of rough equality which, though not exact, is sufficient for carrying on the business of common life' (pp. 48–49). On the question of skilled labour, Whitaker, however, objects: 'The attempt to reduce skill to disutility by urging that the higher wages of skill are in proportion to the disutility of acquiring the skill is futile. The tendency of the wages of skilled labor to proportion themselves to the comparative disutility of that labor — i.e., to the sum of disutility daily felt plus some share or other of the past disutility cost of acquiring the skill — is so completely submerged beneath other forces that it is negligible. In addition to this, much skill is not acquired but is inborn without having entailed any disutility cost of acquisition to its possessor' (Whitaker 1904: 38). It should be noted that Adam Smith, rightly or wrongly, does not consider 'inborn' differences among human beings to be significant.

value. He purchases them sometimes with a greater and sometimes with a smaller quantity of goods, and to him the price
of labour seems to vary like that of all other things. It appears
to him dear in the one case, and cheap in the other. In reality,
however, it is the goods which are cheap in one case, and dear
in the other (p. 51).

Given that the labourers constitute a vast majority of the population and the *Wealth of Nations* was particularly concerned with the
welfare of this particular group of people,[2] it made eminent sense for
Adam Smith to measure the rise and fall in the values of commodities on the basis of whether the labourer had to sacrifice more or less
'toil and trouble' to buy that commodity. The reader should note that
Smith's proposed measure of value is entirely *objective* — how many
hours a labourer must work to purchase a commodity at any given
point of time is an objective measure, and is not affected by the differences in the subjectivities of labourers regarding how they feel about
the work. It is also quite clear, however, that even when real wages are
taken to be given from outside, the real value of commodities at any
given point in time is not immediately determined, as wage is a basket
of goods and thus how much labour-time a labourer must sacrifice to
acquire any commodity (either belonging to or outside of that basket)
can only be determined when the relative values or prices of all commodities against a *numéraire* are known at that point in time. For a
modern reader, Smith's reversal of the *subject* position on this question
amounts to using the wage basket as the *numéraire* for the price determination of commodities at any point in time.

Such reversals of the *subject* position are possible on this question due to the fact that quantitatively the answer remains the same
whether it is looked at from the point of view of the labourer wanting

2 As Adam Smith writes: 'Is this improvement in the circumstances of the lower ranks
of the people to be regarded as an advantage or as an inconveniency to the society?
The answer seems at first sight abundantly plain. Servants, labourers and workmen of
different kinds, make up the far greater part of every great political society. But what
improves the circumstances of the greater part can never be regarded as an inconveniency to the whole. No society can surely be flourishing and happy, of which the far
greater part of the members are poor and miserable. It is but equity, besides, that they
who feed, cloath and lodge the whole body of the people, should have such a share of
the produce of their own labour as to be themselves tolerably well fed, cloathed and
lodged' (p. 96).

to acquire a commodity through the sacrifice of his labour or whether it is looked at from the point of view of the owner of a commodity who directly or indirectly exchanges direct labour services for the commodity. For example, let us posit the labourer as the *subject* and ask the question: how much of labour must a labourer sacrifice to obtain a commodity? In a 'rude' society the value of a commodity must be equal to the time it takes to produce the commodity. If the labourer can produce 2 kg of corn in six hours, then the value of 1 kg of corn would be three hours of labour to him. But in a capitalist society, the labourer does not have direct access to production. He sells his labour for wage; say eight hours of labour a day for 2 kg of corn. Thus the value of 1 kg of corn is equal to four hours of labour to him. In this scenario, suppose that at period 1, one unit of a commodity x exchanges for 4 kg of corn. Thus the value of commodity x will be equal to 16 hours of labour to the labourer in period 1. Now suppose that in period 2 the worker still sells eight hours of labour for 2 kg of corn, but one unit of commodity x exchanges for 2 instead of 4 kg of corn. The exchange ratio between corn and x could change for reasons intrinsic to corn or x or both. However, from the labourer's perspective the value of corn has remained the same but the value of x has fallen to half, from 16 hours to eight hours. Thus as long as the relationship between corn and labour remains constant, corn could be used as an invariable scale of measure to measure changes in the value of all other goods. Further, suppose that in period 2 the worker has to work 16 hours for 2 kg of corn. In this case, the value of x remains constant but the value of 1 kg of corn rises to eight hours. We can repeat the exercise by inverting the *subject* and ask how much of labour-time a unit of the commodity x can command and verify that the quantitative answers remain the same. The only problem in the second case is that there seems to be no particular reason why it would be important to the owner of a commodity to reckon the value of his commodity in terms of the quantity of labour services it can exchange for and not money or some other commodity. Though it makes perfect sense for the labourer to measure the value of a commodity in terms of the quantity of labour he will have to sacrifice to acquire it, the *raison d'être* for labour to be the measure of value apparently ceases to exist with the inversion of the *subject* from the labourer to the owner of the commodity. [3]

3 Meek (1966), Dasgupta (1960) and Kaushil (1973) argue that Adam Smith was theoretically concerned with accumulation and growth, and thus it made eminent sense for him to measure commodity-values in terms of quantity of direct labour

Though it may be helpful for a modern reader of Smith to separate the notion of 'real value' from the notion of 'labour commanded' as a *numéraire* for price determination, Adam Smith apparently did not see it in such terms. As we will explain at the end of our reading, for Smith 'real value' is represented by the 'command of labour' of a commodity and the 'command of labour' of a commodity is at the same time represented by its 'real value'. The two notions cannot be separated. Thus the 'real value', which is the ground for comparing changes in values over periods of time, provides at the same time the measure for relative values at any point in time as well.

---

commanded — in other words, to treat commodities as capital (or variable capital in Marx's terms). Schumpeter (1954), on the other hand, identifies Smith's choice of the measure of 'real price' as labour commanded by a commodity as simply a choice of *numéraire* in Walrasian manner: 'And these real prices he in turn replaces, in ignorance of index number method already invented in his time, by prices expressed in terms of labor (after having considered corn for the role): in other words, he chooses the commodity labor instead of the commodity silver or the commodity gold as *numéraire* — to use the phrase brought into general use by L. Walras' (Schumpeter 1954: 188). In the same vein Hollander (1973a, 1992) maintains that the choice of labour-commanded measure represented a rough index number with the added dimension of a welfare measure in the negative sense of effort counterpart of national or private income. In opposition to Schumpeter and Hollander, Bladen (1975) argues that Smith's measure of labour commanded was designed to measure productivity changes in particular sectors and not as a measure of aggregate output. O'Donnell (1990) argues that Smith's 'real' measure of value was intended for measuring changes in values of commodities due to changes in methods of production in general, and in this context Schumpeter's and Hollander's measure loses its relevance. O'Donnell's contention crucially depends on his argument that Smith assumed constant corn wages for any given stage of development, a point earlier made by Sylos-Labini (1976). This assumption, however, is simply incorrect as we shall see later in the chapter. Smith was quite clear that 'corn or real' wages and the rate of profits change with changes in the rate of growth of the economy — he did not associate a state of development as thriving, stagnating or declining societies with a singular steady-state rate of growth. He advocated fixation of rent in terms of corn only because 'A rent therefore reserved in corn is liable only to the variation in the quantity of labour which a certain quantity of corn can purchase. But a rent reserved in any other commodity is liable, not only to the variations in the quantity of labour which any particular quantity of corn can purchase, but to the variations in the quantity of corn which can be purchased by any particular quantity of that commodity' (p. 53). Hence there was no assumption of fixed corn wage. In any case, all these interpretations suffer from one simple problem. In all these cases, Adam Smith's claim that the scale remains invariable over periods of time becomes invalid. This was, however, the reason why labour was chosen as the 'real' measure as opposed to the 'nominal' measure. Gorden (1968), however, has interpreted Smith on this issue in a vein somewhat similar to mine.

Resolution of Value into Wages, Profits and Rents

Chapter VI is entitled 'Of the Component Parts of the Price of Commodities'. It begins with a proposition regarding the determination of exchange ratio between two commodities at a point of time and place — the proper and fundamental question of a theory of value. According to Smith:

> In the early and rude state of society which precedes both the accumulation of stock and the appropriation of land, the proportion between the quantities of labour necessary for acquiring different objects seems to be the only circumstance which can afford any rule for exchanging them for one another. If among a nation of hunters, for example, it usually cost twice the labour to kill a beaver which it does to kill a deer, one beaver should naturally exchange for or be worth two deer. It is natural that what is usually the produce of two days or two hours labour, should be worth double of what is usually the produce of one day's or one hour's labour (p. 65).

Here we have a statement of what later came to be known as the *labour theory of value*. Let us follow this proposition closely. Adam Smith claims that in a society of only labourers, the 'natural rule' for exchanging commodities would be to exchange them in proportion to the labour-time spent in their production. He then goes on to add:

> In this state of things, the whole produce of labour belongs to the labourer; and the quantity of labour commonly employed in acquiring or producing any commodity, is the only circumstance which can regulate the quantity of labour which it ought commonly to purchase, command or exchange for (p. 65).

That is, 'in this state of things' where labour is the only recipient of all income produced, the real value of the commodity coincides with the labour-time needed to produce the commodity and thus it is the only circumstance that could regulate the labour-commanded measure of the value of a commodity.

But what happens when a capitalist arrives on the scene, i.e., when society is divided into two classes — labourers and capitalists?

> In this state of things, the whole produce of labour does not always belong to the labourer. He must in most cases share

10

it with the owner of the stock which employs him. Neither is the quantity of labour commonly employed in acquiring or producing any commodity, the only circumstance which can regulate the quantity which it ought commonly to purchase, command, or exchange for. An additional quantity, it is evident, must be due for the profits of the stock which advanced the wages and furnished the materials of that labour (p. 67).

In other words, 'in this state of things' the 'real price' of a commodity will not be governed by the labour-time needed to produce the commodity as the emergence of profit is possible only if the amount of labour services a commodity can command, or the amount of labour services a labourer must sell to buy the commodity, is larger than the amount of time needed to produce the commodity. Though 'in this state of things' it is clear that the 'real price' of a commodity will be larger than the labour-time needed to produce the commodity, it is yet not settled how much larger it ought to be. In other words, Smith has not yet provided the 'natural rule' or the principle that would govern the 'real price' of commodities in a society divided into labourers and capitalists.

Similarly, when the class of landlords appears on the scene, then the labourer must sacrifice another portion of the total produce as rent to the landlord. Thus the total produce or the real value of the total produce usually gets divided into three components: one goes to the landlords as rent, another goes to the capitalists as profit, and the third goes to the labourers as wages. Thus the 'real price' of every commodity must resolve itself into rent, profit and wages:

> In every society the price of every commodity finally resolves itself into some one or other, or all of those parts; and in every improved society, all the three enter more or less, as component parts, into the price of the far greater part of commodities (p. 68).

Before proceeding any further, let us note two important points. Adam Smith opens the chapter with a statement of the *labour theory of value* as a principle that regulates exchange ratios between commodities in a society of labourers only. This proposition is neither established nor rejected but simply dropped once his analysis moves on to a capitalist society with two or three classes. We shall come back to this issue at the end of our reading. It should, however, be noted that if a principle of determining relative exchange ratios of commodities could be established, then, given the wages, the labour commanded or the real value of any commodity is also immediately determined. Similarly, if a principle is established by which the labour commanded or the real value of any commodity is directly determined, then it also immediately determines the relative exchange ratios of all commodities. It seems that Smith simply follows the second approach of establishing a principle that regulates the labour-commanded measure of value of any commodity instead of the first approach that directly aims at determining the relative exchange ratios of commodities irrespective of any particular *numéraire*.

Before we move on to the next chapter, it would be appropriate to comment on an important, albeit controversial and poorly understood argument of Smith in this chapter. Smith argues that the price of a commodity ultimately resolves into wages, profit and rent. But it is obvious that the cost of raw materials and depreciated fixed capital, which is not an element of either wages or profit or rent in the production of a particular commodity, must also constitute a part of its price. Here is what Smith has to say on this point:

> In the price of corn, for example, one part pays the rent of the landlord, another pays the wages or maintenance of the labourers and labouring cattle employed in producing it, and the third pays the profit of the farmer. These three parts seem either immediately or ultimately to make up the whole price of corn. A fourth part, it may perhaps be thought, is necessary. In the price of corn, for example, one part pays the rent of the landlord, another pays the wages or for replacing the stock of the farmer, or for compensating the wear and tear of his labouring cattle, and other instruments of husbandry. But it must be considered that the price of any instrument of husbandry, such as labouring horse, is itself made up of the same three parts; the rent of the land upon which he is reared, the labour of tending and rearing him, and the profits of the farmer who advances such a rent of this land, and the wages of this labour. Though the price of the corn, therefore, may pay the price as well as the maintenance of the horse, the whole price still resolves itself either immediately or ultimately into the same three parts of rent, labour, and profit (p. 68).

Clearly, Smith is not denying that the price of the horse is included in the price of the corn. What he is stating is that the price of the horse itself can be further broken into wages, profit and rent, and its raw materials in turn can further be broken into wages, rent and profit, and on and on. The procedure is exactly the same as is used for calculating the embodied labour content of a commodity. To calculate the 'indirect' labour-time in the production of a commodity, one needs to go further and further in the production chain of the raw materials and fixed capital equipments to gather the direct labour-time spent in their production till the residue of raw materials and fixed capital equipments becomes negligible. Adam Smith proposes exactly the same procedure to gather the wages, rent and profit components of the raw materials and the depreciated fixed capital equipments used up in producing a commodity. That is why he insists that the price of a commodity *ultimately*, and *not* necessarily *immediately*, resolves itself into wages, rent and profit. Thus one could say that for Smith, the price of a commodity is constituted by *direct* and *indirect* wages, rent and profit.

Adam Smith's style of writing has been a reason for confusion among many readers of his book. For example, after arguing that the price of any good must ultimately resolve into wages, rent and profit, he goes on to say:

> As the price or exchangeable value of every particular commodity, taken separately, resolves itself into some one or other or all of those three parts; so that of all the commodities which compose the whole annual produce of the labour of every country, taken complexly, must resolve itself into the same three parts, and be parcelled out among different inhabitants of the country, either as wages of their labour, the profits of their stock, or the rent of their land. The whole of what is annually either collected or produced by the labour of every society, or what comes to the same thing, the whole price of it, is in the manner originally distributed among some of its different members. Wages, profits, and rent, are the three original sources of all revenue as well as of all exchangeable value. All other revenue is ultimately derived from someone or other of these (p. 69).

In the forthcoming paragraphs I show that Adam Smith is consistent and correct in his reasoning and all the charges against him of inconsistency and mistakes on this point are the result of misinterpretation. First of all, Smith is quite clear that National Income, which is divided into wages, profits and rent, is made up of 'value added' and not the total prices of gross outputs. For example, he writes:

> As soon as stock has accumulated in the hands of particular persons, some of them will naturally employ it in setting to

work industrious people, whom they will supply with materials and subsistence, in order to make a profit by the sale of their work, or *by what their labour adds to the value of the materials*. In exchanging the complete manufacture either for money, for labour, or for other goods, over and above what may be sufficient to pay the price of the materials, and the wages of the workmen, something must be given for the profits of the undertaker of the work who hazards his stock in this adventure. *The value which the workmen add to the materials, therefore, resolves itself in this case into two parts, one which pays their wages, the other the profits of their employer upon the whole stock of materials and wages which he advanced* (pp. 65–66, emphasis added).

Smith's reasoning can be understood by following a simple example. Let us take a one-good world of corn, where corn is the only raw material as seed and wages are paid in terms of corn as well. Let us suppose that 2 units of corn are produced by 1 unit of corn seed, 8 hours of labour, and 1 unit of land. Let us also suppose that wage is equal to ½ unit of corn for 8 hours of labour and the rate of profit is 20 per cent. In this case, the 'real price' of corn is 16 hours of labour. Now, given the 'real price' of corn as 16 hours of labour, from our production equation we know that, on average, 1 unit of corn production requires ½ unit of corn, ½ unit of land, and 4 hours of labour. Thus the 'real price' of corn in the first place resolves into 4 hours of labour to workers plus $(8 + 4) \, 0.2 = 2.4$ hours of labour as profit plus 8 hours as raw materials plus the remaining 1.6 hours as rent. Now, the 'real price' of raw materials used in producing 1 unit of corn can be further broken into 2 hours to workers as wages plus $(4 + 2) \, 0.2 = 1.2$ hours as profit plus 4 hours as raw materials plus the remaining 0.8 hours as rent. Similarly, the 'real price' of raw material of this round of production can again be broken into the shares of wages, profits and rent plus the 'real value' of the raw materials, and on and on until the raw material element becomes negligible. Now if we add up the 'real prices' of all the wages, profits and rents, we get the total wage share = $(4 + 2 + 1 + 0.5 + ...)$, the total profit share = $(2.4 + 1.2 + 0.6 + ...)$, and the total rent share = $(1.6 + 0.8 + 0.4 + ...)$. The three geometrical series converge to 8 hours of labour, 4.8 hours of labour, and 3.2 hours of labour respectively. Thus the 'real price' of corn is resolved into 8 hours as wages, 4.8 hours as profit and 3.2 hours as rent. Now we can check that in our original example of 2 units of gross output or 1 unit of net output of corn production, the direct share of wages, profits and rent amounts to exactly 8, 4.8 and 3.2 respectively. That is, when the 'real price' is ultimately resolved into wages, profits and rent, it equals the direct share of three classes in the production of one unit of the net output.

The example can be easily generalised for the complicated case of n goods in the system. But before we get to that, it is important to point out that, as we later argue in the section on rent, Adam Smith maintains that land that is capable of producing food always pays rent, which is interpreted as *physical surplus* produced in the agricultural sector. Thus, in a sense 'corn' is the only 'basic good'[4] in his system. Now let us suppose that there is another good 'iron' that requires both corn and iron for its production. For example:

¼ ton of corn + ¼ ton of iron + 8 hrs of labour + 1 acre of land
→ 1 ton of iron.

This implies:

$$(¼ \, p_C + ¼ \, p_I + 8 \text{ hrs of labour}) (1 + r) + 1.t = p_I.$$

From our corn example we already know that 'real price' of 1 ton of corn (p_C) is 16 hours of labour, the rent of 1 acre of land (t) is 3.2 hours of labour and the rate of profit (r) is 20 per cent. After plugging these values in the above production equation of iron, we get price of 1 ton of iron (p_I) = 25.14 hours of labour. Similarly, if we add another good, say 'coal', in the system, where both 'coal' and 'iron' along with 'corn' are needed in the production of both 'coal' and 'iron', then we can accordingly represent the system of production of both 'coal' and 'iron' as follows:

¼ ton of corn + ¼ ton of iron + ½ ton of coal + 8 hrs of labour + 1 acre of land → 1 ton of iron.

¼ ton of corn + ¼ ton of iron + ¼ ton of coal + 8 hrs of labour + 1 acre of land → 1 ton of coal.

---

4 The concept of 'basic goods' was introduced by Sraffa (1960). A basic good is a good that enters directly or indirectly into the production of all other goods; whereas a 'non-basic good' either does not enter into the production of any good or only into the production of a sub-set of non-basic goods.

This implies:

$$(\tfrac{1}{4}\, p_C + \tfrac{1}{4}\, p_I + \tfrac{1}{2}\, p_{CO} + 8 \text{ hrs of labour}) (1 + r) + 1.t = p_I$$

$$(\tfrac{1}{4}\, p_C + \tfrac{1}{4}\, p_I + \tfrac{1}{4}\, p_{CO} + 8 \text{ hrs of labour}) (1 + r) + 1.t = p_{CO}$$

Again, plugging the values of price of 'corn' and the rent of land from the corn model and the given r = 20%, we can solve for price of iron and price of coal in terms of hours of labour commanded by 1 unit of these commodities. This example can be easily generalised for the *n* non-basic goods case on the assumption that the system is productive in the sense that all commodities as inputs are either less than or equal to their outputs; i.e., the Hawkins-Simon condition holds, and the prices are either strictly positive or zero. The same idea can be translated in Smith's reasoning in the following manner:

$$(Ap + H)(1 + r) + tL = p,$$

where A is an nxn matrix of commodity inputs a_{ij}, which represents the quantity of good j required to produce, on average, 1 unit of good i. We take good one as corn with a_{11} positive and all other a_{ij} elements as zero in the first row of matrix A. H, L, and p represent vectors of labour time, land units and the 'real price' or labour-time commanded respectively. We can represent our production system in terms of Adam Smith's price equations as:

$$(H + rH + tL) = p - Ap(1 + r) = [I - A(1 + r)]p$$

$$p = [I - A(1 + r)]^{-1} (H + rH + tL);$$ on the assumption that $[I - A(1 + r)]p$ is invertible.

This can be expanded as:

$$p = [I + A(1 + r) + A^2(1 + r)^2 + A^3(1 + r)^3 + ...] (H + Hr + tL)$$

This resolves all prices into wages, profits and rent.[5] Let us note two aspects of this solution here: (a) both wages and the rate of profits

---

5 'Smith's value-added accounting is shown to be correct by Leontief-Sraffa modelling' (Samuelson 1977: 42). Our procedure given above is similar to Sraffa's (1960) dated labour approach and his statement in the beginning of the Chapter VI that 'prices ... "resolve themselves"' is a clear reference to Adam Smith. I am indebted to Antoine

are taken as given, whereas (*b*) rent is determined as residual. I shall elaborate on this point later when we come to Smith's explanation of distribution.

Of course, Smith did not solve the simultaneous equation problem, but he did think in terms of a one-commodity corn model, and thought that the argument would carry through for a more-than-one-good case. It should be noted, however, that Adam Smith also made statements that show that the complete logic of such resolutions was not clear to him. For example, at one point he states:

> In the most improved societies, however, there are always a few commodities of which the price resolves itself into two parts only, the wages of labour, and the profits of stock; ... In the price of sea-fish, for example, one part pays the fisherman, and the other the profits of the capital employed in the fishery. Rent very seldom makes any part of it ... (p. 69).

Now, if 'corn' is the basic good in his system, then the resolution of the raw materials of fishing into income categories would at some stage bring corn and rent into the picture. If, however, it is assumed that there are no raw materials or the raw materials at any stage do not need 'corn', then of course it must be treated as a separate system; but in this case, given the wages, the rate of profit must come out as a solution to the simultaneous equation system and cannot be taken as given *a priori*. Of course, it is quite easy to see all this after Sraffa (1960), but it was not so easy for people who came before him.

From our foregoing analysis it is clear that in a multicommodity world the 'real price' of a commodity cannot be known prior to the knowledge of the profits and the technique of production in use along with the knowledge of the fertility of land, if land directly or indirectly enters into the production of the commodity. After establishing that the 'real price' of a commodity resolves itself immediately or

---

Rebeyrol for the mathematical representation of my idea. It should be noted that Adam Smith's system can be generalised for n basic goods system. In this case, we first take real wages as given and derive the 'maximum rate of profits', given the wages, by putting the rent (t) as equal to zero. Since the system is taken to satisfy the Hawkins-Simon condition, i.e., there is positive surplus after the payment of real wages in the system, we can be sure that the 'maximum rate of profits' will be positive. On the assumption that the given rate of profits is always below the 'maximum rate of profits', we can determine n - 1 relative positive prices and the rent (t) per unit of land by solving the simultaneous equation problem.

ultimately into wages, profits and rent, Adam Smith, in Chapter VII, introduces a notion of 'natural price' in contradistinction to 'market price'. So we now turn to Smith's discussion on the natural and market prices of commodities.

Natural Price in Contradistinction to Market Price

Adam Smith begins Chapter VII with the claim that: 'There is in every society or neighbourhood an ordinary or average rate both of wages and profit. ... There is likewise in every society or neighbourhood an ordinary or average rate of rent ...' (p. 72). In other words, for determining the 'real price' of commodities in a given market at a point in time, ordinary rates of wages, profits and rent can be taken as given. These ordinary rates are then defined as 'natural' rates, and the price of a commodity as 'natural' price, if the sale of a commodity at that price ensures that the workers, capitalists and the landlords associated with the production of the commodity receive just their 'natural' wages, profits and rent, no more and no less. In other words, the price that remunerates the three classes at their 'natural' rate is the 'natural price':

> When the price of any commodity is neither more nor less than what is sufficient to pay the rent of the land, the wages of the labour, and the profits of the stock employed in raising, preparing, and bringing it to market, according to their natural rates, the commodity is then sold for what may be called its natural price (p. 72).

The 'natural' price is the minimum price at which a commodity can be offered in the market for a considerable period of time. If the price falls below the natural price, then one or the other or all the players involved in bringing the commodity to the market would receive their remuneration below their natural rates, which would induce them to move their factor of production from the present employment to some other employment which pays higher remuneration. Similarly, if the price is above the natural rate, then in the case of perfect liberty, the sector would get crowded in by the factor that is receiving higher than its natural rate. Furthermore, the quantity demanded of a commodity at its 'natural' price is called its 'effectual' demand. It is so called because it is the minimum price at which the supply of the commodity can be effectuated in the long run. When the supplied quantity of a commodity falls short of or exceeds its 'effectual' demand, then, in effect, the commodity is sold at a price higher or lower than its 'natural' price. This will happen because in the case of short supply:

> ... all those who are willing to pay the whole value of the rent, wages, and profit, which must be paid in order to bring it thither, cannot be supplied with the quantity which they want. Rather than want it altogether, some of them will be willing to give more. A competition will immediately begin among them, and the market price will rise more or less above the natural price, according as either the greatness or the deficiency, or the wealth and wanton luxury of the competitors, happen to animate more or less the eagerness of the competition (pp. 73–74).

The opposite will happen in the case of supply exceeding the effectual demand. Thus, the price of a commodity that is paid in the market is called its 'market' price. The market price seldom coincides with the natural price as it would be by accident only that the supply of a commodity would exactly equal its effectual demand. By how much the market prices deviate from the natural prices would depend upon the proportion of supply exceeding or falling short of its effectual demand and the nature of the commodity, such as whether it is a necessity or a luxury or to what extent its supply could be withdrawn from the market for some time. But in any case, market prices are always gravitating toward the natural prices because a price above or below the natural price brings in the corrective mechanism into play by either increasing or decreasing the supply of the commodity through the movement of one or all factors in or out of the sector.

> The natural price, therefore, is, as it were, the central price, to which the prices of all commodities are continually gravitating. Different accidents may sometimes keep them suspended a good deal above it, and sometimes force them down even somewhat below it. But whatever may be the obstacles which hinder them from settling in this centre of repose and continuance, they are constantly tending towards it (p. 75).[6]

---

6 The reader might have noted that Adam Smith does not use the word 'equilibrium' for the long-term natural price. Peter Groenewegen points out that 'Smith studiously avoids the use of the word "equilibrium" in this analysis' and argues that Smith would have regarded such mechanical analogy inappropriate to the phenomenon he was studying (Groenewegen 1982: 7). Emma Rothschild also argues that the word

Thus, by introducing the notion of 'natural price' in contradistinction to the 'market price', Adam Smith is able at the same time to remove the forces of demand and supply from an explanation of the long-term prices of commodities and also introduce the role of the forces of demand and supply in explaining the deviation of 'market prices' from the 'natural prices'.

The question, however, remains: has this result been achieved on an implicit assumption of *constant cost*? The answer seems to be yes. As we have noted, Smith defines natural price as the lowest price that could prevail in the long-term and that this price prevails when the quantity supplied is equal to its effectual demand. Now suppose that diminishing returns or rather increasing costs prevail. In such a case, if supply is reduced by x per cent, the total cost per unit of output would fall by a larger amount than x per cent, implying that the given natural rates of wages, profits and rent could still be paid when the price is lower than what it was when supply was equal to the effectual demand (and vice-versa for increasing returns or decreasing costs). Thus, there will not be just one 'natural price' but infinite natural prices for every given level of output. In this context, therefore, it would be incorrect for Adam Smith to define 'natural' price as the 'equilibrium' price. Smith's 'effectual demands' are apparently determined by the total income created by the observed outputs. As Smith explains:

> ... those who are willing to pay the natural price of the com-
> modity may be called the effectual demanders, and their
> demand the effectual demand; a very poor man may be said
> in some sense to have a demand for a coach and six; he might

---

'equilibrium' was in circulation during Smith's time, but he purposely shies away from such 'metaphors of celestial and fluid mechanics' and points out that Smith used the term only once in connection with the doctrine of the exact balance of trade, which he characterised as 'nothing, however, can be more absurd' (Rothschild 2001: 143–44). Myers points out that Smith was capable of presenting a market equilibrium model in mathematical form but did not do so because he did not think that an economy 'actually operate[s] with a precision akin to that of physical law' and thus 'the exactness of mathematics would be inappropriate for depicting its operation' (Myers 1976: 413). Piel, on the other hand, from the perspective of the continuity between Smith's *Moral Sentiments* and *The Wealth of Nations*, argues that 'Smith's description of *natural price* should remind us that this price is not the long-run market price caused by ongoing interaction of the market. It is of a different order than the *market price*. That is to say that the *natural price* is part of society's prevailing value patterns which provide the articulation of people's behaviour and action ... ' (Piel 1999: 142).

like to have it; but his demand is not an effectual demand, as the commodity can never be brought to market in order to satisfy it (p. 73).

Thus if the effectual demands for the various commodities are not the same as the observed outputs, then the gravitation mechanism ensures that the *given* total employed labour is reallocated in such a manner that outputs match the given effectual demands for the commodities. But this is possible only on the implicit assumption of constant returns to scale and given that the reallocation of labour does not have any influence on the given natural rates of wages, profits and rents, it amounts to an implicit assumption of constant costs as well.[7]

The rest of Book I is devoted to an analysis of the determination and secular changes in wages, profits and rents. Before we conclude our reading of Adam Smith's theory of value, let us briefly describe his treatment of the determination of distributional variables.

Of the Wages of Labour

Chapter VIII deals with the determination of wages. Here Smith argues that the interest of the employers is to keep the wages as low as possible whereas the workers would, of course, like to raise them as much as possible. In this struggle over wages, the employers usually have the upper hand.

> The workmen desire to get as much, the masters to give as little as possible. The former are disposed to combine in order to raise, the latter in order to lower the wages of labour.
>
> It is not, however, difficult to foresee which of the two parties must, upon all ordinary occasions, have the advantage in the dispute, and force the other into a compliance with their terms. The masters, being fewer in number, can combine much more easily; and the law, besides, authorises, or at least does not prohibit their combinations, while it prohibits those of the workmen. ... In all such disputes the masters can hold out much longer. A landlord, a farmer, a master manufacturer, or merchant, though they did not employ a single workman, could generally live a year or two upon the stocks which they

---

7 See Dupertuis and Sinha (2009a) for a critique of the classical theory of gravitation mechanism. We have shown that the classical gravitation mechanism does not work.

have already acquired. Many workmen could not subsist a week, few could subsist a month, and scarce any a year without employment. In the long-run the workman may be as necessary to his master as his master is to him; but the necessity is not so immediate (pp. 83–84).

However, there is a floor to wages below which it cannot be kept for a long time as it will adversely affect the supply of labour. This floor is given by the 'subsistence wage' — a wage that is just sufficient to maintain the worker and enable him to raise two children.[8] In other words, subsistence wage is a wage that is consistent with zero rate of population growth in the long run. Adam Smith, along with Cantillon, reckons that the subsistence wage must be equal to at least twice the maintenance of the worker to rear two children to adulthood, with the wife's wages being equal to her own maintenance. Now, when the demand for labour grows continually with the growth in the economy, then '[t]he scarcity of hands occasions a competition among masters, who bid against one another, in order to get workmen, and thus voluntarily break through the natural combination of masters not to raise wages' (p. 86). On the other hand, higher wages reduce the infant mortality rate among the working class population and thus lead to a positive rate of population growth. For given techniques of production, an economy can grow at a certain rate only if the labour force grows at the same rate as well. If the rate of population growth is lower than the rate of growth of the economy, then the economy will experience shortages of hands and thus the competition among the employers will increase the wages that will in turn lead to a further fall in infant mortality rate and a consequent rise in the rate of population growth. The opposite will happen if the economy is growing at a rate slower than the rate of population growth. Therefore, for every given rate of growth of the economy there is a particular 'equilibrium' wage that generates the supply of labour force such that the demand for labour is equal to the supply. Thus the level of real wages depends upon the rate of growth of the economy (given the nature of technical change that accompanies growth) — the higher the rate of growth of

8 It should be noted that Adam Smith did not consider the subsistence wage to be a biological minimum. He not only took account of given food cultures, such as rice eating or potato eating, but went to the extent of arguing that: 'By necessaries I understand not only the commodities which are indispensably necessary for the support of life, but whatever the custom of the country renders it indecent for creditable people, even of the lowest order, to be without' (pp. 869–70).

the economy, the higher will be the wages. Thus, at any given point in time, the level of real wage depends upon the historical circumstance of the economy — namely, whether it is a thriving (and how fast), stagnant or declining (and at what rate) state:

> Every species of animals naturally multiplies in proportion to the means of their subsistence, and no species can multiply beyond it. But in civilized society it is only among the inferior ranks of people that the scantiness of subsistence can set limits to the further multiplication of the human species; and it can do so in no other way than by destroying a great part of the children which rather fruitful marriages produce.
>
> The liberal reward of labour, by enabling them to provide better for their children, and consequently to bring up a greater number, naturally tends to widen and extend those limits. It deserves to be remarked too, that it necessarily does this as nearly as possible in the production which the demand for labour requires. If this demand is continually increasing, the reward of labour must necessarily encourage in such a manner the marriage and multiplication of labourers, as may enable them to supply that continually increasing demand by a continually increasing population. If the reward should at any time be less than what was requisite for this purpose, the deficiency of hands would soon raise it; and if it should at any time be more, their excessive multiplication would soon lower it to this necessary rate. The market would be so much under-stocked with labour in the one case, and so much over-stocked in the other, as would soon force back its price to that proper rate which the circumstances of the society required. It is in this manner that the demand for men, like for that any other commodity, necessarily regulates the production of men; quickens it when it goes too slowly, and stops it when it advances too fast. It is this demand which regulates and determines the state of propagation in all the different countries of the world, in North America, in Europe, and in China; which renders it rapidly progressive in the first, slow and gradual in the second, and altogether stationary in the last.
>
> The liberal reward of labour, therefore, as it is the effect of increasing wealth, so it is the cause of increasing population. To complain of it is to lament over the necessary effect and cause of the greatest publick prosperity (pp. 97–99).

Of the Profits of Stock

We now turn to the second component of price, the rate of profits. His treatment of the determination of the rate of profits is highly complex and confusing. An understanding of the full scope of his argument is possible only if we succeed in separating the various abstract layers of his arguments. In Chapter VI Adam Smith proclaims:

> The profits of stock, it may perhaps be thought, are only a differ-ent name for the wages of a particular sort of labour, the labour of inspection and direction. They are, however, altogether differ-ent, are regulated by quite different principles, and bear no pro-portions to the quantity, the hardship, or the ingenuity of this supposed labour of inspection and direction. They are regulated altogether by the value of the stock employed, and are greater or smaller in proportion to the extent of this stock (p. 66).

In Chapter IX, entitled 'Of the Profits of Stock', he says:

> The rise and fall in the profits of stock depend upon the same causes with the rise and fall in the wages of labour, the increas-ing or declining state of the wealth of the society; but those causes affect the one and the other very differently (p. 105).

After this, he goes on to list empirical observations that suggest that economies that are growing faster have higher wages and lower rates of profits, with the notable exception of the North American and West Indian colonies where both wages and profits are high simultaneously. The exceptional case of the North American and West Indian colonies is explained on the grounds that the new colonies were both under-stocked and under-populated in proportion to the extent of their ter-ritories. After putting the exception aside, the empirical evidence of an inverse relation between wages and profits is established. As we have already explained, Adam Smith had already theoretically established a positive relationship between the rate of growth of the economy and the level of wages. In the current chapter he argues that the same phenomenon also implies a negative relationship between the rate of growth of the economy and the rate of profits on capital stock. This proposition is established on the ground that:

> The increase of stock, which raises wages, tends to lower profit. When the stocks of many rich merchants are turned

into the same trade, their mutual competition naturally tends to lower its profit; and when there is a like increase of stock in all the different trades carried on in the same society, the same competition must produce the same effect in them all (p. 105).

This argument of Smith's is almost universally considered to be false, as it apparently commits the fallacy of composition — what may be true for one sector taken in isolation may not be true for all the sectors taken together. It is true that if the economy is growing at a certain rate, then increase in the stocks of capital in all the sectors at that rate should not cause a crowding effect leading to a fall in the rate of profits. But before we judge the game and set in favour of Smith's critics on this point, let us see whether the proposition that 'rising wages imply falling profits' is true or not.[9]

In Smith's theoretical analysis, it is assumed that wage goods consist only of 'corn' or food in general. In his case the agricultural sector and the manufacturing sector are sharply separated and his proposition of a rise in real wages may be represented as a rise in money wages with no increase in the money price of 'corn'. The question is: will this rise in the share of wages in the total corn produced be absorbed by a fall in profits or rents? The immediate effect of a rise in money wages with a constant money price of corn would be a fall in the rate of profits in the agricultural sector. If the manufacturing sector is able to raise its money prices to compensate for the rise in money wages, then it will engender an outflow of capital from the agricultural sector to the manufacturing sector, reducing the rate of profits in the manufacturing sector to the level of the rate of profits in the agricultural sector. The question then arises: why doesn't the migration of capital from the agricultural to the manufacturing sector create pressure on rent so that the agricultural rate of profits could be brought back to the old level? The answer to this question lies in the cause of the rise in wages in the first place. Smith does not contemplate the effect of a rise in real wages on either profits or rent in a static context. In his theoretical framework the real wages rise because capital is growing faster than the rate of population growth. It is this growth in capital that actually strengthens the bargaining position of the landlords vis-a-vis the farmers or the agricultural capitalists, who are simply unable to shift the burden of the rise in real wages on to the shoulders of the

---

9 Several arguments of this section and section on Rent rely heavily on 'In Defence of Adam Smith's Theory of Value' (Sinha forthcoming).

landlords. As Smith says: '[E]very improvement in the circumstances of the society tends either directly or indirectly to raise the real rent of land, ... The extension of improvement and cultivation tends to raise it directly' (p. 264).

This point is crucial in distinguishing the impact of rising real wages on the rate of profits from the impact of a tax on real wages or wage goods. The scenario of a tax on wages or wage goods is a static one. In this case, the migration of capital from agricultural sector to the manufacturing sector increases the bargaining strength of the farmers or the agricultural capitalists vis-a-vis the landlords, which eventually leads to the burden of taxes ultimately falling on rent in the agricultural sector and a compensatory rise, to the extent of the rise in money wages, in prices of the manufacturing goods, leaving the original rate of profits unchanged before and after the taxes.[10] Thus it appears that Professor Hollander is mistaken in arguing that:

> [T]here is no reason to believe that the secular rise in *per capita* wages in consequence of an increasing rate of capital accumulation was treated differently than a tax on wages or on wage goods. The increase in wage costs in this case too would be passed on in the form of higher prices and reduced rents (Hollander 1973 a: 181).

The dynamic case of rising wages due to capital accumulation is not the same as the static case of a rise in wages due to a tax on wages.

Now, the question is: how would the fall in the rate of profits work out in the economy? Let us suppose that after the rise in money wages, all the capitalists raise the prices of their goods in equal proportion to the rise in money wages. If they succeed in selling all their goods at those prices, it would amount to only a general inflation with real wages and the rate of profits remaining constant. But this contradicts the initial proposition that wages have risen. Thus a rise in wages implies that the capitalists will not be able to sell all their goods at a price that gives them the same rate of profits, that is, all the sectors will experience a general glut, and a competition among the capitalists

---

10 'While the demand for labour and the price of provisions therefore remain the same, a direct tax upon the wages of labour can have no other effect than to raise them somewhat higher than the tax' (p. 864). And 'It [taxes on necessaries of life or wage goods] ... operates exactly in the same manner as a direct tax upon the wages of labour' (p. 871).

would lead to a fall in prices along with a fall in their general rate of profits. It appears that Smith is simply alluding to the general glut situation that will prevail in all the sectors on the old rate of profits. As a matter of fact, Smith explicitly states that it is the rise in wages that *cause* the rate of profits to fall:

> In a thriving town the people who have great stocks to employ, frequently cannot get the number of workmen they want, and therefore bid against one another in order to get as many as they can, *which raises the wages of labour, and lowers the profits of stock*. In remote parts of the country there is frequently not stock sufficient to employ all the people, who therefore bid against one another in order to get employment, *which lowers the wages of labour, and raises the profits of stock* (p. 107, emphasis added).[11]

Game and set to Adam Smith.

Until now we have been concerned with the relationship between wages and the rate of profits in a growing economy.

But what about their relationship in a stagnant economy? The case of a stagnant economy is different. In this case both the rate of profits and the wages will simultaneously be at their minimum. Smith's logic is as follows. He maintains that there is a natural limit to growth. Thus a growing economy must naturally turn into a stagnating one. Now, a stagnating economy cannot employ more labour than what it employs currently. Given the positive rate of population growth for the economy that was previously growing, the result will be an excess supply of labour, which will lead to a fall in wages and rate of population growth in accordance with Smith's population principle. This wage and population adjustment will continue until the rate of population growth becomes zero, a rate that is compatible with the minimum subsistence wage. As far as the rate of profits is concerned,

---

11 This is not to deny that Adam Smith was also of the opinion that there are natural limits to growth for every sector of the economy and thus a growing economy must eventually stagnate. He also thought that increase in capital in any sector would lead to fall in the residual monopoly powers and thus a fall in the average rate of profits. O'Donnell (1990) argues that in Smith's scheme the rate of profits fall because of the rising proportion of capital over revenue in the course of historical development. But, in our opinion, this conclusion is incorrect as Smith's proposition regarding rise in capital vis-a-vis revenue was predicated on the proposition regarding the falling rate of profits (see *WN* II, iii, 10 & 11, pp. 334–35).

the stagnation of the economy is due not to lack of investment but because of the natural limits to growth. During the period when wages are falling, profits may rise; but eventually, when wages settle at the subsistence level, every fresh capital investment must share in the same amount of profits as neither can wages be reduced any further nor outputs be increased, leading to a fall in the rate of profits. This scenario plays out in the market as overcrowding of capital stock in all the sectors till profits fall to their minimum level, which according to Smith, 'must always be something more than what is sufficient to compensate the occasional losses to which every employment of stock is exposed' (p. 113):

> In a country which had acquired that full complement of riches which the nature of its soil and climate, and its situation with respect to other countries allowed it to acquire; which could, therefore, advance no further, and which was not going backward, both the wages of labour and the profits of stock would probably be very low. In a country fully peopled in proportion to what either its territory could maintain or its stock employ, the competition for employment would necessarily be so great as to reduce the wages of labour to what was barely sufficient to keep up the number of labourers, and, the country being already fully peopled, that number could never be augmented. In a country fully stocked in proportion to all the business it had to transact, as great a quantity of stock would be employed in every particular branch as the nature and extent of the trade would admit. The competition, therefore, would everywhere be as great, and consequently the ordinary profit as low as possible (p. 111).

Thus, like the determination of wages at any given time, the natural rate of profits also depends upon the state of the economy at any given time. It should be kept in mind that the proposition regarding the relationship between wages and the rate of profits is proven on the assumption that the techniques of production remain constant. Smith, however, is also of the opinion that rising wages are usually associated with greater division of labour and labour-saving technical changes leading to increase in labour productivity:

> The same cause, however, which raises the wages of labour, the increase of stock, tends to increase its productive powers, and to make a smaller quantity of labour produce a greater

quantity of work. The owner of the stock which employs a great number of labourers, necessarily endeavours, for his own advantage, to make such a proper division and distribution of employment, that they may be enabled to produce the greatest quantity of work possible. For the same reason, he endeavours to supply them with the best machinery which either he or they can think of. What takes place among the labourers in a particular workhouse takes place, for the same reason, among those of a great society. The greater their number, the more they naturally divide themselves into different classes and subdivisions of employment. More heads are occupied in inventing the most proper machinery for executing the work of each, and it is, therefore, more likely to be invented. There are many commodities, therefore, which in consequence of these improvements, come to be produced by so much less labour than before, that the increase of its price is more than compensated by the diminution of its quantity (p. 104).

In the case of rising labour productivity, the inverse wage-profit relationship cannot be established in a straightforward manner. Nevertheless, according to Smith, in the real world the inverse wage-profit relationship holds empirically.

What about the relationship between the rate of profits and the rate of interest? According to Smith:

It may be laid down as a maxim, that wherever a great deal can be made by the use of money, a great deal will commonly be given for the use of it; and that wherever little can be made by it, less will commonly be given for it (p. 105).

The rate of interest is thus a function of the rate of profits. Like the lowest rate of profits, the lowest rate of interest must 'be something more than sufficient to compensate the occasional losses to which lending, even with tolerable prudence, is exposed' (p. 113). And, '[t]he proportion which the usual market rate of interest ought to bear to the ordinary rate of clear profit, necessarily varies as profit rises or falls' (p. 114). This proportion is conventionally determined for a given range of profits; for example:

Double interest is in Great Britain reckoned, what the merchants call, a good, moderate, reasonable profit; terms which

I apprehend mean no more than a common and usual profit. But the proportion between interest and clear profit might not be the same in countries where the ordinary rate of profit was either a good deal lower, or a good deal higher. If it were a good deal lower, one half of it perhaps could not be afforded for interest; and more might be afforded if it were a good deal higher (p. 114).

And what about the relationship between the rate of interest and the price of land? According to Smith:

The ordinary market price of land, it is to be observed, depends every where upon the ordinary market rate of interest. The person who has a capital from which he wishes to derive a revenue, without taking the trouble to employ it himself, deliberates whether he should buy land with it, or lend it out at interest. The superior security of land, together with some other advantages which almost every where attend upon this species of property, will generally dispose him to content himself with a smaller revenue from land, than he might have by lending out his money at interest. These advantages are sufficient to compensate a certain difference of revenue; but they will compensate a certain difference only; and if the rent of land should fall short of the interest of money by a greater difference, nobody would buy land, which would soon reduce its ordinary price. On the contrary, if the advantages should much more than compensate the difference, every body would buy land, which again would soon raise its ordinary price. When interest was at ten per cent, land was commonly sold for ten and twelve years purchase. As interest sunk to six, five, and four per cent, the price of land rose to twenty, five and twenty, and thirty years of purchase. The market rate of interest is higher in France than in England; and the common price of land is lower. In England it commonly sells at thirty; in France at twenty years purchase (pp. 358–59).

Thus, when the economy is growing fast, the price of land will be high and when the economy is growing slowly, the price of land will be low.

Of the Rent of Land

We now turn to the third component of price, the rent of land. Adam Smith argues that:

> Rent ... enters into the composition of price of commodities in a different way from wages and profit. High or low wages and profit are the causes of high or low price; high or low rent is the effect of it. It is because high or low wages and profit must be paid, in order to bring a particular commodity to market, that its price is high or low. But it is because its price is high or low; a great deal more, or very little more, or no more, than what is sufficient to pay those wages and profit, that it affords a high rent, or a low rent, or no rent at all (p. 162).

But why should a commodity's price be 'high' enough that it affords rent? Is it because, at any given time, the supply of the commodity is falling short of its effectual demand, thereby raising its market price and allowing the monopoly power of the landlord to extract as rent all the excess profits over and above the given natural rate of profit? If that is the case, then increase in the supply of the commodity should reduce its market price and eliminate the rent. Smith argues that in the case of 'corn' or food for the working class in general, a supply response does not affect the price because in the case of food, both supply and effectual demand move simultaneously and in parallel to each other:

> As men like all other animals, naturally multiply in proportion to their means of their subsistence, food is always, more or less, in demand. It can always purchase or command a greater or smaller quantity of labour, and somebody can always be found who is willing to do something, in order to obtain it (p. 162).

Smith seems to believe that there are always some unemployed labourers in the system who can be immediately employed against the excess food or that the population mechanism works instantaneously. But Smith elsewhere argues that the market price of agricultural produce in general fluctuates much more than that of industrial goods:

> The price of the one species of commodities [industrial goods] varies only with the variations in demand: That of the other

[agricultural goods] varies, not only with the variations in the demand, but with the much greater and more frequent variations in the quantity of what is brought to market in order to supply that demand (p. 76).

Thus it is safe to assume that the context of the discussion on rent is the long-term context and not the market-period context. The point Smith seems to be making is that the 'high' price of food that allows a rent cannot be explained on the basis of supply shortages in relation to its effectual demand as, in this particular case, an increase in supply brings forth with it an increase in effectual demand. Though this might explain why the price of food will not fall due to supply response, it does not explain why the price of food *must* be 'high' enough to always afford a positive rent to begin with. This proposition cannot be established through the price mechanism; it must be established through the notion of physical *surplus.*

It should be noted that the notion of surplus can only be defined from a particular point of view. From a purely scientific point of view, no surplus can be produced in nature; from a technical point of view, all the net outputs after deducting the total physical inputs used in the production process from the gross outputs must be treated as surplus (Sraffa's position); in Classical Political Economy the notion of surplus has been defined from particular class positions, e.g., both Ricardo and Marx took the capitalist point of view in defining surplus, where wages are taken as part of the necessary cost and thus part of the inputs and the rest of the output is treated as surplus; it is our contention that, unlike Ricardo and Marx, Adam Smith takes the landlord's point of view in defining surplus — he considers both wages and a normal profit as necessary cost, treating only rent as surplus. We use the term 'surplus' in this strict sense and distinguish it from its common usage, e.g., Smith frequently uses the word 'surplus' for expressing 'over and above', which is not always identical to our conceptual notion of 'surplus'. The following argument shows that in this context Smith maintained the fundamental Physiocratic proposition that rent is a *surplus,* which is a gift of nature:

But land, in almost any situation, produces a greater quantity of food than what is sufficient to maintain all the labour necessary for bringing it to market, in the most liberal way in which that labour is ever maintained. The surplus too is always more than sufficient to replace the stock which employed that labour, together with its profits. Something, therefore, always remains for a rent to the landlord (p. 163).

Here we have Smith's reasoning in terms of the 'corn model' in embryo. This confirms the procedure we have applied in determining Smith's prices by taking rent as residual. The notion of rent as residual was also present in the quotation cited on page 33, where Smith states that:

> But it is because its price is high or low; a great deal more, or very little more, or no more, than what is sufficient to pay those wages and profit, that it affords a high rent, or a low rent, or no rent at all.

And it is further confirmed by his notion of the maximum rate of profit: 'The highest ordinary rate of profit may be such as, in the price of the greater part of commodities, eats up the whole of what should go to the rent of the land, and leaves only ... the bare subsistence of the labourer' (p. 113). Thus the allegation that Adam Smith did not have a constraint binding on his distributional variables is simply not true.

Furthermore, our claim that Smith's proposition regarding rent is Physiocratic in nature is confirmed by both the nature of his critique of the Physiocratic doctrine as well as the application of his theory to the principle of direct taxation. In his critique of the Physiocratic system, Smith claims that: 'This system, however, with all its imperfections is, perhaps, the nearest approximation to the truth that has yet been published upon the subject of political economy ... ' (p. 678). The 'imperfections' mainly allude to the treatment of manufacturing labour as sterile or unproductive by the Physiocrats. From the point of view of determining the nature of surplus, Smith's objection to such characterisation of manufacturing labour, however, boils down to just a semantic quibble, as he claims:

> [T]his class [the class of manufacturers], it is acknowledged, reproduces annually the value of its own annual consumption, and continues, at least, the existence of the stock or capital which maintains and employs it. But upon this account alone the denomination of barren or unproductive should seem to be very improperly applied to it. We should not call a marriage barren or unproductive, though it produces only a son and a daughter, to replace the father and mother, and though it did not increase the number of the human species, but only continued it as it was before. Farmers and country labourers, indeed,

over and above the stock which maintains and employs them, reproduce annually a neat produce, a free rent to the landlord. As a marriage which affords three children is certainly more productive than one which affords only two; so the labour of farmers and country labourers is certainly more productive than that of merchants, artificers and manufacturers. The superior produce of the one class, however, does not render the other barren or unproductive (pp. 674–75).[12]

However, when it comes to identifying the nature and the origin of rent, he completely identifies with the Physiocratic notion of rent as a 'gift of nature'. He states:

No equal capital puts into motion a greater quantity of productive labour than that of the farmer. Not only his labouring servants but his labouring cattle, are productive labourers. In agriculture too nature labours along with man; and though her labour costs no expense, its produce has its value, as well as that of the most expensive workmen. The most important operations of agriculture seem indeed, not so much to increase, though they do that too, as to direct the fertility of nature towards the production of the plants most profitable to man. ... The labourers and labouring cattle, therefore, employed in agriculture, not only occasion, like the workmen in manufactures, the reproduction of a value equal to their own consumption, or to the capital which employs them, together with its owners profits; but of a much greater value. Over and above the capital of the farmer and all its profits, they regularly occasion the reproduction of the rent of the landlord. This rent may be considered as the produce of those powers of nature, the use of which the landlord lends to the farmer. It is greater or smaller according to the supposed extent of those powers, or in other words, according to the supposed natural or improved fertility of the land. It is the work of nature which remains after deducting or compensating every thing which can be regarded as the work of man. It is seldom less than a fourth, and frequently more than third of the whole produce. No equal quantity of productive labour

12 It should, however, be noted that it was important for Smith to distinguish between the manufacturing labour that reproduces its own cost, from service labour that does not, and is thus unproductive in his opinion.

employed in manufactures can ever occasion so great a reproduction. In them nature does nothing; man does all; and the
reproduction must always be in proportion to the strength of
the agents that occasion it. The capital employed in agriculture,
therefore, not only puts into motion a greater quantity of productive labour than any equal capital employed in manufactures,
but in proportion too to the quantity of productive labour which
it employs, it adds a much greater value to the annual produce
of the land and labour of the country, to the real wealth and
revenue of its inhabitants. Of all the ways in which a capital can
be employed, it is by far the most advantageous to the society
(pp. 363–64).

Clearly the 'power of nature' results in physical output, the extent of
which is given by the fertility of land. Since there is no price paid for
nature's contribution to the physical output, it turns into a pure *surplus* and is appropriated by the landlord as rent.

One way of determining whether an original income category is a
necessity or a surplus within a theory is to observe the effect of a direct
tax on such an income category. If the income category is a necessity
then the incidence of direct tax will not stick there and will cause
'disruptions' to productive activities in the entire system. On the other
hand, if the income category is a surplus, then the incidence of direct
tax on such income will stick and will not have a 'disruptive' impact
on the entire system.

In the case of rent of land, we find that the landlords are unable to
pass on the incidence of a direct income tax on rent of land to the consumers or any other class, and that this does not have any 'disruptive'
impact on the entire system of production. For example:

A land tax which ... is assessed upon each district according
to a certain invariable canon ... has no tendency to diminish
the quantity [and therefore] it can have none to raise the price
of the produce. It does not obstruct the industry of the people.
It subjects the landlord to no other inconveniency besides the
unavoidable one of paying the tax (pp. 828–29).

Similarly, in the case of a variable tax according to a fixed percentage
of the real rent:

If by such a system of administration a tax of this kind could
be so managed as to give, not only no discouragement, but,

on the contrary, some encouragement to the improvement of land, it does not appear likely to occasion any other inconveniency to the landlord, except always the unavoidable one of being obliged to pay the tax (p. 834).

In the case of wages, the matter is quite different however:

In all cases, a direct tax upon the wages of labour must, in the long-run, occasion both a greater reduction in the rent of land, and a greater rise in the price of manufactured goods, than would have followed from the proper assessment of a sum equal to the produce of the tax, partly upon the rent of land, and partly upon consumable commodities. ... The declension of industry, the decrease of employment for the poor, and diminution of the annual produce of the land and labour of the country, have generally been the effects of such taxes [direct taxes on wages] (p. 865).

But what about the third original source of revenue, the profit? Smith deals with this category as 'revenue arising from stock', which is divided into two parts: one as 'profit' that goes to the agent who employs the stock, and the other as 'interest', which goes to the owner of the stock who does not employ it himself but lends it to the person who employs it. In the case of profit to the person who employs the stock, the matter is straightforward:

This ... part of profit is evidently a subject not taxable directly. It is the compensation, and in most cases it is no more than a very moderate compensation, for the risk and trouble of employing the stock. The employer must have this compensation, otherwise he cannot, consistently with his own interest, continue the employment. If he was taxed directly, therefore, in proportion to the whole profit, he would be obliged either to raise the rate of his profit, or to charge the tax upon the interest of money; that is, to pay less interest. If he raised the rate of his profit in proportion to the tax, the whole tax, though it might be advanced by him, would be finally paid by one or other of two different sets of people, according to the different ways in which he might employ the stock of which he had the management. If he employed it as a farming stock in the cultivation of land, he could raise the rate of his profit only by retaining a greater portion, or what comes to the same thing, the price of a greater portion of the produce of the land; and as this could be done only by a reduction of rent, the final payment of the tax would fall upon the landlord. If he employed it as a mercantile or manufacturing stock, he could raise the rate of his profit only by raising the price of his goods; in which case the final payment of the tax would fall altogether upon the consumers of those goods. If he did not raise the rate of his profit, he would be obliged to charge the whole tax upon that part of it which was allotted for the interest of money. He could afford less interest for whatever stock he borrowed, and the whole weight of the tax would in this case fall ultimately upon the interest of money. So far as he could not relieve himself from the tax in one way, he would be obliged to relieve himself in the other (p. 847).

However, what about a direct tax on the interest of money? As far as a tax on interest is concerned, Smith's practical position is that it would encourage the stock to flee from the country where it was taxed to a country where it was not. In that case, such a tax would be extremely harmful to the economic health of the country that imposes the tax. However, in a theoretical case of a closed economy, he draws a parallel between the interest of money and rent of land:

The interest of money seems at first sight a subject equally capable of being taxed directly as the rent of land. Like the rent of land, it is a neat produce which remains after completely compensating the whole risk and trouble of employing the stock. As a tax upon the rent of land cannot raise rents; because the neat produce which remains after replacing the stock of the farmer, together with his reasonable profit, cannot be greater after the tax than before it: so, for the same reason, a tax upon the interest of money could not raise the rate of interest; the quantity of stock or money in the country, like the quantity of land, being supposed to remain the same after the tax as before it. The ordinary rate of profit, it has been shown in the first book, is everywhere regulated by the quantity of stock to be employed in proportion to the quantity of the employment, or the business which must be done by it. But the quantity of the employment, or of the business to be done by stock, could neither be increased nor diminished by any tax upon the interest of money. If the quantity of the stock to be employed, therefore, was neither increased

nor diminished by it, the ordinary rate of profit would necessarily remain the same. But the portion of this profit necessary for compensating the risk and trouble of the employer,
would likewise remain the same; that risk and trouble being in
no respect altered. The residue, therefore, that portion which
belongs to the owner of the stock, and which pays the interest of money, would necessarily remain the same too. At first
sight, therefore, the interest of money seems to be subject as fit
to be taxed directly as the rent of land (pp. 847–48).

Now the question is whether interest of money is part of what Adam
Smith defines as 'natural rate of profit'. If it is a part of the 'natural
rate of profit', then the profit income has two elements: one is a necessity and the other is a surplus. If that is the case, then it is not clear
where this surplus comes from. I shall, however, argue that in Smith's
scheme of things, interest of money is not a part of the natural rate of
profit and it does not constitute an original source of income.

First of all, as we have already noted, Smith has a notion of minimum rate of profit, which is defined as 'something more than what is
sufficient to compensate the occasional losses to which every employment of stock is exposed' (p. 113). When the natural rate of profit is at
or near the minimum rate, interest of money vanishes as no employer
can afford to pay any interest on borrowed stock. When the rate of
profit rises beyond the minimum level, then emerges a 'neat' or 'clear'
profit from which a rate of interest could be afforded:

> It is this surplus only which is neat or clear profit. What is
> called gross profit comprehends frequently, not only this sur-
> plus, but what is retained for compensating such extraordi-
> nary losses. The interest which the borrower can afford to pay
> is in proportion to the clear profit only (p. 113).

Now the question is: is this clear profit a surplus? To answer this question, we first need to recall Adam Smith's definition of 'natural rate of
profit':

> His profit, besides, is his revenue, the proper fund of his sub-
> sistence. As, while he is preparing and bringing the goods to
> market, he advances to his workmen their wages, or their
> subsistence; so he advances to himself, in the same manner,
> his own subsistence, which is generally suitable to the profit
> which he may reasonably expect from the sale of his goods.

> Unless they yield him this profit, therefore, they do not repay
> him what they may very properly be said to have really cost
> him (p. 73).[13]

Here we can see that there is no trace of surplus in the notion of natural rate of profit. Could it be that Smith identifies the natural rate of
profit with the minimum rate of profit? The answer is no, as he clearly
states that:

> The natural price itself varies with the natural rate of each
> of its component parts, of wages, profit, and rent; and in
> every society this rate varies according to their circumstances,
> according to their riches or poverty, their advancing, station-
> ary, or declining condition (p. 80).

Furthermore, the rate of interest is not necessarily equal to the 'clear'
profit; rather, it is in proportion to the clear profit — a proportion
that itself changes with changes in the 'natural rate of profits'. Thus,
whenever the natural rate of profits is higher than the minimum rate
of profits, there is always a part of 'clear' profit that is appropriated by the capitalist who employs the stock. But still, Adam Smith
nowhere suggests that a tax on profits appropriated by the capitalist
who employs the stock will have no disruptive impact on the system
of production. Thus the part of profit that is 'neat' or 'clear' is not
necessarily a surplus category, though the level of clear profit may
rise or fall with changes in the historical situation; for a given historical situation, it can be understood as a conventional 'normal' cost of
capital investment.

In the chapter on 'Of the Component Parts of the Price of Commodities', Smith makes it quite clear that interest is not a part of profit
and that it is a derivative rather than an original income category:

> Whoever derives his revenue from a fund which is his own,
> must draw it either from his labour, from his stock, or from
> his land. The revenue derived from labour is called wages.
> That derived from stock, by the person who manages or
> employ it, is called profit. That derived from it by the person
> who does not employ it himself, but lends it to another, is

---

13 A.K. Dasgupta, in my opinion, mistakenly identifies this statement with Smith's
    notion of minimum rate of profit. See Dasgupta (1985: 47).

called the interest of the use of money. It is the compensation which the borrower pays to the lender, for the profit which he has an opportunity of making by the use of the money. Part of the profit naturally belongs to the borrower, who runs the risk and takes the trouble of employing it; and the part to the lender, who affords him the opportunity of making his profit. The interest of money is always a derivative revenue, which, if it is not paid from the profit which is made by the use of the money, must be paid from other source of revenue. ... The revenue which proceeds altogether from land, is called rent, and belongs to the landlord. ... All taxes, and all the revenue which is founded upon them, all salaries, pensions, and annuities of every kind, are ultimately derived from some one or other of those three original sources of revenue, and are paid either immediately or mediately from the wages of labour, the profits of stock, or the rent of land (pp. 69–70).

There are, therefore, three distinct groups of people in this story. One group of people employs their *own* stock and earns a normal or 'natural' rate of profit as their income, which is defined as their 'proper fund of subsistence'. Any tax on this category of income would disrupt the real economy because '[u]nless they yield him this profit, therefore, they do not repay him what they may very properly be said to have really cost him'. A second group of people does not own any stock. They could either earn their income as wages by offering their labour for hire or borrow stock from a group of people who owns stock but does not employ it themselves. This group of people earns a minimum income as a reward for taking the risk of employing capital. Any tax on this income will also disrupt the economy because it will take away the minimum incentive to employ the borrowed stock. The third group of people lends the stock to the second group of people and receives interest as their income, which is a part of the total profits earned by the investment of their stock. This group of people has no impact on the real economy as it is in their interest to lend their stock so long as it brings an interest earning larger than zero. Therefore, this income category can be taxed without causing any disruption to the real economy. Thus we can conclude that the natural rate of profit does not contain any *surplus*.[14] However, when the natural rate of

14 Krishna Bharadwaj writes: 'Smith acknowledged that surplus arose not only in agriculture (as was the view of the Physiocrats in France), but also in manufactures' (Bharadwaj 1989: 22). She, however, provides no evidence in support of

profit happens to be higher than the minimum rate, then it becomes worthwhile for some employers who do not have enough stock of their own to borrow from those who are willing to lend and then share the 'clear' profit with the moneylenders at some conventionally determined rate. Here the interest payment could be understood as expenditure out of profit income and a tax on interest to be a tax on transferred income.[15]

After establishing Adam Smith's Physiocratic credentials and establishing that the rent of land, which produces food for human

---

her claim. Her reading of Smith is an example of an attempt to read Sraffa's interpretation of Ricardo into Smith. Also Maurice Dobb (1973), without providing any evidence, simply interprets Smith's 'productive labour' as productive of 'surplus', and thus identifies profits with surplus. O'Donnell tries to read Smith from the perspective of Garegnani's (1984) 'surplus approach' framework. He confuses Smith's concept of *revenue* with the concept of *surplus* and therefore mistakenly declares profits to be a surplus in Smith's system. This leads him to inevitable frustration, as he notes: 'However, what is striking about these surplus relationships is that they were not used by Smith to develop a theory of the *rate* of *profit*, his concern being, almost exclusively, the *amount* of surplus and its implications for accumulation' (O'Donnell 1990: 52). The source of such misinterpretations lies in accepting Marx's (and also Quesnay's) proposition, which establishes a one-to-one relationship between 'productive labour' and 'surplus production' as well as the idea that savings can come only from 'surplus', as universally valid for all political economy. Smith, however, does not identify 'productive labour' with 'surplus'-producing labour, as he is quite clear that even though manufacturing produces no surplus (a marriage that produces only two children), the manufacturing labour is productive. He also maintained that savings need not come from 'surplus' as not only the bulk of savings came from profits (which he did not classify as 'surplus') but even wages, could generate savings as some of the workers consumptions could be classified as 'luxuries' such as tobacco, spirituous liquors, sugar, tea, etc., and that a tax on these items would not have any effect on money wages. Vivienne Brown has also argued that Smith's 'revenue components theory was a challenge to the view that agriculture alone is productive' (Brown 1994: 176). However, she fails to notice that Quesnay had identified productive labour with the labour that produces surplus, whereas Smith simply changes the meaning of productive labour without challenging the fundamental Physiocratic notion of surplus.

15 In his attempt to deny Smith's Physiocratic foundation on this issue, Hollander (1973a: 170) argues that: 'A well known statement referring to landlords as "the only one of the three orders whose revenue costs them neither labour nor care, but comes to them, as it were, of its own accord, and independent of any plan or project of their own" must, therefore, be qualified. This proposition distinguishes the return to *labour* and to *entrepreneurship* from that of *land*, but neglects to take into account interest payments, which in principle should be classified together with rent.' But as we have argued above, there is no reason to qualify Smith's statement since he does not consider interest payments as an original source of revenue.

consumption, is determined by the physical surplus, let us get back to the question of rent in general. The rent of land that produces food for human consumption also regulates rents of lands that produce other commodities; for example, if the rent of land for pasture is higher than rent of land for corn, more corn land will be converted to pasture and vice-versa, till the rent of all lands that are capable of producing food are brought to parity. It should, however, be noted that though Smith, unlike Ricardo, does not put much theoretical emphasis on differing fertility of land, he does recognise that all lands are not of the same fertility and some lands have situational advantages that generate differing rents: 'The rent of land not only varies with its fertility, whatever be its produce, but with its situation, whatever be its fertility' (p. 163).[16]

But what about the rent of lands that are not capable of producing food, such as coalmines, etc.? In such cases, for example whether a coalmine will afford a rent to its landlord would depend exclusively on the price of coal. The minimum price of coal has to be at least so much that, after replacing all the raw materials and machines used up in its production, it should be able to pay the natural wages and the natural profits prevailing at that time. If the price is at its minimum, then there will be no rent. If the price is higher than this minimum, then a positive rent will arise. But why should its price be higher than its minimum? It is simply because the supply of coal cannot be increased in the same manner as the supply of any industrial or agricultural goods. In other words, such cases are necessarily non-competitive, and in these special cases it is the level of demand, given the supply, that influences the price and determines whether the land will afford any rent or not.[17] As Smith argues:

> The most fertile coal mine too, regulates the price of coals at all the other mines in its neighbourhood. Both the proprietor and the undertaker of the work find, the one that he can get a greater rent, the other that he can get a greater profit, by somewhat underselling all their neighbours. Their neighbours

16 On the question of rent of land that produces food, Professor Stigler's comment is pertinent: 'He [Adam Smith] consistently treated the rent of land as it should be treated: any one use of land had to pay a rent, which was a cost of production, to draw the land from other uses; whereas for all uses combined, rent was a residual' (Stigler 1976: 465). The same point is made by Buchanan (1929) as well.

17 The same logic applies to the case of timber on wild forest or the hide of wild animals.

are soon obliged to sell at the same price, though they cannot so well afford it, and though it always diminishes, and sometimes takes away altogether both their rent and their profit. Some works are abandoned altogether; others can afford no rent, and can be wrought only by the proprietor (p. 184).

But why doesn't the landlord of a more fertile land that produces food for human consumption do the same thing? It is simply because when it comes to food production all the inputs (including wages paid to labourers) and outputs are the same goods and a physical surplus remains even on the least fertile land after accounting for all the expenses of production, including an ordinary profit on stock. However, what happens when equally fertile or more fertile mines are discovered? Smith says: 'If the mines were discovered as much superior to those of Potosi as they were superior to those of Europe, the value of silver might be so much degraded as to render even the mines of Potosi not worth the working' (p. 191).

And what will happen if more fertile lands were suddenly discovered? In the short run it may create a glut in the food market; but in the long run it will increase population and restore food prices to such a level that all land under cultivation will generate a positive rent. Thus the case for separate theoretical categories: one based on rent due to physical surplus, and the other based on long-term shortage of supply, given the effectual demand, is strong. In this context Ricardo's comments are most pertinent:

Adam Smith sometimes speaks of rent, in the strict sense to which I am desirous of confining it [rent is that portion of the produce of the earth, which is paid to the landlord for the use of the original and indestructible powers of the soil], but more often in the popular sense, in which the term is usually employed. He tells us that the demand for timber, and its consequent high price, in the more southern countries of Europe, caused a rent to be paid for forests in Norway, which could afford no rent. Is it not, however, evident, that the person who paid what he thus calls rent, paid it in consideration of the valuable commodity which was then standing on the land, and that he actually repaid himself with a profit, by the sale of the timber? If, indeed, after the timber was removed, any compensation were paid to the landlord for the use of the land, for the purpose of growing timber or any other produce, with a view to future demand, such compensation might justly be called rent, because it would be paid for the productive powers of the land; but in the case stated by Adam Smith, the compensation was paid for the liberty of removing and selling the timber, and not for the liberty of growing it. He speaks also of the rent of coal mines, and of stone quarries, to which the same observation applies — that the compensation given for the mine or quarry, is paid for the value of the coal or stone which can be removed from them, and has no connection with the original and indestructible powers of land (Ricardo 1951: 67–68).[18]

Round Up

Before we go any further, let us round up our understanding of Smith's theory of value. Our discussion has led us to understand that for Adam Smith, the natural price of a commodity was determined by the aggregate of direct and indirect natural wages, natural profits, and natural rent generated in the production of one unit of gross output of the commodity. Both the natural wages and the natural profits are necessities in the system, whereas the natural rent is the surplus. That is why some commodities such as coal, etc., could be supplied in the long run at their *sufficient price* — a price that contains only natural wages and profits but no rent. Given the natural wages and natural profits at any given point of time, the natural rent is determined by the physical surplus produced in the agricultural sector devoted to producing food. However, when it comes to the determination of natural wages and natural rate of profits at any given point of time, Smith identifies their minimum and maximum levels and argues that they rise or fall within those limits according to the rate of growth of the economy. However, nowhere does he give a theoretical description of how exactly could the level of wages or the rate of profits be determined for any given rate of growth of the economy. Here it appears that Smith defers to social convention in determining the exact rate of profits and the level of wages.[19]

---

18 Ricardo, however, seems to overlook his own argument while criticising Smith's theory of rent when he claims that 'If he [Adam Smith] had adverted to this principle, he would have made no distinction between the law which regulates the rent of mines and the rent of land' (Ricardo 1951: 329). Marshall pulled Ricardo up for this slip (Marshall 1890 [1949]: 139, f.n.1).

19 See Garegnani (1983b) for an emphasis on social convention in Smith's theory of distribution. Mark Blaug (1962), on the other hand, is apparently quite unsympathetic in his judgement of Adam Smith when he claims that 'A cost of production

In the end let us come back to our original puzzle: why did Adam Smith need to develop a 'theory' of value, and that too before discussing his theory of distribution? The answer to this question lies in understanding the nature of his 'contradictory' juxtapositions. The epistemological background of Smith's theory is not the same as the modern epistemological background of unidirectional *cause and effect* relationship. Smith simply does not recognise our persistent question: is it the distributional variables that determine the value of a commodity or is it the value of the commodity that determines the distributional variables? For Smith, a determination of a thing takes place only through its *representation* in something else — as if to exist, we need to see our image in the mirror! In this representational framework value is represented by its division into wages, profit and rent, and at the same time wages, profit and rent are represented as components of value. They function as a *sign* for each other and 'determine' each other simultaneously. For Smith, the problem of value and the problem of distribution cannot be separated in the sense we now recognise. This explains why he does not even recognise the so-called *labour theory of value,* which he had supposedly propounded and which played such an important role in subsequent theories of political economy since Ricardo. For Smith, its meaning is exhausted by the fact that when value resolves itself only in wages, then the real price is represented by the embodied labour of the commodity. However, once value is no longer resolvable in wages only, the embodied labour of a commodity is unable to mirror the real price and thus the matter ends right there. This brings us to the question of the other 'contradictory' juxtaposition of 'real value' as toil and trouble as well as the command of labour by the commodity. In Smith's representational framework, though the real value of a commodity is measured by the toil and trouble the labourer has to sacrifice to buy that commodity, this real value comes into existence only through its representation in the amount of labour that a commodity can command. Again, these two measures determine each other simultaneously as mirror images and it would be wrong to think that one is a measure for measuring changes over time

---

theory of the value of a commodity is obviously empty and meaningless if it does not include some implication of how the prices of productive services are determined. But in fact Adam Smith had no consistent theory of wages and rents and no theory of profit or pure interest at all' (Blaug 1962: 41).

and the other is a *numéraire* for measuring value at any given point of time.[20]

Part II
Some Significant Other Interpretations and Criticisms of Smith

After presenting my reading of Adam Smith on the question of value and distribution, I now turn to some other significant readings and criticisms of Smith on this question, starting from Smith's own contemporaries to our own times. It should be noted that I shall not focus on points of agreements but rather concentrate on points of disagreements and criticisms of Smith that I find unjustified.

Smith's Contemporaries

It is well known that Smith's good friend David Hume, in a letter dated 1 April 1776, wrote to Smith that: 'If you were here at my fireside, I should dispute some of your principles. I cannot think that the rent of farms makes any part of the price of the produce, but that the price is determined altogether by the quantity and the demand' (Mossner and Ross 1987: 186). It is not known whether this issue was ever discussed by Hume's fireside, as Hume fell ill rather seriously and died soon after on 25 August 1776. There is, however, no mention of this issue in Smith's few extant letters to Hume during this period. It is clear, however, that Smith did not make any changes in the second edition on this score, implying that he was not convinced by Hume's criticism. As I have suggested earlier, Hume's case would apply only to monopoly cases where supply is restricted given the effectual demand, and not generally.

Another of Smith's contemporaries, Governor Pownall, in his open letter dated 25 September 1776, wrote long and varied criticisms of the *Wealth of Nations*. On the question of value, he took objection to Smith's proposition that labour is the 'real price' of all commodities. He argued that a commodity is always a mixture of labour and some object, and thus its price cannot be reduced to labour alone. He further went on to develop an example of a strong and churlish man who takes possession of a 'tree loaded with the spontaneous fruits of

---

20 From this point of view, Adam Smith's reasoning falls more within what Foucault (1973) described as 'Classical' episteme rather than the 'modern' episteme.

nature' and who could force another weaker but industrious man to collect fruits for him if the weaker man needed to collect fruits for his necessities. By this example, Pownall challenged Smith's proposition that the 'real price' of a commodity is the amount of labour its possessor could command. According to Pownall, the fruits in the hands of the weaker man cannot command anybody's labour. Though his first criticism was simply a reflection of his misunderstanding of Smith's 'real measure' of value, his second had the potential of developing in a Marxist line by emphasising the relation of command over labour with the notion of property rights rather than commodity relations as such. In any case, Adam Smith invited Pownall for a discussion, which perhaps did take place, and the final result of this discussion is summed up by Smith in his letter of 26 October 1780 to Andreas Holt:

> I published more than two years ago a second edition of the inquiry concerning the Wealth of Nations, in which though I have made no material alteration, I have made a good number of corrections, none of which, however, affect even in the slightest degree, the general principles, or plan of the system. ... In the edition I flattered myself that I had obviated all the objections of Governor Pownall. I find however, he is by no means satisfied, and as Authors are not much disposed to alter the opinions they have once published, I am not much surprised at it (Mossner and Ross 1987: 250, letter 280).

Ricardo

Ricardo, who can be credited for establishing the theoretical foundations of classical political economy, criticises Adam Smith for abandoning the true theory of value to 'that early and rude state of society'. He objects to Smith's measure of 'real value' as labour commanded by a commodity on the ground that wage as *numéraire* is as variable as any money-commodity: 'Adam Smith, after most ably showing the insufficiency of a variable medium, such as gold and silver, for the purpose of determining the varying value of other things, has himself, by fixing on corn or labour, chosen a medium no less variable' (Ricardo 1951: 14).

However, most significantly, as is clear from Sraffa's account (1951, see 'Introduction' to Ricardo, Vol. I), Ricardo recognises that Smith did not investigate why the simple labour theory of value, which was valid for the 'early and rude state', could no longer be valid once profits and rents emerged as other sources of income. Adam Smith simply abandons his ingenious hypothesis without investigation and pro-pounds another hypothesis that value is made up by *adding up* wages, profits and rents. One implication of the 'adding up' theory, accord-ing to Ricardo, is Smith's erroneous proposition that 'the money price of corn regulates that of all other home-made commodities' (p. 509). This, Ricardo considers Adam Smith's 'original error' and argues that:

> In considering a rise in the price of commodities as a necessary consequence of a rise in the price of corn, he [Adam Smith] reasons as though there were no other fund from which the increased charge could be paid. He has wholly neglected the consideration of profits, diminution of which forms that fund, without raising the price of commodities. If this opinion of Dr. Smith were well founded, profits could never really fall, whatever accumulation of capital there might be (Ricardo 1951: 308).

Now, as I have argued, Adam Smith is quite clear that in the context of accumulation the causes that raise wages also cause profits to fall. A rise in wages in real terms (i.e., in terms of the labour-commanded measure of value) implies a fall in the real value of all commodities, and this fall can come about only if the rate of profits falls (given rent). Thus Ricardo is not right in charging Smith of neglecting the inverse wage-profit relation in the context of accumulation.[21] As a matter of fact, Smith is quite clear that a rise in wages may not lead to a rise in prices because of the compensating effect of a fall in the rate of profits:

> In countries which are fast advancing to riches, the low rate of profit may, in the price of many commodities, compensate the high wages of labour, and enable those countries to sell as cheap as their less thriving neighbours, among whom the wages of labour may be lower (p. 114).

---

21 Ricardo (1951: 289) misinterprets Smith's position with respect to a rise in wages due to accumulation of capital as 'a temporary rise, proceeding from increased funds before the population is increased. ...' This leads him to think that in the long run Smith has no means of showing a fall in the rate of profits due to accumulation of capital other than his logically flawed argument of overcrowding of capital stock. However, as we have seen, Smith's theory of wages allows for the long-term rise in real wages due to accumulation of capital.

In any case, Smith's proposition that 'the money price of corn regulates that of all other home-made commodities' is made not in the context of accumulation but in the context of bounty on the export of corn; and Ricardo's criticism implies that Smith simply adds the increased wages (due to high price of corn) to given profits to arrive at the conclusion that all prices will rise. Here 'price' does not refer to 'real price' but rather to the nominal price (in terms of silver). Now, the logic of Smith's proposition is as follows. Wages are given in terms of corn and they are fixed. Given the wages in terms of corn, a rise in the silver price of corn (due to a fall in the average supply of corn in the home market because of increase in export due to the bounty on corn exports) will lead to a rise in the nominal wages. A rise in the nominal price of corn will also lead to a rise in the nominal prices of all other 'rude' produce of land, since they must maintain a certain proportion to the price of corn — a proposition that he had established earlier. This implies a rise in the nominal price of both labour and raw materials of manufactures and thus a proportionate rise in their nominal prices as well. Of course, Smith is assuming that silver is not produced at home. In other words, the impact of bounty on corn export will be a general inflation. There is a problem with Smith's reasoning here, which lies in the fact that in his account the system settles back at the same level in real terms, with a reduced amount of corn supply on the average. How can the effectual demand for corn be reduced when nothing in real terms is changing? And if the effectual demand for corn remains the same, then the fall in supply must lead to a relative rise in the 'market price' of corn, causing an immediate rise in the rate of profit in the corn sector. This would lead to a flow of capital from manufacturing to the corn sector and an eventual rise in the supply of corn before the system settles back again. Apparently, Smith erroneously balances the fall in the supply of corn with a rise in the inflow of money or silver — as if, contrary to his own major stand against the mercantilist doctrine, money could compensate for real changes.[22] Let us follow Ricardo's argument further. He goes on to explain:

> ... If, when wage rose, the farmer could raise the price of his corn, and the clothier, the hatter, the shoemaker, and every

---

22 O'Donnell (1990) argues that inflow of silver due to bounty on export of corn leads to an increase in 'specie points' and thus a general rise in prices becomes permanent. He, however, forgets that a bounty on export of corn does not only increase the inflow of specie but also reduces the average supply of corn in the home market, which would have some real consequences in the system.

other manufacturer, could also raise the price of their goods in proportion to the advance, although estimated in money they might be all raised, they would continue to bear the same value relatively to each other. Each of these trades could command the same quantity as before of the goods of the others, which, since it is goods, and not money, which constitute wealth, is the only circumstance that could be of importance to them; and the whole rise in the price of raw produce and of goods, would be injurious to no other persons but to those whose property consisted of gold and silver, or whose annual income was paid in a contributed quantity of those metals, whether in the form of bullion or of money. Suppose the use of money to be wholly laid aside, and all trade to be carried on by barter. Under such circumstances, could corn rise in exchangeable value with other things? If it could, then it is not true that the value of corn regulates the value of all other commodities; for to do that, it should not vary in relative value to them. If it could not, then it must be maintained, that whether corn be obtained on rich, or on poor land, with much labour, or with little, with the aid of machinery, or without, it would always exchange for an equal quantity of all other commodities (Ricardo 1951: 308–09).

The first question that arises here is: how would Smith's arguments run if money is taken out of picture? Though Smith did not discuss such a case explicitly, we could argue that in Smith's case, as has been explained earlier, the first impact of a bounty on the export of corn is a reduction in the average supply of corn in the home market. This, given the effectual demand for corn, will raise the price of corn vis-a-vis all other commodities immediately. But this is a short-term situation. A rise in the market price of corn above its natural price will bring higher profits to the farmers of corn, which will attract capital from the manufacturing sector to corn production, thereby bringing the relative prices back to parity. And here we come to the crux of Ricardo's critique: how can Smith deny that the relative price of corn would not rise even if the increased supply of corn came from much poorer quality lands? And thus the impact of bounty on corn export would be a permanent increase in rent. But the answer to this question is simple. Let us look at its impact on the natural price of corn first. As we have seen, rent is determined as residual in Smith's system and the indirect element of wages, profits and rent in his price equation takes account of the inputs per unit of output. Thus any change in the technique of production will have an impact on rent, as well as, given real wages and the rate of profits, on the relative prices. Smith, however, would not necessarily assume that the increased supply of corn must come from poorer quality land. Second, if the increase in the supply of corn comes from poorer quality land, its impact would be to reduce the average residual rent on land, as the rate of profits is given as a necessary cost at any given point of time.

As a matter of fact, Ricardo does not see that the role of productive technique in the determination of prices is taken into account by Smith through his 'ultimate' resolution of prices into wages, profits and rent. He incorrectly thinks that Smith's rejection of the so-called labour theory of value in an advanced society is a denial of any role to technique of production in the determination of prices. As Ricardo wrote to James Mill in 1818:

> He [Torrens] makes it appear that Smith says that after capital accumulates and industrious people are set to work the quantity of labour employed is not the only circumstance that determines the value of commodities, and that I oppose this opinion. Now I want to show that I do not oppose this opinion in the way that he represents me to do so, but Adam Smith thought, that as in the early stage of society, all the produce of labour belonged to the labourer, and as after stock was accumulated, a part went to profits, that accumulation, necessarily, without any regard to the different degree of durability of capital, or any other circumstance whatever, *raised* the price or exchangeable value of commodities, and consequently that their value was no longer regulated by the quantity of labour necessary to their production. In opposition to him, I maintain that it is not because of this division into profits and wages — it is not because capital accumulates, that exchangeable value varies, but it is in all stages of society, owing only to two causes: one the more or less quantity of labour required, the other the greater or less durability of capital: — that the former is never superseded by the later, but is only modified by it (Ricardo 1951–52, Vol. VII: 377).

Though Ricardo is right in what he says, it should be noted that while the relative prices will not change with emergence of profits if the ratio of means of production to labour is the same for all the commodities, Adam Smith's 'real' value of all commodities would nevertheless rise due to the emergence of profits. Further, as we have suggested, for

Smith, the significance of the so-called 'labour theory of value' is not that it gives the principle for determining relative exchange values of commodities, but rather that it determined the 'real' value of commodities in that early and rude stage of society.

Ricardo also criticises Smith's theory of rent from the vantage point of his assumption of diminishing returns on land. He argues that even when there is no poorer quality land available for cultivation, the marginal dose of capital on land must not pay any rent:

> But if it were true that England had so far advanced in cultivation, that at this time there were no lands remaining which did not afford a rent, it would be equally true, that there formerly must have been such lands; and that whether there be or not, is of no importance to this question, for it is the same thing if there be any capital employed in Great Britain on land which yields only the return of stock with its ordinary profits, whether it be employed on old or new land. If a farmer agrees for land on lease of seven or fourteen years, he may propose to employ on it a capital of 10,000*l.*, knowing that at the existing price of grain and raw produce, he can replace that part of his stock which he is obliged to spend, pay his rent, and obtain a general rate of profit. He will not employ 11,000*l.*, unless the last 1000*l.* can be employed so productively as to afford him the usual profits of stock. In his calculation, whether he shall employ it or not, he considers only whether the price of raw produce is sufficient to replace his expenses and profits, for he knows that he shall have no additional rent to pay (ibid., Vol. I: 328–29).

Before we take up Smith's plausible answer to this criticism, let us note two fundamental facts: (*i*) Smith does assume that in all 'great countries' there was no more opportunity for 'extension' of cultivation, as all his examples of increase in production of one sort of vegetable crop comes at the cost of fall in the cultivation of some other sort (also his example of potatoes [p. 176ff.] shows that his interest was only in examining the case when population had risen enough to ensure that all lands were under cultivation);[23] and (*ii*) Smith does not assume

---

23 Gee (1981) quotes Smith: 'In all the great countries of Europe, however, much good land still remains uncultivated, and the greater part of what is cultivated is far from being improved to the degree of which it is capable', to argue that Smith does not maintain that extension of cultivation is not possible. In this context it should be

that the landlords were competing to let their lands to the farmers; his assumption is that the farmers were competing to rent the lands from the landlords. Given that no more land was available, the landlords were able to extract the maximum rents from the farmers.[24] On Ricardo's specific argument that the marginal dose of capital on any given land must not pay rent, it must be admitted that Adam Smith never poses this question to himself. However, it should also be noted that Ricardo's argument rests on the tacit assumption that there is a smooth declining curve to the returns on successive doses of capital on land — which is an assumption and not a logical necessity. Smith may very well have assumed a fixed coefficient technology between capital, labour and natural land, where returns on all investments designed to augment land are calculated as profits and not rent; and thus having no impact on the original rent of the original and indestructible quality of land.

The Ricardians

A contemporary of Ricardo's, David Buchanan interprets Smith's theory of rent as a result of scarcity price and criticises him for differentiating the nature of rent from the nature of extraordinary profits due to secrets in manufacture:

The high price which leaves a surplus or rent to the landlord, after paying wages and profit, being no way necessary to production, must be accounted for on a different principle and it

---

noted that the passage quoted in the text is taken from a context where Smith is criticising the government policies that have 'unnaturally' created better investment conditions for capital in the manufacturing and trading sectors, and that it is not a statement that related to his theoretical model. Furthermore, it is pertinent to note that the same passage goes on to state that 'What circumstances in the policy of Europe have given the trades which are carried on in towns so great an advantage over that which is carried on in the country, that private persons frequently find it more for their advantage to employ their capitals in the most distant carrying trades of Asia and America, than in the improvement and cultivation of the most fertile fields in their own neighbourhood, I shall endeavour to explain at full length in the two following books' (Smith 1976: 374–75). The point to note here is that Smith talks about 'improvements of the most fertile lands' and not 'extension' of cultivation.

24 In this scenario every increase in total output of food could come about only through improvement in the quality of land through investment (i.e., land-augmenting technical change), a return to which must be calculated as profit.

seems accordingly to arise from the comparative scarcity in which articles that yield a rent are generally produced. It is clear that the quantity of a commodity consumed, can never for any length of time exceed the quantity produced; and it is by a rise of price that the consumption is confined within the limits of the supply; while, in the case of a more abundant supply, the consumption is accelerated by a fall of price. The price is, in this manner, the great regulator of consumption; and where a commodity is sold at such a price as to leave a surplus after paying all the necessary expenses of its production, it will always be found that this high price is required to proportion the consumption to the supply. It is necessary, for example, that the yearly supply of corn should last until the produce of the succeeding season reach the market; and the price, by which the daily and weekly consumption is regulated, according to the supply of the year, is always such as to leave a rent or surplus above wages and profit. The price of every commodity which affords a rent is regulated in the same manner. ... When Dr. Smith considers the extraordinary profit derived from secrets in manufacture as the high price of manufacturer's private labour, he clearly mistakes the nature of this profit, which is in no respect different from the rent of land (Buchanan 1817, in Mizuta 2000, Vol. II: 79–80).

As we have argued earlier, for Adam Smith the rent of land that produces food is not due to shortage of supply or some kind of monopoly but rather due to nature being bountiful. However, even J.S. Mill (1848), also erroneously, interprets Smith's theory of rent of land as based on the idea of monopoly price:

It was long thought by political economists, among the rest even by Adam Smith, that the produce of land is always at a monopoly value, because (they said) in addition to the ordinary rate of profit, it always yields something further for rent. This we now see to be erroneous. A thing cannot be at a monopoly value, when its supply can be increased to an indefinite extent if we are only willing to incur the cost. If no more corn than the existing quantity is grown, it is because the value has not risen high enough to remunerate any one for growing it. Any land which at the existing price, and by the existing processes, will yield the ordinary profit, is tolerably certain, unless some artificial hindrance intervenes, to be cultivated, although nothing may be left for rent. As long as there is any land, fit for cultivation, which at the existing price cannot be profitably cultivated at all, there must be some land a little better, which yield the ordinary profit, but allow nothing for rent: and that land, if within the boundary of a farm, will be cultivated by the farmer; if not so, probably by the proprietor, or by some other person on sufferance. Some such land at least, under cultivation, therefore can scarcely fail to be (Mill 1848: 559).

The reader can see that Mill's reasoning is based on the implicit assumption of diminishing returns on land — an assumption that Adam Smith does not maintain.

Another contemporary of Ricardo's, J.R. McCulloch (1838) criticises Smith's additive theory of value from a pure labour theory of value perspective. He simply asserts that values of commodities would not change with changes in distribution as long as the labour-time needed to produce the commodities remains the same. He also criticises Smith's theory of rent from the vantage point of Ricardo's theory. Wakefield, however, correctly points out that a fall in the rate of profits would affect prices of different commodities differently 'for simple reason, because the proportion which capital bears to labour is not the same in all employments' (Wakefield 1843, in Mizuta 2000, Vol. III: 510).

Marx

Marx is also critical of Smith for abandoning the 'correct' theory of value in favour of the 'incorrect' *additive* theory of value and points to a logical contradiction between the two:

Adam Smith first explains that exchange-value resolves itself into a certain quantity of labour and that after deducting raw materials etc., the value contained in exchange-value is resolved into that part of labour for which the labourer is paid and that part for which he is not paid, the latter part consists of profits and rent (the profit in turn may be resolved into profit and interest). Having shown this, he suddenly turns about and instead of resolving exchange-value into wages, profit and rent, he declares these to be the elements forming exchange-value, he makes them into independent exchange-values that form the exchange value of the commodity from the values of wages, profit and rent, which are determined independently and separately. Instead of having their source in value, they become the source of value (Marx 1968, *TSV II*: 217).

If I define the lengths of the three straight lines independently, and then make these three lines 'components' of a fourth straight line equal in length to their sum, this is in no way the same procedure as if I start with a given straight line and divide this for some purpose or other — 'resolve' it, so to speak — into three parts. The length of the line in the first case invariably changes with the length of the three lines whose sum it forms; in the latter case the length of the three segments is limited from the beginning by their forming parts of a line of a given size (Marx 1992, *Capital II*: 459).

If our reading of Adam Smith is accepted, then it is clear that even though Smith's language here and there gives this false impression of a logical contradiction, his theoretical position recognises the constraint binding on distribution and accordingly treats rent as the residual income category.

Marx further accuses Adam Smith for arguing in a circle; for example, if the wages represent the independent component of value, then how can the price of wages or the price of the worker's necessary means of subsistence be determined? In Marx's opinion, Smith would have to say that: 'The price of wages is determined by the price of the means of subsistence and the price of the means of subsistence is determined by the price of wages' (Marx 1968, *TSV II*: 222). Though it is not clear what exactly Marx has in mind here, on the face of it his criticism does not appear to be justified. As we have seen, Smith measures 'real value' by the labour-time a commodity can buy or command. A given wage in real terms implies that the labour-time commanded by the wage basket is directly given, which is the 'real price' of wages. Thus it simply does not make sense to say that 'Adam Smith would have to say: The price of wages is determined by the price of means of subsistence. ...' It would make sense only if price is measured in terms of any arbitrary *numéraire,* but Smith does not proceed that way. As we have shown, his determination of real prices or real values is consistent and does not involve any circular reasoning.

Marx also criticises Smith for omitting the constant capital (i.e., raw materials and depreciated fixed capital) element in the value of a commodity. This, according to Marx, is not merely an oversight on Smith's part but rather essential for his additive theory of value:

> One can see here too why Adam Smith — despite his considerable scruples on this point — resolves the entire value of the commodity into rent, profit and wages and omits constant capital, although of course he admits its existence for each 'individual' capitalist. For otherwise he would have to say: The value of a commodity consists of wages, profit, rent and that part of the value of the commodity which does not consist of wages, profit, rent. It would therefore be necessary to determine value independently of wages, profit and rent (ibid.: 219).

But if Marx is right, then the value of a commodity will *immediately* resolve into wages, profit and rent. There would be no need for Smith to add that the value of a commodity immediately or *ultimately* resolves itself into wages, profit and rent. It would be too far-fetched to assume that Adam Smith acknowledged 'constant capital' (in Marx's terminology) for individual capitals but thought that they simply disappeared into thin air when they were all aggregated. However, in *Capital, Vol. II*, Marx goes on to further argue that:

> The statement that the entire price of commodities is either 'immediately' or 'ultimately' resolvable into v + s [wages + surplus] would only cease to be an empty subterfuge if Smith could demonstrate that the commodity products whose price is immediately resolved into c (the price of the means of production consumed) + v + s are finally compensated for by commodity products which entirely replace these 'consumed means of production', and which are for their part produced simply by the outlay of variable capital [wage advances only], i.e., capital laid out on labour-power. The price of these latter commodities would then immediately be v + s. And in this way the price of the former, too, c + v + s, where c stands for the component of constant capital, would be ultimately resolvable into v + s. Adam Smith himself did not believe he had given such a proof ... (Marx 1992, *Capital II*: 450).

As I have argued earlier, Adam Smith neither omits the constant capital element in resolving the value of a commodity into wages, profit and rent, nor resolves it by making them to be ultimately produced by only labourers, unassisted by any means of production. It forms the *ultimate* part of the resolution, though not in the manner Marx proposes. Ironically, Smith's procedure to calculate the 'ultimate' part of this resolution is similar to Marx's own procedure of calculating the labour-embodied part of the constant capital used in the production of a commodity.

Marx is also not happy with Smith's theory of rent. Even though he rightly acknowledges the Physiocratic basis of Smith's theory, he argues that: 'Smith forgets altogether, that it is a question of *price,* and derives rent from the ratio between the amount of *food* yielded by agriculture and the amount of *food* consumed by the agricultural worker' (Marx 1968, *TSV II:* 355). He goes on to elaborate further:

> But why does his product always pay a rent? Why is its *ordinary price* always higher than its *sufficient price* [the price that covers only wages and profit]? Smith leaves price out of account here and reverts to the physiocratic theory. What runs through it, however, is that the demand is always so great because the product itself creates the demand (since it creates) its own consumers. Even provided that this were so it is incomprehensible why the demand should rise above the supply and thus force the price **above** the sufficient price (ibid.: 358).

Let us take the minor issue of demand first. As we have argued earlier, in cases of monopoly the role of demand becomes critical in determining whether that land will pay any rent or not. In the case of food, however, Smith's argument that population adjusts to the supply of food in the long run was only to deny the role of demand and supply in determining the price of food or the rent of land that produces food. Smith's explanation is built on the supposition that when the aggregate supply of food is equal to its effectual demand, every individual unit of land produces a physical surplus over and above all the raw materials, wages and profits deducted in the same physical unit. The landlords appropriate this physical surplus as rent. This rent is always realised in the market as it is assumed that the aggregate supply is equal to the effectual demand. So whatever happens to be the price of food, it must incorporate the value of rent that is already appropriated in physical terms. Marx here is clearly mistaken in thinking that when it is accepted that even the worst land produces physical surplus that converts into rent, Adam Smith still needs to prove that the price of food would be higher than its *sufficient price*.[25] We should, however, keep in mind that we have taken Marx's criticisms from his notes, which he did not publish in his lifetime. We cannot be sure which ones he would have published and in what form after further reflection.

Following in the footsteps of Marx, A.K. Dasgupta claims: 'There is no doubt that Adam Smith's value analysis involves a contradiction' (Dasgupta 1985: 49). To prove this, he first assumes that an output Q is produced by L hours of labour only. The Q is then divided into subsistence wages W and surplus S, which is appropriated by the capitalist as P (i.e., rent is submerged into profit). If wage rate is given by w, then the real value of wages is equal to $W/w = L$ and real value of profit is equal to $P/w = m$ (say). Now, the rate of profit r will be given by: $r = P/wL$. Therefore, $m = P/w = rL$. From these identities, he derives the real value of Q as

$$Q/w = L + m = L + rL = L(1 + r).$$

On the basis of this equation he argues that:

> We are thus led on to the conclusion that the value of output Q is a function of the rate of profits, while the rate of wages remains the same. This of course could not happen if Q were taken as given, as it should be. With Q given, the rate of wages should fall as the rate of profits rises, and vice versa. Failure to show this inverse relationship between wages and profits is a lacuna in Smith's system — a 'ridiculous blunder', as Marx would put it (ibid.: 49).

It is not clear which contradiction Dasgupta is referring to here. Given that $r = P/wL$ and that both w and L are given, then r could move only with movements in P. But he himself has defined $P = (Q - W)$, where

---

25 Schumpeter also identifies Smith's theory of rent with the monopoly theory only: 'Smith not unnaturally — though wrongly — arrives at the conclusion that the phenomenon of rent can be due only to a "monopoly" in land.' (Schumpeter 1954: 190). If our interpretation is accepted, then Smith's reasoning would be that if land was free, then the physical surplus of land would be appropriated as profit. However, once it becomes private property, the landlords are able to convert the physical surplus from being part of profits to rent. This, however, is quite different from the idea that landlords by monopolising land restrict food supply compared to its effectual demand, which raises its price and generates rent on land.

both Q and W are given. If there is any apparent problem here, then it lies with clubbing the rent and profits together into a single category called 'profits' and then misattributing to Smith the notion that total surplus or the value of total surplus is determined independently from outside. But as we have argued earlier, Smith did not say anything of the sort. When profit reaches its maximum, the rent goes to zero and the profit is determined as the residual given the subsistence wage. However, as long as profit remains below its maximum and the rent is positive, then it is the rent that is determined as residual given the rate of profits independently from outside the system. There is no such contradiction in Adam Smith. Such contradictions only emerge when we forget the special status of rent in his theory.

The Neoclassicists

A.C. Whitaker argues that:

> Adam Smith states that since under the division of labor any man must derive almost all his necessaries, conveniences and luxuries from the labor of other people, he must be rich, in the sense of possessing things of value, in proportion to the quantity of this labor which he can command. The assumption implicit in this is that the quantity of labor expended upon the production of things for this man, as *labor-cost*, determines their values. For if the economic goods obtained by him from the labor of others, which he is enabled to command, should have values out of proportion to the quantity of labor so commanded, namely, their labor-cost, this man would not be rich or poor merely in proportion to the labor which he commands. Since, therefore, the labor-command standard of value is made to depend upon labor-cost regulation of value, according to the principal argument advanced by Smith, it follows that Smith is really estopped [sic] from applying the labor-command standard as he does under the conditions of advanced society. For he himself has stated that labor-cost regulation of value fails under these conditions (Whitaker 1904: 39–40).

Though it is true, as we have noted earlier, that in the early phase of his book Adam Smith appears to argue that the labour-commanded measure of value runs in parallel with the 'labour-cost' or labour-embodied measure of value and that Whitaker is right in pointing out that from the perspective of the owner of a commodity, it cannot be argued that he or she is richer or poorer by the measure of its direct command of labour, for a commodity that commands less labour directly may have cost more labour-time to produce than a commodity that commands more direct labour. However, Smith's real measure of value was designed for measuring changes in value over periods of time and it was designed from the perspective of the labourer as the subject who needed to acquire any given commodity the value of which was being compared over a period of time. In this context, Whitaker's contention that along with the fall of the 'labor-cost regulation' of value, the labour-commanded measure of it must *ipso facto* fall, does not hold water.

Edwin Cannan writes:

A theory of value should explain in general terms why commodities and services are exchanged for one another in the ratios in which they are exchanged, and also why from time to time these ratios are subject to alteration.

As an answer to the first of these two questions Adam Smith's theory does not seem even plausible. ... The pair of slippers and the book became worth the same because the same total expenses in wages, profits, and rents is required to produce them. This does not seem plausible to us because we can see that the equality of the wages, profits, and rents with the price is no proof that the price is caused by the wages, profits, and rents: it may be the other way round.

Adam Smith's answer to the second question seems much more plausible. If the particular wages, profits, and rents payable for the production of any commodity rise, we expect that commodity to rise in price. Suppose, for instance, that the coalminers of the world were attacked by some disease which reduced their numbers, and at the same time growing refinement cause greater reluctance of new persons to enter the business, coal would rise, and it would be natural to ascribe the rise to the increased wages: or suppose that frightened by strikes and rumours of syndicalism, no one would put more capital into mining, coal again would rise and it would be natural to ascribe the rise to the increased profits which must be paid to keep some capital in the industry: suppose that owing to the spread of towns or something else there were more reluctance to allow mining to be carried out at the expense of damaging the surface, coal once more would rise, and it would be natural to ascribe the rise to the increased amount paid as rent or royalty.

But the price of coal could not rise an atom if the same quantity of coal continued to be put on the market: it rises because the quantity coming to market is reduced, and its rise is not in the least dependent on the higher wages, profits, or rents paid. If the number of miners were reduced to one-half, the price of coal would rise just the same if the miners still employed did not get any penny more than they did before. Each of the suppositions involves a rise in the price of coal not because a particular factor of production is better paid, but because that factor is shorter in supply, and its shortness causes a shortness in the supply of coal. There is no harm in saying that the rise of price is due to diminished supply of labour, capital, or land required for the production of coal, but we must not say that it is caused by the rise of the wages, profits, or rents. It is undeniably rather plausible to say so, but it is incorrect (Cannan 1929: 170–72).

As far as the first criticism is concerned, we have already discussed it enough and there is no need to cover the same ground again. As for the second criticism: Cannan's argument clearly rests on the assumption of a given, downward-sloping demand curve and a vertical supply curve. He says that a rise in the price of coal is possible only if the vertical supply curve (given the demand curve) shifts to the left, and not necessarily because of a rise of some income category. If this were a shortterm phenomenon then, as we have seen earlier, Smith would characterise an immediate rise in the price of coal as its market price deviating from its natural price. In this case, either wages or profits or rent would rise above its natural rate and bring the equilibrating mechanism of the market into play. Notice that in all such adjustments of market prices to natural prices, it is the market prices that *cause* the income categories to deviate from their natural rate and not the other way around. Thus, for the short run, Cannan's interpretation of Smith is simply wrong — Smith does not claim that it is movements in income categories that move the market prices from their natural prices.

However, Cannan's argument seems to imply long-term changes. If that is the case, then Smith would argue that the increased disagreeableness of coalmining or higher risk of capital investment in coalmining or long-term shortage of supply due to monopoly would permanently raise the wages or the rate of profits or the rate of rent. And this would cause the natural price of coal to rise. In this case, the causality will run the other way around — the rise of some income category will lead to a rise in the natural price of coal. Cannan's point that this could not happen unless there was a leftward shift in the supply is simply a tautology, given his fixed, downward-sloping demand curve. Smith's proposition rests on the argument that in the new long-term situation, there would be zero supply of coal if the price was not higher than the previous natural price. The extent of the supply of coal would depend on the effectual demand for it. Even if we accept Cannan's assumption that the level of demand curve stays put before and after the changes, in Smith's reasoning it would imply a fall in the effectual demand for coal. It should be noted here that in this case the rise in the price of coal is not caused by a fall in the supply; rather, a rise in the natural price is caused by a rise in an income category, which brings about the equilibrium of supply and effectual demand at a lower level of output of coal than previously.

Following Marshall,[26] Samuel Hollander (1973a, 1992) has provided the most detailed and comprehensive neoclassical interpretation of Adam Smith's theory of value.[27] It should, however, be noted that the sort of value theory Smith had inherited was not an objective or a cost of production theory but rather, as his *Lectures* testify, a subjective theory of value.[28] Robertson and Taylor argue that 'Adam Smith felt that this sort of subjective analysis was leading nowhere. It had not so far proved capable of being employed in any actual quantitative measurement', and given that Smith needed a real measure of wealth over periods of time in the *Wealth of Nations*, he had to abandon the subjective arguments and develop 'some unifying standard of value' (Robertson and Taylor 1957:82).[29] D.P. O'Brian argues that Smith's shift of emphasis from subjective to a cost of production theory of value is due to the consideration of a theory of distribution in the *Wealth of Nations*, which is absent in his *Lectures*:

Smith's *Wealth of Nations* contained a theory of distribution, though his *Lectures* did not. Without the concept of marginal

26 'His [Adam Smith's] highest claim to have made an epoch in thought is that he was the first to make a careful and scientific inquiry into the manner in which value measures human motive, on the one side measuring the desire of purchasers to obtain wealth, and on the other the efforts and sacrifices (or "Real Cost of Production") undergone by its producers' (Marshall 1949: 627).

27 Also see Blaug (1962), Kaushil (1973) and Larsen (1977) for similar neoclassical interpretations of Smith.

28 See Kauder (1953) for subjective elements in economic valuation since Aristotle and Smith's break from it.

29 The page number is from J.C. Woods (ed.), *Adam Smith: Critical Assessment*.

productivity, there was no very obvious way of linking distribution to value except by a cost of production theory of value. Having thought it necessary to introduce a theory of distribution, Adam Smith had to rework his value theory (1975: 92).

Paul Douglas (1928) argues that:

> Smith had considered the possibility of utility but dismissed it because of the paradox which Locke, Hutcheson, Law, and Harris had pointed out before him between the relative value of water and diamonds. ... The main reason why Smith and those who followed him abandoned utility as determinant of value was, of course, because they were comparing the total utilities yielded by varying types of objects rather than their marginal utilities (1928: 78).

Hollander (1973a, 1992), on the other hand, argues that the idea of cost price was as prevalent in the period prior to the publication of the *Wealth of Nations* and that 'on the contrary, his [Smith's] concern with these matters fell within the mainstream of development of contemporary economic thought' (Hollander 1992: 62). He further argues that the so-called water-diamond paradox had little to do with the role of utility in determining the value of a commodity; rather, it was meant to show that physiological needs had little to do with the valuation of commodities. Anyway, the most interesting aspect for our purpose is his claim that 'a price-theoretic orientation to the *Wealth of Nations* which in substance, if not expression, has a "modern" [i.e., neoclassical] flavour cannot be gainsaid; no one has yet been able to show that the unfamiliar formulation affects the substance of the analysis' (ibid.: 61).

Hollander first emphasises the market prices in Smith's scheme to draw out the notions of demand and supply. As we have acknowledged earlier, in the case of market supply falling short of the effectual demand, the market price of the commodity would rise above the natural price; however, the extent of the rise will depend upon the extent of the shortage as well as the nature of the commodity and the situation of the buyers. From these commonsensical notions of Smith, Hollander concludes that Smith has a notion of a downward-sloping demand schedule with proper elasticity properties. This demand schedule is supposed to pass through the independently determined point of effectual demand at the 'natural price'. Hollander also argues that the notion of an upward-sloping supply curve is also present in Adam Smith:

> The possibility was recognized of withdrawing supplies to add to inventory as prices fall, and conversely drawing from inventories as prices rise, thus generating a supply curve with a positive slope. ... Supply elasticity will thus depend on the possibility of withdrawing products from the market and holding them in stock. We may therefore attribute to Smith a positively sloped (market) supply curve as well as negatively sloped demand curve (Hollander 1992: 68–69).

As a matter of fact, an upward-sloping supply schedule of the neo-classical variety cannot by itself tell us whether the supply is greater or smaller than the effectual demand. Smith, of course, takes the supply as a given quantity brought to the market, which determines the quantity of either excess demand or excess supply at the given natural prices. It is only *after* a certain quantity has been brought to the market that the question of withdrawing some of the supply or adding from inventory to the given supply arises. The so-called market supply curve in Smith's analysis is drawn from the point of given market supply at the level of given natural price, which explicitly shows, given the 'supply elasticity' of the commodity, how much of the supply has been withdrawn from the market or added from the inventory, as the price in the market will be determined by the point of intersection of the market supply and the demand curves. In other words, there is no independent upward-sloping supply schedule in Smith; the market supply curves are drawn on the basis of the given excess market supply at the natural prices (see Figure 1.1).

The next step in Hollander's argument is to show that in the case of 'market prices' not being equal to the given 'natural prices', the resource movements will shift the market supply curves towards the 'natural prices'. Now, as far as this is descriptive of how market prices gravitate toward the natural prices in Smith's framework, it is quite faithful to Smith. However, the identification of Smith's notions of demand and supply with neoclassical notions of demand and supply has serious problems. The Smithean notions of demand and supply are *descriptive* in nature rather than being mathematical *functions* of price, as in neoclassical economics. In Smith's case,

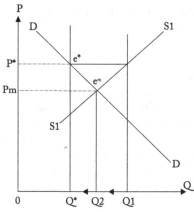

Gravitation Mechanism for a single commodity

e* is the point of effectual demand and P* is the long-term equilibrium or the natural price. DD is the demand curve that passes through e*. Q1 is the initial quantity brought to the market. S1S1 is the supply curve that passes through quantity Ql. Pm is the market price and Q1Q2 is the quantity added to the inventory. Q* is the equilibrium supply.

Figure 1.1

both the effectual demand and the market supply are given quantities and the so-called market demand and supply curves are drawn on the basis of these given quantities, which is not the case with neoclassical demand and supply curves. The central question of value determination in Smith's analysis is: how, at any given point of time, is the 'natural' price of a commodity determined? On this question, Hollander's answer is that Smith 'assumes constant-cost conditions in all industries' (ibid.: 72). If that is the case, then by assumption the role of demand is removed from the determination of 'natural' prices and that demand can only affect the allocation of resources. The reader should note that in a general equilibrium context, which is what Hollander ascribes to Smith, an assumption of constant returns to scale is not sufficient to ensure constant cost, since a rise in demand for a relatively 'capital intensive' good in comparison to a 'labour intensive' good would amount to an increase in the demand for capital vis-a-vis labour, which will increase the interest on capital compared to wages and thus cause a shift in techniques for all goods in favour of relatively more 'labour intensive' techniques resulting in changes in all the prices. This prompts Hollander to argue:

> It is thus implied both that factor proportions are identical from industry to industry — only then will the average ratios of returns remain constant following a change in the structure

of industry in response, for example, a changed pattern of demand — and that factor proportions in each productive unit are constant (Hollander 1973a: 122).

Hollander, however, does not provide any evidence from Smith that suggests he made any such assumption. Such an implied assumption on Smith's system of analysis is based on the conclusion arrived at by attributing a general equilibrium framework to Smith, resulting in a sort of a circular reasoning.

Hollander further argues that Smith assumes 'constant cost' only for his basic expository model; in general, however, he assumes variable cost conditions with the level of demand playing a role in determining the prices. The fundamental question in this respect is: to what extent do variable cost conditions play a role when supplies adjust to effectual demands during the course of gravitation of 'market prices' to 'natural prices'? In section entitled 'Natural Price in Contradistinction to Market Price', we have argued that Smith seems to maintain a constant cost assumption in this respect. Hollander, however, uses a different strategy. He asks the question: what happens to prices when demand shifts? If a shift in demand brings a change in prices, then he concludes that as evidence of variable cost conditions. But this conclusion crucially depends on the highly questionable assumption that the presumed supply curve stays put while the demand curve slides up or down the given supply curve. Let us briefly examine his various examples of the evidence of variable cost conditions in Adam Smith. In his latest textbook (Hollander 1992: 72–74), he provides four examples to buttress his case — (*i*) The example of rare birds: In this case the supply is fixed. In such cases it is well accepted that demand plays a crucial role in determining prices. However, the law of competition does not operate in such cases, which are therefore considered to be outside the realm of the theory of value; (*ii*) the example of wild animals and the price of butcher's meat: In this case Smith argues that when the supply of wild animals is superabundant, then the price of meat cannot be higher than the labour cost of catching the animals. But with the passage of time and falling natural supply of wild animals and rising demand for meat, the price of meat rises to the level where it can cover the natural price of wages, profits and rent. Up to this point the price is governed by the level of demand; but once the price rises to the level where it can pay the natural price of wages, profits and rent, then the butcher's meat can be produced commercially. This is when the butcher's meat becomes a commodity governed by the law of competition and the theory of value. But once that happens then, as Hollander himself points out, 'A (long-run) price ceiling is thus ultimately imposed as demand for butcher's meat continues to rise: "When it has got so high it cannot well go higher. If it did, more land and more industry would soon be employed to increase their quantity" ([Smith] p. 220)' (Hollander 1992: 73). In other words, demand plays a role in fixing the price only until the supply is fixed and the competitive mechanism does not operate. However, once a good qualifies for the condition of competitive supply, the role of demand disappears from the determination of its price; (*iii*) the case of sea fish: Here Adam Smith argues that with the rise of population and a substantial rise in demand (Smith takes an example of a rise in demand from 1,000 tons to 10,000 tons) for fish can only be met by going a greater distance and employing larger vessels and all sorts of machineries, which amounts to a proportionately larger increase in average cost. This example, yet again, deals with a dwindling given natural supply and increasing demand in the context of the growth of the economy. It is quite far-fetched to think that the two supply points are connected by a given supply schedule; and (*iv*) in the context of a polemic against the East India Company's argument that open trade with India had on the one hand raised the price of goods bought in India and lowered the price of goods sold in England to the extent that no profit on trade could be made, Smith argues that though it was plausible that competition could lower the price in the English market, it was simply not plausible that it could raise the price in the Indian market because

> as all the extraordinary demand which that competition could occasion, must have been but a drop of water in the immense ocean of India commerce. The increase of demand, besides, though in the beginning it may sometimes raise the price of goods, *never fails to lower it in the* long-run. *It encourages production, and thereby increases the competition of the producers, who, in order to undersell one another, have recourse to new divisions of labour and new improvements of art, which might never otherwise have been thought of* (p. 748, emphasis added).

Again, the evidence is far from a description of a movement along a given supply curve, as Smith's explicit reference to 'new improvements of art, which might never otherwise have been thought of' clearly points out. The theoretical dispute is not about whether or not demand has any influence on prices in any circumstances, but rather, whether there is a rising or falling supply curve along which demand could be conceived to slide up or down. Hollander's examples do not establish that Smith had any such supply curve or schedule in mind.[30]

Rosenbluth (1969) claims that there is an apparent redundancy in Smith's Chapter 8 on wages and deficiency in the treatment of rent on land that always produces rent. He argues that once the labour-commanded measure is taken as the *numéraire* in the system, the value of wages by definition is equal to one, and if the prices of commodities are determined by adding up given profits, rent and wages, then the real wage basket is automatically determined once the prices are determined by given profits, rents and unity wages. On the other hand, rent on land that always pays rent cannot be determined unless the price of food or corn is known. He argues that the significance of Chapter 8 on wages lies in determining the 'real' price of corn, which is used in the chapter on rent to determine rent as a residual. Hollander (1973a: 173ff.) agrees with Rosenbluth's reasoning but goes on to add that the 'money price' of corn is not determined by his general principle of price determination for other commodities, but rather by 'specie distribution', i.e., by the international flow of money supply. Thus the real wages in terms of corn determined in the chapter on wages simultaneously determine the money wages, given the money price of corn. Now given the money price of corn, the money wages and the rate of profits, the rent on corn land is determined as a residual on the assumption that the money price of corn is always high enough to generate a residual rent. Neither Rosenbluth nor Hollander, however, explains why the money price of corn must always be larger than what Smith calls the *sufficient price*, i.e., a price that covers only the natural wages and natural profits of corn. I find an immediate problem with their explanation. The 'real' corn wages as well as money wages determined in Chapter 8 on wages

---

30 In a private e-mail correspondence with me, Professor Hollander acknowledges that 'though I agree that Smith did not distinguish properly between shifts and movements along curves', he nevertheless maintains that 'the fact remains that he [Smith] takes for granted that at higher industry outputs cost price normally does fall'.

by no means guarantee that there would be a positive rent on land that produces corn. Smith's proposition, however, is that such lands always produce rent. This proposition cannot be established through the price mechanism; it must be established through the notion of physical surplus.[31]

31 In a private e-mail correspondence with me, Professor Hollander agrees that 'the notion of lands always yielding positive rent relates to the physical surplus', but maintains that a corn surplus assures a value surplus because the price of corn remains constant with increase in supply, which in this special case brings an increase in demand with it. However, as we have argued, Smith's argument that demand for corn rises with the rise in the supply of corn, was designed to show that rent could not be explained on the ground of high demand for corn compared to its supply. Once it is admitted that rent is a physical surplus, then whatever natural price of corn happens to be it must ensure a positive rent. Thus the explanation based on the specific mechanism of corn demand rising along with corn supply becomes redundant.

2

THE THEORY OF VALUE IN RICARDO'S *PRINCIPLES*

Part I

Distribution: The Problem

In the 'Preface' to the *Principles of Political Economy and Taxation*, Ricardo argues that 'the produce of the earth' is divided among the landlords, the owners of the stock, and the labourers. However, the *proportion* in which the whole produce is divided among the three classes in the name of rent, profits and wages depends 'on the actual fertility of the soil, on the accumulation of capital and population, and on the skill, ingenuity, and instruments employed in agriculture'. From here he goes on to claim that '[to] determine the laws which regulate this distribution, is the principal problem in Political Economy.' It should, however, be noted that though the idea of a proportional division of a given output refers to a point in time, his reference to the *law* that regulates this distribution refers to a *dynamic law*, as his critical remark that his predecessors, such as Turgot, Stuart, Smith, Say, Sismondi and others, had provided little satisfactory information 'respecting the *natural course* of rent, profits, and wages' (emphasis added, p. 5; all references to the *Principles* are from Ricardo 1951–52, *Works I*) testifies to. He further goes on to claim that without the knowledge of the true doctrine of rent, for which he gives credit to Malthus and Edward West, 'it is impossible to understand the effect of the progress of wealth on profits and wages…'. Thus, according to Ricardo, a correct understanding of the theory of rent is central to the understanding of the *law of distribution*.

The book, however, does not begin with a theory or law of distribution but with a theory of value. The third edition (the final edition published by Ricardo) of the book is divided into 32 chapters. The first seven chapters are devoted to the basic theoretical framework, while the rest of the book is devoted to the application of the theoretical principles to the general areas of public finance and particular policy questions, as well as two chapters dealing separately with 'Doctrine of Adam Smith concerning the Rent of Land' and 'Mr. Malthus's opinion on Rent' and a new chapter on 'Machinery'. If we compare Ricardo's division of the theoretical section of his book with Adam Smith's *Wealth of Nations*, we find a remarkable affinity between the two with one critical difference. After establishing the causes that increase the wealth of a nation, Adam Smith begins his theoretical analysis by first considering the nature of 'value' and then proceeding to analyse wages, profits and rent respectively. Ricardo also begins with 'value', but immediately moves to 'rent' in the second and third chapters. Only after analysing the nature of rent does he introduce a chapter on 'Natural and Market Prices', which is part of the consideration of 'value' in Adam Smith. After this, two chapters on 'Wages' and 'Profits' follow.[1] Clearly, the theoretical status of 'rent' is different for the two authors.

The Chapter on Value

Ricardo does not provide any reason for beginning the analysis of distribution with a consideration of value except for the claim that 'for from no source do so many errors, and so much difference of opinion in that science proceed, as from the vague ideas which are attached to the word value' (p. 13). Let us begin by following Ricardo's exposition and then come back to the question: why begin with value?

The chapter on 'Value', as presented in the third edition, is divided into seven sections. In Section I, following Adam Smith, he distinguishes between the use-value and exchange-value of commodities. He argues that the values of commodities that are in fixed supply are determined solely by their scarcity. However, such commodities form a very small part of the mass of commodities and the supply of the vast majority of commodities can be increased without any practical limit by the application of labour. It is only such commodities that the theory takes into consideration, and following Adam Smith again, Ricardo declares that: 'In the early stages of society, the exchangeable value of these commodities, or the rule which determines how much of one shall be given in exchange for another, depends almost exclusively on the comparative quantity of labour expended on each' (p. 12). As a corollary of this hypothesis, he further argues that the

---

1 Chapter 7 is devoted to the theory of foreign trade, which will not be dealt with in the present chapter.

cause of changes in the relative values of commodities can be discovered by locating the changes in the expenditure of labour needed to produce the commodities.

In Section II, Ricardo argues that the existence of different qualities of labour does not vitiate his original hypothesis. Again following Adam Smith, he declares that the market-adjusted wage differentials for different kinds of labour provide an appropriate scale for reducing various qualities of labour into a homogeneous quantity. He argues that as long as it can be assumed that the causes of wage differentials remain the same, it is of 'little importance to examine into the comparative degree of estimation in which the different kinds of human labour are held' (pp. 21–22). This is because 'the inquiry to which I [Ricardo] wish to draw the reader's attention, relates to the effect of the variations in the relative value of commodities, and not in their absolute value ... ' (p. 21).

In Section III, he brings the existence of means of production into consideration and argues that the values of commodities are not regulated only by the direct labour expended in their production, but must also take into account the indirect labour, i.e., the labour expended in producing the means of production:

> Even in the early state to which Adam Smith refers, some capital, though possibly made and accumulated by the hunter himself, would be necessary to enable him to kill his game. Without some weapon, neither the beaver nor the deer could be destroyed, and therefore the value of these animals would be regulated, not solely by the time and labour necessary to their destruction, but also by the time and labour necessary for providing the hunter's capital, the weapon, by the aid of which their destruction was effected (pp. 22–23).

He further argues that on the assumption of equal direct to indirect labour ratios for all commodities, an emergence of equal rate of profits on capitals or an equal rise and fall of wages in all sectors will not have any impact on the relative values of commodities as:

> The proportion which might be paid for wages, is of the utmost importance in the question of profits; for it must at once be seen, that profits would be high or low, exactly in proportion as wages were low or high; but it could not in the least affect the relative value of fish and game, as wages would be high or low at the same time in both occupations. If the hunter urged the plea of his paying a large proportion, or the value of

a large proportion of his game for wages, as an inducement to the fisherman to give him more fish in exchange for his game, the latter would state that he was equally affected by the same cause; and therefore under all variations of wages and profits, under all the effects of accumulation of capital, as long as they continued by a day's labour to obtain respectively the same quantity of fish, and the same quantity of game, the natural rate of exchange would be one deer for two salmon (p. 27).

In Sections IV and V, this assumption is relaxed. The cases of different ratios of direct and indirect labour in terms of different combinations of fixed and circulating capital, different durability of fixed capitals and differing lengths of time taken to bring the final goods to the market are introduced. Ricardo argues that in such cases the relative values of commodities cannot be regulated solely by the relative direct and indirect labour-time expended in the production of the commodities. All these cases could be reduced to differences in the 'length of time which must elapse before [the commodities] can be brought to market' (p. 37). The reason why the labour-time ratio does not determine the value ratios in this context is that the rate of profits on capital accrues on the basis of a *compound rate* and so the value ratios must diverge from labour ratios to ensure an equal rate of profits on equal capital with unequal lengths of existence.[2] But more importantly, Ricardo argues that once this phenomenon is recognised, it cannot be denied that relative value ratios will change not only because of changes in labour expenditure but also because of changes in wages. As wages rise or fall, the capital that circulates faster will be impacted more by it, and thus the relative value of the commodity produced by this capital must rise or fall relative to the capital that circulates slowly; otherwise the rate of profits on the two capitals will not remain equal. However, after admitting that labour is not the sole cause of variation in the value of commodities and that changes in distribution are another cause, Ricardo goes on to argue that the variations caused by changes in distribution are of minor magnitude compared to those caused by changes in labour expenditure. He believes that in the real world changes in

---

2 ' ... The second year the manufacturers and farmer will again employ 5,000l. each in the support of labour, and will therefore again sell their goods for 5,500l., but the men using the machines, to be on par with the farmer, must not only obtain 5,500l. for the equal capital of 5,000l. employed on labour, but they must obtain a further sum of 550l.; for the profit on 5,500l., which they have invested in machinery, and consequently their goods must sell for 6,050l' (p. 34). Also see footnote 45.

distribution cannot cause more than 6 to 7 per cent changes in relative values and thus for all practical purposes they could be ignored in considering the cause of changes in the values of commodities:

> The reader, however, should remark, that this cause of the variation of commodities is comparatively slight in its effects. With such a rise of wages as should occasion a fall of one per cent in profits, goods produced under the circumstances I have supposed, vary in relative value only one per cent; they fall with so great a fall of profits from 6,050*l* to 5,995*l*. The greatest effects which could be produced on the relative prices of these goods from a rise of wages, could not exceed 6 or 7 per cent; for profits could not, probably, under any circumstances, admit of a greater general and permanent depression than to that amount. ... In estimating then, the causes of the variations in the value of commodities, although it would be wrong wholly to omit the consideration of the effect produced by a rise or fall of labour, it would be equally incorrect to attach much importance to it; and consequently, in the subsequent part of this work, though I shall occasionally refer to this cause of variation, I shall consider all the great variations which take place in the relative value of commodities to be produced by the greater or less quantity of labour which may be required from time to time to produce them (pp. 36–37).

This has led Professor Stigler (1958) to characterise Ricardo's theory as a 93 per cent labour theory of value. It should, however, be noted that Ricardo's statement only refers to the cause of change in the relative values. As far as the divergence of value ratios from their labour ratios due to differences in the time-structures of capitals is concerned, it could be considerable. It is true that the causes for both the divergences are the same; e.g., if the rate of profits were zero, then the relative values of commodities would coincide with their labour ratios and they would diverge as wages fell or the rate of profits rose. But the larger the rate of profits, the larger would be this divergence, given the differences in the time-structures of capitals. The largeness of the rate of profits would depend on the given real wages and the productivity of the production techniques in use. Thus, assuming that the rate of profits is large, one could start off with a considerable divergence of value ratios from their labour ratios. However, when it comes to contemplating a rise or fall in the rate of profits from a given level, one could reasonably argue that this would not be considerable over a moderate period of time simply because a fall in the rate of profits from 10 per cent to 5 per cent would be considered extremely large as it represents a 50 per cent fall in profits, though a 10 per cent rate of profits in itself may not be considered large. It appears that Ricardo usually assumes that the time-structures of capital of most of the commodities are rather close, and so from this point of view the divergence of value ratios from labour ratios is not large, as Ricardo's letter to Malthus, dated 9 October 1820, shows:

> You say that my proposition 'that with few exceptions the quantity of labour employed on commodities determines the rate at which they will exchange for each other, is not well founded'. I acknowledge that it is not rigidly true, but I say that it is the nearest approximation to truth, as a rule for measuring relative value, of any I have ever heard (Ricardo 1951–52, *Works VIII*: 279).

To which Malthus responded by asking: 'Do fifty oak trees valued at 20£ each contain as much labour as a stone wall in Gloucestershire which has cost 1000£?' (ibid.: 286, Letter dated 26 October 1820). On 24 November 1820, Ricardo responded:

> Fifty oak trees valued at £20 each do not contain as much labour as a stone wall in Gloucestershire which costs £1000. I have answered your question, let me ask you one. Did you ever believe that I thought fifty oak trees would cost as much labour as the stone wall? I really do not want such propositions to be granted in order to support my system (Ricardo 1951–52, *Works VIII*: 303).

It should be noted that Ricardo's results have no general validity and are the products of his particular example. The variations in value would be much larger if Ricardo started from a much higher rate of profits and thus allowed a larger fall in it. Furthermore, the variations in value would be much larger if the two goods were far apart in terms of their composition of direct and indirect labour-time. As a matter of fact, Ricardo was well aware of this and in the first edition of the *Principles* he had worked out examples of variations in the relative values of two commodities produced by equal amounts of capital investment, but with one produced by labour only and the other produced by machine only. Ricardo showed that a fall in the rate of profits from 10 per cent to 3 per cent would cause the relative values to vary '68%

if the machine would last 100 years; 28% if the machine would last 10 years; 13% if the machine would last 3 years; and little more than 6% if the machine would last only 1 year' (ibid., *Works I*: 60).[3] It appears that Ricardo's comments in the third edition relate to the relative value deviation from his chosen 'money-commodity', which was supposed to be produced by a capital composition close to the average of 'most of the commodities produced', leaving out the extreme cases.

In Section VI, the problem of the *invariable measure of value* is introduced. Ricardo argues that:

> When commodities varied in relative value, it would be desirable to have the means of ascertaining which of them fell and which rose in real value, and this could be effected only by comparing them one after another with some invariable standard measure of value, which should itself be subject to none of the fluctuations to which other commodities are exposed (p. 43).

The problem Ricardo is grappling with here is a theoretical rather than a practical one. He argues that if labour is the sole cause of variation in the values of commodities, then even though it would be impractical to think that any commodity would in all times and places be produced by the same amount of labour, in theory at least one could imagine or assign such a property to a commodity and know for sure that this particular commodity will remain invariable. However, as he discovers that in the case of different time-structures of capitals, labour is not the sole cause of variation in the values of commodities and that relative value varies also due to changes in wage rates or rate of profits, he finds that it is simply 'impossible' to find a commodity that will remain invariable since even the commodity whose labour content remains constant will be affected by changes in distribution: 'Neither gold then, nor any other commodity, can ever be a perfect measure of value for all things' (p. 45). But again Ricardo takes refuge in practicality. In keeping with his argument that the influence of changes in distribution on variation of value could only be minor, he proposes to ignore this effect and proceeds to assume that gold is produced with the same amount of labour all the time, with its ratio of direct to indirect labour being somewhere near the average employed in the production of most commodities:

> If, then, I may suppose myself to be possessed of a standard so nearly approaching to an invariable one, the advantage

3 See Barkai (1967), Wilson and Pate (1968) and Groenewegen (1972).

77

is, that I shall be enabled to speak of the variations of other things, without embarrassing myself on every occasion with the consideration of the possible alteration in the value of the medium in which price and value are estimated (p. 46).

In the last section, Section VII, Ricardo points out that changes in the value of money can only create nominal effects; that is, it cannot change the relative value of all the other commodities. He further goes on to explain that by rise or fall in wages, profits and rent, he only means their proportional, and not their absolute, rise or fall.

Before going any further, two methodological points should be noted. First, Ricardo begins with a proposition that is considered to be logically correct within highly restrictive parameters — the labour theory of value under Adam Smith's 'that early and rude state of society'. He then introduces the conditions of capitalist production one by one to see how the correctness of the original proposition is affected by adding these conditions. Interestingly, he finds that the original proposition regarding the labour theory of value is not contradicted by the emergence of capital and the rate of profits, as was, according to his understanding, argued by Adam Smith. However, he does find that differences in the time-structures of capitals of different commodities do cause the original proposition to be 'modified'. But instead of giving up the original proposition in this case, he goes on to argue that empirically, the modification called for due to the other discovered cause is minor and should be ignored. Second, it appears that for him a theory of value is identical to a search for the cause(s) of *changes* in value. Once he realises that the pure labour theory of value does not correctly predict the exact relative values of commodities at any point in time, he simply gives up the attempt to find a theory that would determine the exact value ratios and concentrates instead on finding the cause that explains the variation in values from one point of time to another, as his statement regarding the so-called 93 per cent labour theory of value suggests.[4]

---

4 'There are, it is true, many passages in his chapter on value which seem at first sight to indicate an acceptance of the labour theory. But on closer examination it will be found that most of them refer not to values but to variations in values, that almost all the others refer to special simplified cases, and that the few remaining statements which do relate to the actual valuation process are merely survivals from the earlier stages of his thinking and are entirely contradicted by what he wrote later in the amended editions of his book and his letters. ... So engrossing, indeed, was his interest in the question of the *"variation in relative value"* that those very words or their equivalents occur no less than 200 times in this one short chapter, an average of 7

On Rent

Following the methodology outlined in the preceding section of relaxing the restrictive assumption of the theory and step by step bringing it closer and closer to the capitalist economic system, Ricardo, in Chapter 2 'On Rent', asks: Will the emergence of landed property and rent vitiate the proposition regarding the labour theory of value, as Adam Smith claims? His answer to the question is an emphatic no! He argues that if, like air and water, land is practically unlimited in quantity, then it will be free and no one will pay any rent for the use of it. A rent on land implies that land is 'scarce'. According to Ricardo, scarcity of land can show up in two ways: (*i*) when extension of cultivation necessitates bringing inferior quality land under cultivation; and (*ii*) a further application of equal amounts of capital and labour on the same land gives less return than the previous dose of capital and labour. Thus, if population rises and the demand for food reaches a level that cannot be met by the application of capital and labour on the best quality land available, then either production must be extended to some next best quality land or the farmer has to be content with lower output from the further application of capital and labour on the best quality land. In either case, the difference in the output received by the application of equal amounts of capital and labour must form a separate category of income, as there cannot be two rates of profits on an equal amount of capital investment. This is the *cause* of rent as a separate category of income in the system. For Ricardo, at any stage of a society's development, there is a marginal land whose status is equivalent to natural air or water and therefore there is no rent on this marginal land (or the application of the last dose of capital and labour on any land must not pay rent, which he defines as the intensive margin of land). Rent accrues only to the intra-marginal land whose fertility is higher than that of the marginal land.

The question is: does rent enter in the price of the produce of land? Ricardo argues that land with lower fertility is brought into cultivation only because the high demand due to economic growth and rise in population cannot be met by cultivating only the best

---

times on every page' (Cassels 1935, in Woods 1985, Vol. II: 44–45). Whitaker (1904: 51ff.) also highlights Ricardo's move away from the determination of values to the explanation of the cause(s) of their variations. He argues that this was because of Ricardo's failure to explain away the difficulty of skilled labour in the explanation of labour theory.

quality land. Thus the excess demand caused by rise in population raises the price of the agricultural produce, which in turn makes it possible for a less productive method to be operated with profit. Thus the value of agricultural produce is regulated by the labour-time needed to produce it on the marginal land (or the return on the marginal *dose* of capital and labour on any land). And as the marginal land pays no rent, it does not enter into the price of agricultural produce:

> The reason then, why raw produce rises in comparative value, is because more labour is employed in the production of the last portion obtained, and not because a rent is paid to the landlord. The value of corn is regulated by the quantity of labour bestowed on its production on that quantity of land, or with that portion of capital, which pays no rent. Corn is not high because a rent is paid, but a rent is paid because corn is high ... (p. 74).
>
> If the high price of corn were the effect, and not the cause of rent, price would be proportionally influenced as rents were high or low, and rent would be a component part of price. But that corn which is produced by the greatest quantity of labour is the regulator of price of corn; and rent does not and cannot enter in the least degree as a component part of its price. Adam Smith, therefore, cannot be correct in supposing that the original rule which regulated the exchangeable value of commodities, namely, the quantity of labour by which they were produced, can be at all altered by the appropriation of land and the payment of rent (pp. 77–78).

In the next chapter Ricardo maintains that the same principle applies on the rent of mines.

Centre of Gravitation

Chapter IV introduces Smith's idea of the long-term centre of gravitation of market prices in a competitive economy. Though Ricardo maintains that '[i]n the 7th chap. of the Wealth of Nations, all that concerns this question is most ably treated', we should note one similarity and one fundamental difference from Adam Smith here. First of all, it appears that, along with Adam Smith, Ricardo also implicitly assumes constant costs in the operation of the gravitational principle.

For example, at one point he explains the adjustment mechanism by taking a case of shift in demand:

> Let us suppose that all commodities are at their natural price, and consequently that the profits of capital in all employments are exactly at the same rate, or differ only so much as, in the estimation of the parties, is equivalent to any real or fancied advantage which they possess or forego. Suppose now that a change of fashion should increase the demand for silks, and lessen that for woollens; their natural price, the quantity of labour necessary to their production, would continue unaltered, but the market price of silks would rise, and that of woollens would fall; and consequently the profits of the silk manufacturer would be above, while those of the woollen manufacturer would be below, the general and adjusted rate of profits. Not only the profits, but the wages of the workmen, would be affected in these employments. This increased demand for silks would however soon be supplied, by the transference of capital and labour from the woollen to the silk manufacture; when the market prices of silks and woollens would again approach their natural prices, and then the usual profits would be obtained by the respective manufacturers of those commodities (p. 91).

A careful reading of the passage suggests that Ricardo is 'implicitly assuming' constant costs. First of all, Ricardo's phrase, 'when the market prices of silks and woollens would *again* approach their natural prices', suggests that the natural prices are the same as they were before the adjustments in the quantity supplied took place, as clearly 'again' refers to the old position. Second, once the two commodities settle down to their natural prices again, then the respective manufacturers again obtain the *usual* profits. But the 'usual profits' refer to the profits received by all manufacturers before the shift in demand. If variable costs prevailed in the two manufactures, then in all likelihood the quantity adjustments would have changed the 'usual' rate of profits if the goods were *basics* in the system (though silk would be considered a 'luxury' by Ricardo, woollens would not be necessarily so characterised; in any case, here the example is simply chosen to illustrate the principle of the market adjustment mechanism and not necessarily so that its possible impact on the rate of profits could be avoided). Therefore, Ricardo's contention that the usual rate of profits remains the same before and after the quantity adjustments implies a 'constant costs' assumption.

Ricardo, however, has an apparent problem here that Adam Smith did not have. Though his reasoning is all right for purely manufactured commodities, one could argue that the same reasoning cannot apply to agricultural commodities, as Ricardo assumes diminishing returns in agriculture. This requires us to sharpen our understanding of the meaning of diminishing returns in agriculture in Ricardo's case. Unlike the modern notion of diminishing returns, which applies to individual commodity production functions, Ricardo's notion of diminishing returns applies only to total agricultural production. In other words, diminishing returns come into operation only in the context of growth where the total land under cultivation is extended or total capital and labour on agriculture as a whole is increased. If there is movement of capital and labour from one type of crop to another, then such increase in the output of one crop at the cost of another crop may not give rise to diminishing returns. But of course, if the misallocation of labour and capital is between manufacturing and agriculture in aggregate, then the problem will have to be faced. One way to deal with it would be to assume that diminishing returns in agriculture is not a continuous but a step function, and the adjustments of supply to bring market prices to natural prices take place on the flat segments (i.e., the constant returns segments) of the step function. But this cannot be accepted as a general solution to the problem as one cannot always assume that the actual system is not close to the edge of the step. In a continuous diminishing returns scenario, a supply adjustment of agricultural goods (say, 'corn') as a whole must result in changes in cost of production and thus the natural price itself. Further, when we take into account the indirect use of land for manufacturing such as cotton textile, etc., then it cannot be denied that a change in taste could affect the total demand for land and thus its margin (see Samuelson 1978). It would be fair to say that Ricardo has not thought through this issue. He is more interested in working out the relationship between distribution and prices on the assumption that market prices have adjusted to natural prices.[5] It should also be noted that, like Adam Smith, Ricardo does not have the modern notion of production functions. As far as the difference with Smith is concerned, we must note that in Smith the market price of not only commodities but also wages, profits and

---

5 See Barkai (1965), Brens (1960) and Pasinetti (1960) for further discussion on this issue.

rent could be either higher or lower than their natural prices at any given time, which prompts the adjustment mechanism to come into play on that factor. In Ricardo, however, the concept of market and natural prices does not operate on rent — it has no part in a theory of value.[6]

Now we turn to Ricardo's law of distribution. As we have seen, through his theory of rent, Ricardo is able to 'get rid' of rent from the consideration of a theory of value. Thus his law of distribution proper deals with the relationship between value and wages and profits, where rent is a passive element that is affected by the movements in the three variables but has no independent impact on them. First we turn to Ricardo's theory of wages and its dynamics.

On Wages

On the question of real wage determination and its long-term trend, Ricardo presents a theory that is subtly different from that of Adam Smith's. Following Smith, Ricardo defines subsistence wage as the wage 'which is necessary to enable the labourers, one with another, to subsist and to perpetuate their race, without either increase or diminution' (p. 93).[7] However, he adds a great deal of confusion to this by defining, contra Smith, subsistence wage as the 'natural wage' or

---

6 In Chapter I on Smith we have noted that Dupertuis and Sinha (2009a) have shown that the classical notion of the centre of gravitation is not a sound concept. It is interesting to note that on this question, in response to Ricardo, William Whewell (1831) had argued that: 'It appears to be by no means clear that the irregular fluctuations and transitory currents by which the elements of wealth seek their natural level may be neglected in the investigation of the primary laws of their distribution. It is not difficult to conceive that the inequalities and transfers produced by the temporary and incomplete action of the equalizing causes, may be of equal magnitude and consequence with those ultimate and complete changes by which the general tendency of such causes is manifested. A panic may produce results as wide and as important as a given fall in profit' (Whewell 1831, in Yeo 2001: 167–68).

7 Again, following in the footsteps of Adam Smith, Ricardo goes on to qualify subsistence wage in these terms: 'It is not to be understood that the natural price of labour, estimated even in food and necessaries, is absolutely fixed and constant. It varies at different times in the same country, and very materially differs in different countries. It essentially depends on the habits and customs of the people. An English labourer would consider his wages under their natural rate, and too scanty to support a family, if they enabled him to purchase no other food than potatoes, and to live in no better habitation than a mud cabin; yet these moderate demands of nature are often deemed sufficient in countries where "man's life is cheap", and his wants easily satisfied. Many of the conveniences now enjoyed in an English cottage, would have been thought luxuries at an earlier period of our history' (pp. 96–97).

'natural price of labour', which gives the impression that he believes that a real wage either higher or lower than subsistence can only be short-lived disequilibrium 'market wage', and thus a long-term analysis must take 'subsistence wage' as the equilibrium 'natural wage'.[8] Some of his comments in the early part of the chapter on wages give such an impression. For example:

> However much the market price of labour may deviate from its natural price, it has, like commodities, a tendency to conform to it...
>
> When, however, by the encouragement which high wages give to the increase of population, the number of labourers is increased, wages again fall to their natural price, and indeed from a reaction sometimes fall below it (p. 94).

In these examples, however, Ricardo is dealing with the case of a stagnant economy receiving one shot of positive capital investment. In the case of an economy that is growing at a positive rate, Ricardo, appearing to follow Adam Smith, admits that the real wages of labour will be consistently higher than the subsistence wage. But unlike Smith, he adds to the confusion by calling such a persistently higher-than-subsistence wage the 'market price' as opposed to the 'natural price' of labour:

> Notwithstanding the tendency of wages to conform to their natural rate, their market rate may, in an improving society, for an indefinite period, be constantly above it; for no sooner may the impulse, which an increased capital gives to a new demand for labour be obeyed, than another increase of capital may produce the same effect; and thus, if the increase of capital be gradual and constant, the demand for labour may give a continued stimulus to an increase of people (pp. 94–95).

The reason for Ricardo's unusual terminology, or departure from Smith's well-established terminology, lies in his adherence to the

---

8 This is a position taken by, among others, Böhm-Bawerk (1890), Ashley (1891), Knight (1956), Pasinetti (1960), Blaug (1962), O'Brien (1975, 2004), and Stigler (1952, 1981). Earlier, Whewell also interpreted Ricardo in the same vein: 'Mr. Ricardo assumes that the natural rate of wages is invariable, that is, that the labourer's command of food and other necessaries is never permanently augmented or diminished' (Whewell 1831: 159).

Malthusian theory of population along with his belief in diminishing returns in agriculture. As we have seen in Chapter 1, Smith believes that every positive growth of population is associated with a particular real wage. But Ricardo, following Malthus, believes that the 'power of population continues always the same' and 'in favourable circumstances population may be doubled in twenty five years' (p. 98). In other words, there is a natural tendency for population to grow at a rate that doubles itself in 25 years, if there is no resource constraint put before it. The implication of this is that there is a maximum limit to the rate of growth of labour. Thus, if demand for labour is growing faster than the rate that doubles itself in 25 years, then the 'market wages' must keep rising till the rate of growth of capital accumulation is brought within the limits of the natural rate of population growth. In other words, there is no 'equilibrium wage' or 'natural wage' possible for an economy where the demand for labour is growing at a faster rate than the rate that doubles itself in 25 years. So the question that Ricardo poses to himself is: how, in such cases, will the 'market wage' tend towards an 'equilibrium wage'? And the answer to this question is provided by the diminishing returns in agriculture:

> In new settlements, where the arts and knowledge of countries far advanced in refinement are introduced, it is probable that capital has a tendency to increase faster than mankind: and if the deficiency of labourers were not supplied by more populous countries, this tendency would very much raise the price of labour. In proportion as these countries become populous, and land of a worse quality is taken into cultivation, the tendency to an increase of capital diminishes; for the surplus produce remaining, after satisfying the wants of the existing population, must necessarily be in proportion to the facility of production, viz., to the smaller number of persons employed in production. Although, then, it is probable, that under the most favourable circumstances, the power of production is still greater than that of population, it will not long continue so; for the land being limited in quantity, and differing in quality, with every increased portion of capital employed on it, there will be a decreased rate of production, whilst the power of population continues always the same (p. 98).

In other words, diminishing returns in agriculture will ensure that the rate of increase in the demand for labour is continuously declining, but this process does not stop once the rate of growth of demand for labour becomes equal to the maximum rate of population growth. So long as the rate of population growth is positive, the diminishing returns in agriculture must accompany it, till the economy comes to a stationary state and the rate of population growth becomes zero. Thus, contrary to Smith's position, there is no rate of wages above the subsistence wage which could be characterised as the long-term 'equilibrium' or 'centre of gravitation' wage. It is because of this reason that Ricardo finds himself compelled to move away from Smith's terminology and declare all wages above the subsistence level to be 'market wages'. But again, the concept of a secular wage trend, which is what he describes in the case of a growing economy, gets characterised as the same thing as a short run adjustment process, which no doubt creates a great deal of theoretical confusion.[9] It should be noted in passing that Ricardo held a theory of wages similar to that of Adam Smith's in his *Essay*, at least as a simplifying assumption (see Ricardo 1951–52, *Works IV*: 12), but appears to have broken from his old position in the *Principles*.

Let us follow the causal sequence of Ricardo's wage theory closely. Given that the rate of growth of population or the supply of labour (g^s_L) is a positive function of real wage (w), with $g^s_L = 0$ when w is equal to subsistence wage (w_s) and has a Malthusian maximum; the rate of growth of demand for labour (g^d_L) is a positive function of the rate of profit (r) in the economy with $g^d_L = 0$ when r approaches zero (as one must grant a certain minimum consumption level for the capitalist class); and the rate of profit (r) is inversely related to the labour-time needed to produce the real wage (w). Begin the analysis with real wages higher than subsistence wage and hence a positive rate of population growth. A positive rate of population growth leads to production of food (a major wage-good) on less fertile land, which

9 In response to Malthus's criticism of his definition of 'natural wage', Ricardo writes: 'By natural price I do mean the usual price, but such a price as is necessary to supply constantly a given demand. The natural price of corn is the price at which it can be supplied affording the usual profits. With every demand for an increased quantity the market price of corn will rise above this price and probably is never at the natural price but either above or below it ... the same may be said of the natural price of labour' (Ricardo 1951–52, *Works II*: 227–28). However, in an earlier draft of this response, Ricardo had written: 'I am however very little solicitous to retain my definition of the natural price of labour — Mr. Malthus's would do nearly as well for my purpose' (ibid.: 228). Malthus had defined the natural price of labour as 'that price which, in the actual circumstances of the society, is necessary to occasion an average supply of labourers, sufficient to meet the average demand' (ibid.: 228). Ricardo, however, did not change his terminology in the third edition of the *Principles*.

amounts to an increase in the labour-time needed to produce the given real wage (say w^0). This leads to fall in the rate of profit from r^0 to r^1. This in turn leads to a fall in the rate of growth of demand for labour. Now, given the old rate of population growth based on w^0, it leads to an excess supply of labour and thus a fall in real wages from w^0 to w^1, which is followed by a fall in the rate of population growth. At this stage, we must note that since real wage has fallen from w^0 to w^1, this in turn should lead to a rise in the rate of profit for two reasons: one, because it would take less labour-time to produce the smaller wage basket even if the marginal land remains the same; and two, the productivity of the marginal land would also rise as some land that was marginal previously would be given up because now less food is needed to be produced. The question is: will the rebound effect on the rate of profit be strong enough to send it back from r^1 to r^0 or even higher? If this happens, then Ricardo's dynamic movement of wages and the rate of profits would simply oscillate within a band or oscillate explosively. Thus for Ricardo's story to hold, it is imperative that the rebound effect on the rate of profits be less than the initial effect. But this must be the case since for all wages higher than subsistence level the rate of population growth is positive and therefore the value of wages must rise continuously due to the diminishing returns on land.

However, Ricardo's story hangs on the proposition that the rise in the labour-time needed to produce the wage basket must lead to a fall in the rate of profits. Most of Ricardo's theoretical concerns with respect to value are designed to establish this proposition.

In the foregoing story, we assumed that 'the rate of growth of demand for labour (g^d_L) is a positive function of the rate of profit (r) in the economy with $g^d_L = 0$ when r approaches zero'. In general, Ricardo assumes a fixed relation between the rate of accumulation and the rate of growth of demand for labour, i.e., taking the ratio of the means of production to labour as constant. However, in his new chapter on Machinery in the third edition of the *Principles,* he relaxes this assumption and argues that as accumulation leads to a rise in the value of wages and a fall in the rate of profits, there is an incentive for capitalists to substitute machines for labourers. Thus the demand for labour is a positive but decreasing function of the accumulation of capital. Such a development would, of course, somewhat retard the development towards the stationary state:

> With every increase of capital and population, food will gen-
> erally rise, on account of its being more difficult to produce.
> The consequence of a rise of food will be a rise of wages, and

> every rise of wages will have a tendency to determine the saved capital in a greater proportion than before to the employment of machinery. Machinery and labour are in constant competition, and the former can frequently not be employed until labour rises. ... The demand for labour will continue to increase with an increase of capital, but not in proportion to its increase; the ratio will necessarily be a diminishing ratio (p. 395).

Let us note here that Ricardo does not subscribe to Barton's claim (see Ricardo 1951–52, *Works I*: 395–96, f.n.) that under certain circumstances such a tendency to replace labour with machines might be so strong that accumulation would lead to no increase in the demand for labour.[10] In that case, there will be no upward pressure on the value of wages and thus no fall in the rate of profits. Furthermore, if the new machines bring improved productivity with them, then their effect could be an increase in the rate of profits, which might lead to an overall increase in the demand for labour. In that case we will have rising profits with rising wages. Such a scenario would clearly contradict Ricardo's basic proposition that real wages tend towards subsistence and the rate of profits tends towards zero. Therefore, it would be fair to conclude that Ricardo does not take into account the output (or change in technology) effect of the machinery; he only looks at it from the perspective of substitution of labour. The introduction of machinery is an *effect* of a rise in real wages, which in turn is an *effect* of a rise in the demand for labour. In this context, Ricardo's conclusion is robust. His static example in the early part of the chapter is only designed to illustrate the impact of substitution of labour for machines on the demand for labour and cannot be taken as an argument for accommodating unemployment of labour in his theoretical system.[11]

In any case, along with the idea that real wages have a tendency to fall towards subsistence wage, Ricardo points out that this does not imply that money wages would also fall. On the assumption that

10 'It is not easy, I think, to conceive that under any circumstances, an increase in capital should not be followed by an increased demand for labour; the most that can be said is, that the demand will be in a diminishing ratio' (Ricardo 1951–52, *Works I*: 396 f.n.).

11 Also see Eltis (1985) and Hollander (1973b, 1979), who also maintain that Ricardo's chapter on Machinery does not admit of unemployment of labour as part of his theory.

the value of the money-commodity remains constant, he argues that diminishing returns in agriculture lead to a rise in the value of food grains, the most important wage-goods, and thus falling real wages are quite compatible with rising money wages. Furthermore, it should be noted that Ricardo accepts that wages are not spent solely on food; a small proportion is also spent on manufactured goods. Although the progress of society leads to increasing prices of food grains, it also, due to technical progress in manufacturing, leads to a fall in the prices of manufactured goods. Thus by slightly changing the consumption basket by sacrificing a little food for manufactured goods, a worker can to some extent maintain a healthy standard of living:

> From manufactured commodities always falling, and raw produce always rising, with the progress of society, such a disproportion in their relative values is at length created, that in rich countries a labourer, by the sacrifice of a very small quantity only of his food, is able to provide liberally for all his other wants (p. 97).

On Profits

In a quintessential manner, Ricardo declares profits to be a surplus in the system: 'The remaining quantity of the produce of the land, after the landlord and the labourer are paid, necessarily belongs to the farmer, and constitutes the profits of the stock' (p. 112). The reader should note that the status of profit in Ricardo differs significantly from Adam Smith. While profit is a necessity and not a surplus in Smith's theoretical framework (see Chapter 1), it is a purely surplus category in Ricardo. Thus, in order to treat (or measure) profits as 'physical surplus' in agriculture, Ricardo needs to first 'get rid' of rent.[12] If rent also features as surplus on marginal lands, then there is no way of determining profits. That the status of profits in Ricardo is different from Smith is clearly evident in Ricardo's treatment of the implication of a direct tax on profits:

> If a tax in proportion to profits were laid on all trades, every commodity would be raised in price. But if the mine, which supplied us with the standard of our money, were in this

---

12 See Ricardo's letter to McCulloch dated 13 June 1820 (Ricardo 1951–52, *Works VIII*: 194).

country, and the profits of the miner were also taxed, the price of no commodity would rise, each man would give an equal proportion of his income, and every thing would be as before (pp. 205–06).

The theoretical implication of this is clear: profit is a pure surplus. Contrast this with Adam Smith's position presented in Chapter 1.[13]

The problem of the chapter 'On Profits' is to determine 'the cause of the permanent variations in the rate of profits'. Ricardo argues that the value of the produce of the marginal land is divided only between the labourer and the capitalist and thus the rate of profits must fall if the value of real wages rises. According to him, the value of real wages can rise due to two causes: (*i*) the techniques of production remain the same but the real wages rise, and (*ii*) the real wages remain the same but it takes more labour-time to produce the wage-goods. What Ricardo needed for his fundamental proposition regarding the effect on the rate of profits of a rise of wages was that any combination of the two causes just listed should lead to an increase in the labour-time needed to produce the wage basket. A simple rise in real wages given constant techniques of production, or a constant real wage with a rise in the difficulty of producing wage-goods, or even a fall in real wages more than compensated by a rise in the difficulty of producing the real wages, are all equivalent propositions for him as far as the impact on the rate of profits is concerned. Thus Ricardo's basic proposition regarding 'permanent variations in the rate of profits' boils down to this: when the net output is reduced to its labour-embodied content, then a rise in the proportionate share of wages of the total labour-embodied content of the net output must lead to a fall in the rate of profits. To prove this proposition, Ricardo maintains his assumption that he is in possession of a money-commodity which requires a constant labour-time to produce it and which is not affected by the variation in wages or the distribution of total income between wages and profits. Given this assumption, it is clear that if we assume a simple rise in real wages with no change in techniques, then the produce of the marginal land remains constant and as the real share of the labourer in it rises, a smaller share is left for profit; and since the impact on prices

---

13 In a response to Malthus, Ricardo wrote: 'Profits come out of the surplus produce; if profits were taxed, the tax would come out of the surplus produce, but it would not therefore come out of rent. Here Mr. Malthus identifies surplus with rent' (Ricardo 1951–52, *Works II*: 128).

due to changes in distribution is ignored, the value or prices of all the goods remain constant; and so the rate of profits must fall. Alternatively, let us suppose that due to diminishing returns in agriculture the value of wage-goods rises. Given the assumption that the value of the money-commodity is constant, a constant real wage implies a rise in money wages. If some manufactured commodities do not use any agricultural commodities as raw materials and if the changes in prices due to changes in the distribution are ignored, then the values of those manufactured commodities must remain the same. However, they will have to pay higher money wages, which will lower their rate of profits. And since competition must equalise the rate of profits across the board, the rate of profits in general will fall. Ricardo argues that the rise in the value of agricultural goods will not compensate the farmer for the rise in money wages because the farmer would not only have to pay higher money wages but would also have to employ more workers to produce the same amount of commodities due to diminishing returns. The value of agricultural goods rises only to the extent of the additional labour-cost of producing the same amount on marginal land (for the produce on intra-marginal lands this rise in price transforms into additional rent) and thus the rise in money wages has the same impact on farmers' profits as on the manufacturers' profits:

> Thus in every case, agricultural as well as manufacturing profits are lowered by a rise in the price of raw produce, if it be accompanied by a rise of wages. If the farmer gets no additional value for the corn which remains to him after paying rent, if the manufacturer gets no additional value for the goods which he manufactures, and if both are obliged to pay a greater value in wages, can any point be more clearly established than that profits must fall, with a rise of wages? (p. 115).

The implication of the law of inverse relation between the value of wages and the rate of profits is clear. The rate of profits has a tendency to fall as the economy and population grows. The reader should keep in mind that though Ricardo assumes constant real wages to work out his examples of fall in the rate of profits due to diminishing returns, the argument remains valid even when real wages are falling — so long as the fall in real wages is not large enough to warrant falling or constant money wages; in other words, the argument remains valid so long as money wages are rising and the value of money is assumed as constant and the cause of deviation in prices due to changes in distribution is ignored. He also considers the fact that either fall in real wages or development in agricultural technology may keep this tendency at bay for some time but maintains that in the end the secular trend of the rate of profits must be towards zero:

> It may be said that I have taken it for granted, that money wages would rise with a rise in the price of raw produce, but that this is by no means a necessary consequence, as the labourer may be contented with fewer enjoyments. It is true that the wages of labour may previously have been at a higher level, and that they may bear some reduction. If so, the fall of profits will be checked; but it is impossible to conceive that the money price of wages should fall, or remain stationary with a gradually increasing price of necessaries; and therefore it may be taken for granted that, under ordinary circumstances, no permanent rise takes place in the price of necessaries, without occasioning, or having been preceded by a rise in wages (p. 118).
>
> The natural tendency of profits then is to fall; for, in the progress of society and wealth, the additional quantity of food required is obtained by the sacrifice of more and more labour. This tendency, this gravitation as it were of profits, is happily checked at repeated intervals by the improvements in machinery, connected with the production of necessaries, as well as by discoveries in the science of agriculture which enable us to relinquish a portion of labour before required, and therefore to lower the price of the prime necessary of the labourer (p. 120).

Thus there is a secular tendency for real wages to fall to subsistence level and the rate of profits to fall towards zero and the economy to come to a stationary state. However, there is one class that stands to gain during this entire process, and that is the class of landlords. Not only the absolute size of the rent on all intra-marginal land rises as the economy moves to lesser and lesser fertile land, but their [the landlords'] purchasing power also rises as the value of agricultural produce rises vis-a-vis the manufactured goods: '[N]ot only is the landlord's money rent greater, but his corn rent also; he will have more corn, and each defined measure of that corn will exchange for a greater quantity of all other goods which have not been raised in value' (p. 102).

It should be noted, however, that these trends in real wages, rate of profits and rents do not prove any trend in the share of wages, profits and rent in the total produce. For example, a marginal fall in the productivity of land may be small enough compared to the rise in total output such that the total increase in rent is proportionately smaller than the increase in total output. In that case, the share of rent in total output would decline rather than rise. And given that the share of rent in total output may decline, it is quite plausible that the share of profits in total output may rise even though the rate of profits is falling. As far as the share of rent is concerned, by the time the third edition of the *Principles* was published Ricardo had come to realise that: 'It is according to the division of the whole produce of the land of *any particular farm*,[14] between the three classes of landlord, capitalist, and labourer, that we are to judge of the rise or fall of rent, profit, and wages ... ' (p. 49, emphasis added).[15] In any case, to this extent Ricardo fails to fulfil the promise of his 'Preface', wherein he has identified distribution with 'proportions of the whole produce of the earth'. It is nevertheless clear that since Ricardo 'gets rid' of rent from his scheme of economic valuation, his law of proportional distribution can only apply to profits and wages, as the relevant agricultural technique used for determining total agricultural output is given by marginal land and thus excludes all rent income from the account of total agricultural produce.

Before closing this section, I would once again like to emphasise that Ricardo does not come up with any theory of profits, i.e., the determination of the rate of profits at any given time. The purpose of the chapter was solely to determine '*the cause of the permanent variations in the rate of profits*'. At one place in the 'Introduction' to Ricardo's *Principles* (*Works I*), Sraffa appears to suggest that the labour theory of value provided Ricardo with an alternative to the 'corn model' to determine the rate of profits. According to him:

> It was now labour, instead of corn, that appeared on both sides of the account — in modern terms, both as input and output: as a result, the rate of profits was no longer determined by the ratio of the corn produced to the corn used up in production, but, instead, by the ratio of the total labour of the country to the labour required to produce the necessaries for that labour (Sraffa 1951: xxxii).

14 In the first edition it reads, 'It is according to the division of the whole produce of the land and labour of the country. ' (p. 64).
15 See H. Barkai (1959), E. Cannan (1929), P. Davidson (1959) and Dobb (1973) for details on this question. Also see Hicks (1972) who shows that under certain assumptions, such as proportion of demand of agricultural to manufactured goods being fixed, fixed capital intensity, and fixed real wages, Ricardo's original proposition can be proven to be valid.

The major reference cited in support of this thesis is as follows:

> A rise in wages, from an alteration in the value of money, produces a general effect on price, and for that reason it produces no real effect whatever on profits. On the contrary, a rise in wages, from the circumstance of the labourer being more liberally rewarded, or from a difficulty of producing the necessaries on which wages are expended, does not, except in some instances, produce the effect of raising price, but has a great effect in lowering profits. *In the one case, no greater proportion of the annual labour of the country is devoted to the support of the labourers; in the other case, a large portion is so devoted* (pp. 48–49, emphasis added).

I have emphasised the last sentence because this is what has been cited as the evidence in support of Sraffa's thesis. But the context makes it clear that what Ricardo means here is that a nominal rise of wages will have no impact on the rate of profits; but a real rise of wages (or the value of wages), which amounts to a greater proportion of the annual labour of the country being devoted to the support of the labourers, will lower the rate of profits. There is no evidence here of a theory for determining the rate of profits by taking the ratio of the total labour of a country to the labour necessary to produce total wages. In any case, such a proposition would be valid only if total capital is equal to total wage advances. But Ricardo was keenly aware of the existence of non-wage capital and their differing time-structures, which renders the simple labour-value calculations invalid and thus also any such method to calculate the rate of profits.

Interestingly, in a footnote to what I have quoted from Sraffa's 'Introduction', he writes: 'See the statement that profits depend upon the "proportion of the annual labour of the country [which] is devoted to the support of the labourers", below, pp. 48–49, and "the same conclusion" on p. 126 below' (Sraffa 1951: xxxii, f.n. 5). Here Sraffa's use of the word 'depend' could mean either its level or the movement of its level. As far as Ricardo is concerned, he does not use the word 'depend' in either of the quotations cited and his preferred word for describing the relations between variables is usually 'regulate'. Again, the reference reads:

> Each man may, and probably will, have a less absolute quantity; but as more labourers are employed in proportion to the whole produce retained by the farmer, the value of a greater proportion of the whole produce will be absorbed by wages,

and consequently the value of a smaller proportion will be devoted to profits. This will necessarily be rendered permanent by the laws of nature, which have limited the productive powers of land (p. 126).

Here again, the statement simply refers to a fall in profits due to an increase in the difficulty of producing the given wage basket and not the determination of its rate.

I suspect Maurice Dobb's direct hand in the framing of this proposition, not only because it is clearly in a Marxian vein and because Dobb repeats the argument almost word for word later (Dobb 1973: 74), but more importantly because this argument stands in sharp contrast to the rest of Sraffa's 'Introduction'. For example, Sraffa emphasises that 'Ricardo was not interested for its own sake in the problem of why two commodities produced by the same quantities of labour are not of the same exchangeable value' (Sraffa 1951: xlix). Had Ricardo been interested in the question of why the same quantities of labour are not of the same exchangeable value, as Marx was, then he would have to, as Marx had to, get interested in the determination of the rate of profits and not just in its permanent movements.

Dmitriev also argues that Ricardo's contribution is to *determine* the rate of profits:

> Too much importance is often attached to this Ricardian hypothesis [the inverse wage-profit relation]. Ricardo's main contribution to the theory of profit does not lie here, but in his establishment of the laws governing the *absolute* level of profit. ... whenever a known quantity of some product has been up in the production of and we can obtain a larger quantity of *the same* product within some finite period of time as a result of the production process, the profit rate in the given branch of industry will be fully-determined quantity greater *than zero, irrespective of the price of the product* (Dmitriev (1974) [1904]: 57 f.n. 62).

Here we have an anticipation of Sraffa's 'corn-model' interpretation of Ricardo's early theory of profit. Sraffa, however, did not have an opportunity to read Dmitriev's work before the 1960s.[16] In any case, it is clear that Ricardo did not work with such simplified models in

16 I am indebted to Professor Heinz Kurz for this information.

the *Principles* and Dmitriev fails to show how Ricardo could have determined the absolute level of profits in a model with more than one *basic* good.

The Significance of the 'Invariable Measure of Value': Ricardo's LTV

So what is the nature of Ricardo's theory of value? As we have noted earlier, Ricardo recognises that differences in the time-structures of capitals along with the condition of equal rate of profits on capital investments vitiate or deviate the relative values of commodities from their respective labour-embodied ratios. But how much would the deviation be? Ricardo has no answer to this question, as he needs the relative values to be able to determine the rate of profits; on the other hand, relative values cannot be determined without knowledge of the rate of profits. Ricardo tries to get out of this circularity by giving up the idea of *determining* the relative values of commodities and concentrating on a search for the *cause of variation* in the relative values (given whatever the relative values happen to be). But the corollary of the first problem shows up again as he realises that in this case labour is not the only cause that could change the relative values of commodities, but that a change in distribution also appears to cause changes in the relative values. This is where his concern for the 'invariable measure of value' comes into play.[17]

As we shall see, Ricardo recognises 'the supposition of the invariability of the precious metals as a standard of value' as part of the sheet anchor on which all his propositions are built. However, we have also noticed that in the *Principles* he fails to find the theoretical conditions that would make his standard of measure 'invariable'. He takes refuge in practicality by proposing to ignore the effect of the rise or fall of wages on the standard of measure by declaring its effects to be minor. But this was definitely not theoretically satisfactory. Ricardo was well aware of it, and in his last unfinished theoretical piece entitled, *Absolute Value and Exchangeable Value [A Rough Draft]*, which he wrote only a few weeks before his untimely death on 11 September 1823, he acknowledges that:

> ... but difficulty or facility of production is not absolutely the only cause of variation in value, there is one other, the rise

---

17 The arguments of this section rely heavily on 'A Note on Ricardo's Invariable Measure of Value' (Sinha forthcoming).

or fall of wages, which though comparatively of little effect and rarer occurrence yet does effect the value of commodities and must not be omitted in this important enquiry (Ricardo 1951–52, *Works IV*: 368).[18]

The question is: what problem did Ricardo think the 'invariable measure of value' could solve? Let us suppose that there is a commodity that remains invariable in the face of changes in wages or in the rate of profits.[19] On the assumption that the labour-time embodied in this commodity remains constant, one could ascertain which commodity has changed in value by comparing it with this particular commodity at two points of time. However, one would still be unable to tell whether the commodity has changed in value because of changes in its labour content or because of changes in wages or both. Since Ricardo identifies his theory of value with the search for the cause(s) of changes in value, it is apparent that his 'invariable measure of value' cannot be of much help here.

The clue to the problem can be found in Ricardo's letter to McCulloch dated 13 June 1820, wherein he wrote:

I sometimes think that if I were to write the chapter on value again which is in my book, I should acknowledge that the relative value of commodities was regulated by two causes instead of by one, namely, by the relative quantity of labour necessary to produce the commodities in question, and by the rate of profit for the time that the capital remained dormant, and until the commodities were brought to market. Perhaps I should find the difficulties nearly as great in this view of the

---

18 In a letter to McCulloch dated 19 March 1822, Ricardo wrote: 'If 1000 bricks vary in relative value to a certain quantity of muslin, produced by the aid of valuable machinery, it may be owing to one or two causes: more or less labour may be required to produce one of them; or wages may have risen or fallen generally. With respect to the first being a cause of variation we entirely agree, but you do not appear to admit that although the same quantities of labour shall be respectively employed on the bricks and the muslin that their relative values may vary solely because the value of labour rises or falls, and yet the fact appears to me undeniable. To this second cause I do not attach near so much importance as Mr. Malthus and others but I cannot wholly shut my eyes to it.' (Ricardo 1951–52, *Works IX*: 178).

19 'It is a great desideratum of Polit. Econ. to have a perfect measure of absolute value in order to be able to ascertain what relation commodities bear to each other at distant periods' (ibid., *Works IV*: 396).

subject as in that which I have adopted (Ricardo 1951–52, *Works VIII*: 279–80).

What is enigmatic about this statement is that in the first two editions of the *Principles* Ricardo repeatedly makes the point that: 'If the fixed and circulating capitals were in different proportions, or if the fixed capital were of different durability, then the relative value of the commodities produced, would be altered in consequence of a rise of wages' (ibid., *Works I*, first edition of the *Principles*: 56). Given this, what did Ricardo mean in his letter by suggesting that he had not acknowledged that the relative value of commodities is regulated by *two* causes? Sraffa points out that this was merely a passing mood and that Ricardo had soon come to the conclusion that 'My first chapter will not be materially altered — in principle I think it will not be altered at all' (ibid., *Works VIII*: 280, letter to Malthus dated 9 October 1820; also quoted in Sraffa 1951: xl), and that 'in fixing on the quantity of labour realized in commodities as the rule which governs their relative value we are in the right course' (ibid., *Works VIII*: 344, letter to McCulloch dated 25 January 1821; also quoted in Sraffa 1951: xl). Thus the problem is: how do we reconcile the fact that the first chapters of all three editions are replete with explicit statements acknowledging the second cause — which is the rise and fall of wages and the rate of profits — of the variation in relative value of commodities with the statement in his letter to McCulloch that he apparently had not acknowledged it?[20]

20 Peach also finds Ricardo's statement 'puzzling' and goes on to add: After all, Ricardo had allowed for a "considerable modification" to the "pure" labour theory in the published versions of his first chapter and to that extent, the "two causes" had been acknowledged already. I can only suggest that he thought he should be even more explicit in terms of the newly adopted "labour profile" framework, although this suggestion is avowedly tentative' (Peach 1993: 197). Of course, it simply is a non-sequitur. It is strange that though Peach notices that 'All distribution-induced price changes were now considered to be indicative of a "defect" *in the standard*' (ibid.: 198), he fails to put two and two together here. Samuel Hollander (1979: 221–23), on the other hand, suggests that Ricardo may be suggesting a new cause of change in prices, namely, the exogenous changes in the period of investment. He, however, acknowledges that this was neither taken up in the third edition nor in any subsequent correspondence. Both Hollander and Peach fail to notice that in the later letter to McCulloch [dated 25 January 1821] Ricardo reverts back to indicating only one cause of change: 'in fixing on the quantity of labour realized in commodities as the rule which governs their relative value we are in the right course'.

The solution to this riddle lies in the fact that Ricardo separates the nature of the two causes. Though the first cause, i.e., change in the labour content of the commodity, is considered the *real* cause; the second cause, i.e., the rise or fall of wages or the rate of profits, is considered only an *apparent* cause. Ricardo seems to think that the variations in the relative values of commodities brought about by changes in wages or the rate of profits are solely due to the absence of 'an invariable measure of value' in nature. As he writes in his notes on 'Absolute and Exchangeable Values':

> If the commodity chosen for Mr. Ricardo's measure, whose value confessedly consists of profits and labour, were divided in the proportion of 90 for labour and 10 for profit — it is manifest that with every rise of 1 pc^t. in labour a commodity produced by labour alone would rise one per cent. *If the measure was perfect it ought not to vary at all* (Ricardo 1951–52, *Works IV*: 373; emphasis added).

Again, after a couple of pages, he writes: 'To me it appears to be a contradiction to say a thing has increased in natural value while it continues to be produced under precisely the same circumstances as before' (ibid.: 375). This is the context in which we can understand Ricardo's statement regarding changes in the proportions of capital and labour due to changes in distribution:

> The two commodities change in relative value. ... Can it be said that the proportions of capital we employ are in any way altered? or the proportions of labour? Certainly not, nothing has altered but the rate of distribution between employer and employed ... this and this only is the reason why they alter in relative value (Ricardo 1951–52, *Works IX*: 355–56, draft letter to McCulloch, 15 August 1823).

What Ricardo implies here is that the changes in the proportions of capital brought about by changes in distribution are only nominal and if there was an 'invariable measure of value' then it could be shown that no such changes occur. This point is further emphasised in the defence of his selection of the money-commodity to be produced by the 'mean' composition of capital: ' ... and the mean will in most cases give a much less deviation from *truth* than if either of the extremes were used as a measure' (ibid., *Works IV*: 405, emphasis added). The *truth*, of course, stands for zero deviation! Thus when Ricardo speaks of changes in 'real' or 'absolute' value, he refers to the changes in value caused solely by the changes in its labour content, as is indicated in his letter to Trower dated 22 August 1821:

> In speaking of exchangeable value you have not any idea of real value in your mind — I invariably have. ... The exchangeable value of a commodity cannot alter, I say, unless either its real value, or the real value of the things it is exchanged for alter. This cannot be disputed[21] (ibid., *Works IX*: 38).[22]

But, of course, Ricardo is wrong in assuming that changes in distribution will have no effect on relative values if they were measured against an 'invariable measure of value' for the simple reason that changes in distribution do affect the relative values of commodities and thus logically there cannot be any commodity against which the relative values of commodities could remain constant in the face of changes in distribution. As usual, Sraffa is most perceptive on this score:

> In this attempt to extend the application of absolute value to the second problem (that of distinguishing the two sorts of changes in exchangeable value) Ricardo was confronted with this dilemma: whereas the former application presupposes an exact proportionality between relative and absolute value, the latter implies a variable deviation of exchangeable from absolute value for each individual commodity. This contradiction Ricardo never completely succeeded in resolving, as is apparent from his last paper (Sraffa 1951: xlvii).

If our interpretation is accepted, then the widely held opinion propagated by Professor Stigler (1958) that Ricardo had only an *empirical*, but no *analytical* labour theory of value must be rejected.[23]

---

21 Sraffa writes: 'On the other hand, Ricardo was not interested for its own sake in the problem of why two commodities produced by the same quantities of labour are not of the same exchangeable value. He was concerned with it only in so far as thereby relative values are affected by changes in wages. The two points of view of difference and change are closely linked together; yet the search for an invariable measure of value, which is so much at the centre of Ricardo's system, arises exclusively from the second and would have no counterpart in an investigation of the first' (Sraffa 1951: xlix).

22 Also see Meek (1966).

23 'I can find no basis for the belief that Ricardo had an analytical labour theory of value. ... On the other hand, there is no doubt that he held what may be called

Before we close this section, let me point out that in addition to what I have said, Sraffa provides another and more widely held interpretation of Ricardo's problem of the 'invariable measure of value'. He argues that:

> This preoccupation with the effect of a change in wages arose from his approach to the problem of value which, as we have seen, was dominated by his theory of profits. The 'principal problem of Political Economy' was in his view the division of the national product between classes and in the course of that investigation he was troubled by the fact that the size of this product appears to change when the division changes. Even though nothing has occurred to change the magnitude of the aggregate, there may be *apparent* changes due solely to change in measurement, owing to the fact that measurement is in terms of value and relative values have been altered as a result of a change in the division between wages and profits. This is particularly evident in the extreme case where the aggregate is composed of the same commodities in the same quantities, and yet its magnitude will appear to have changed as measured in value (Sraffa 1951: xlviii).

As we will see in Chapter 4, an ingenious solution to this problem was found by Sraffa (1960) himself in his book, *Production of Commodities by Means of Commodities*.[24] However, Sraffa does not provide any direct evidence to the effect that 'in the course of

---

an empirical labour theory of value, that is, a theory that the relative quantities of labour required in production are the dominant determinants of relative values' (Stigler 1958: 60). Schumpeter (1954: 594), on the other hand, thinks that for Ricardo labour is more fundamental and important. He, however, maintains that once 'the murder was out', i.e., the fact that the rate of profits had influence on value, his theorem could only be maintained as an 'approximation'.

24 Sraffa (1960: 22ff.) shows that if the Standard commodity is used as the *numéraire* and wages are expressed in terms of the Standard commodity, then there exists a straight line inverse relationship between the wage rate and the rate of profits for any given empirical system. This relationship is given by the equation: $r = R(1 - w)$, where r, R and w are the rate of profits, the maximum rate of profit of the system and the wage rate expressed in the Standard commodity respectively. This proves that when the Standard commodity is used as the *numéraire*, then the value of the net output remains constant as the rate of profits takes on the values from zero to its maximum R.

that [division of national product between classes] investigation he [Ricardo] was troubled by the fact that the size of this product appears to change when the division changes'. His thesis hangs on two pegs: (*i*) by *absolute* or *real* value Ricardo means the value of a commodity measured against the 'invariable measure of value'; and (ii) Ricardo identifies the search for an 'invariable measure' with the search for the correct theory of value itself.

On the question of *absolute* or *real* value in Ricardo, Sraffa writes:

> The idea of an 'invariable measure' has for Ricardo its necessary complement in that of 'absolute value'. This concept appears in the *Principles* at first (in ed. I) as 'absolute value' and later (in ed. 3) as 'real value', it comes out from time to time in his letters, and takes more definite shape in his last paper on 'Absolute Value and Exchangeable Value'. In one of the drafts for that paper he writes: 'No one can doubt that it would be a great desideratum in political Economy to have such a measure of absolute value in order to enable us to know[,] when commodities altered in exchangeable value[,] in which the alteration in value had taken place' (Sraffa 1951: xlvi).

However, he immediately goes on to add:

> In another draft he [Ricardo] explains what he means by a test of whether a commodity has altered in value: 'I may be asked what I mean by the word value, and by what criterion I would judge whether a commodity had or had not changed its value. I answer, I know no other criterion of a thing being dear or cheap but by the sacrifices of labour made to obtain it' (ibid.: xlvi).

Thus the second (actually the earlier) draft makes it clear that the *real* change in value for Ricardo always means change in its labour content only. Now, when we put the two positions together, that is, (*a*) a change in 'absolute value' or 'real value' is the change measured against the 'invariable standard', and (*b*) a change in 'absolute value' is a change in its labour content, then we come up with the inescapable conclusion that the changes in value of any commodity caused by changes in distribution must disappear (become zero) when measured against the 'invariable standard'. This is the property of the 'invariable measure' that Ricardo was looking for.

Let us now look at the second peg in Sraffa's argument:

> The search for what has been called 'the chimera of an invari-
> able standard of value' preoccupied Ricardo to the end of his
> life. However, the problem which mainly interested him was
> not that of finding an actual commodity which would accu-
> rately measure the value of corn or silver at different times
> and places; but rather that of finding the conditions which
> a commodity would have to satisfy in order to be invariable
> in value — and this came close to identifying the problem of
> a measure with that of the law of value: 'Is it not clear then
> that as soon as we are in possession of the knowledge of the
> circumstances which determine the value of commodities, we
> are enabled to say what is necessary to give us an invariable
> measure of value?' (Ricardo to McCulloch, 21 August 1823).
> (ibid.: xl-xli).

Now it is clear that Ricardo was quite worried by his inability to find
the 'invariable measure', but it does not appear that he held for too
long the position that he expresses in the letter to McCulloch that has
been cited by Sraffa. For, this position implies that if Ricardo came to
the conclusion that the 'invariable measure of value' is a chimera, then
he would have to conclude that a correct theory or the law of value is
also a chimera. However, as we have seen, Ricardo is quite confident
about what he means by 'value' and the cause of its change in the first
draft of the 'Absolute and Exchangeable Value'; in fact, just one day
after he wrote the cited letter to McCulloch, we find him writing to
Trower quite confidently that: 'The exchangeable value of a commodity cannot alter, I say, unless either its real value, or the real value of
the things it is exchanged for, alter. This cannot be disputed.' Only a
week later, though, we again find him writing: '... if we were in possession of the knowledge of the law which regulates the exchangeable
value of commodities, we should be only one step from the discovery
of a measure of absolute value' (Ricardo 1951–52, *Works IX:* 377,
Ricardo to Trower, 31 August 1823).

However, in the end Ricardo appears to have come to the conclusion that the 'invariable measure of value' is truly a chimera; as in his
last letter dated 5 September 1823, he wrote to Mill:

> I have been thinking a good deal on this subject lately but
> without much improvement — I see the same difficulties as
> before and am more confirmed than ever that strictly speaking

> there is not in nature any correct measure of value nor can any
> ingenuity suggest one, for what constitutes a correct measure
> for some things is a reason why it cannot be a correct one for
> other (ibid.: 372).

The reader should note that Ricardo's point that 'what constitutes
a correct measure for some things' refers to those things with equal
ratios of labour to means of production. In such cases, when one
commodity is used as the standard of measure against another, the
impact on their prices due to changes in distribution would be zero.
Moreover, the idea that 'a correct measure' could be found for a subset
of commodities clearly shows that Ricardo's 'correct measure' is not
about maintaining the value of aggregate net output constant. In this
context, it might be helpful to remind the reader that in the *Production
of Commodities* Sraffa acknowledges that: 'It should perhaps be stated
that it was only when the Standard system and the distinction between
basics and non-basics had emerged in the course of the present investigation that the above [corn-model] interpretation of Ricardo's theory
suggested itself as a natural consequence' (Sraffa 1960: 93).

   Though Sraffa's interpretation has now become orthodoxy, there are
several other Ricardo scholars who have over the years demurred.[25]
One common ground of all the critics of Sraffa on this issue has been
the argument that Ricardo sought to establish an inverse wage-profit
relation in the context of diminishing returns on land, and thus the
whole idea of a given size of the cake being cut in different proportions
is simply not relevant to Ricardo's case. As Peach writes:

> Ricardo's standard was to sanction the use of the labour
> theory in demonstration of his 'agricultural' thesis: the proof
> that 'permanent' reductions in general profitability must
> result when an increasing corn output requires proportionally
> greater inputs of labour. Sraffa's analytical devices would have
> no relevance in this Ricardian context (Peach 1993: 290).

Though it is true that Ricardo is concerned primarily with the impact
of changes in distribution on the relative values of commodities in the
context of diminishing returns on land, it would be incorrect to suggest that this is the sole context of his search for an 'invariable measure

---

25 See for example, Caravale and Tosato (1980), Ong (1983), Caravale (1985) and
   Peach (1993).

of value' and that he does not separate the problem from the context of growth and diminishing returns on land. It should be noted that Ricardo introduces the problem of the 'invariable measure of value' in Chapter I, before the theories of rent and wages are introduced. Thus at the formal level, the problem caused by the effect of changes in distribution on relative prices is completely independent of the context of growth and diminishing returns on land. For example, in Section III of Chapter I, Ricardo deals with the question of a rise and fall of wages and its impact on relative prices when the 'time-structures of capitals' are assumed to be uniform. In this context, he argues:

> Under different circumstances of plenty or scarcity of capital, as compared with labour, under different circumstances of plenty or scarcity of food and necessaries essential to the support of men, those who furnished an equal value of capital for either one employment or for the other, might have a half, a fourth, or an eighth of the produce obtained, the remainder being paid as wages to those who furnish the labour; yet this division could not affect the relative value of those commodities, since whether they were 50, 20, or 10 per cent or whether the wages of labour were high or low, they would operate equally on both employments (p. 24).

Clearly, Ricardo is here contemplating a rise or fall of real wages with the techniques remaining the same. If the change in wages were being contemplated on the basis of a change in the technique of producing the wage-goods, then, on the basis of the 'labour theory of value' Ricardo could not hold the relative values to be constant. Further on, Ricardo makes it clear that he is contemplating a rise or fall of wages caused not only by diminishing returns on land, but also due to changing circumstances in the labour market:

> ...a rise of wages, *from the circumstance of the labourer being more liberally rewarded*, or from a difficulty of producing the necessaries on which the wages are expended, does not, except in some instances, produce the effect of raising prices, but has a great effect of lowering profits (pp. 48–49, emphasis added).

This point is reiterated in his 'Notes on Malthus':

> I have invariably insisted that high or low profits depend on low and high wages, how then can it be justly said of me that

105

the only cause which I have recognized of high or low profits is the facility or difficulty of providing food for the labourer. I contend that I have also recognized the other cause, the relative amount of population to capital, which is another of the great regulators of wages (Ricardo 1951–52, *Works II*: 264–65).

Why Begin with Value?

This brings us to the close of the exposition of Ricardo's presentation of his theory of value proper. Before we move on to a consideration of criticisms and other interpretations of his theory, let us recall our question: why begin with value? In his celebrated 'Introduction' to Volume I of *The Works and Correspondence of David Ricardo* (i.e., Ricardo's *Principles of Political Economy*), Sraffa (in collaboration with Maurice Dobb) gives an interesting answer to this question. According to Sraffa, Ricardo in around 1814, as well as in his *Essay on the Influence of a Low Price of Corn on the Profits of Stock* which was published in February 1815, was working on the basic principle that 'it is the profits of the farmer that regulate the profits of all other trade'. He argues that Ricardo had a 'corn model' in mind, which provided the 'rational foundation' of this principle. According to Sraffa, Ricardo assumes that in agriculture, both capital (including wage advances) and products are the same goods, and thus a rate of profit in agriculture can be determined on the basis of the physical data without any need for a theory of value. And since in a competitive market an equal rate of profits must prevail, the prices of manufactures and other commodities have to be so adjusted as to allow the same rate of profits on their capital investments. In this framework, an inverse and proportional relationship between the rate of profits and real wages can be directly observed through the microcosm of the agricultural sector. Apparently, Malthus had objected to Ricardo's reasoning on the ground that:

> In no case of production, is the produce exactly of the same nature as the capital advanced. Consequently we can never properly refer to a material rate of produce. ... It is not the particular profits or rate of produce upon the land which determines the general profits of stock and the interest of money (letter dated 5 August 1814, quoted in Sraffa 1951: xxxi–xxxii).

Under such criticism Ricardo had to abandon his 'corn model', which exposed him to the problem of aggregating heterogeneous commodities, as the measure of capital required some device to homogenise a heterogeneous collection of goods. This led Ricardo to search for a general theory of value, which would then allow him to get a measure of the produce and capital in terms of their value. Thus the problem of value had to be solved before the question of distribution could be dealt with. As Ricardo, in the early stages of the preparation of the *Principles*, wrote to James Mill: 'I know I shall be soon stopped by the word price'[26] (Ricardo 1951–52, *Works VI:* 348, letter dated 30 December 1815, quoted in Sraffa 1951: xiv).

Another interesting story about why Ricardo needed a general theory of value is told by J.H. Hollander (1904). According to Hollander, Ricardo's proposition that 'it is the profits of the farmer that regulate the profits of all other trade' was challenged by Malthus on the ground that Ricardo's proposition was no more true than its converse. Thus an increase in the rate of profits in the sector of foreign commerce would raise the general rate of profits and consequently the rate of profits of the farmer.[27] Hollander writes that:

> ... With the greatest precision of thought brought by this controversy, and even more by Malthus's explanation of the cause and nature of rent, a few months later Ricardo appears to have become aware of a vulnerable point in his theory of the inverse relation between wages and profits. It was impossible to prove that a rise in wages was the exclusive cause of a fall in profits, if it were true that a rise in wages necessarily occasioned a rise in prices. Were the latter the case, the manufacturer simply recouped himself from out of the higher prices of his product for the higher wages he was obliged to pay, and profits remained unchanged. Thus the validity of Ricardo's theory of profits became, in large measure, dependent upon his ability to prove that prices did not necessarily increase as wages rose (Hollander 1904, in Wood 1985, Vol. I: 26).

26 Sraffa's 'corn-model' story generated a huge controversy between Samuel Hollander (1973b, 1975), who was joined on this issue by Peach (1993), and the Sraffians such as Eatwell (1975a), Garegnani (1982) and de Vivo (1985, 1996). But for our purpose the controversy is not important as nobody has claimed that Ricardo had a 'corn-model' in the Principles. Also see Faccarello (1982).

27 J.H. Hollander (1904) also mentions two other independent causes pushing Ricardo in this direction: (i) McCulloch's Essay on a Reduction of the Interest of the National Debt; and (*ii*) the general apprehension that removal of restrictions on the importation of corn would be followed by a disastrous fall in general prices (this argument is also made by Malthus).

Sraffa agrees that parallel to Ricardo's concern for a general measure of capital ran this particular theme of proving that all prices do not necessarily rise with a rise in wages. He further argues that:

> At once a proper understanding of the matter appears to him [Ricardo] as involving: (a) the distinction between causes which affect the value of money and causes which affect the value of commodities; (b) the supposition of the invariability of the precious metals as a standard of value; (c) the opposition to the view that the price of corn regulates the prices of all other commodities. These three things, which are so closely connected in his mind as to be almost identified, are what he calls 'the sheet anchor on which all my propositions are built' (f.n. letter to Mill of 30 December 1815, *Works VI*, 348) (Sraffa 1951: xxxiv).

It should be noted that even in his *Essay* of 1815 Ricardo had come to question the proposition that the price of corn regulates the prices of all other things, as in a footnote he writes:

> It has been thought that the price of corn regulates the prices of all other things. This appears to me to be a mistake. If the price is affected by the rise or fall of the value of the precious metals themselves, then indeed will the price of commodities be also affected, but they vary, because the value of money varies, not because the value of corn is altered. Commodities I think, cannot materially rise or fall, whilst money and commodities continue in the same proportion, or rather whilst the cost of production of both estimated in corn continues the same (Ricardo 1951–52, *Works IV*: 21).

Thus a rise of wages should not cause a rise in the price of a manufactured commodity since the price in terms of corn of the money-commodity is equally affected. But the discovery that a rise of wages would affect different commodities differently led to the conclusion that a rise in wages would lower the price of most of the commodities produced with the aid of machinery and fixed capital if the money-commodity chosen was produced with only labour (a position held in the first edition of the *Principles*), or some will rise and some will fall if the money-commodity was chosen close to the composition of the average of most of the commodities (a proposition held in the third edition). This discovery was essential in establishing that Adam Smith was wrong in proposing an *additive* theory of value, where value was arrived at by adding up given wages, profits and rent, which implied that a rise in wages (given profits and rent) would invariably lead to a rise in the prices of all the commodities — a proposition Ricardo considered Adam Smith's 'original error respecting value' (Ricardo 1951–52, *Works VII:* 82, letter to James Mill dated 14 October 1816).[28]

The problem with both these accounts is that they are told from the perspective of the author and the particular theoretical problem he was tackling before the writing of the book, rather than from the perspective of the book itself. From the perspective of the book, however, as we have seen, Ricardo needed to establish the proposition that the rate of profits on capital must fall as it becomes more difficult to produce wage-goods. Of course, in a 'corn model' set-up this proposition is obviously true as a fall in the marginal product of land with fixed wages would directly reduce the rate of profits, or alternatively, a rise in wages, given the output on the marginal land, will directly reduce the rate of profits. But as we have seen, in a general multiple-commodity case, Ricardo needed to go via money prices and money wages. For Ricardo the proof of the proposition required that the rise in the difficulty of producing wage-goods must lead to a rise in the money wages, with the price of some manufacturing goods remaining invariant. This required the proposition that changes in relative prices must be caused *only* by changes in the difficulty or facility of producing the goods. Ricardo needed to establish his version of the labour theory of value before he could establish his proposition that wages and the rate of profits were inversely related. But he could not completely succeed in achieving his goal as he could not eliminate the disturbances in prices caused by the changes in wages. Without it, however, he had no means of showing that his proposition would be valid even if such changes were allowed. Thus he took refuge in 'expediency' by ignoring this effect on prices on the dubious argument that they were small.

---

28 See Chapter 1 for a critique of Ricardo's critique of Smith on this point. It should, however, be noted that the proposition that 'the price of corn regulates the prices of all other commodities' had become an established doctrine by Ricardo's time, as McCulloch had declared in the *Edinburgh Review* of June 1818: 'Nothing in the whole science of political economy was reckoned better established, than that a rise or a fall of the rate of wages was attended by a proportionable increase or diminution of the price of commodities' (Quoted in Hollander 1904: 40). Also see *Malthus's Observations on the Effects of the Corn Laws* (1815) and J.-B. Say's *A Treatise on Political Economy* (1818) [1803].

Part II
Some Significant Readings and Criticisms of Ricardo

Now let us turn to some other significant readings and criticisms of Ricardo on the question of his theory of value starting from his contemporaries to our own times. It should be noted that instead of focusing on points of agreements, I shall concentrate on points of disagreements and criticisms of Ricardo that I find unjustified.

Ricardo's Contemporaries

Among Ricardo's contemporaries, J.B. Say and Thomas Malthus were the two most important critics of his book. Both Say and Malthus were apparently defending Smith from Ricardo's onslaught and thus their attacks on Ricardo were quite similar and conservative in nature — even though Say and Malthus diametrically disagreed on the question of the possibility of a general glut in the economy. J.B. Say (1821 [1971]) took the opportunity of the publication of the fourth edition of his *Treatise* in 1818 to briefly comment on Ricardo's *Principles* in a scattered manner and in the 'Introduction' criticised Ricardo for adopting a method characterised by a long chain of *deduction* as opposed to what he considered the correct method for economic reasoning — which for him was primarily *inductive* and one that drew relations between known facts.[29] In the French edition of Ricardo's *Principles* (1821), Say, however, took the opportunity to make several comments on Ricardo's specific arguments in terms of supplementary notes to the publication. He criticised Ricardo for neglecting the true foundation of the value of a good, i.e., its *utility*. It is the utility, according to him, that gives rise to a demand for a good, whereas the cost of production makes it rare by limiting its supply. He went on to argue that when the cost of production rises and the value of the good also rises, then it must require that the demand for the good rises at the same time. And if the demand falls, everything else being the same, it is impossible that

---

29 On Ricardo's method, Robert Torrens wrote: 'Though Mr. Ricardo has done more for the science of Political Economy than any other writer, with the single exception perhaps of Dr. Adam Smith, yet he sometimes falls into a species of error to which men of great original genius seem particularly exposed, and in the ardour of discovery, generalizes too hastily, and fails to establish his principles on a sufficiently extensive induction. In the inventive faculty, and in the power of pure and continuous ratiocination, he has seldom been surpassed; but in the capacity for accurate observation, his preeminence is less apparent' (Torrens 1821: iv).

the value will not fall. The value of a good cannot rise solely with the rise in its cost of production:

> M. Ricardo me semble à tort ne considérer ici qu'un des éléments de la valeur des choses, c'est-à-dire le travail, ou pour parler plus exactement, l'étendue des sacrifices qu'il faut faire pour les produire. Il néglige le premier élément, le véritable fondement de la valeur, l'utilité. C'est l'utilité qui occasionne la demande qu'on fait d'une chose. D'un autre côté, le sacrifice qu'il faut faire pour qu'elle soit produite, en d'autres mots, ses *frais de production* font sa rareté, bornent la quantité de cette chose qui s'offre à l'échange. Sa valeur s'élève *d'autant plus* qu'elle est plus demandée et moins offerte, et s'élève *d'autant moins* qu'elle est moins demandée et plus offerte. Ce principe est fondamental en économie politique; il est confirmé par une expérience constante; il est expliqué par le raisonnement. (Voyez mon *Traité d'Economie politique, liv. II, chap.I.*) Ce ne sont donc pas les frais de production *seuls*, ce que M. Ricardo, d'après Smith, appelle le *prix naturel* d'une chose, qui règle sa valeur échangeable, son prix courant, si l'on veut exprimer cette valeur en monnaie. Lorsque les frais de production augmentent, pour que la valeur échangeable augmentât aussi, il faudrait que le rapport de l'offre et de la demande restât le même; il faudrait que la demande augmentât aussi; et il est de fait qu'elle diminue; il est impossible, toutes ces circonstances étant d'ailleurs les mêmes, qu'elle ne diminue pas. La valeur échangeable ne peut donc pas monter comme les frais de production. C'est pour avoir perdu de vue ce fait constant, et par conséquent ce principe fondamental, que M. Ricardo a été entraîné, je crois, dans quelques erreurs, que je prendrai la liberté de relever dans l'intérêt de la science, et sans m'écarter des égards que mérite l'auteur par ses qualités personnelles autant que par ses talents. (J.B. Say in Fonteyraud 1847: 8–9).[30]

30 ['It seems to me that Mr Ricardo here wrongly considers only one element of the value of things, that is labour, or to say it in a more precise way, the sacrifices that are required to produce them. He neglects the first element, the real basis of value, which is the utility. It is because of utility that one wants to get a thing. On the other hand, the sacrifice required to produce it, in other words, its *costs of production*, creates its scarcity and limits the quantity of that thing available in the market. The value of it *rises* as more of it is demanded and less of it is produced, and it *falls* as less of it is demanded and more of it is produced. This is a fundamental principle

Clearly, Say's arguments are a good case of muddled reasoning. It is one thing to say that the *market price* of a good would rise or fall in relation to the rise or fall in its demand, other things being the same, but quite another thing to say that the *natural price* of the good would rise or fall in relation to a rise or fall in its cost of production only. Say argues that the rise in cost of production would increase the 'exchange value' only if the quantity supplied and demanded remains constant or the quantity demanded rises. He further goes on to argue that in fact a rise in the cost of production would lead to a fall in the quantity demanded and thus, given the quantity supplied, cause a fall in the 'exchange value'. But this fall in the exchange value, or rather, market price, can happen only if the price had first risen. But in any case, it is easy to see that the long-term price or Ricardo's natural price would eventually rise with the rise in cost of production. Suppose that the quantity demanded at the price equal to the higher cost of production is lower than the original demand or the quantity supplied. This would lead to a fall in the market price, which would imply a fall in the rate of profit in this sector, given the higher cost of production. This, in turn, would lead to an exit of some capital from the sector, lowering its supply until the market price rises to the new 'equilibrium' or natural price at the higher cost of production level. Say clearly mixes up the causes that have an immediate impact on *market prices* with the causes that have a permanent impact on *natural prices*, with which Ricardo's propositions are solely concerned.[31]

of political economy, proven by the constant experience and explained by reasoning (see my *Traité d'Economie politique*, liv. *II*, chap.*I*). It is therefore not only the costs of production, that Mr Ricardo, following Smith, calls the *natural price* of a thing, that regulates its exchange value, its current price, if one wants to express its value in money terms. When the costs of production rise, for the exchange value to also rise, it would require the relation of supply and of demand to remain the same; it would also require the demand to rise; but it is a fact that it goes down; in these circumstances it is impossible that it does not go down. The exchange value cannot rise as the costs of production do. It is because he has not kept in mind this constant fact, and so this fundamental principle, that Mr Ricardo has made some mistakes that I will feel free to underline in the interest of science even though I do not forget how honourable he is because of his personal qualities as well as his skills.']

31 In the controversy with Ricardo on the role of 'utility' on values of commodities, Say, in a letter of 19 July 1821 explained that he maintained that commodities possessed two kinds of utilities: the first derived from nature without any addition of labour on it, and the second derived exclusively from expenditure of labour on it and it was the second type of utility that was responsible for the value of commodities. To which Ricardo responded: 'Although I cannot quite approve of the terms

Say also criticises Ricardo's notion of 'invariable measure of value' by claiming that it is a pure chimera:

> La vérité est que la valeur des choses étant une qualité essentiellement variable d'un temps à un autre, d'un lieu à un autre; la valeur d'une chose (fût-ce celle du travail) ne peut servir de mesure à la valeur d'une autre chose, si ce n'est pour un temps et pour un lieu donnés. C'est pour cela que, pour chaque lieu, il y a, tous les jours, un nouveau prix courant des marchandises, et un nouveau cours du change (qui n'est que le prix courant des diverses monnaies). Une mesure invariable des valeurs est une pure chimère, parce qu'on ne peut mesurer les valeurs que par des valeurs, c'est-à-dire par une quantité essentiellement variable. Il n'en résulte pas que la valeur soit chimérique; elle ne l'est pas plus que la chaleur des corps qui ne peut pas se fixer davantage. (Fonteyraud 1847: 10).[32]

Now, if one (along with Sraffa's 1951 'Introduction') holds that Ricardo's 'invariable measure of value' was designed to ensure that the measuring rod was not affected by the changes in the distribution of the net output between wages and profits, then Sraffa (1960) has shown that such a measure can theoretically be constructed and thus is definitely not a chimera (see Chapter 4 of this book). On the other hand, if one holds (along with *our* interpretation) that Ricardo thought that the 'invariable measure of value' would ensure that changes in the distribution of the net output between capitalists and workers will not

---

used to explain this truth, yet I do now, and always have substantially agreed in the reasoning which proves it, for I have always contended that commodities are valuable in proportion to the quantity of labour bestowed upon them, and when you say that they are valuable in proportion as they are useful, and they are useful in proportion to the quantity of labour or industry bestowed upon them, you are in fact expressing the same opinion in other words' (Ricardo 1951–52, *Works IX*: 169, Letter of 5 March 1822).

32 ['The truth is that the value of things is a quality that by essence varies from time to time, from place to place; the value of a thing (even if it is the value of work) can be used to measure the value of another thing only for a certain time and place. That is why there is for every place, everyday a new current price of goods and a new exchange rate (that is only the current price of different currencies). An invariable measure of values is a pure illusion, because one can only measure values by using values, that is to say a quantity that by essence varies. It doesn't mean that the value is an illusion; it is not an illusion as in the case of the heat of bodies which, in the same way, cannot remain constant.']

cause the money-value of commodities to change, then of course, it is a chimera. However, it should be noted that Say had not understood the purpose of Ricardo's search for the 'invariable measure of value'.

As we remarked earlier, Malthus makes similar criticisms of Ricardo's cost of production theory of value. Sraffa (in Ricardo 1951–52, *Works II:* vii) contends that Malthus's *Principles* was foremost 'intended as an answer to Ricardo'.[33] Malthus's critique of Ricardo's theory of value has two aspects: (*a*) that value is determined by supply and demand and the consideration of cost is subordinate to it; and (*b*) that Ricardo's measure of value is incorrect and reveals the weakness of his theory. In the following paragraphs we take up both controversies successively. My references are from Volume II of *Works and Correspondence of David Ricardo* edited by Sraffa (Ricardo 1951–52), which provides the text from Malthus's *Principles* along with Ricardo's notes on them.[34]

On the first point, Malthus argues:

> If for instance, all the commodities that are consumed in this country, whether agricultural or manufacturing, could be produced, during the next ten years, without labour, and yet could only be supplied exactly in the same quantities as they would be in natural state of things; then, supposing the wills and the powers of the purchasers to remain the same, there cannot be a doubt that all prices would also remain the same. But, if this be allowed, it follows, that the relation of the supply to the demand, either actual or contingent, is the dominant principle in the determination of prices whether market or natural, and that the cost of production can do nothing but in subordination to it, that is, merely as this cost affects actually or contingently the relation which the supply bears to the demand. (ibid., *Works II:* 46–47).

This criticism, however, can be easily dismissed from Ricardo's theoretical perspective. It is obvious that if labour is not required in

---

33 In a letter to Ricardo dated 3 December 1817, Malthus wrote: ' … I am meditating a volume as I believe I have told you, and I want to answer you, without giving my work a controversial air. Can you tell me how to manage this?' (Ricardo 1951–52, *Works VII:* 229).

34 These notes were not published, though Ricardo wavered between publishing and not publishing them.

production, then a 'labour theory of value' of any kind will have no meaning. Let us suppose that in Malthus's example the supplies every year fell from the sky in the exact amounts he specifies. Such a case would be similar to the case of rare piece of art, etc., where supply is a fixed quantity. In these cases, Ricardo had already contended that their prices would be governed by supply and demand and that such cases were left out of the consideration of the general theory of value. The real test of Malthus's argument is in imagining that the cost of production of a commodity falls because of a new innovation, although the total supplies and demands in the market remain the same. In this case, the old set of prices would generate a higher rate of profit in this sector compared to others. This will bring the competitive forces and the gravitational mechanism into play. If demand is a fixed quantity, then a fall in the cost of the commodity will lead to capital influx in the sector and thus excess supply. This excess supply must prevail till the price comes down to the level where the rate of profit is again equal to the old level. At this stage the supply must contract to the level of the given demand because the persistence of excess supply would cause the prices to fall further and thus the rate of profit to fall below the original level triggering a fall in supply. Thus, when the dust settles, the price of the commodity under question must fall, even if its supply eventually comes back to the old level. If Malthus contends that the demand schedule of all commodities are fixed downward sloping curves on the price-quantity plane, then Ricardo's centre of gravitation at the lower price will eventually require a higher supply of the commodity, but this change in supply is subordinate to the principle that prices must be proportional to cost rather than the other way round. Curiously, Ricardo remains silent on this point made by Malthus, though elsewhere he indirectly responds to it by noting: 'I do not say that the value of a commodity will always conform to its natural price without an additional supply, but I say that the cost of production regulates the supply, and therefore regulates the price' (1951–52, *Works II*: 48–49).[35]

---

35 In a letter to Malthus dated 30 January 1818, Ricardo wrote: ' ... However abundant the demand it can never permanently raise the price of a commodity above the expense of its production, including in that expense the profit of the producers. It seems natural therefore to seek for the cause of the variation of permanent price in the expenses of production. Diminish these and the commodity must finally fall, increase them and it must as certainly rise. What has this to do with demand?' (ibid., *Works II*: 250–51).

Malthus's second line of attack moves away from a general denial of the labour theory of value to a specific attack on Ricardo's theory:

> But if, at the same place and at the same time, the relative values of commodities are not determined by the labour which they have cost in production, it is clear that this measure cannot determine their relative values at different places and at different times (Ricardo 1951–52, *Works II*: 76).

Clearly he believes that Ricardo's labour theory of value is tied to the proposition regarding the *cause* of *changes* in relative values and not the determination of relative values as such. He, however, simply asserts a correct point without proving it. As we have argued earlier, Ricardo's concern for the 'invariable measure of value' centres on this problem. Malthus's critique of Ricardo's 'measure of value', however, fails to go to the heart of it. He keeps arguing that since a rise or fall in wages or profits could affect the relative prices of commodities, it is proof that the labour theory of value is invalid (see ibid.: 65–66 and 81–82). Ricardo's response was that he had never denied it except that his contention is that its effect on relative values is minor. Of course, Ricardo's choice of gold as his measure of value was not made on any empirical consideration but was simply a theoretical abstraction, as he himself explains: 'It was never contended that gold under the present circumstances was a good measure of value, it was only hypothetical, and for the purpose of illustrating a principle, supposed that all the known causes of the variability of gold, were removed' (ibid., *Works II:* 81–82). But more polemically, Ricardo counters Malthus's criticism by questioning the basis on which Malthus talks about the rise and fall in wages and prices. According to Ricardo, Malthus must implicitly assume that 'money was stationary in value' and if so, then:

> That definition which he calls arbitrary he nevertheless adopts. If he says that the medium I have chosen is variable, then none of his conclusions are just: if he admits its invariability, then there is an end of his objection against the medium under the conditions I have supposed as a measure of real value (Ricardo 1951–52, *Works II*: 64–65).

However, this argument of Ricardo's is a non-sequitur. As Ricardo was well aware, the proof of the variability of the unit of measure in the face of a rise or fall in the rate of profits or wages does not require the assumption of an invariable measure of value. He produces another defensive non-sequitur against Malthus when he argues:

'I object to your measure of value, says Mr. Malthus, because it is not so invariable as you represent it, — there are causes of variation which affect it for which you have not made due allowance.' Who would not suppose then that when he proposed a measure of value [Malthus had proposed Smith's labour commanded measure] he would propose one free from these objections? He does quite the contrary, he proposes a measure which is not only variable in itself, but is particularly variable, on account of its connection with other variable commodities. (ibid.: 90–91).

This line of attack has meaning only if Malthus had accepted Ricardo's theoretical *problematique* to begin with. There is no doubt that Ricardo was most vulnerable on this point. Even though Malthus may not have been entirely convincing, he nevertheless exposed a chink in Ricardo's armour, of which Ricardo himself was well aware.

Given the importance of the theory of rent in Ricardo's overall theoretical structure, another major issue of contention between him and Malthus turned out to be Ricardo's theory of rent; Say also joined hands with Malthus on this issue. As the reader will note, Ricardo had credited Malthus for his theory of rent and was quite upset to learn that Malthus had decided to attack him on this point: 'He [Mr. Malthus] has altered his opinion you know about there being land in every country which pays no rent, and appears like M. Say to think that when that is proved, my doctrine of rent not entering into price is overthrown.' (ibid., *Works VII*: 372, Ricardo's letter to Mill, dated 22 December 1818).

Malthus's basic argument was that given that there is positive rent in an economy, it implies that the total revenue in terms of money after the sale of all the agricultural supply (say, corn) is larger than the total cost of production in money, including all the wages and profits paid to the labourers and the farmers (or the capitalists) employed in the agricultural sector. This implies that there is a surplus of 'corn' after the payment of both wages and profits. At this stage, the theoretical question Malthus raised to himself was: why does this surplus corn not create an excess supply of corn leading to a fall in its price such that the total revenue falls to the extent that only wages and profits can be paid out of the total revenue and rent is completely wiped out? His answer to this question was that corn is a special commodity. The supply of corn always brings about its own demanders according to his theory of population. This special property of corn is responsible for maintaining the proportion of supply and demand and hence the high price of corn, which affords a rent.[36]

In this scenario the idea of differential fertilities of land is not a cause of rent. Even if all lands were homogeneous but fertile enough to produce more corn than the cost of its production including wages and profits, then, once all the lands were brought under cultivation, a rent would arise on all the lands. Differential fertilities of land can only explain differential rent on different plots of land but cannot explain the existence of rent itself. It is also possible that the marginal land, in the case of differential fertilities of land, does not pay any rent because its fertility is so low that it does not produce any surplus beyond the expenses of wages and usual profits on that land. But this scenario has nothing to do with the existence of rent as such.

Malthus's theory of rent rests on two intertwined hypotheses: (*i*) the value of a commodity is determined by the forces of demand and supply in contradistinction to Ricardo's theory that value is determined by cost of production; and (*ii*) surplus 'corn' will lead to population growth. Both these hypotheses are highly suspect and Ricardo's self-defence or rather attack on Malthus concentrates on the second hypothesis. As long ago as 21 October 1817, Ricardo, in his comment on the fifth edition of Malthus's *Essay on Population*, had written to Malthus: 'In every part you are exceedingly clear, and time only is wanted to carry conviction to every mind. The chief difference between us is whether food or population precedes' (Ricardo 1951–52, *Works VII*: 201). The crucial difference between Malthus's and Ricardo's propositions on this issue is that for Malthus a surplus supply of corn brings about increase in population and the demanders of that corn, thereby preventing the 'surplus' from turning into excess supply; whereas for Ricardo a 'surplus' of corn of Malthus's type would not fail to create an excess supply in the short run and thus reduce the market price of corn below its natural price. Therefore, it would be simply irrational for any farmer (or capitalist producer) to produce such 'surplus' output intentionally. According to Ricardo, the rise in population causes the demand for corn to rise, leading to a rise in the market price of corn at the old supply level. This leads to an increase

36 'Rent then being the excess of price above what is necessary to pay the wages of the labour and the profits of the capital employed in cultivation, the first object which presents itself for inquiry, is, the cause or causes of this excess price' (Malthus in ibid., *Works II*: 103).

in the farmers' rate of profits, which attracts more capital into the corn sector and increases its supply to match the increased demand. Thus there is nothing special about corn. It follows the same logic as any other commodity — its supply adjusts to changes in demand.

> Corn is produced because it is reasonably anticipated, but should not on that account be justified in saying that corn raises up its own demanders, or that its plenty bribes people to come into existence, because that always supposes a price of corn below the natural or remunerating price, and it is no man's interest to produce it on such terms. ... Pray understand that I am answering Mr. Malthus who contends that there is something peculiar about corn which gives it a character of being able to raise up demanders different from all other things — I contend on the contrary, that there is no difference between them that nothing is produced until it is wanted unless from mistaking and miscalculation (ibid., *Works VIII*: 235–37, Ricardo's letter to Trower dated 15 September 1820).

On the question of marginal land paying rent, Ricardo stopped insisting that there is always a marginal land in the physical sense that does not pay rent. Instead, he argued that a corollary of his argument is that the marginal capital employed on land did not pay any rent — it was in the capitalists' self-interest to go on investing capital on a given plot of land until the last unit of capital investment resulted in returns from land exactly equal to the wage bill plus the prevailing rate of profits. This is the simple rule of profit maximisation under diminishing returns. He insisted that neither Malthus nor Say were able to touch this proposition, which amounted to leaving his theory of rent intact: '... they neither of them [Malthus and Say] advert to the other principle which cannot be touched, of capital being employed on land, already in cultivation, which pays no rent' (Ricardo 1951–52, *Works VII*: 372, Ricardo's letter to Mill dated 22 December 1818). Again, in a letter to Say dated 11 January 1820, Ricardo wrote:

> You appear to me to have mistaken also an opinion of mine on which you comment in a note of the translation of my book. My argument respecting rent, profit and taxes, is founded on a supposition that there is land in every country which pays no rent, or that there is capital employed on land before in cultivation for which no rent is paid. You answer the first position,

but you take no notice of the second. The admission of either will answer my purpose (ibid., *Works VIII*: 149–50).[37]

In his response dated 2 March 1820, Say concedes Ricardo's second point:

> J'avoue que je ne vois pas trop comment la seconde partie de la proposition fait passer la premiere. N'importe: si la critique est juste pour cette premiere partie, je conviendrai volontiers que vous avez raison pour la seconde (ibid.: 161).[38]

On the question of Ricardo's theory of profit, Malthus raised one fundamental question. He argued that Ricardo's proposition that, given the total output, a rise in wages must lead to a fall in the rate of profits, is built on the assumption that the money-commodity remained invariable in the face of a rise or fall in wages. According to Malthus, since Ricardo's money-commodity is not invariable, he cannot presume that the value of the total output ('mass of commodities') would remain constant when money wages are increased or diminished. If the value of the total output changes due to changes in wages, how can Ricardo argue that a rise in wages must lead to a fall in the rate of profits?

> This theory of profits depends entirely upon the circumstances of the mass of commodities remaining at the same price, while money continues of the same value, whatever may be the variations in the price of labour. This uniformity in the value of wages and profits taken together is indeed assumed by Mr. Ricardo in all his calculations, from one end of his work to the other; and if it were true, we should certainly have an accurate rule which would determine the rate of profits upon any given rise or fall of money wages. But if it be not true, the whole theory falls to the ground. We can infer nothing respecting

---

37 In a letter to Mill dated 28 December 1818, Ricardo wrote: 'I did not expect that you would be satisfied by Say's notes. Some of them are ingenious, but he does not grapple with the real question in dispute, he makes a shew of answering it, but he completely evades it. ... I think of making no other answer to M Say's observations but that of remarking that he has left my main position respecting the regulator of rent unanswered' (ibid., Works VII: 378–79; see also Works I: 413, f.n).

38 ['I must admit that I don't really see how the second part of the proposition allows the first one to go through. Anyway: if the critique is right for this first part, I will fully recognise that you are right about the second one.']

the rate of profits from a rise of money wages, if commodities, instead of remaining of the same price, are very variously affected, some rising, some falling, and a very small number indeed remaining stationary. But it was shown in a former chapter [Chapter II] that this must necessarily take place upon a rise in the price of labour. Consequently the money wages of labour cannot regulate the rate of profits (Ricardo 1951–52, *Works II*: 285–86).

This comes close to what Sraffa has identified to be at the core of Ricardo's search for an 'invariable measure of value'. Interestingly, Ricardo remains silent on this point. Though he was convinced of the truthfulness of his proposition that wages and rate of profits are inversely related, since in a corn economy set-up this appeared obvious, he was unable to prove his proposition in a multiple-commodity scenario without assuming the invariability of his measuring rod.[39]

Before closing this sub-section, it may not be out of place to make a brief comment on Robert Torrens, who is among the first of Ricardo's contemporaries to write a bitter critique of Ricardo's first edition of the *Principles* in the October 1818 issue of the *Edinburgh Magazine*. His main attack concentrated on his misunderstanding of Ricardo's labour theory of value:

> The relative worth of all things is determined, not by the quantities of labour required to produce them, but by the universally operating law of competition, which equalizes the profits of stock, and consequently, renders the results obtained from the employment of equal capitals of equal value in exchange ... when capitalists and labourers become distinct, it is always the amount of capital, and never the quantity of labour ...

---

39 In a letter to McCulloch dated 13 June 1820, Ricardo wrote: 'By getting rid of rent, which we may do on the corn produced with the capital last employed, and on all commodities produced by labour in manufactures, the distribution between capitalist and labourer becomes a much more simple consideration. The greater the portion of the result of labour that is given to the labourer, the smaller must be the rate of profits, and vice versa. Now this portion must essentially depend on the facility of producing the necessaries of the labourer — if the facility be great, a small proportion of any commodity, the result of capital and labour, will be sufficient to furnish the labourer with necessaries, and consequently profits will be high. The truth of this doctrine I deem to be absolutely demonstrable, yet I think that Mr. Malthus does not fully admit it' (ibid., *Works VIII*: 194–95).

which determines the exchangeable values of commodities (Torrens 1818: 336–37).

Of course, it was never Ricardo's doctrine that the relative worth of all things are determined by the quantities of labour required to produce them.[40] In any case, the biggest problem with Torrens's own alternative, that 'it is the amount of capital that determines the exchangeable values of all commodities', is that one does not know how to measure the 'amount of capital'.

In his *An Essay on the Production of Wealth*, Torrens suggests that the capital should be measured by the total labour-time embodied in capital goods:

> Are we to understand by the expression, 'the labour expended on production', immediate labour or accumulated labour, or both? And in which of these senses is it true, that the labour expended on production determines exchangeable value? The Author conceives, that in his chapter upon Value, he has given, for the first time, the correct solution of these fundamental questions, and has shown, that it is neither the immediate labour, nor the sum of the immediate and accumulated labour, but solely the accumulated labour expended on production, which determines the quantity of one article which shall be exchanged against a given quantity of another (Torrens 1821: vii).

This closely anticipates Marx's measure of capital and his derivation of 'prices of production' from it. But Ricardo was well aware of the fundamental problem with such a procedure of measuring capital — it fails to take account of the fact that profit is accrued on a *compound* rather than a simple rate. As Ricardo explained in his letter to McCulloch dated 21 August 1823:

> You explain this by saying that you estimate the labour bestowed on a commodity by the labour bestowed on the

40 In a letter to Mill, dated 28 December 1818, Ricardo wrote: 'But, say my opposers, Torrens and Malthus, capital is always of unequal durability in different trades, and therefore of what practical use is your enquiry? Of none, I answer, if I pretended to show that cloth should be at such a price, shoes at such another — muslins at such another and so on — this I have never attempted to do, — but I contend it is of essential use to determine what the causes are which regulate exchangeable value, although they may be so complicated, and intricate, that practically, the knowledge may be very little useful' (ibid., *Works VII*: 377–78).

capital or agent by which the commodity is produced. This I think is Torrens mode of estimating value, for it is in fact saying that commodities are valuable according to the value of the capital employed on their production, and the time for which it is employed. ... [B]ut value is compounded of two elements wages and profit mixed up in all imaginable proportions; it is in vain, therefore, to attempt to measure accurately, unless your measure agrees precisely in the proportions of wages and profits with the commodity measured (Ricardo 1951–52, *Works IX*: 359–61).

Samuel Bailey

Within two years of Ricardo's death, Samuel Bailey (1825, 1826) published an influential critique of Ricardo's theory of value.[41]

Though the spectrum of Bailey's attack was wide, its main concentration was on what he considered the confusion in the conceptualisation of the notion of value in Ricardo. We will keep to those of Bailey's criticisms that fall within the frame of Ricardo's basic theoretical assumptions. According to Bailey, the concept of value is inherently a *relative* one. He argues that the analogy of length and its invariable measure in a yardstick as usually invoked in explaining the notion of value and its measure is misleading. It is worth quoting Bailey at length on this issue:

It has been taken for granted that we measure value as we measure extension, or ascertain weight; and it has been consequently imagined, that to perform the operation we must possess an object of invariable value.

Let us examine, therefore, how far measuring value and measuring space are similar operations. In every case of measuring we merely ascertain ratios — the ratio which one thing bears to another. In measuring the length of an object we

---

41 According to Schumpeter, 'Bailey ... attacked the Ricardo-Mill-McCulloch analysis on a broad front and with complete success. His *Dissertation*, which said, as far as fundamentals are concerned, practically all that can be said, must rank among the masterpieces of criticism in our field, and it should suffice to secure to its author a place in or near front rank in the history of scientific economics' (Schumpeter 1954: 486). On the other hand, in Marx's opinion, 'It [Bailey's *Dissertation*] seeks to overturn the foundation of the doctrine — value. It is definitely worthless except for the definition of the "*measure of value*", or rather money in this function' (Marx 1971: *TSVIII*: 125).

find what ratio it bears to the length of some other object, or in other words, how many times one is contained in the other. We measure the longitudinal extension of a piece of timber, for example, by a foot-rule; that is, we find how often the length of the latter is contained in the former, and this is effected by the actual application of the rule to the timber. *It is a physical operation,* by which we obtain the knowledge of a fact before unknown, the ratio of length subsisting between the object and the instrument we employ.

In measuring value, what resemblance to this operation can possibly be discovered? We may place two objects by the side of each other, or apply one to the other in any way we please, but we shall never be able by such means to discover the relation of value existing between them. We shall never extort from them a single fact with which we were before unacquainted. What then is it possible to do in the way of measuring value? What kind of measurement is intended, when the term is so frequently employed? All that is practicable appears to be simply this: if I know the value of A in relation to B, and the value of B in relation to C, I can tell the value of A and C in relation to each other, and consequently their comparative power in purchasing all other commodities. This is an operation obviously bearing no resemblance at all to the process of measuring length. There is no unknown fact discovered by a physical operation: *it is in truth a calculation from certain data, a mere question in arithmetic.* It is not, let it be observed, what on a first glance it may appear, like ascertaining the comparative length of two pieces of timber which cannot be brought into juxtaposition, by means of a foot-rule or other instrument which we apply first to one and then to the other: it is far from being so much as this: it is merely like calculating the ratio of length between two pieces of timber, after we are informed how many feet are contained in each. For of each commodity A and C the value in relation to B must be given, or, in other words, their value must be expressed in a common denomination, before their mutual relation can be ascertained; just as in the case supposed the relation of each piece of timber to the foot-rule must be given, before their relation to each other can be deduced. *The actual application of the foot-rule is that part of the process which is alone entitled to the appellation of measuring,* the rest being mere calculation, but to this there is nothing at all analogous in any possible attempt to ascertain value. The way in which the commodity B would be used, in the above instance, is in truth as a medium of comparison, not a measure, yet it is the only process which bears any analogy to measurement (Bailey 1825: 94–97, emphasis added).

Bailey makes an important point that length is a physical property of a thing and the knowledge of its measure can be ascertained only by the physical act of measuring it by a 'foot-rule'. Value, on the other hand, is not a physical property of a commodity. It is an expression of a *relation* between two commodities, such as the notion of *distance*:

> In the circumstance, that it denotes a relation between two objects, and cannot be predicated of any commodity without an express or implied reference to some other commodity, value bears a resemblance to distance. As we cannot speak of the distance of any object without implying some other object, between which and the former this relation exists, so we cannot speak of the value of the commodity but in reference to another commodity compared with it. A thing cannot be valuable in itself without reference to another thing, any more than a thing can be distant in itself without reference to another thing (Bailey 1825: 5).

If the analogy of 'distance' is accepted in the case of value, then it follows that the notion of 'absolute' value must be deemed absurd. But does this imply, as a corollary, that the notion of the 'invariable' measure of value must also be deemed absurd? Bailey thinks so. According to Bailey, the very idea of comparing values of a commodity over a period of time or speaking of a rise or fall in the value of a commodity is absurd. For example, let us say that point A is two miles from point B at a point of time 0. At time 1, point A moves further away from point B and the distance between them becomes three miles. Bailey argues that a statement of the nature that 'A has increased in distance from B by one mile' is nonsensical since it cannot be denied that 'B has, at the same time, increased in distance from A by one mile'. What we have here is the distance between two points at two different points of time from which one cannot derive an *increase* or *decrease* in the distance of A from its old to its new position.

> But in relation to what object is it wished to measure the value of A and its fluctuations? We cannot speak of value, as I have before shown, without meaning value in something, and as

only A and the standard commodity which may be called B are here in question, the value of A must mean its value in B. It is wished therefore to measure the relation between A and B at two different periods by B, which if it has any significance must imply, that it is wished to ascertain the value of A and B relatively to each other at two different periods. These are historical facts, and when we have learned them as we learn other facts, we shall certainly know the fluctuations which the relation between A and B has undergone; but B is, in this procedure, by no means a measure of value, or a medium of comparison, any more than A (ibid.: 101).

But of course one can. As in our example, we have stated that 'A has moved'. So one can easily measure the distance between A's old point and its new point and furthermore since B has not moved, the change in the distance between A and B must be equal to the change in the position of A from its old to its new position. What Bailey denies in his description of the problem is that we have knowledge of the fact that A has moved and B has not. According to Bailey, all we have is the data of the distance between A and B at two points of time. From this data alone we cannot infer which has risen and which has fallen from their old position. But Ricardo never claimed any such thing. Ricardo's position was that we know the *cause* of change in value. Thus during the period 0 to 1, if that cause is operative in A and absent in B, then one can measure the difference in the old and the new positions of A by measuring the difference in the relative positions of A and B, or alternatively, one can *predict* the difference in the relative positions of A and B based on the knowledge of the cause operating on A and absent on B.

On this fundamental issue, Bailey flounders. First, he insists that since Ricardo claims that labour is the only cause of changes in value, by comparing the two positions of A against the fixed position of B, all Ricardo could discern was the changes in the amount of labour needed to produce A and not changes in the value of A. He simply insists that the ratios of A and B at two points of time are the given historical data, so the inference can only be about changes in the labour needed to produce A.[42] He further goes on to claim that in practical terms

42 'It is curious enough that he [Ricardo] should never have clearly discerned what such a commodity would really serve to indicate: it would not, as he asserts, serve to indicate the variations in the value of commodities, but the variations in the circumstances of their production. It would enable us to ascertain, not any fluctuations in

it is quite difficult to ascertain the labour-time needed to produce a commodity independently.[43] All this is, of course, beside the point and appears to be a deliberate attempt to skirt the theoretical issue.

Later on Bailey admits that:

> The value of A and B is the effect of causes acting on both, but a change in their mutual value may arise from causes acting on either: as the distance of two objects is to be referred to the circumstances which have fixed both of them in their particular situation, while an alteration of the distance between them might originate in circumstance acting on one alone (1825: 184).

However, he ends up simply claiming that the value of commodities is caused by many factors but primarily by the cost of 'capital', and the thesis that labour is the sole cause of change in value is wrong as Ricardo himself admits when he says that changes in wages could change the relative values of commodities without any change in the labour needed to produce them:

Now this cannot be true if we can find any instances of the following nature:

1. Cases in which two commodities have been produced by an equal quantity of labour, and yet sell for different quantities of money.
2. Cases in which two commodities, once equal in value, have become unequal in value, without any change in the quantity of labour respectively employed in each (ibid.: 209).

Though Bailey quite correctly exposes the confusing use of the term *value* in Ricardo's writings and also points out various reasons such as 'insalubrity', 'disagreeableness' and 'danger' as causes of differences in wages that cannot be homogenised by Ricardo's formula, he does not succeed in going beyond Malthus on the core theoretical issue. Not a very rich harvest in the end!

---

value, but in which commodity those fluctuations had originated. He has in truth confounded two perfectly distinct ideas, namely, *measuring the value of commodities, and ascertaining in which commodity, and in what degree, the cause of value have varied*' (Bailey 1825: 121–22).

43 'But it is to be recollected, that the circumstance of a commodity having been always produced by the same quantity of labour, is an historical fact quite as difficult to ascertain as the variations of another commodity' (ibid.: 132).

Karl Marx

Marx is a quintessential retrospective reader. He takes his own theory as being the correct one and reads all other authors from that vantage point. Though Marx was a great admirer of Ricardo and it could be said that his own theory depended largely on the theoretical break-through inaugurated by Ricardo,[44] he nevertheless wrote voluminous criticisms of Ricardo, particularly in *Theories of Surplus Value Part II* (Marx 1968, henceforth *TSV*). Here we will take up only the criticisms[45] that I think go to the heart of his (mis)understanding of Ricardo's theory of value and distribution. Since Marx's criticisms are based on his own theory, I assume that the reader is familiar with his basic theoretical concepts. If not, then the reader is advised to read the next chapter on Marx before reading this section.

As we will see in the next chapter, Marx had developed a theory of relative exchange ratios of commodities (which he called 'prices of production') in the regime of equal rate of profits on all capitals employed, and from this vantage point he criticises Ricardo for passing over the problem of the discrepancy that he encounters between the theory of determination of relative values (or exchange values) on the basis of labour-time and the cost of production:

> *Ricardo does not dwell on the conclusion which follows from his own illustrations*, namely, that — *quite apart* from the rise or fall of wages — on the assumption of constant wages, the cost-prices of commodities must differ from their values, if cost-prices are determined by the same percentage of profit. But he passes on, in this section [Chapter I, section V], to the influence which the rise or fall of wages exerts on *cost-prices* to which the values have already been levelled out (*TSV II*: 191).

But the determination of cost prices was not Ricardo's concern. As we have argued earlier, Ricardo acknowledges that the existence of differing time-structures of capital would vitiate the exchange ratios of commodities from their labour ratios because of the requirement of an equal rate of profits throughout the system. How much this vitiation

---

44 'But at last Ricardo steps in and calls to science: Halt! The basis, the starting-point for the physiology of the bourgeois system — for the understanding of its internal organic coherence and life process — is the determination of *value by labour-time*' (Marx 1968, *TSV II*: 166).

45 For an exhaustive treatment of Marx's critique of Ricardo, see Steedman (1982).

would be was none of Ricardo's concern. From here on he was mainly concerned with the cause(s) of changes in the exchange ratios of commodities, whatever they happened to be. As cited earlier in footnote 39, Ricardo had made it clear that 'this [the determination of cost prices] I have never attempted to do, — but I contend it is of essential use to determine what the causes are which regulate exchangeable value...' (Ricardo 1951–52, Works VII: 377–78).

Marx's purpose in bringing this up, however, was deeper. His own theory of 'prices of production' was built on a particular theory of the determination of the rate of profits based on his theory of surplus value. Again, from this vantage point, he criticises Ricardo for failing to develop a theory of the determination of the rate of profits:

> If one did not take the definition of value as the basis, the *average profit*, and therefore also the cost-prices, would be purely imaginary and untenable. The equalisation of the surplus-values in different spheres of production does not affect the absolute size of the total surplus-value; but merely alters its *distribution* among the different spheres of production. The *determination of this surplus-value* itself, however, only arises out of the determination of value by labour-time. Without this, the average profit is the average of *nothing*, pure fancy. And it could then equally well be 1,000 per cent or 10 per cent (*TSV II*: 190).

But again, all Ricardo was interested in showing is that the rate of profits must fall when the proportion of total labour going to wages rises and vice-versa; and not why the rate of profits happen to be 10 per cent and not 1,000 per cent. Leaving aside whether the questions Marx was interested in were more profound than Ricardo's, it cannot be a criticism of Ricardo's theory that he failed to solve Marx's problem. So where does the crux of Marx's critique of Ricardo lie? It must lie in the proof that from Marx's theoretical vantage point some of Ricardo's crucial propositions can be shown to be false. And this is what Marx claims, that Ricardo's contention that a rise in the share of wages in total labour must lead to a fall in the rate of profits and vice-versa is not necessarily true:

> Ricardo concludes quite wrongly, that because 'there can be no rise in the value of labour without a fall in profits', there can be no rise of profits without a fall in the value of labour. The first law refers to surplus value. But since profit equals

the proportion of surplus-value to the total capital advanced, profit can rise though the value of labour remains the same, if the value of constant capital falls. Altogether Ricardo mixes up surplus-value and profit. Hence he arrives at erroneous laws on profit and the rate of profit (*TSV II*: 193).

Though Marx's language is not very clear here, it appears that he thinks that Ricardo's proposition is true only if the constant capital is assumed away from the model and the rate of profits is identified with the rate of surplus value, as in other places Marx repeatedly accuses Ricardo for abstracting from constant capital and thus identifying the rate of profit with the rate of surplus value (see ibid.: 373, 414, 426, 439). What Marx is contending is that the rate of profits, according to his theory, is determined by the formula $r = S/(C + V) = (S/V)/(C/V + 1)$. Therefore, even if S/V remains constant, r could rise if C/V falls and vice-versa. Leaving aside the correctness of Marx's formula for determining the rate of profits (we will take up this issue in the next chapter), Marx's example is not faithful to Ricardo's case. What Ricardo had argued is that in the face of increase in the difficulty of production of wage-goods, the rate of profits must fall and vice-versa. When we translate Ricardo's proposition into Marx's concepts, a rise (or fall) in the difficulty of production of wage-goods given fixed real wages would lead directly to a fall (or rise) in S and also a general rise (or fall) in (C + V). Thus, there is a simultaneous movement of both S and (C + V) that reinforces the movements in the rate of profits predicted by Ricardo according to Marx's own theory of the rate of profits. The possibility of an independent fall in C/V leaving S/V constant is a case that is simply irrelevant to Ricardo's proposition. In passing, one should note that in developing his theory of profits Marx did not show much appreciation for the theoretical problem in measuring capital due to compounding of profits — a consideration about which Ricardo was keenly aware.[46]

---

46 In his last written letter to Mill dated 5 September 1823, Ricardo wrote: '... John does not allow for profits increasing at a compound rate. The profits for 5 years are more than 5 times the profits of one, and the profits of one year more than 52 times the profits for one week, and it is this which makes the great part of the difficulty. Beg him to consider this and let me know if I am wrong in my critique on his paper.' (Ricardo 1951–52, *Works IX*: 387). The 'John' in the letter was apparently John Stuart Mill. The paper Ricardo is referring to has not been found.

The Neoclassical Readings

The early protagonists of neoclassical economics took Ricardo to be the primary adversary and undertook to develop their theory in opposition to his. It is well known that Jevons (1957b) [1879] accused Ricardo for being an able but wrong-headed man who 'shunted the car of economic science on to a wrong line'.[47] Walras (1954) [1874], who perhaps admired Ricardo's theoretical acumen in many ways, criticised 'English economists' for determining two variables with one equation. He argued that the cost of production theory of prices claims that prices are determined by adding up wages, profits and rent. After taking rent out of the equation on the ground that marginal land does not pay any rent, they are left with the equation that price is equal to wages plus profit. They determine wages directly, based on 'the theory of wages', and then claim that profit is equal to price minus wages. This, according to Walras, explains why 'English economists are completely baffled by the problem of price determination; for it is impossible for I [profit] to determine P [price] at the same time that P determines I. In the language of mathematics one equation cannot be used to determine two unknowns' (Walras 1954: 425). Later, Dmitriev (1974) [1904] defended Ricardo on the ground that Ricardo had used 'corn' as the only *basic* good (to use Sraffian terminology) in the system and thus the rate of profits is mathematically and rigorously determined in the system without involving the problem of two unknowns in one equation. If, however, our reading of Ricardo is accepted, then it appears that Walras-Dmitriev controversy is no longer pertinent as Ricardo did not take up the problem of determining either the price ratios or the rate of profits. His concern was simply to show that the rate of profits would fall if the difficulty of producing the wage basket increased.

Wicksell (1934) criticises Ricardo's '...cost of production' theory of price on the ground that '...costs of production and exchange values cannot stand in the simple relation of cause and effect which Ricardo supposed. ...*they are mutually conditioned* like the various elements in a single economic system in equilibrium' (Wicksell 1934: 25–26). He argues that Ricardo's margin in the 'corn' sector depends on the

---

47 Later on, Frank Knight went on to present the problem of his essays on 'The Ricardian Theory of Production and Distribution' in the following manner: 'On the assumption that the primary interest in the "ancients" in such a field as economics is to learn from their mistakes, the principal of this discussion will be the contrast between the "classical" system and "correct" views' (Knight 1935: 87).

demand for corn: 'Their [classical theory] margin of production is not a fixed limit, given *a priori,* but is variable and itself depends, among other things, upon the actual exchange value of the goods in question and, to that extent upon what it has to explain' (ibid.: 24).[48] However, he goes on to recognise that: '[T]hey regarded demand or consumption [of corn] (and therefore also the extension of the margin of production), as given by the size of the *population.*' Therefore, in the end the theoretical criticism winds up with 'Statistics have not confirmed this: largely owing to indirect methods of use, the demand for and consumption of corn and other foodstuffs is almost as elastic and variable as that of other goods' (ibid.: 26).[49]

It may not be out of place to introduce the Austrian capital theorist Eugen von Böhm-Bawerk at this stage. Böhm-Bawerk also argues that it is illegitimate for Ricardo to take his margin of cultivation as *given.* According to him, the consumption-saving decision of the capitalist class determines the rate of growth of the economy and thus the size of the population and the margin of cultivation in Ricardo's system. Thus the rate of profits cannot be determined independently of demand:

> For instance, suppose that the motives to which interest, generally speaking, owes its origin, and which Ricardo unfortunately does so little to explain, demand for a given capital a yield of 30 tons, and that the workers employed by this capital need for their combined subsistence 80 tons. Then cultivation will have to cease at the point where the labour of so many men as can live on 80 tons produces 110 tons. If the 'motives of accumulation' demanded only 10 tons, then cultivation could be extended to the point where the least productive labour produced 90 tons. The cultivation of land less

---

48 For a modern reincarnation of this argument, see Samuelson (1978): 'The point is obvious that any classicist who thinks he can separate "value" from "distribution" commits a logical blunder. He also blunders if he thinks that he can "get rid of land and rent as a complication for pricing" by concentrating on the external margin of no-rent land: where that external margin falls is an *endogenous* variable that shifts with tastes and demand changes so as to vitiate a hoped-for labour theory of value or a wage-*cum*-profit rate theory of value' (Samuelson 1978: 1420).

49 Wicksell also criticised Ricardo's labour theory of value on the ground that it is inapplicable in the case of joint-production: 'Here the only question which arises is whether the total selling value of the products will cover the total costs of production, for the separate costs cannot be imputed' (Wicksell 1934: 26). Of course, Ricardo did not consider joint-production cases. On the problem of joint-production, see Chapter 4 on Sraffa.

productive than that will always be economically impossible, and this will define the limit for the expansion of population for the time being. ... So that interest, no less than wages, may be said to stem from independent motives. To have ignored those motives completely is the decisive blunder committed by Ricardo (Böhm-Bawerk 1959: 63–64).

Since Böhm-Bawerk grants the labour theory of value and subsistence wage to Ricardo in order to develop his purely logical argument, we too will take them for granted in developing our defence of Ricardo. Böhm-Bawerk would not deny that at any given point of time an empirical economy is given with its margin of cultivation already determined. Thus, given the subsistence wage, the profit can be determined as a *residual*. Let us suppose that the rate of profits at the given margin happens to be 10 per cent. Böhm-Bawerk's argument is that it is 10 per cent because the capitalist class is satisfied by a 10 per cent return on the total capital employed. If, however, they were satisfied by only a 5 per cent return, then they would have extended the cultivation to the point where the rate of return on capital would have fallen to 5 per cent. And here we detect a fundamental confusion between a dynamic and a comparative-static argument. Given that the total land is arranged in terms of its productivity, we know the margin when the system reaches a stationary state. Ricardo's model gives us the whole trajectory of the economy from any given point of intra-marginal land to the margin of stationary state. The consumption-savings decision of the capitalist class can only affect the *speed* with which the economy will approach the stationary state, but not its trajectory (e.g., a high saving propensity would give a high speed whereas a low propensity to save will give a low speed). However, for determining the rate of profits at any *point of time* the knowledge of the speed of the trajectory is irrelevant; all one needs to know is the margin the economy has reached up till that point of time. This is why the *subjective* element of the propensity to save plays no role in Ricardo's theoretical scheme.

Alfred Marshall

Marshall [1890] (1949), on the other hand, tried to incorporate Ricardo into the neoclassical fold. Though he admits that Ricardo did emphasise the supply or the objective cost side of the price equation, he nevertheless detects that 'in a profound, though very incomplete, discussion of the difference between "Value and Riches" he [Ricardo] seems to be feeling his way toward the distinction between marginal and total utility' (Marshall 1949: 814). Further on, he argues that:

> [I]n Section V [Ch. 1] he [Ricardo] sums up the influence which different lengths of investment, whether direct or indirect, will have upon relative values; ... His argument is avowedly provisional; in later chapters he takes account of other causes of differences in profits in different industries, besides the period of investment. But it seems difficult to imagine how he could more strongly have emphasized the fact that Time and Waiting as well as labour is an element of cost of production than by occupying his first chapter with this discussion (ibid.: 815–16).

Leaving aside the question of 'marginal utility' as there is no evidence of it in Ricardo, and as we cannot enter Ricardo's mind to 'see' in which direction he was feeling his way, let us take the more substantial argument that the differences in the time-structures of capitals influence the determination of relative prices as well as their changes. Is this a good enough proof that Ricardo considers 'Time and Waiting' as an element of cost on a par with labour? As we have seen earlier, whenever it came to defining 'cost of production' Ricardo included profit in it. But the question is: did Ricardo treat 'Time and Waiting' as a *cause* of profit? But then, we have never found Ricardo posing the question: where does profit come from? We have, however, seen that Ricardo defines profits in physical terms: 'The remaining quantity of the produce of the land, after the landlord and the labourer are paid, necessarily belongs to the farmer, and constitutes the profits of the stock' (Ricardo 1951–52, *Works I*: 112). Furthermore, he argues that the emergence of capital and a rate of profits do not vitiate the principle that prices are determined by the ratio of direct and indirect labour-time needed to produce the respective commodities, so long as the time-structures of capitals are uniform in the system. Thus, 'Time and Waiting' have no role here in the determination of prices, even though there are positive profits in the system. Profits begin to have an impact on prices only when the time-structures of capitals are not the same for all the capitals. But this in itself does not explain the origin of profits. As we have observed earlier, the impact of unequal time-structures of capitals on prices is considered only an *apparent* impact and not a *real* one by Ricardo.

Moreover, if profits could be explained on the basis of 'Time and Waiting', then of course a rise or fall in the relative price of any commodity would cause a change in the general rate of profits. But as Ricardo argues, a tax on luxury goods has no impact on the general rate of profits, whereas a tax on wage-goods must reduce the general rate of profits:

> Taxes on those commodities, which are generally denominated luxuries, fall on those only who make use of them. A tax on wine is paid by the consumer of wine. A tax on pleasure horses, or on coaches, is paid by those who provide for themselves such enjoyments, and in exact proportion as they provide them. But taxes on necessaries do not affect the consumers of necessaries, in proportion to the quantity that may be consumed by them, but often in a much higher proportion. A tax on corn, we have observed, not only affects a manufacturer in proportion that he and his family may consume corn, but it alters the rate of profits of stock, and therefore also affects his income. Whatever raises the wages of labour, lowers the profits of stock; therefore every tax on any commodity consumed by the labourers, has a tendency to lower the rate of profits (ibid.: 205).

The same argument must apply even if the rise in the price of a luxury good is due to a change in its technique of production (i.e., a change in the 'Time and Waiting' element). The rate of profits in Ricardo's theory clearly stands in a particular relation with the productivity of the wage-goods (or rather *basic* goods) sector and the wages. In this framework, no separate cause of profits can be introduced from outside.[50]

Samuel Hollander

In the contemporary period, Samuel Hollander (1979, 1992 and 1995) has presented the most comprehensive neoclassical interpretation of Ricardo. Though Hollander paints a large canvas, we will take up only what I consider the crux of his argument in favour of a neoclassical reading of Ricardo on the question of his theory of value and distribution. Hollander emphasises the *problematique* of resource allocation in Ricardo's treatment of the mechanism adjusting 'market prices' to 'natural prices'. This in itself is not problematic from our perspective,

---

50 Also see Ashley (1891) for a critique of Marshall's interpretation of Ricardo.

as we have already explained the resource allocation mechanism that comes into play when 'market prices' gravitate to their 'natural prices'. What is problematic in Hollander's story is that he maintains that the determination of the wage rate and rate of profits in the system is dependent upon the adjustment mechanism itself, e.g., if tastes shift from a 'labour-intensive' commodity to a 'capital-intensive' commodity, then the demand for labour will fall leading to a fall in wages and a rise in the rate of profits:

> If, then, we assume differential capital (machinery)-labour ratios, given aggregate capital (machinery and working capital combined) and aggregate labour, an increase in the demand for a capital-intensive good at the expense of that for a labour-intensive good will disturb the profit-rate and the price structure. There will follow in consequence an expansion of the first category of commodities and a contraction of the second. But as a result the fixed capital or machinery component of total capital will rise at the expense of wage capital as resources are transferred between industries. The wage rate (given the total labour force) must be lower and the general profit rate correspondingly higher in the new compared with the original equilibrium (Hollander 1979: 300).

However, as we have seen earlier in the section on the 'gravitation mechanism', Ricardo maintains that the rate of profits comes back to its *original* level after the system adjusts due to the shift in demand from woollens to silk. As a matter of fact, Hollander does not provide any evidence from the *Principles* to show that the adjustment mechanism does affect wages and the rate of profits. He argues that the lack of evidence is due to an *implicit* assumption that Ricardo had made to simplify his illustrations. Supposedly, the implicit assumption is that the 'capital-labour' ratio throughout the economy is *uniform*:

> A second 'extension' of the Ricardian analysis relates to the consequences of a change in the pattern of tastes, which Ricardo did not formally make, it must be said. We have seen earlier that changes in the pattern of demand affect the factor returns in particular industries generating appropriate adjustments of industry size while the general levels of profits and wages remain unaffected. Now it is the assumption of uniform factor proportions which permit the neglect of any 'play-back' on the wage rate itself emanating from changes in

the pattern of demand, and allows the treatment of the factor returns as *parameters* in the analysis of price (ibid.: 299–300).

Though it is true that Ricardo considered that for most of the commodities the 'labour-capital' ratios were rather close and he left out the extreme cases from his theoretical frame, it would be difficult to maintain that Ricardo assumed the ratios to be uniform as his central theoretical problem with respect to a theory of value emanated from the condition of *diverse* 'capital-labour' ratios. The problem with Hollander's story at this stage can be located in his claim that during the adjustment process Ricardo takes 'aggregate capital (machinery and working capital combined)' as *given*. Hollander does not provide any evidence in support of this claim. Perhaps he thinks it is self-evident. I, on the other hand, think that this is the crucial point where his interpretation goes wrong. For the purposes of illustration, let us assume a two-sector economy of corn and iron where both corn and iron are used as inputs in the production of iron and only corn in the production of corn and all wages are paid in corn (in Sraffian terminology, corn is the only basic good). We begin with an equilibrium point and assume that the capitalists' consumption demand for iron rises at the cost of corn. This would cause the price and the rate of profit in the iron sector to rise vis-a-vis the corn sector. Now, when the corn sector contracts, it only releases corn; so how does the iron sector expand? Obviously because a rise in the rate of profit in the iron sector increases its demand as a capital-good and so some of the net output of iron is ploughed back into producing more iron and this process continues till the system reaches its new equilibrium with the rate of profits becoming uniform in the two sectors once again. In this mechanism, the 'aggregate capital' is not 'given'; rather, it adjusts itself in the process. The crucial theoretical issue involved here is the notion of *effectual demand*.

As we have seen in the previous chapter, Adam Smith has defined 'effectual demand' as a demand backed by real income and Ricardo has accepted this without any criticism. The real income of an economy is given by its total output. Both Smith and Ricardo begin their analysis by taking an economy as empirically given. We know the techniques used, the labour employed and the output produced. Given the total labour employed and the techniques in use, the economy can produce several combinations of outputs by reallocating the total labour in use (given constant returns to scale). All such possible reallocation of labour give a vector of combinations of gross outputs, all of which could serve as effectual demands for the system. Let us suppose that the output combination of the empirically given economy is not the same as the preferred effectual demand combination; the adjustment mechanism would then reallocate the total labour to produce the preferred combination. The same would be the case when tastes change from one preferred effectual demands to another. So the gravitation mechanism takes only the total labour employed as *given* and not the 'aggregate capital' as well.

At this stage, however, Ricardo had to face an additional complication. In his system the agricultural sector is characterised by diminishing and not constant returns. Thus the technique used at the margin in the agricultural sector depends on the demand for agricultural goods. Ricardo gets around this problem by removing the possibility of shift in taste when it came to the case of 'corn'. He argues that there is a one-to-one relationship between the size of the population and the demand for 'corn'. Thus, the demand for corn is determined by the size of the population and can be therefore taken as *given* and fixed during the allocation mechanism.[51] Hollander, in my understanding, agrees with this interpretation. Barkai (1965) and Rankin (1980), however, have advanced a few citations from Ricardo's writings that purport to invalidate this claim. They argue that Ricardo does not take demand for corn as a given vertical straight line in the price-quantity space; rather, he takes the usual downward sloping demand curve for 'corn' as well. Therefore, the quantity of 'corn' demanded depends upon its price. The evidence they cite are from: (i) *On Protection of Agriculture* (which was published in 1822), where Ricardo argues that in the case of a good harvest the price of 'corn' will fall and its consumption will rise (Ricardo 1951–52, *Works IV:* 219–20); and (ii) the *Principles*, where he says that '[a] bad harvest will produce a high price of provisions, and the high price is the only means by which the consumption is compelled to conform to the state of the supply' (p. 162). But what Barkai and Rankin fail to notice is that such rise and fall in the price of 'corn' does not affect the *margin* of cultivation. Here Ricardo is simply taking note of the natural fact that the output of 'corn' is not only dependent on the techniques used and the amount of inputs that go into its production, but that it randomly fluctuates with fluctuations in the weather. Given the population, the average size of the demand for 'corn' is given and this is what determines the margin of cultivation. However, fluctuations in supply from the average due to the weather

---

51 Also see Blaug (1958: 22ff.).

factor are accommodated by the rise and fall in its price and thus have no impact in determining the margin of cultivation.

Though Hollander correctly highlights the fact that neither Smith nor Ricardo had a notion of vertically given demands on the price and quantity plane, he accepts the fact that both Smith and Ricardo nevertheless take effectual demands as given points, and the downward sloping demand curves must pass through these points. The effectual demands, however, cannot be taken as *given* unless the size of the economy, defined by the total labour and techniques in use, is taken to be *given*. In this scheme, the *given* total labour is the only resource that is allocated among various sectors according to the effectual demands. Hollander's scheme implies that Ricardo's adjustment process does not begin with *given outputs* but rather with *given endowments*. But if this is true, then the notion of effectual demands as given *points* in quantity space will have no meaning — all we can have are demand schedules, with equilibrium points being determined as a result of the interaction between the demand and supply schedules.[52]

Hollander interprets the *given* wage argument to be based on an alternative theory of wages, which takes real wages as given by the socio-historical conditions of an economy, independently of demand and supply conditions in the labour market. He cites Dobb (1973) for holding such a theory, which is perhaps not entirely fair to Dobb. But in any case, he has seized upon this misrepresentation to show that in a dynamic context of growth, Ricardo is quite explicit that real wages are not fixed and it is precisely the persistence of excess demand or

---

52 It is also interesting to note Kenneth Arrow's remark on the question of demand in Ricardo's system: 'The main thrust of Ricardo's system is a bold attempt to determine values independent of demand considerations. I do not mean that Ricardo thought of the alternative of a role for demand in determining values and rejected it. Rather he did not really conceive of this alternative. Clearly he lacked that very elementary tool, the demand schedule. ... I do not think, as some neo-Ricardians seem to, that there was in any sense an intended repudiation of the demand schedule. Indeed, some of Ricardo's analysis can only be made sensible on the basis of such a concept. Thus, if there is more capital in an industry than is needed to meet the demand, it is asserted that the market price will fall, so that the capital will be earning less than the normal rate of return and therefore will exit. Evidently, the price falls so that demand will rise to use the excess capacity' (Arrow 1991: 75). The reader should note that Arrow makes no comment on the classical notion of 'effectual demand'. The point that a fall in price should lead to a rise in the quantity demanded sounds like common sense, which both Adam Smith and Ricardo had. The crucial difference lies in assigning the level of the 'demand schedule'. In the classical case the level is assigned by a point in a price-quantity space independently of the schedule, which is not the case with the neoclassical theory.

excess supply conditions in the labour market that explains the movement of real wages (our reading of Ricardo's theory of wages in the
dynamic context is largely in agreement with Hollander's).[53] The problem, however, arises when he uses evidence from the context of growth
to buttress a claim that he makes in the context of resource allocation.
The theoretical context of resource allocation, however, amounts to
cutting a slice *at a point of time* from a continuous growth context. As
we have argued earlier, the resource allocation context takes the going
real wages and the total labour employment as given data irrespective
of the labour market situation — the time involved in the allocation
process is purely 'logical' or 'notional' time and not 'historical' or 'real'
time (all the 'natural prices' for any given set of effectual demands are
the same). Hollander's application of arguments from the growth context to a resource allocation context is contingent on his treatment of
resource allocation from the perspective of *given endowments*, but this
is not, in our opinion, Ricardo's perspective.[54] In this context I should
point out that a significant fact has been overlooked by Hollander and
other commentators: Ricardo *does not* assume homogeneous labour
in his theory; he homogenises heterogeneous labour by multiplying
them by their wage differentials. Thus Ricardo *must* take wages as
given before he can calculate the labour content of commodities.

It is, however, true that in his new chapter on Machinery, Ricardo
discusses the question of shift in demand patterns — such as a shift
in the demand pattern of capitalists and landlords from luxury goods
to employment of menial servants (p. 393 ff.). He argues that in such
cases the total demand for labour will rise and that this will raise the
wages. Hollander (1989) has emphasised such examples from Ricardo
to buttress his position. The question, however, is: could this be a centre of gravitation with higher wages? The answer is: no. Let us suppose
that there are only capitalists and labourers in the system and the capitalists spend all their profits on a luxury good (say, silk) and the system

---

53 Also see Hicks and Hollander (1977), Casarosa (1978, 1985) and Cannan [1893]
    (1997: 247–57).

54 'In the first place, Ricardo was no Marshallian. He maintained, consistently, that
    prices are determined by cost; demand has nothing to do with them. It may indeed
    be objected that when he lets the (marginal) cost of food production rise, under
    pressure of population, he is admitting demand; it is the increased demand for food
    which forces the extension of cultivation. I do not believe that Ricardo looked at
    the matter like that. His sequence, I have insisted, was a succession of equilibria. It
    is not a change in demand which marks the transition from one equilibrium to its
    successor; it is the increase in population itself' (Hicks 1985: 317).

initially is at the centre of gravitation. Now suppose that the capitalists decide to switch their consumption from silk to direct services of menial servants. The idea is that when the silk sector reduces to zero, all the direct and indirect labour released due to its disappearance is smaller than the total direct demand for labour generated by the total profit revenue in the system. If the size of the labour force is taken to be fixed, then the excess demand for labour must lead to rise in wages. Now the rise in wages must reduce the demand for menial servants to the exact amount of the total direct and indirect labour released from the silk sector (we assume linear techniques in the basic goods sectors for simplicity's sake). However, the rise in wages must lead to a fall in profits (let us also assume an equal 'capital-labour' ratio in the basic good sectors so that a rise in wages has no effect on relative prices), which implies that the demand for menial servants must fall leading to a fall in wages such that the current profit revenue is able to demand the total direct and indirect labour released from the silk sector. However, as the wages fall, the profits yet again rise and we are back with an excess demand for labour. Thus the system may keep oscillating. And the reason for such oscillation is that the set of all possible effectual demand points changes when wages change. That is why such changes are not compatible with a gravitation mechanism with fixed labour supply. They are better dealt with in the growth context, where the system has more flexibility both in terms of labour supply and substitution between labour and machines, as Ricardo's context of such discussions appears to be.

The detractors of Hollander and the neoclassical interpretation of Ricardo have, on the other hand, chosen to join the battle on his interpretation of Ricardo's theory of wages. Garegnani (1983a, b and c; 1990a, b, c and d; 2007), for example, argues that the real wages are a given datum in Ricardo's analysis irrespective of demand and supply conditions in the labour market. He buttresses his claim by pointing to the fact that Ricardo, like Adam Smith, emphasises the role of historical and social conventions in determining real wages, as well as to his new chapter on Machinery that raises the theoretical possibility of unemployment of labour. Garegnani's position relies too much on the theoretical possibility of unemployment of labour in the Machinery chapter. But, as we have highlighted in our discussion, Ricardo did not think that introduction of labour-saving machines in the process of economic growth would or could create long-term unemployment of labour. He was of the opinion that labour-saving machines are generally introduced in response to rising real wages, i.e., as a response to excess demand for labour. The theoretical possibility of unemployment was presented in a static framework for illustrative convenience. The possibility of change in techniques, on the other hand, was dealt with only in a dynamic framework. Though it is true that Smith, and to a lesser extent Ricardo, showed their awareness of historical and social conventions with regard to real wage determination much more than the present-day neoclassical theory does, they did not, however, think that these conventions could counter the forces of excess demand or excess supply in the growth context.

Though Garegnani (2007) correctly (in my opinion) points out the conflation between the static demand and supply functions and the dynamic rate of growth of demand and supply of labour in Samuelson's (1978) 'canonical classical model' and other neoclassical interpretations, he unfortunately throws the baby away with the bath water by claiming that the 'classicists' (e.g., Adam Smith and David Ricardo) had a 'bargaining' theory of wages, where wages are determined by the 'relative strength of the competing parties' and not by the forces of demand or supply of labour in the growth context. He argues that Ricardo's position that a tax on necessaries would immediately increase the money wages to compensate the workers cannot be explained on the basis of the forces of demand and supply of labour since its impact through the population mechanism would take a long time (Garegnani 2007: 218ff.). On the other hand, he argues:

> Indeed, the tax has presumably left that 'relative strength' unchanged and it would only be reasonable to say as Ricardo does, that the compensatory wage rise is 'in the interest of all parties': it would be only rational for capitalists to yield straightaway what they would otherwise have to yield after useless conflict (ibid.: 219).

I find both arguments unconvincing. In a dynamic context, if a fall in real wages due to tax on necessaries has a slight immediate impact on the supply of labour, then it should immediately create an excess demand for labour and pull the wages up to restore the supply balance. There is no need to assume a one-generation time lag for this process to work itself out. On the other hand, it simply makes no sense to argue that an individual capitalist would 'know' that the tax has not changed the relative strength between the two classes and so they should relent immediately, without a fight. As a matter of fact the tax policy itself is an important site of class struggle — a tax on necessaries is most likely a sign that the relative strength has tilted in favour of the capitalist class. There is no reason to think that the capitalists would relent 'immediately', without a fight.

The problem with Garegnani's position is that there is no evidence in Ricardo's writing of such class struggles in wage determination. The word 'labour union' does not even get a mention in his book. Garegnani is aware of this fact and thus argues that: 'It is from Adam Smith that the above interpretative line gets its most direct support: and it is a safe rule to assume that Ricardo implicitly defers to Smith whenever he does not explicitly disagree with him' (ibid.: 220). But even in Adam Smith the combination is noticed only of employers and not workers. Again, Garegnani is aware of this fact and so argues that when Adam Smith and Ricardo speak of the 'proportion of the supply to the demand for labour', they mean the relative strengths of the competing parties. However, as we have seen in the previous chapter, when it came to explaining the rise in real wages, Adam Smith explicitly states:

> When in a country the demand for those who live by wages [...] is continually increasing [...] the workmen have no occasion to combine in order to raise their wages. The scarcity of hands occasions a competition among masters, who bid against one another, in order to get workmen, and thus voluntarily break through the natural combination of masters not to raise wages (WN, p. 86; also quoted in Garegnani 2007: 221–22).

This is clearly a statement in favour of the demand and supply mechanism in the growth context determining the changes in wages against both the 'cultural' determination of wages and the 'relative bargaining strength' hypotheses. The cultural aspect is unable to counteract the persistent force of excess demand or excess supply, and even though the employers' strength vis-a-vis the workers remains the same, as workers are unable to combine, the forces of excess demand compels them to break through their own combination. In Garegnani's interpretation of classical wage theory there is no role for the population mechanism. This clearly points to the fact that there is something seriously missing in his interpretation.

Peach appears to have joined hands with the fix-wage interpreters. He quotes from Ricardo's Chapter XXI on 'Effects of Accumulation on Profits and Interest', where Ricardo writes that: 'If the necessaries of the workman could be consistently increased with the same facility, there could be no permanent alteration in the rate of profits or wages, to whatever amount capital might be accumulated'(p. 289, quoted in Peach 1993: 114ff.). From this Peach concludes that it is a refutation of the so-called 'new view' interpretation of wages, as here Ricardo admits that accumulation will have no impact on wages. The other evidence he provides for his supposed refutation of the 'new view' interpretation is a passage from further down in the same chapter where Ricardo writes:

> ... however abundant capital may become, there is no other adequate reason for a fall of profit but a rise of wages, and further it may be added, that the only adequate and permanent cause for the rise of wages is the increasing difficulty of providing food and necessaries for the increasing number of workmen (p. 296, quoted in Peach 1993: 114ff.).

The two passages quoted by Peach, however, do not refute the so-called 'new view' at all. Even in the 'new view', the impact of accumulation on wages comes about precisely due to the assumption of diminishing returns on land, which is the point that Ricardo is emphasising here. If there were constant returns on land as well, then Ricardo's system would be similar to Adam Smith's except for one important difference. Adam Smith, as we have seen in the previous chapter, has argued that capital accumulation by increasing competition among capitals in every sector would bring about a general fall in the rate of profits. Ricardo opposes Smith's reasoning (on the basis of 'Say's law') and his chapter on the 'Effects of Accumulation on Profits and Interest' is designed to highlight the argument that Smith's idea that accumulation by itself would reduce the rate of profits is false:

> Adam Smith, however, uniformly ascribes the fall of profits to accumulation of capital, and to the competition which will result from it, without ever adverting to the increasing difficulty of providing food for the additional number of labourers, which the additional capital will employ (p. 29).

Caravale and Tosato (1980) and Caravale (1985) argue that Ricardo's definitions of 'market' and 'natural' wages in his chapter on Wages is an inadvertent mistake on his part. They suggest that Ricardo had not broken from Adam Smith's terminology by citing his position of the Essay. Their own position, however, seems to be untenable. Ricardo was well aware of his break from Smith on this issue and when Malthus (see footnote 9, this chapter) raised questions about the appropriateness of Ricardo's terminology, he admitted that it was somewhat confusing but still did not revert back to Smith's terminology and maintained his original one, which avowedly was not the ideal one in his own opinion.[55] Caravale and Tosato also emphasise Ricardo's definition of 'natural price' in the context of any commodity and try to draw a parallel with the 'natural price' of labour. But they forget a crucial difference between a commodity and labour. Since there are n commodities in the system, a shift in the demand for one commodity at the cost of another would bring the reallocation mechanism into play through the movement of market prices to natural prices. However, when it comes to labour, its demand and supply (which is relevant to wage determination) is treated only in aggregate. Change in the demand for labour takes place only in the context of growth and not in the context of allocation. To maintain the assumption of fixed real wage above the subsistence level, Caravale and Tosato (1980) assume that the rate of population growth is always equal to the rate of capital growth. But why should population grow in tandem with capital when growth in capital has no impact on wages? Not only is there no evidence of such a theory of population in Ricardo, but it would be hard to defend it on the basis of any rational theory of population.[56]

We have also noted that many scholars have maintained that Ricardo assumes a subsistence real wage throughout his analysis. As Blaug put it: 'In the Ricardian system, therefore, economic growth is viewed as if all demographic adjustments to a long-run equilibrium had already taken place, while the process of capital accumulation had not yet been completed' (Blaug 1962: 84). Pasinetti (1960) assumes that with every positive dose of capital investment, the population adjusts instantaneously; whereas O'Brien (2004: 47ff.) argues that capital accumulation and 'market wages' move in spurts. A positive dose of capital accumulation increases 'market wages' above subsistence level, which brings about an increase in the labour force through the population mechanism and consequently the wages back down to subsistence with the same cycle continuing with every new dose of capital accumulation.[57] This again seems untenable, as Ricardo was

---

55 Caravale and Tosato's position is closer to Torrens's position in his Essay on the External Corn Trade (1827). See Cannan (1997: 248ff.) [1893] for an argument of a subtle break in Ricardo's Principles from Torrens's position. Also see Rosselli (1985).

56 Also see Casarosa (1985).

57 Also see Edelberg (1933) for a similar explanation. But Edelberg, in an Austrian manner, defines physical capital in terms of 'time' and treats substitution of capital and labour in terms of rise and fall of the ratio of total indirect labour-time to living

clear that the population adjustment mechanism took a long period of time to work and a continuous capital accumulation process would not give enough time for the population mechanism to bring the wages back to subsistence level.

It is common to allude to Chapter XVI on 'Taxes on Wages' of the *Principles* in support of the subsistence wage hypothesis. In this chapter Ricardo argues that 'A tax on wages is wholly a tax on profits' (p. 215). From here it is contended that wages had to be at subsistence level for labourers to not afford any tax on their income. O'Brien quotes from Chapter IX on 'Taxes on Raw Produce' where Ricardo writes:

> A tax, however, on raw produce, and on the necessaries of labourers, would have another effect — it would raise wages. From the effect of the principle of population on the increase of mankind, wages of the lowest kind never continue much above that rate which nature and habit demand for the support of the labourers. This class is never able to bear any considerable proportion of taxation; and, consequently, if they had to pay 8s per quarter in addition for wheat and in some smaller proportion for other necessaries, they would not be able to subsist on the same wages as before, and keep up the race of labourers (p. 159, quoted in O'Brien 1981: 367).

This sounds like a subsistence wage hypothesis. However, the meaning of the last phrase — 'and keep up the race of labourers' — is not yet clear. Further down the chapter, we are told:

> An accumulation of capital naturally produces an increased competition among the employers of labour, and a consequent rise in its price. The increased wages are not always immediately expended on food, but are first made to contribute to

---

labour-time. In his framework, given wages at subsistence level with zero rate of growth of population, a fresh savings from profits add to the indirect labour part of the capital, leading to increase in the productivity of labour and thus rise in real wages (apparently on the basis of marginal productivity theory of wages), which in turn leads to an increase in population, which is again brought back by the diminishing returns on land. And the cycle continues with the next round of capital investment. As we will see in Chapter 4 on Sraffa, the idea of having a measure of capital in terms of a 'roundabout' method of production independently of a rate of profits is illogical. Further, Edelberg does not provide convincing evidence from Ricardo for the marginal principles he uses in his explanation.

the other enjoyments of the labourer. His improved condition however induces, and enables him to marry, and then the demand for food for the support of his family naturally supersedes that of those other enjoyments on which his wages were temporarily expended (p. 163).

Now a relationship of higher wages with a positive rate of population growth is made via the early demand for marriage. Then, when we move on to the chapter on 'Taxes on Wages', we find Ricardo claiming:

> Does not Mr. Buchanan allow all that is contended for, when he says, that 'were he (the labourer) indeed reduced to a bare allowance of necessaries, he would then suffer no further abatement of his wages, as he could not on such conditions continue his race?' Suppose the circumstances of the country to be such that the lowest labourers are not only called upon to continue their race, but to increase it; their wages would be regulated accordingly. Can they multiply *in the degree required*, if a tax takes from them a part of their wages, and reduces them to bare necessaries? (p. 220, emphasis added).

Clearly, the necessity of a particular level of wage with the requirement of the rate of population growth is now established. Incidentally, the phrase, 'in the degree required', was added only in the third edition to make this point unambiguous. Ricardo completely concurs with Adam Smith on this point. His only difference with Smith is that though Smith, as we have argued in the last chapter, considers profits to be a necessity and thus argues that a tax on wages would be completely shifted to rent, Ricardo argues that it will be completely shifted to profits, as profits are surplus in his system and marginal land pays no rent. Thus a tax on wages would reduce the rate of profits, which in turn would reduce the rate of accumulation and the rate of growth in the demand for labour, which in turn would reduce the real wages and rate of population growth:

> ... for, *so far as these taxes affect the labouring poor*, they will be almost wholly paid by the diminished profits of stock, a small part only being paid by the labourers themselves in the diminished demand for labour, which taxation of every kind has a tendency to produce (p. 233).

Michio Morishima

Morishima (1989) has presented a mathematical interpretation of Ricardo's *Principles* which claims that:

> In fact, his [Ricardo's] political economy is nothing other than mathematical economics without mathematical symbols and formulas. It can easily be translated into mathematical language and one may find, as we shall do in this book, a general equilibrium system (that is very similar to Walras) concealed within (1989: 3).

Morishima's 'short-run' equilibrium system, however, takes the 'wage fund', the total 'capital stock', and 'the labour force' as *given* (see ibid.: 104ff.). Given the labour force (with the assumption of full employment) and wage fund, the real wages are already determined. Thus in Morishima's system one of the distributional variables, the real wages, is taken as given and is not determined in the process of efficient resource allocation. Furthermore, he takes the workers' consumption basket as given and their propensity to save as zero; the demand of the landlord class is also given as a fixed demand for corn and the rest of rent income as a demand for gold; and the capitalists' consumption demand is taken to be zero. In other words, Morishima assumes given vertical straight-line demands on the price and quantity plane. Such a restrictive system is far from Walrasian. As a matter of fact, since he assumes that the total demand for food is given, the determination of the 'marginal' land is already established and thus the techniques of production are not determined from within the system of equations but are rather taken as *given*. In every respect, Morishima's 'short-run' equilibrium model is equivalent to a model that takes real wages, techniques of production and total outputs as given.

3

THE THEORY OF VALUE IN MARX'S *CAPITAL*

Part I

Introduction

Among the four classics discussed in this book, Marx's *Capital* is the only one that was not originally written in English. The first German edition of *Capital*, Volume I, was published in 1867. The complete work was intended to be divided into four 'books' but three volumes. Marx, however, did not complete them in a publishable form during his lifetime. From a mass of handwritten manuscripts, Marx's close collaborator and friend Friedrich Engels published the 'books' II and III in two separate volumes, Volumes II and III of *Capital*, in 1885 and 1894 respectively. The intended fourth 'book' or the third volume was published in 1905–10 by Karl Kautsky. It was entitled *Theories of Surplus Value* and had three separate volumes of its own. This clearly shows that Marx had intended a much more substantial editing of his manuscripts, which could not be achieved by others.[1] The first volume of *Capital* deals primarily with 'the process of production of capital' and is divided into eight parts: (*i*) commodities and money; (*ii*) the transformation of money into capital; (*iii*) the production of absolute surplus-value; (*iv*) the production of relative surplus-value; (*v*) the production of absolute and relative surplus-value; (*vi*) wages; (*vii*) the process of accumulation of capital; and (*viii*) primitive accumulation. And in Marx's own words:

> The second volume of this work will deal with the process of the circulation of capital (Book II) and the various forms of the process of capital in its totality (Book III), while the third and

1 In a letter to Engels dated 13 February 1866, Marx wrote: 'Although finished, the manuscript, gigantic in its present form, could not be made ready for publication by anybody but me, not even by you' (quoted in Hollander 2008: 2–3).

last volume (Book IV) will deal with the history of the theory (Marx 1977).

For our purpose, Volumes I [1867] and III [1894] of *Capital* are the most important. In this chapter, I follow the English translation of the German *Das Kapital* Volume 1 by Ben Fowkes and of Volumes 2 and 3 by David Fernbach published by Vintage/ Penguin Books in 1977 and 1992, 1991 respectively.

In the 'Preface' to the first edition of *Capital*, Volume I, Marx begins by stating that this work is in continuation of his earlier publication, *A Contribution to the Critique of Political Economy*, published in 1859. He explains that the *substance* of the earlier work is summarised in the first chapter (which in later editions was divided into three chapters) and that the 'presentation is improved'. Further on in the 'Preface', he warns the reader of the difficulty of understanding the first chapter on 'the commodity'. He argues that the value-form of a commodity, 'whose fully developed shape is the money-form', 'is very simple and slight in content'. The difficulty, however, lies in getting to the 'bottom of it'. Apparently, the difficulty lies not in the analysis of the value-form of the commodity but rather in the *discovery* of the *essence* of the value-form or the money-form of the commodity. He himself raises the question: why is it so difficult?, and then answers it in the following words: 'Because the complete body is easier to study than its cell ... for bourgeois society, the commodity-form of the product of labour, or the value-form of the commodity, is the economic cell form' (Marx 1977: 90). Apart from the first chapter, the rest of the volume, according to Marx, 'cannot stand accused on the score of difficulty'.

Marx identifies his object of examination as 'the capitalist mode of production, and the relations of production and forms of intercourse that correspond to it'. This statement, combined with the metaphors of 'body' and 'cell' that he uses, suggests that he sees his examination of the capitalist mode of production as an act of *surgery* performed on a body or an examination of a cell under a microscope. While this would imply a rather static operation, he hastens to add that 'it is the ultimate aim of this work to reveal the economic law of motion of modern society ... ', which by its very nature would be a study of a dynamic process.

Finally, he makes an interesting statement pointing towards his fundamental philosophical position on 'historical materialism':

> To prevent possible misunderstandings, let me say this. I do not by any means depict the capitalist and the landowner in rosy colours. But individuals are dealt with here only in so far as

they are the personifications of economic categories, the bearers [*Träger*] of particular class-relations and interests. My standpoint, from which the development of the economic formation of society is viewed as a process of natural history, can less than any other make the individual responsible for relations whose creatures he remains, socially speaking, however much he may subjectively raise himself above them (Marx 1977: 92).

The statement reveals a basic difference between Marx's approach and that of the classical economists who preceded him. The motives and actions of the agents or the economic actors are not taken to be 'natural', based on some kind of given immutable 'human nature'. The idea here is to *discover* the law of motion of the capitalist mode of production independently of 'human nature' or human psychology as such, and to show that the actors behave according to their position in the system and in accordance with the laws of motion of that system. In other words, the analysis takes as *given* the 'mode of production' in which the individuals are caught, and their psychology is determined by their position in and the dynamics of the system.

In the 'Postface' to the second edition of *Capital*, Volume I, which was written in January 1873, Marx first identifies the major changes that were made in this edition:

In Chapter 1, Section 1, the derivation of value by analysis of the equations in which every exchange-value is expressed has been carried out with greater scientific strictness; similarly, the connection between the substance of value and the determination of the magnitude of value by the labour-time socially necessary, which was only alluded to in the first edition, is now expressly emphasized. Chapter 1, Section 3 (on the form of value), has been completely revised, a task which was made necessary by the two-fold presentation of it in the first edition, if by nothing else. ... The last section of the first chapter, 'The Fetishism of Commodities, etc.', has been altered considerably. Chapter 3, Section 1 (on the measure of values), has been carefully revised, because in the first edition this section was treated carelessly. ... Chapter 7, particularly Section 2, has been re-worked to a great extent (Marx 1977: 94).

This is evidence of the fact that Marx was facing a serious difficulty with the presentation of the subject matter of Chapter 1, which might not have been just a problem of presentation.

He also takes this opportunity to clarify the method of analysis used in this work, in particular its relation to Hegelian dialectics. The statement from the 'Preface' alluded to earlier, that '[w]ith the exception of the section on the form of value, therefore, this volume cannot stand accused on the score of difficulty' was already pointing to the fact that the ordinary or the commonplace method of analysis was used in this volume. In the 'Postface' Marx takes pains to further clarify the matter by approvingly quoting Professor Sieber's review of the first edition of Capital, Volume I, where Sieber says that 'the method of Marx is the deductive method of the whole English school, a school whose failings and virtues are common to the best theoretical economists'. He also appreciatively quotes M. Block's remark that: 'With this work, M. Marx can be ranged among the most eminent analytical thinkers.' Finally, he describes the 'Hegelian mode of expression' of Chapter 1 as mere flirtation. Marx explains the reason for this in detail:

> I criticized the mystificatory side of Hegelian dialectic nearly thirty years ago, at a time when it was still the fashion. But just when I was working at the first volume of *Capital*, the ill-humoured, arrogant and mediocre epigones who now talk large in educated German circles began to take pleasure in treating Hegel in the same way as the good Moses Mendelssohn treated Spinoza in Lessing's time, namely as a 'dead dog'. I therefore openly avowed myself the pupil of that mighty thinker, and even, here and there in the chapter on the theory of value, coquetted[2] with the mode of expression peculiar to him (ibid.: 102–03).

However, he goes on to add that:

> The mystification which the dialectic suffers in Hegel's hands by no means prevents him from being the first to present its general forms of motion in a comprehensive and conscious manner. With him it is standing on its head. It must be inverted, in order to discover the rational kernel within the mystical shell (Marx 1977: 103).

A statement of the 'inverted' dialectic was earlier alluded to in the 'Postface' by, yet again, a long quotation from a review of the first

---

2 In German the word 'coquet' is loosely understood as 'flirtation'. However, the original French expression *'faire la coquette'* is used for a conscious attempt to look pretty, particularly by women of advancing age. Interestingly, in the 'Preface' to the French edition, Marx elided this expression.

edition in *European Messenger* (*Vyestnik Evropy*). According the reviewer:

> While Marx sets himself the task of following and explaining the capitalist economic order from this point of view, he is only formulating, in a strictly scientific manner, the aim that every accurate investigation into economic life must have. ... The scientific value of such an inquiry lies in the illumination of the special laws that regulate the origin, existence, development and death of a given social organism and its replacement by another, higher one. And in fact this is the value of Marx's book (ibid.: 102).

This, of course, is nothing but a description of a dynamic analysis of an evolving system. But, as pointed out earlier, it stands in contradiction with the idea of an 'examination of a body' and its cells. It is, however, entirely possible that Marx used both the static and dynamic methods for analysing different aspects of the system, as indeed Adam Smith and David Ricardo had done before him: the analysis of value was conducted in a static context whereas that of the distribution of income was conducted in a dynamic context. Ironically, Marx uses the 'Hegelian mode of expression' in the static context of value analysis.

It should also be noted that dialectics, as distinct from analytical 'method', comes into its own only when one of the tenets of logic, *the law of excluded middle,* does not hold. For example, let us suppose that an entity 'A' transforms into entity 'B' over a period of time. Now both before 'A' transforms into 'B' and after 'A' has transformed into 'B', the law of excluded middle holds. However, during the period of transition there would be a time when it is no longer possible to say that it is either 'A' or 'not-A'. It is at the time when the proposition 'A' *or* 'not-A' gives way to the proposition 'A' *and* 'not-A' that dialectics comes into its own — it is supposed to be a logic of transition *par excellence.* However, as we shall see, in the case of Marx's analysis in *Capital,* the object of his analysis or examination remains fixed. Though he analyses the dynamics of the capitalist mode of production, he nowhere ventures into an analysis of the moment of transition of the capitalist mode into a socialist or some other mode of production. It is the fixity of the object of analysis in *Capital* — 'What I have to examine in this work is the capitalist mode of production, and the relations of production and forms of intercourse that correspond to it' — that rules out the use of dialectics as a 'method of analysis'.[3]

The Commodity

In the very first few pages of Chapter 1, Marx establishes one of the fundamental propositions of his work with blinding speed. He argues that in an exchange-relation two commodities 'express something equal' and it 'cannot be anything other than the mode of expression, the "form of appearance", of a content distinguishable from it' (Marx 1977: 127). The common element of the two commodities is quickly identified as 'being products of labour' (ibid.: 128), as, Marx argues, no aspect of the two commodities that makes them useful to human beings can be put in a quantitative relation. But a similar objection could be raised for 'labour', as there exist very different kinds of labour. For example, the labour of a goldsmith and the labour of an ironsmith are quite different in nature and cannot be put in a direct quantitative relation. Marx then turns the argument 180 degrees. He argues that since the concrete form of a goldsmith's labour produces a useful thing, such as a gold ornament, and the concrete form of an ironsmith's labour produces another useful thing, such as a sword, these forms of concrete labour cannot be put in any quantitative relation by virtue of the fact that they produce useful things for human beings and, as has already been argued, those useful things cannot be placed in a quantitative relation with each other. Still, he does not reject 'labour' as the common element that appears in the quantitative relation of commodities. He maintains that the common element is 'being products of labour'; and *given* this proposition, he goes on to argue that if the concrete forms of labour cannot be put in a quantitative relation then the labour *must* be 'abstract' labour, i.e., labour that has no concrete form and can only be understood as expenditure of human energy:

> If then we disregard the use-value of commodities, only one property remains, that of being products of labour. But even the product of labour has already been transformed in our hands. If we make abstraction from its use-value, we abstract also from the material constituents and forms which make

3 'Again, the reader must be on his guard against being misled by traces of Hegelian terminology. It will be argued below that Marx did not allow his analysis to be influenced by Hegelian philosophy' (Schumpeter 1954: 392).

it use-value. It is no longer a table, a house, a piece of yarn or any other useful thing. All its sensuous characteristics are extinguished. Nor is it any longer the product of the labour of the joiner, the mason or the spinner, or of any other particular kind of productive labour. With the disappearance of the useful character of the products of labour, the useful character of the kinds of labour embodied in them also disappears; this in turn entails the disappearance of the different concrete forms of labour. They can no longer be distinguished, but are all together reduced to the same kind of labour, human labour in the abstract (Marx 1977: 128).

Several questions must have already cropped up in the reader's mind. First of all, on what grounds can Marx simply assume that a commodity exchange-relation is a relation of equality, i.e., on what grounds can Marx say that when one-quarter of corn exchanges against x cwt of iron, the relationship could be expressed as: '1 quarter of corn = x cwt of iron'? What about the Utilitarian argument that rational individuals exchange commodities only because the utility they receive from the commodity the other party has is always greater than the utility they receive from the commodity they part with? From this perspective an exchange-relation between the two commodities is necessarily a relation of inequality of utilities from an individual's point of view. In response to such objections, Marx argues that he is dealing with a society where commodity-production has become a rule rather than an exception. In such a society exchange is presupposed and production is exclusively for exchange purposes.[4] In this context the utility of

4 'In Condillac, for instance: "It is not true that in an exchange of commodities we give value for value. On the contrary, each of the two contracting parties in every case gives a less for a greater value. If we really exchanged equal values, neither party could make a profit. And yet they both gain, or ought to gain. Why? The value of a thing consists solely in relation to our needs. What is more to the one is less to the other, and vice versa ... It is not to be assumed that we offer for sale articles essential for our own consumption ... We wish to part with a useless thing, in order to get one that we need; we want to give less for more ... It was natural to think that, in an exchange, one value was given for another equal to it whenever each of the articles exchanged was of equal value with the same quantity of gold ... But there is another point to be considered in our calculation. The question is, whether we both exchange something superfluous for something necessary." We see in this passage how Condillac not only confuses use-value with exchange-value, but in a really childish manner assumes that, in a society in which the production of commodities is well developed, each producer produces his own means of subsistence, and throws into circulation only what is superfluous, the excess over his own requirements' (ibid.: 261–62).

his own commodity to a producer is close to zero and it is reasonable to think that in exchange he compares not the utility of the two commodities to himself but rather the cost of obtaining them.

The second question that comes to mind is: if equal labour-times exchange in the market, then would not it be advantageous to be lazy or unskilled? Marx's answer to this question is that in a commodity exchange-relation the labour that counts is the 'socially necessary labour', which is defined as 'the labour-time required to produce any use-value under the conditions of production normal for a given society and with the average degree of skill and intensity of labour prevalent in that society' (Marx 1977: 129).

But a more important question that comes to mind is: on what grounds can Marx equate one hour of an ironsmith's labour with one hour of a goldsmith's labour? Marx's answer to this question appears to be that he does not. He first argues that different kinds of concrete unskilled labour can be treated as 'simple average labour', which is defined as expenditure of human brains, muscles, nerves, hands, etc., that are possessed in his bodily organism by every ordinary man, and so can be equated on the basis of an hour for an hour; but when it comes to equating skilled labour with unskilled labour, he comes up with a curious answer:

> More complex labour counts only as *intensified*, or rather *multiplied* simple labour, so that a smaller quantity of complex labour is considered equal to a larger quantity of simple labour. Experience shows that this reduction is constantly being made. A commodity may be the outcome of most complicated labour, but through its *value* it is posited as equal to the product of simple labour. The various proportions in which different kinds of labour are reduced to simple labour as their unit of measurement are established by a social process that goes on behind the backs of the producers; these proportions therefore appear to the producers to have been handed down by tradition. In the interest of simplification, we shall henceforth view every form of labour-power directly as simple labour-power; by this we shall simply be saving ourselves the trouble of making the reduction (Marx 1977: 135).

This quotation from Marx is significant in highlighting the theoretical tension between the positions taken in the first three chapters of Volume I of *Capital* and the rest of the book. First of all, the so-called 'simple labour' is not conceptually equivalent to 'abstract labour'.

'Abstract labour' is supposed to be a property of the commodity relation, whereas 'simple labour' is nothing but unskilled labour which
exists in the labour process and can be observed and measured in
terms of labour-time or energy expenditure through direct observation
without bringing in any commodity relation into the picture. By substituting 'simple labour' for 'abstract labour', Marx is already prepar-
ing the ground for shifting his theoretical *problematique*.

Second, the simplification alluded to in the last sentence of the quotation is an attempt to assume away a significant theoretical problem. If we follow Marx's explanation, then we must conclude that
he breaks from the classical tradition of Adam Smith and Ricardo on
this crucial issue. As we have noted in the previous two chapters, both
Smith and Ricardo used the wage differential to reduce skilled labour
to unskilled homogeneous labour. Marx, on the other hand, explicitly
adds a footnote stating that:

> The reader should note that we are not speaking here of the
> wages or value the worker receives for (e.g.) a day's labour,
> but of the value of the commodity in which his day of labour
> is objectified. At this stage of our presentation, the category of
> wages does not exist at all (1977: 135, f.n. 15).

Thus, instead of going from the *observation* of labour-time in the
process of production to the *prediction* of the quantitative relation
between commodities, Marx begins with the *observation* of the quantitative relation between commodities and postulates that such a
relation is a relation of *equal abstract or homogeneous labour*. Therefore, if one-quarter of corn exchanges against x ctw of iron and it is
observed that 10 hours of labour produces one-quarter of corn and
five hours of labour produces x ctw of iron, then, according to Marx's
argument, we must conclude that one hour of an ironsmith's labour is
equivalent to two hours of a corn-producing farmer's labour.

Throughout the first three chapters of Volume I of *Capital*, Marx
maintains that commodities are 'products of labour'. Production is
understood as a direct relation between man (the worker, the producer) and nature — even 'raw materials' of labour do not explicitly
show up before the end of Chapter 5 on the 'contradiction in the general formula' of capital. Supposedly, a tailor's labour directly makes
a coat and a weaver's labour directly makes linen. Even if the raw
materials are implicitly assumed, they are placed in a sequential labour
process such that the beginning of the process of producing any commodity can be traced back to a direct relationship between man and

nature. In other words, commodities are not recognised as produced by means of commodities. Therefore, no commodity residue remains when a commodity is reduced to the total direct and indirect labour-time needed to produce it.

Given this restricted framework, we find that Marx continuously shuttles between the idea of exchange as exchange of equal (*labour*) cost and exchange as a representation or manifestation of *equal abstract labour*. In the section on 'Commodity Fetishism' in Chapter 1, Marx presents the argument that the exchange-relation must represent exchange of equal 'simple labour' because exchange must represent equal cost.

He argues that the social division of labour is a natural phenomenon, which is part of all forms of society. He conceives of society as an *organism* that has *needs*, and that the organism must divide the *total* labour at its disposal to satisfy those various needs; e.g., the division of the total labour within a patriarchal peasant family is consciously divided by the patriarch on the basis of sex and age of the family members (Marx 1977: 171), or, for that matter, Robinson Crusoe's division of his own labour while he was stranded on an island, is similarly governed by Robinson himself:

> Necessity itself compels him [Robinson Crusoe] to divide his time with precision between his different functions. Whether one function occupies a greater space in his total activity than another depends on the magnitude of the difficulties to be overcome in attaining the useful effect aimed at. Our friend Robinson Crusoe learns this by experience, and having saved a watch, ledger, ink and pen from the shipwreck, he soon begins, like a good Englishman, to keep a set of books. His stock-book contains a catalogue of the useful objects he possesses, of the various operations necessary for their production, and finally of the labour-time that specific quantities of these products have on average cost him. All the relations between Robinson and these objects that form his self-created wealth are here so simple and transparent that even Herr M. Wirth could understand them. And yet those relations contain all the essential determinants of value (ibid.: 169–70).

Marx's point is that, unlike a peasant household or Robinson Crusoe on an island, in a commodity-producing society there is no conscious determination of the social division of labour. In such a society the social division of labour is maintained through, what he calls, the '*law of value*. Let us suppose that in the market one unit of commodity 'x' exchanges against two units of commodity 'y' and it takes 10 hours of unskilled simple labour for the producers of both 'x' and 'y' to produce one unit of each. In that case, it would pay the producers of commodity 'y' to switch from producing commodity 'y' to producing commodity 'x' (on the assumption that the knowledge of producing different commodities is common), till the exchange ratio between commodity 'x' and 'y' are adjusted such that they exchange at 1:1. In that case, there would be no incentive for either producer to shift. This is supposed to be the *law of value* that maintains the social division of labour in a commodity-producing society.

It should be noted that in this case equal simple labour-times exchange only when the social division of labour is stable or is in 'equilibrium'. It is thus a *result* of the operation of the law of value and not a pre-supposition of exchange of commodities as such. This result is a logical result, given that labour is the only 'cost' in the system. However, we should also keep in mind another important implicit assumption behind such descriptions. It is implicitly assumed that commodities are produced for a year and brought to the annual market for exchange at the end of that year (or harvest cycle). If, however, there was a continuous market and it took different time-periods to bring different commodities to the market, e.g., bread and wine, then the problem of the time of waiting (and not just the labour-time of producing) would have to be taken into account. It is generally assumed by most economists that one puts higher values on present consumption over future consumption. If this is true, then the wine producers would switch to producing bread if wine and bread exchanged one-to-one in terms of simple labour-time of production, since it would take a longer time to bring mature wine to the market than baked bread. Thus the law of value would ensure that commodities do not exchange one-to-one in terms of simple labour-time — this argument was highlighted by Böhm-Bawerk ([1896] 1949). But, of course, this proposition is not as strong as it sounds. The assumption that people prefer consumption today over consumption in the future is based on the fact that in modern society a positive rate of interest exists. If the rate of interest were zero, then it is not obvious that future consumption would always be discounted. But again, it would still be arbitrary to assume that there must be zero discount for future consumption, at least in the case of positive storage charges; for example, if a baker can finance his daily consumption after his daily sale of bread but a farmer has to store his consumption for a year (or a harvest cycle) before he can sell his wheat, then the farmer will need more labour-time in exchange for his wheat against the bread to be able to pay the storage charges on the consumption good for a year. This problem could perhaps be solved by introducing money into the system, with the assumption that there is no cost to storing money. The crucial point, however, is that an intertemporal preference for consumption could create an income category independent of the expenditure of labour in a world of labourers only, which strikes at the heart of the exploitation theory of profits and interest.

Now let us go back to Robinson's story. It is clear that if Robinson needs a certain skill to overcome the difficulties of attaining the useful effect aimed at, he will add the cost of labour-time spent in acquiring the skill into his calculation. In the framework where every use-value production begins with a direct relation between man and nature, the problem of reduction of skilled to unskilled labour does not pose any problem that is different from the problem of depreciation of a means of production that lasts more than one production cycle. Thus, on the assumption that commodities are 'products of labour' and the complications arising from various ratios of past and present labour incorporated in various commodities are ignored, Marx could argue that the total commodities in circulation could be seen as a pool of simple homogeneous labour that a society has, and a commodity could be seen as representing (or containing) a part of the total pool of social labour, which is what Marx terms the value of a commodity: 'As crystals of this social substance, which is common to them all, they are values — commodity values' (Marx 1977: 128).

Parallel to this theme, however, runs another discourse. As we have mentioned earlier, in this framework it is postulated that the exchange-relation between two commodities represents *equal abstract labour.* Here the measure of 'abstract labour' is divorced from its empirical measure by the clock — it is the market that is supposed to do the 'abstraction'. Since the market-relation is always relative, the labour-relation that is supposed to be reflected by the market relation also remains relative. But the idea of the *total* labour-time of a society as well as the value of a commodity requires an *absolute* measure in labour-time unit. Marx solves this problem by identifying one specific commodity, the money-commodity, as the representative of 'abstract labour', and the measure of this 'abstract labour' by the concrete labour that produces the money-commodity:

> [...] the endless series itself is now a socially given fact in the shape of the prices of the commodities. We have only to read the quotations of a price-list backwards, to find the magnitude

160

of the value of money expressed in all sots of commodities. As against this, money has no price. In order to form a part of this uniform relative form of value of the other commodities, it would have to be brought into relation with itself as its own equivalent (Marx 1977: 189).

Before we go any further, it should be noted that unless it is assumed that the money-commodity is produced directly in a relation between man and nature — such as picking silver on a beach, which is completely unassisted by raw materials and means of production — there is no way of measuring the labour-time required to produce the money-commodity without adding various other kinds of concrete labour required for the production of the money-commodity. In other words, one must implicitly assume that abstract labour is nothing but *simple unskilled labour* to be able to calculate the labour-time needed to produce the money-commodity itself.[5]

Second, if the values could be simply read back from a pricelist, then the exercise is akin to converting the price of a commodity to some other currency given the exchange rate between currencies — it is devoid of any analytical content. Furthermore, if the value of a commodity could be simply read backwards from a price-list, then market-price fluctuations must be interpreted as fluctuations in commodity values and the 'total social labour' of the society cannot be taken as *given*, as it must fluctuate with fluctuations in the market prices. Marx recognises the problem and quickly reverts back to defining value only at the 'equilibrium' of the market and by the calculation of simple unskilled labour needed to produce the commodity:

> Price is the money-name of the labour objectified in a commodity. ... But although price, being the exponent of the magnitude of a commodity's value, is the exponent of its exchange-ratio with money, it does not follow that the exponent of this exchange ratio is necessarily the exponent of the magnitude of the commodity's value. Suppose two equal quantities of

---

5 Steedman (1985) has argued that Marx's proposition relates to taking the given money-wage differentials as the multiplication factor for homogenising (or abstracting) various concrete labours, as was the case with classical economists. But this cannot be correct, as Marx develops this idea prior to introducing the wage-labour category in his theory. For Marx, the process of abstraction of labour does not lie at the level of exchange of labour-power against money wages but rather at the level of exchange of commodities.

socially necessary labour are respectively represented by 1 quarter of wheat and £2 (approximately % ounce of gold). £2 is the expression in money of the magnitude of the value of the quarter of wheat, or its price. If circumstances now allow this price to be raised to £3, or compel it to be reduced to £1, then although £1 and £3 may be too small or too large to give proper expression to the magnitude of wheat's value, they are nevertheless prices of the wheat, for they are, in the first place, the form of its value, i.e., money, and, in the second place, the exponents of its exchange-ratio with money. If the conditions of production, or the productivity of labour, remain constant, the same amount of social labour-time must be expended on the reproduction of a quarter of wheat, both before and after the change in price. The situation is not dependent on the will of the wheat producer or on that of the owners of other commodities. The magnitude of the value of a commodity therefore expresses a necessary relation to social labour-time which is inherent in the process by which its value is created. With the transformation of the magnitude of value into the price this necessary relation appears as the exchange-ratio between a single commodity and the money commodity which exist outside it. This relation, however, may express both the magnitude of value of the commodity and the greater or lesser quantity of money for which it can be sold under the given circumstances. The possibility, therefore, of the quantitative incongruity between price and magnitude of value, is inherent in the price-form itself. This is not a defect, but, on the contrary, it makes this form the adequate one for a mode of production whose laws can only assert themselves as blindly operating averages between constant irregularities (Marx 1977: 195–96).

Thus the idea that one could derive the value of commodities from the given exchange-relations in the market or the relations of commodities with money in the market, had to be abandoned. Concrete labours are not 'abstracted' in the market by a market process that goes behind the producers' back; rather, the idea that all unskilled labour in a given economy can be treated as homogeneous labour is a theoretical simplification made for analytical purposes. We find that Marx, after Chapter 3, moves away from the concept of 'abstract labour' in this sense. Even the expression 'abstract labour' begins to disappear and terms such as 'socially necessary labour', 'simple labour', and 'average labour' begin to take its place; and value begins to be simply defined as: '*the value of each commodity is determined by the quantity of labour materialized in its use-value, by the labour-time socially necessary to produce it*' (ibid.: 293, emphasis added).[6] In this sense, Marx's notion of the 'labour-value' of commodities is no different from that of the classical tradition, except for the fact that in the classical tradition, skilled or more complex and intensive labour is reduced to unskilled or simple labour by the wage differentials, whereas for Marx it requires the further analytical procedure of calculating the unskilled labour-time of producing the skill and apportioning it to commodities by the calculation of 'depreciation' of the skill over the average life-span of the workers:

> All labour of a higher, or more complicated, character than average labour is expenditure of labour-power of a more costly kind, *labour-power whose production has cost more time and labour than unskilled or simple labour-power*, and which therefore has a higher value. This power being of higher value, it expresses itself in labour of a higher sort, and therefore becomes objectified, during an equal amount of time, in proportionally higher values (Marx 1977: 305, emphasis added).

It should be noted that in the world of only labourers, Marx's procedure of reducing skilled to unskilled labour must amount to equal returns to labourers on per unit of simple labour so calculated; otherwise it cannot be guaranteed that the total labour input is always equal to total labour output for the system. However, in a capitalist economy with positive profits, it cannot be guaranteed that Marx's reduction factors will necessarily be equal to the wage differentials in the system unless the production of labour-power is taken to be similar to the production of machines or beasts of burden. But in that case, there will be no incentive for the workers to acquire skills. In any case,

---

6 Faccarello (1983, 1997) has discovered four different definitions of 'abstract labour' in Marx's writings. He argues that these definitions end up in contradiction. He also has an interesting discussion on what he calls the 'sociological definition' of 'abstract labour' (Faccarello 1983: ch. 14). In my opinion, the definition of 'abstract labour' as simple labour in the sense of 'productive expenditure of human brains, muscles, nerves, hands, etc.' (Marx 1977: 134) is the only definition that is consistent throughout Marx's theory.

Marx is quite clear that the wage differentials in the real world do not represent the differentials in labour required to acquire the skills:

> The distinction between higher and simple labour, 'skilled labour' and 'unskilled labour', rests in part on pure illusion or, to say the least, on distinctions that have long since ceased to be real, and survive only by virtue of a traditional convention; and in part on the helpless condition of some sections of the working class, a condition that prevents them from exacting equally with the rest the value of their labour-power. Accidental circumstances here play so great a part that these two forms of labour sometimes change places (Marx 1977: 305, f.n. 19).

Thus, once it is admitted that the wage differentials may diverge from the strict accounting of labour-time, it can no longer be maintained that Marx's rate of surplus-value will be uniform for all kinds of labours.[7] One way out of it could be to treat all skilled workers as 'capitalists' who lease out their skills (i.e., capital) at the going rate of profits. But this will not only complicate the analysis considerably, but also move away from Marx's notion of the distinction between workers and capitalists. On the other hand, if we revert back to the classical procedure of homogenising labour through wage differentials, then changes in relative wages would change Marx's labour-values even if such relative wage changes had nothing to do with labour-time accounting at the level of production.

---

7 See Okishio (1963), Morishima (1973) and also Rowthorn (1974, 1980) for an exercise of Marx's method of reduction of skilled to unskilled labour. Morishima (1973) and later Steedman (1985) have shown that several of Marx's fundamental propositions such as 'exploitation of labour is zero when the rate of profits is zero', 'rate of surplus-value must be equal for all labourers in a competitive capitalist economy', etc., require that concrete labour of different kinds must be aggregated via the relative wage rates of those different kinds of labour. Also see Blaug (1982), Elster (1978), Howard and King (1985), Krause (1981, 1982) and Roemer (1986) on this issue. For a critique of Steedman (1985) see Ganssmann (1988); though Ganssmann's basic argument suffers from the mistake that in an input-output framework it is meaningless to talk about 'money-commodity producing labour' as a homogeneous quantity *a priori*, particularly when commodities, including the money-commodity, are produced by means of commodities and labour. Bowles and Gintis (1977) propose to deal with heterogeneous labours in Marx's theory without having a need to homogenise them. However, see Morishima (1978) for a critique of their approach.

Division of Value into its Parts

In Chapter 4, 'The General Formula for Capital', Marx introduces the notion of 'capital'. He distinguishes production of commodities in general from the production of commodities in a specifically capitalist system. According to Marx, in a simple commodity-producing society the immediate *cause or reason* for production is still rooted in the consumption needs of the producers. In this case the general formula for the circulation of commodities could be given by C_1 - M - C_2, where a producer exchanges his commodity C_1 for money M in order to buy another commodity C_2 that he needs. He contrasts this with the general formula for the circulation of capital. He argues that in capitalism a capitalist begins his operation with a certain amount of money, which is his money-capital. He buys commodities with the money in order to sell them and convert them back into money. In other words, the general formula for the circulation of capital appears as M - C - M. It would, however, be patently irrational for anyone to go through the whole process of buying and selling commodities only to end up with the same amount of money one had started with. Thus a rational representation of the circulation of capital must appear as M - C - M', where M'>M. In other words, the *raison d'être* of money as capital is its self-expansion. In this circuit the commodity appears only as a means of self-aggrandisement of the money-capital. The *direct* connection of the production of commodities with human needs is severed and the spiral of the circuit of money-capital becomes limitless.

In the next chapter on the 'Contradictions in the General Formula', Marx argues that the general formula of money-capital raises a serious theoretical question. On the basis of his previous argument that when a market is in 'equilibrium' the exchange of commodities or exchange of commodities for money and vice-versa must represent equal values, he asks how it would be possible to extract more values from simple buying and selling in the market. The answer to this question is provided in Chapters 6 and 7. According to Marx, the secret of M'>M does not lie in buying and selling of commodities but rather in the production of commodities. With his initial money-capital the commodity-producing capitalist buys various commodities as a means of production, such as raw materials and machines, as well as a 'special commodity' called 'labour-power'. He argues that in the exchange of money for raw materials and machines, etc., equal values are exchanged. But in a capitalist system there exists a class of people who own nothing but their capacity to work, and for their livelihood have no other option than to alienate their capacity to work as if it were a commodity, and like any other commodity, offer it in the market for sale. The value of labour-power, therefore, is also determined by the same principle of commodity-production, i.e., the labour-time needed for the reproduction of the worker's capacity to work, which amounts to the labour-time needed to reproduce the worker's subsistence. Thus when it comes to the first half of the circuit M - C, the values on both sides of the equation are equal. However, instead of selling the commodities that he has bought, the capitalist puts them through a process of production and converts them into a new commodity. So the circuit expands to M - C - P - C' - M'. In the process of production the workers are put to work and they add value to the means of production according to the amount of time they put in. Marx argues that a worker's capacity to work is highly elastic in the sense that, given his subsistence, a worker could work much longer hours than the value his subsistence contains. His contention is that capitalists invariably make the workers work longer hours than the value their subsistence or wages contain. It is the difference between the value of the subsistence the workers receive as wages and the value they add to the means of production in the production process that explains the expansion of money in the circuit of money-capital. Marx calls it 'surplus-value' and maintains that it is this surplus-value that is the source of all the various categories of income in the system except wages. On the basis of this exercise, Marx divides the value of any commodity into its three components: the value of the means of production used up in the production process is called 'constant capital' (c), and the total value added to the means of production by the workers is divided into 'variable capital' (v), which represents the value of workers' subsistence or wages, and the 'surplus-value' (s), which is the difference between the total labour-time used up in the production process and the value of the variable capital. Thus if the value of a commodity is represented by λ, then $\lambda = c + v + s$. The ratio s/v is called the 'rate of surplus-value' or the rate of exploitation, and the ratio c/v is called the 'value or organic composition of capital'.

Before going any further, it must be pointed out that Marx obtains the foregoing result on the basis of his analysis of commodities in Chapter 1. But, as we have pointed out, the result of the analysis in Chapter 1 is based on the assumption that commodities are 'products of labour'. In other words, Marx had assumed that a commodity could be reduced to simple labour-time without any commodity residue remaining. But in the analysis presented in the previous paragraph, the commodity is produced not only by labour but by other commodities as well. If all commodities are produced in a similar fashion, then there is no way of reducing a commodity to its labour-time without leaving some commodity residue.[8] In other words, *production, in this case, must be understood as a circular rather than a linear process.* Once we realise this, it becomes clear that it cannot be taken for granted that the commodity exchange-relation represents the exchange of equal labour-time even if we assume an annual post-harvest market, as commodities cannot be removed from the cost side of the equation. For example, let us assume that the price-ratios diverge from the respective value-ratios. In the case where commodities are 'products of labour' alone, it is easy to see that this will lead to a movement of labour resources (of course, on the implicit assumption that knowledge of how all the commodities are produced is common) such that the price-ratios would equilibrate at the value-ratios. In the present case, however, the price-ratios of commodities affect their costs of production and it cannot be said *a priori* that the divergence of price-ratios from the value-ratios is simply due to mal-distribution of labour and not to a return on the investment in commodities as a means of production. It is true that if we assume that returns on investment in the means of production is zero and all income accrues to workers in accordance with their expenditure of labour-time alone, then the price-ratios and value-ratios will coincide. But we must keep in mind that this is a restrictive assumption and *must* necessarily be dropped when we are considering the production of commodities under capitalist relations. Thus the proposition that equal quantities of simple labour-time exchange in an equilibrium market condition can no longer be taken as a result of analysis. *It turns into an assumption.* Quite characteristically, Marx indirectly alludes to this fact in a footnote at the end of Chapter 5:

> How can we account for the origin of capital on the assumption that prices are regulated by the average price, i.e., ultimately by the value of the commodities? I say 'ultimately' because average prices do not directly coincide with the values of the commodities, ... (1977: 269, f.n. 24).

---

8 It is ironical that Marx himself had criticised Adam Smith for forgetting the constant capital element of the production process (see Chapter 1 of this book); and it was Marx's remark, that the rate of profit must have a finite maximum even when wages become zero since there is always some amount of constant capital involved in production, which gave Sraffa (1960: 94) the idea of exploring the analytical property of the 'maximum rate of profit'.

Contrast this with the quotation from Marx (ibid.: 195–96) on page 174. Thus the relevance of the analysis of Chapter 1 is extinguished for the rest of the book. It was an appendage from an earlier work when Marx's economic theory had not matured, and it just did not fit well in the new book.[9]

Transformation of Value into Price of Production

Throughout Volumes I and II of *Capital* Marx maintains the assumption that equal labour-values exchange in the market. It is, however, apparent that if this were so, then the commodity that uses a higher ratio of c/v in its production would have a lower rate of profit compared to the commodity that uses a lower c/v ratio, since the rate of profit in every sector would be given by s/(c + v) or (s/v)/(c/v + 1), with s/v being equal in every sector. This, according to Marx, is not a sustainable situation in a competitive capitalist system since competition among the capitalists brings about a tendency for the rates of profit to equalise, as both Adam Smith and Ricardo had maintained. At the end of Chapter 8 of Volume III of *Capital*, Marx brings this aspect of capitalism to bear upon the notion of value and its components:

> We have shown, therefore, that in different branches of industries unequal profit rates prevail, corresponding to the different organic composition of capitals, and, within the indicated limits, corresponding also to their different turnover times; so that at a given rate of surplus-value it is only for capitals of the same organic composition — assuming equal turnover times — that the law holds good, as a general tendency, that profit stand in direct proportion to the amount of capital, and that capitals of equal size yield equal profits in the same period of time. *The above argument is true on the same basis as our whole investigation so far: that commodities are sold at their values.* There is no doubt, however, that in actual fact, ignoring inessential, accidental circumstances that cancel each other out, no such variation in the average rate of profit exists between different branches of industry, and it could not exist

9 Young (1976) has pointed out that prior to Capital Marx used the term 'value' and 'exchange-value' interchangeably. He argues that the distinction between 'value' and 'exchange-value' of Capital took shape sometime between January 1866 and April 1867, when Marx revised his manuscripts of Capital Vol. I for publication. On this issue also see Hodges (1965).

without abolishing the entire system of capitalist production. The theory of value thus appears incompatible with the actual movement, incompatible with the actual phenomena of production, and it might seem that we must abandon all hope of understanding these phenomena (Marx 1991: 252, emphasis added).

Marx's solution to this problem is simple, but unfortunately incorrect. He proposes to derive the average rate of profit from the given value magnitudes by dividing the aggregate surplus-value in the system by the aggregate of constant and variable capitals in the system. In other words, if $\Sigma s_i = S$ and $\Sigma(c_i + v_i) = (C + V)$, where i = 1, ... n, then Marx's average rate of profit (r) is given by $S/(C + V)$. After so deriving the average rate of profit (r), he applies this rate of profit to mark up the values of each sector's constant plus variable capital by the average rate of profit to derive the so-called price of production of each commodity. In other words, the price of production for each sector or commodity is given by:

$$(c_i + v_i)(1 + r) = (c_i + v_i)\{(C + V + S)/(C + V)\}$$

It is evident from the above equation that $\Sigma(c_i + v_i)(1 + r) = C + V + S$ and $\Sigma(c_i + v_i)r = S$. Marx's contention is that in a competitive capitalist economy commodities do not exchange in proportion to their labour-values but rather in proportion to their prices of production. But this in itself does not invalidate the basis of his analysis of capitalism in terms of labour-values and its three main components, since the average rate of profit and the prices of production are derived from value magnitudes and cannot be derived otherwise; and given the result that the sum of the prices of production is proportional to the sum of values, and the sum of profits is proportional to the sum of surplus-values, it stands as a proof that the source of profit is surplus-value. It should be noted, as we have pointed out in the previous two chapters, that in Adam Smith the natural rate of profit is taken as a conventionally given necessity of production, and Ricardo did not provide a theory to determine its exact magnitude at any given point of time. Put in this context, the above result was of immense importance to Marx (and would have been to Political Economy if it were correct):

> The price of production includes the average profit. And what we call price of production is in fact the same thing that Adam Smith calls 'natural price', Ricardo 'price of production' or

'cost of production', and the Physiocrats '*prix nécessaire*', though none of these people explained the difference between price of production and value. We call it the price of production because in the long term it is the condition of supply, the condition for the reproduction of commodities, in each particular sphere of production. We can also understand why those very economists who oppose the determination of commodity value by labour-time, by the quantity of labour contained in the commodity, always speak of the prices of production as the centres around which market prices fluctuate. They can allow themselves this because the price of production is already a completely externalized and *prima facie* irrational form of commodity value, a form that appears in competition and is therefore present in the consciousness of the vulgar capitalist and consequently also in that of the vulgar economist (Marx 1991: 300).

In Marx's own examples the units for all the variables are given in terms of £ and not labour-time. This, of course, was Marx's practice given his assumption of the exchange of equal values in the market so that the labour-value of half-an-ounce of gold could be directly translated into £1. However, once it is admitted that commodities exchange in proportion to their prices of production and not values, it is clear that in all likelihood the prices of production of gold would also differ from its value. And once that happens, the £ figures for constant and variable capitals in Marx's equations would also change, which means that it would not be possible to take either (C + V) as the measure of total capital, or S as a measure of the total surplus-value or total profits. In other words, the average rate of profit would be unknown and the measure of the surplus-value and the constant and variable capitals would be of no use in determining the rate of profits. The root of the problem is that the measure of capital is itself dependent on the rate of profit — a problem of which Ricardo was well aware and Marx was unsuccessful in getting around it with his transformation of values into prices of production.

As a matter of fact, Marx was aware that he needed to measure capital in terms of prices of production and not values, but at first he thought that it was not a serious obstacle and his results would still remain valid:

This seems contradicted by the fact that the elements of productive capital are generally bought on the market in capitalist production, so that their prices include an already realized profit and accordingly include the production price of one branch of industry together with the profit contained in it, so that the profit in one branch of industry goes into the cost price of another. But if the sum of the cost prices of all commodities in a country is put on one side and the sum of the profits or surplus-values on the other, we can see that the calculation comes out right. Take for example a commodity A; its cost price may contain the profits of B, C, D, just as the profits of A may in turn go into B, C, D, etc. If we make this calculation, the profit of A will be absent from its own cost price, and the profits of B, C, D, etc., will be absent from theirs. None of them includes his own profit in his cost price. And so if there are n spheres of production, and in each of them a profit of p is made (and the symbol for the cost price of a single commodity is k), then the cost price in all together is $k - np$. Considering the calculation as a whole, to the same extent that the profits of one sphere of production go into the cost price of another, to that extent these profits have already been taken into account for the overall price of the final end-product and cannot appear on the profit side twice. They appear on this side only because the commodity in question was itself an end-product, so that its price of production does not go into the cost price of another commodity (Marx 1991: 259–60).

However, this argument of Marx is clearly wrong. First of all, had it been correct, it would apply equally to his measure of capital in terms of labour-values, as the values of both constant and variable capital elements also contain their surplus-value elements. But the problem here is not of 'double counting' either profits or surplus-value. The problem is how to count the capital investment. The 'k' element in Marx's quotation is an unknown. If we look at the system in physical terms, then the problem becomes clearer. Let us say that all the capital and wage goods used up in one production cycle are given by $\Sigma \alpha_i$ and the total output produced in the system is given by $\Sigma \theta_i$, where i = 1, ... n. Thus $(\Sigma \theta_i - \Sigma \alpha_i)$ is the net output or the surplus produced in the system. The problem Marx is dealing with is how to get a single dimensional measure of $\Sigma \alpha_i$ such that $(\Sigma P_i \theta_i - \Sigma P_i \alpha_i) = r\Sigma P_i \alpha_i$, where r is the rate of profit and P_i's are the prices of commodities in terms of a money-commodity (say, gold). It is clear from this equation that there is no 'double counting' involved, as the total profit is completely accounted for by the total net output or the surplus produced in the system. Since Sraffa (1960) it is well known that there exists a solution of P_i's and r that satisfies the above equation. And, as a matter of fact, it appears that Marx himself came to conclude that his above argument was unsatisfactory, as only a few pages further down from the passage just quoted, we find Marx writing:

The development given above also involves a modification in the determination of a commodity's cost price. It was originally assumed that the cost price of a commodity equalled the *value* of the commodities consumed in its production. But for the buyer of a commodity, it is the price of production that constitutes its cost price and can thus enter into forming the price of another commodity. As the price of production of a commodity can diverge from its value, so the cost price of a commodity, in which the price of production of other commodities are involved, can also stand above or below the portion of its total value that is formed by the value of the means of production going into it. *It is necessary to bear in mind this modified significance of the cost price, and therefore to bear in mind too that if the cost price of a commodity is equated with the value of the means of production used up in producing it, it is always possible to go wrong* [emphasis added]. Our present investigation does not require us to go into further detail on this point. It still remains correct that the cost price of commodities is always smaller than their value. ... *As a general rule, the principle that the cost price of a commodity is less than its value has been transformed in practice into the principle that its cost price is less than its price of production* [emphasis added]. For the total social capital, where price of production equals value, this assertion is identical with the earlier one that the cost price is less than the value. Even though it has a different meaning for the particular spheres of production, the basic fact remains that, taking the social capital as a whole, the cost price of the commodities that this produces is less than their value, or than the price of production which is identical with this value for the total mass of commodities produced (1991: 264–65).

This clearly shows that Volume III of *Capital* was still a working manuscript and not ready for publication. In any case, in the foregoing quotation we find that Marx has modified his claim of equality between the sum of profits and the sum of surplus-values and the sum of prices and the sum of values to an assertion that the sum of the costs of production must be less than the sum of values. Again, we need to clarify the dimensional incongruity here. The cost prices as well as the prices of production are given in terms of some *numéraire* or money-commodity, whereas values are given in terms of labour-time. And, as we have argued above, since there is no natural relationship between values and prices of production, Marx's conclusion cannot be established on the basis of an analysis of the value or the price of production accounting. However, let us suppose that we start with prices proportional to labour-values and unequal rates of profit across the sectors. We calculate the total money-price of the total output produced in the system at these prices. Let us suppose that the unit of the money-commodity is chosen such that £ 1 represents one hour of socially necessary labour-time when prices are proportional to labour-values. Now we allow the rate of profits to equalise and the relative prices of production to be formed under the condition that the total money-price of the total output in terms of £ or gold is kept constant in the two regimes. We can do this because the prices of production are ratios and therefore open to arbitrary constraint binding on the total. Given this constraint, it is obvious that if there is positive profit in the system then the total cost price in terms of prices of production must be less than the total value. This is what Marx seems to suggest in the foregoing quotation.

Thus Marx's procedure of transforming values into prices of production can be represented as below:

$$(\lambda_{11}\pi_1 + \lambda_{12}\pi_2 + ... + \lambda_{1n}\pi_n) (1 + r) = \lambda_1\pi_1$$

$$...$$

$$(\lambda_{n1}\pi_1 + \lambda_{n2}\pi_2 + ... + \lambda_{nn}\pi_n) (1 + r) = \lambda_n\pi_n$$
$$\Sigma\lambda_i\pi_i = \Sigma\lambda_i$$

where i = 1, ... n; λ_{ij} represents labour-value of commodity j needed in the production of one unit of commodity i; r is the equal rate of profits and π_i's are the multiplication factors that transform the values into prices of production. We have n + 1 equations to solve for n deviation factors π's and one rate of profits r.

Given this procedure of transforming values into prices of production, it is clear that in general the rate of profits 'r' will not be equal to S/(C + V) and the sum of profits will not be equal to the sum of surplus-values. In other words, the rate of profits cannot be determined at the level of value accounting. This has a serious consequence for

Marx's theory of exploitation. Marx had criticised the claims made by the Ricardian socialists that since labour is the only productive agent it ought to be the only recipient of net income, which it should receive in accordance with the amount of labour put in by the individual workers in the production process. The problem with such a claim is that there is no guarantee that the sum of all the income claims will exactly equal the sum of values of the net output unless there is a theory of value that ensures it.[10] Marx's theory of prices of production was supposed to provide the scientific foundation to the claim that only labour is productive of value by proving that the total profits in the system are nothing but exactly equal to the total surplus-values or what Marx called 'unpaid labour'. Once this claim cannot be maintained, it is no longer possible to hold that *only labour is productive*. The fact of the matter is that in a capitalist economy neither labour nor machines nor raw materials, nor even single sectors can be identified as 'productive'. What is productive is the *system of production as a whole*, if it produces more than what it uses in the process of production.

The idea that 'only labour is productive', lies at the heart of the misunderstandings about Marx's 'transformation problem'. For example, Paul Sweezy, who was the first English-speaking Marxist to have engaged with Bortkiewitcz's critique (see section on 'Controversies about the Transformation Problem'), accepted the conclusion that 'the Marxian method of transformation is logically unsatisfactory' (Sweezy [1942] 1949: 115), but still went on to maintain throughout his book that 'the exchange of commodities is an exchange of the products of the labour of individual producers' (ibid.: 27). This theoretically contradictory position still remains a hallmark of most of the Marxist literature on value and the transformation problem. But this does not imply that the idea that land and capital are also 'productive' has any credence either. There is no logical way of separating the productivities of various elements involved in the process of production. As we have pointed out, it is the system as a whole that can be characterised as productive or unproductive and not its various elements separately.

All this does not mean that Marx's fundamental argument that there is a conflict of interest between the class of capitalists and the class of workers, and that it is in the interest of the capitalists to extend the working day as much as possible given daily wages or reduce the wages to their possible minimum, is incorrect. All these measures, however, increase the rate of profits directly and there is, therefore,

---

10 Gordon (1968) has argued that this was the *raison d'etre* of Marx's labour theory of value.

no formal need to go via a labour theory of value to establish any such claims. The reader should also keep in mind that up to now we have been assuming that every sector produces only one commodity. As we shall see in the section on Controversies as well as in the next chapter, in the case of joint-production it becomes difficult to measure a commodity's labour-value and in such cases one could get paradoxical results — such as a system having positive profits with negative surplus-value. *The lesson of the analysis of prices of production is that no particular claim to the distribution of income can be derived from a theory of prices in a capitalist economy.* It also shows that the nature of the dynamics of technical change in a capitalist economy cannot be inferred from a labour-value and surplus-value analysis.

Falling Rate of Profits

Even though Marx was well aware of the fact that the rate of profits given by $S/(C + V)$ is not necessarily the correct rate of profits, he maintains it to be the correct measure for his analysis of the dynamic trend in the rate of profits. Thus, on the assumption that $r = (S/V)/(C/V + 1)$, it is clear that 'r' will decline if S/V remains constant but C/V rises. Marx's contention is that in a capitalist system the competitive forces engender technical changes and the long-term trend of technical changes is such that both S/V and C/V rise, but the rise in C/V is large enough to more than offset the rise in S/V and bring about a fall in 'r'. However, before we analyse Marx's explanation for this peculiar nature of technical change in the capitalist system, it is important to know whether the explanation is provided as an explanation of an empirical historical trend or as a prediction of his dynamic theory. It appears that, following Adam Smith, Marx accepted that there was a well-established historical trend for the rate of profits to fall, which called for an explanation. For example, he begins Chapter 14 (Volume III) by declaring:

> If we consider the enormous development in the productive powers of social labour over the last thirty years [i.e. 1835–65] alone, compared with all earlier periods, and particularly if we consider the enormous mass of fixed capital involvement in the overall process of social production quite apart from machinery proper, then instead of the problem that occupied previous economists, the problem of explaining the fall in the profit rate, we have the opposite problem of explaining why this fall is not greater or faster (Marx 1991: 339).

If we accept that Marx treats the fall in the rate of profits as an empirical trend requiring an explanation, then given his formula for the rate of profits, it was clear to him that the variables have to move in such a way that they bring about the trend. He provides two separate explanations but intertwines them in a highly confusing manner. One explanation is more like a historical description of capitalist competition leading to centralisation and concentration of capital; and the other is supposedly a theoretical explanation with its accompanying logical necessity or prediction.

On the theoretical side, Marx argues that due to competitive pressures every capitalist is forced to innovate so that he can reduce his cost of production and undercut his competitors. In the beginning the innovators reap higher than the prevailing average rate of profits; however, as new and more productive technology is adopted by most of the capitalists, the new level of productivity becomes 'socially necessary' and the earlier innovators lose their higher-than-average rate of profits. The crucial point that Marx makes here is that when the dust settles, the average rate of profits in the system falls because the technical change is of such a nature that C/V rises, but S/V does not rise enough[11] to offset the downward pull on 'r' caused by the rise in C/V. Marx's point is that the nature of competition is contradictory — what is good for one, when adopted by all, turns out to be bad for all; but since every man is for himself, he continuously acts in his interest bringing woe to all, including himself:

> No capitalist voluntarily applies a new method of production, no matter how much more productive it may be or how much it might raise the rate of surplus-value, if it reduces the rate of profit. But every new method of production of this kind makes commodities cheaper. At first, therefore, he can sell them above their price of production, perhaps above their value. He pockets the difference between their costs of production and the market price of the other commodities, which are produced at higher production costs. This is possible because the average socially necessary labour-time required to produce these latter commodities is greater than the labour-time required with the new method of production. His production procedure is ahead of the social average. But competition makes the new

---

11 'The tendential fall in the rate of profit is linked with a tendential rise in the rate of surplus-value, i.e., in the level of exploitation of labour' (Marx 1991: 347).

procedure universal and subjects it to the general law. A fall in the profit rate then ensues — firstly perhaps in this sphere of production, and subsequently equalized with the others — a fall that is completely independent of the capitalists' will (Marx 1991: 373–74).

Most of the controversy over Marx's 'law of the tendential fall in the rate of profit' has concentrated on the theoretical explanation and we shall deal with it briefly in the section on 'Controversies about the Falling Rate of Profits'. The basic objection against Marx's reasoning is that if the new technique reduces the cost of production or, in other words, is more productive than the old one, then there is no reason to think that its adoption by all the capitalists in the sector would cause the average rate of profits in the system to fall. As a matter of fact, it should, in most cases, lead to a rise in the average rate of profits, given the real wages. The intuition behind this reasoning is simple. Let us assume that a technical change takes place in the production of a commodity that is either a constant capital or a wage good in the system. Let us also assume that the technical change does not introduce any new commodity but only represents a more efficient way of producing the same commodity with the same inputs. Based on Marx's labour theory of value the innovator can temporarily reap higher than the average rate of profits only if the value of the commodity produced by the new technique is lower than the value of the commodity produced by the old technique. This can happen only if the value of the constant capital used up by the new technique is smaller than the value of the constant capital used up by the old technique per unit of output, as the length of the working day and the value of the variable capitals remain the same for both the new and the old techniques (at this stage the values for both techniques are accounted by the old technique). Thus, when we compare the two systems with identical constant capital and total labour employment, we find that the total physical outputs in the system with only the new technique is higher than the total physical outputs in the system with only the old technique. This will necessarily increase the rate of profits as the physical ratio of surplus over total capital investments rises and the effects of price changes due to technical change are neutralised on both sides of the equations. (Technically, the ratio of Standard net product over the aggregate of Standard inputs will always be higher for the system with the new technique than the old one; and since the given real wages are part of the inputs in both the systems, those ratios are also the respective average rate of profits of the two systems — see the next chapter for an understanding of the Standard system and the Standard net product.) If, however, the technical change takes place in a luxury-good sector, then the fall in the price of the luxury good due to technical change cannot be neutralised by a fall in the price on the input side. In this case, it can be shown that the fall in the price would neutralise the rise in the physical output of the luxury good, leaving the rate of profits unchanged.

It should, however, be noted that Marx's incorrect result was perhaps also due to the requirement of his theory of surplus-value and profits. If the nature of technical change in the system is such that C/V is continuously rising, then the rate of profits could stay constant (or at least not tend to zero) if and only if S/V is continuously rising as well. This implies that with the passage of time the rate of surplus-value or the rate of exploitation tends to infinity. And this undercuts Marx's fundamental proposition that the sole source of profit is surplus-labour. As Dmitriev ([1904] 1974) shows, a productive economy with zero direct labour input can easily have positive prices and a finite rate of profits. Such a possibility could be denied only if one could argue that the rate of profits tends to zero when the relative importance of direct labour in the system tends to zero. The fact that the rate of profits need not tend to zero when C/V is continuously rising is another theoretical blow to the idea that only labour is productive and the secret of profit lies in the 'surplus-value'.

Marx, however, has another explanation for the tendency of the rate of profits to fall. He argues that modern techniques are characterised by increasing returns to scale, and in the competitive battles amongst the capitalists each one tries to amass greater and greater capital so that they can establish larger and larger capacities to produce at lower and lower costs to undercut their competitors. Of course, if these large firms produce at capacity levels then such technical changes would, in effect, represent an increase in productivity and therefore result in an increase in the rate of profits too, given wages. But there could be a twist in the tale. One can further argue that the large capacities are not always created to produce at such large levels permanently; rather, they are used as weapons to wipe out the smaller competitors: by producing at such large levels and driving down the prices, they ensure that the smaller fish do not survive for long. After the small competitors are vanquished, the large firms reduce their output and raise the prices, but retain their excess capacity to threaten potential competitors. In this scenario the change in technique is in effect less productive for the system as a whole but still rational and meaningful for individual capitalists as their control over a larger share of the market increases their total profit even though their rate of profit falls.

Thus the contradiction between the individual and the collective is located here — for the system as a whole it would be optimum to maximise the average rate of profits, but for the individual it is optimal to maximise his total profit and not necessarily its rate. The extent to which Marx was conscious of such an explanation is not clear, but as evident from the following quotation, it is obvious that he did come very close to formulating it:

> We have seen how it is that the same reasons that produce a tendential fall in the general rate of profit also bring about an accelerated accumulation of capital and hence a growth in the absolute magnitude or total mass of the surplus labour (surplus-value, profit) appropriated by it. Just as everything is expressed upside down in competition, and hence in the consciousness of its agents, so too is this law — I mean this inner and necessary connection between two apparently contradictory phenomena. It is evident that, on the figures given above, a capitalist controlling a large capital will make more profit in absolute terms than a smaller capitalist making apparently high profits. The most superficial examination of competition also shows that, under certain conditions, if the bigger capitalist wants to make more room for himself on the market and expel the smaller capitalists, as in times of crisis, he makes practical use of this advantage and deliberately lowers his profit rate in order to drive the smaller ones from the field (Marx 1991: 331).

But then it cannot be denied that this will in turn affect the 'law of value' by affecting the assumption of free competition. Thus the natural tendency of capitalism is to grow in a manner that negates the 'law of value'. Marx was well aware of this problem as he noted that natural monopolies such as large investments in railways, etc., as well as major joint-stock companies 'simply yield interest ... These do not therefore enter into the equalization of the general rate of profit, since they yield a profit rate less than the average' (ibid.: 347–48). However, he fell short of providing any guidelines as to how, in such situations, could prices and profits be accounted for on the basis of labour-value accounting.

Theory of Ground-Rent

Marx's theory of ground-rent is amongst his least discussed theories. His theory of rent is effectively an attempt to fuse Ricardo's theory of rent with that of Adam Smith's. He agrees with Ricardo as far as his theory of differential rent goes:

> The following statement of Ricardo's is completely correct: 'Rent (i.e. differential rent; he assumes that there is no other rent in existence besides this) is always the difference between the produce obtained by the employment of two equal quantities of capital and labour.' He should have added 'on equal quantities of land', in as much as he is dealing with ground-rent and not with surplus profit in general (ibid.: 788).

However, he disagrees with Ricardo's position that there cannot be any rent on marginal land. He argues that even marginal land usually pays positive rent, which he calls 'absolute ground-rent'. Here he draws from Adam Smith's theory of rent based on rent as part of monopoly price rather than his theory of rent based on high productivity of land that produces food:

> Smith stresses very strongly, that it is landed property, the landlord who as *landlord* 'demands the rent'. [Regarded] as a mere effluence of *landed property*, rent is *monopoly price*, this is perfectly correct, since it is only the intervention of landed property which enables the product to be sold for more than the cost-price, to be sold at its value (Marx 1968: 343).

Marx again builds his argument on the basis of his incorrect theory of prices of production defined by $[(c_i + v_i)\{1 + S/(C + V)\}]$. He argues that historically the manufacturing and agricultural sectors have grown in such a way that it is an empirical fact that the organic composition of capital in the agricultural sector is lower than the organic composition of capital in the manufacturing sector. Now, if there were no landed property, the capitalist competition would ensure that the prices of production of the agricultural goods would be below their values and the prices of production of the manufactured goods would be higher than their values. Marx's contention is that the difference between the value of the agricultural good and its price of production creates the possibility for the landed property to demand a rent on marginal land such that it raises the price of the agricultural good higher than what it would be if there was no rent. In effect, a part of the surplus-value produced in the agricultural sector is prevented from flowing to the manufacturing sector through price and the profit equalisation mechanism and is appropriated by the landlords as monopoly profit over and above the average rate of profit on capital:

> But whether this absolute rent is equal to the whole extra value over and above the price of production, or only to a part of this, agricultural products are always sold at the monopoly price, not because their price stands above their value but above their price of production. Their monopoly consists in this, that their value is not levelled down to their price of production as it is with other industrial products whose value stand above the general price of production. ... It finally follows that in this case it is not the rise in the product's price that is the cause of the rent but rather the rent that is the cause of the rise in price. ... If the average composition of agricultural capital were the same as that of the average social capital, or even higher than this, the result would be the disappearance of absolute rent in the sense developed above, namely a rent that is different from both differential rent and from rent depending on an actual monopoly price (Marx 1991: 897, 899).

This establishes a sharp theoretical dichotomy between the industrial and the agricultural sector in Marx's reasoning. Though capital is affected by competition and competitive profits everywhere, it is the capital invested and the surplus-value produced in the industrial sector alone that determines the average rate of profits, with the capital invested and the surplus-value produced in the agricultural sector playing a purely passive role. Leaving aside the problems with reasoning in terms of the values and prices of production, there still remains some serious problems with Marx's reasoning, e.g., he yet again reasons as if commodities actually exchange in proportion to their values and then the competitive mechanism enters to establish the prices of production, and in this process the landlords, due to their monopoly over land, are somehow able to maintain the prices of production of agricultural goods in proportion to their values. But, of course, there is no basis to think that the transformation of values to prices of production occurs in historical time; and even if one accepts this as a working hypothesis, it is not clear why the landlords were unable to demand absolute ground-rent when the commodities were exchanging in proportion to their values. The competitive mechanism or the equalisation of the rate of profits does not increase the power of the landlords vis-a-vis the capitalists in any respect. If the landlords are able to raise the price of agricultural goods above their prices of production when the organic composition of capital in the agricultural sector is lower than that in the industrial sector, then they should be able to do so even when the organic composition of capital is equal to or even higher than that in the industrial sector. Marx needed to establish that the landlords' power vis-a-vis the capitalists is related to the organic composition of capital in both the agricultural and industrial sectors. But he has not done so, and I cannot think of any reason to make such connection.[12]

As far as the long-term trend of ground-rent is concerned, Marx, surprisingly, does not say anything. It is, however, clear from his theory of ground-rent that if the industrial rate of profit is falling, then the absolute ground-rent in agriculture must proportionately be rising.

On Wages

As mentioned earlier, Marx maintains that the value of labour-power is given by the labour-time needed to reproduce the labourer's normal mental and physical capabilities to work. This, however, also needs to take into account the continuous withdrawal of labour-power from the market due to wear and tear and death. In other words, the value of the labour-power must ensure a stable or positive rate of population growth:

> The owner of labour-power is mortal. If then his appearance in the market is to be continuous, and the continuous transformation of money into capital assumes this, the seller of labour-power must perpetuate himself 'in the way that every living individual perpetuates himself, by procreation' [Petty]. The labour-power withdrawn from the market by wear and tear, and by death, must be continually replaced by, at the very least, an equal amount of fresh labour-power. Hence the sum of means of subsistence necessary for the production of labour-power must include the means necessary for the worker's replacements, i.e., his children, in order that this race of peculiar commodity-owners may perpetuate its presence on the market (Marx 1977: 275).

As with Adam Smith and Ricardo, Marx's main concern regarding wages is also with its short- and long-term trends. First of all, Marx takes into account the cyclical nature of capitalist accumulation in the short run. Given the stylised fact of the decennial cycle of boom

---

12 Also see Howard and King (1985) and Fine (1979).

and bust, Marx argues that the system *requires*, on an average, some surplus population (the reserve army of labour) so that when the system needed to expand from the bottom of the cyclical phase, it has the required labour force available to do that. Thus in the context of a cyclical upswing, Marx believed that neither the introduction of labour-saving technical changes nor the population mechanism could be relied upon as the time period was too short:

> It would be utterly absurd, ..., to lay down a law according to which the movement of capital depended simply on the movement of the population. Yet this is the dogma of the economists. Higher wages stimulate the working population to more rapid multiplication, and this goes on until the labour-market becomes over supplied, and hence capital becomes insufficient in relation to the supply of labour. Wages fall, and now we have the obverse side of the medal. ... This would indeed be a beautiful form of motion for developed capitalist production! Before the rise in wages could produce any positive increase of the population really fit for work, the deadline would long since have passed within which the industrial campaign would have to have been carried through, and the battle fought to a conclusive finish (Marx 1977: 790–91).

Within the framework of a business cycle, the real wages of the workers are supposed to rise and fall along with the rise and fall in the rate of capital accumulation. The argument is that given a supply of labour, a rising accumulation of capital leads to a rising demand for labour, which in turn leads to rising wages. However, rising wages cause the rate of profits to fall and thus a fall in the rate of capital accumulation, bringing about a falling demand for labour and thus falling wages:

> It is these absolute movements of the accumulation of capital which are reflected as relative movements of the mass of exploitable labour-power, or rather its price, to be in excess. It is these absolute movements of the accumulation of capital which are reflected as relative movements of the mass of exploitable labour-power, and therefore seem produced by the latter's own independent movement. To put it mathematically: the rate of accumulation is the independent, not the dependent variable; the rate of wages is the dependent, not the independent variable. ... the relation between capital, accumulation and the rate of wages is nothing other than the relation between

the unpaid labour which has been transformed into capital and the additional paid labour necessary to set in motion this additional capital. It is therefore in no way a relation between two magnitudes which are mutually independent, i.e., between the magnitude of capital and the numbers of working population; it is rather, at bottom, only the relation between the unpaid and the paid labour of the same working population. If the quantity of unpaid labour supplied by the working class and accumulated by the capitalist class increases so rapidly that its transformation into capital requires an extraordinary addition of paid labour, then wages rise and, all other circumstances remaining equal, the unpaid labour diminishes in proportion. But as soon as this diminution touches the point at which the surplus labour that nourishes capital is no longer supplied in normal quantity, a reaction sets in: a smaller part of revenue is capitalized, accumulation slows down, and the rising movement of wages comes up against an obstacle. The rise of wages is therefore confined within limits that not only leave intact the foundations of the capitalist system, but also secure its reproduction on an increasing scale (Marx 1977: 770–71).

The question is: how, on an average, is a reserve army of labour created and maintained? The answer to this question lies in the analysis of accumulation in the long run. Marx assumes a positive rate of population growth as exogenously given, which he considers 'natural'. His position is that, in the long run, the rate of growth of capital accumulation is greater than the given natural rate of population growth: 'Capitalist production can by no means content itself with the quantity of disposable labour-power which the natural increase of population yields' (ibid.: 788). Thus there is a problem of excess demand for labour to be solved. According to Marx, the system solves this problem by regularly introducing labour-saving technical changes. His contention is that the rate of population growth plus the rate at which labourers are regularly thrown out of their jobs due to technical changes is larger than the rate of increase in the demand for labour in the long run. Thus, not only is a reserve army of labour created by labour-saving technical changes, but in the long run there is a tendency for the size of the reserve army of labour to grow in proportion to the size of the employed labour force:

This accelerated relative diminution of the variable component, which accompanies the accelerated increase of the total capital and moves more rapidly than this increase, takes the inverse form, at the other pole, of an apparently absolute increase in the working population, an increase which always moves more rapidly than that of the variable capital or the means of employment. But in fact it is capitalist accumulation itself that constantly produces, and produces indeed in direct relation with its own energy and extent, a relatively redundant working population, i.e., a population which is superfluous to capital's average requirements for its own valorization, and is therefore a surplus population (Marx 1977: 782).

It is the increase in the proportion of the size of the reserve army of labour in relation to the size of the employed labour force that leads to the 'increasing misery' of the working class. This thesis of 'increasing misery' has two dimensions: First of all, the very rise in the proportion of the unemployed compared to the employed part of the total working class must increase the misery of the working class as a whole, as the living conditions of unemployed workers are miserable when compared to those employed workers. On the other hand, the same phenomenon reduces the bargaining strength of the employed working class, which leads to overwork and a long-term trend for real wages to fall, if the wages had started from a sufficiently higher than the subsistence level:

> If the means of production, as they increase in extent and effective power, become to a lesser extent means for employing workers, this relation is itself in turn modified by the fact that in proportion as the productivity of labour increases, capital increases its supply of labour more quickly than its demand for workers. The over-work of the employed part of the working class swells the ranks of the reserve, while, conversely, the greater pressure that the reserve by its competition exerts on the employed workers forces them to submit to over-work and subjects them to the dictates of capital. The condemnation of one part of the working class to enforce idleness by the over-work of the other part, and *vice versa*, becomes a means of enriching the individual capitalist, and accelerates at the same time the production of the industrial reserve army on a scale corresponding with the progress of social accumulation (ibid.: 789–80).

Taking them as a whole, the general movements of wages are exclusively regulated by the expansion and contraction of the industrial reserve army, and this in turn corresponds to the periodic alternations of the industrial cycle. They are not therefore determined by the variations of the absolute numbers of working population, but by the varying proportions in which the working class is divided into an active army and a reserve army, by the increase or the diminution of the relative amount of the surplus population, by the extent to which it is alternately absorbed and set free (Marx 1977: 790).

A Comment on the Nature of Marx's Reasoning

In the last two chapters we have seen that both Adam Smith and Ricardo rooted some essential aspects of the dynamics of capitalism in 'nature'. For example, the productivity of land (or surplus as a gift of nature) and population dynamics played important roles in explaining the nature and the dynamics of capitalism in Adam Smith; and it was the falling productivity of land along with the Malthusian population dynamics that played an important role in Ricardo's understanding of the system. Marx, however, seems to be particular about severing all such ties of capitalism with nature. In his framework, capitalism is a self-sufficient historical system with its own set of dynamics. He takes pains to remove all connections with nature; for example, the trends in regard to fall in the rate of profit as well as the 'increasing misery' of the working class do not depend on either the natural limit to growth or falling productivity of land or population dynamics, but are explained in terms of the specific logic of capitalist dynamics. The capitalist nature of rent as absolute ground-rent is also explained on the basis of specific capitalist logic rather than 'nature' as such. In this context, the character of Marx's arguments is highly *functional*. However, when it comes to the explanation of prices and commodity relations in capitalism, Marx's arguments become *essentialist*. He seems to be convinced that there is an 'essence' of the apparent price-relation, which must be discovered by digging deep. It is curious that Marx did not think of applying the same *functional* approach to prices that he used for the analysis of the capitalist system as a whole. Had he done so, he would have not fallen into the abyss of the 'labour theory of value'.

Part II
Comments on Some Other Readings

Most critiques of Marx's economic theory have concentrated on his transformation of values to prices of production and the theory of the falling rate of profits. In this section, I will first discuss a few important criticisms and interpretations of Marx's theory of value presented in

Volume I of *Capital*, and then take up the controversies on the transformation problem, his theory of the falling rate of profits and his
theory of wages respectively.

In 1884, two independently written, powerful critical reviews of
Volume I of *Capital* appeared almost simultaneously. One, by P.H.
Wicksteed, was published in a socialist journal *TO-Day*, and the
other, by Eugen von Böhm-Bawerk, appeared in Böhm-Bawerk's first
edition of *Capital and Interest*. Both reviewers recognised that Marx's
labour theory of value as presented in *Capital*, Volume I, was in 'contradiction with reality', which resulted from 'the law of equal profits'
(Böhm-Bawerk [1884] 1959); and that Marx was perfectly aware

> [t]hat his view of the origin of all 'surplus value' appears to
> stand in glaring contradiction to experience and to the his-
> torical order in which the successive forms of capital have
> been evolved, and that this apparent contradiction can only
> be removed by a long chain of reasoning which is *not* given
> in the published volume of *Das Kapital*, though it seems to be
> promised in a future portion of the work. (Wicksteed [1884]
> 1938: 707, f.n. 1).

However, even though there are overlaps in the arguments of the two
reviewers, there is a significant difference in their focus.

Wicksteed [1884] (1938) summarises Marx's arguments in three
theses: (*i*) the exchange value of a commodity is determined by the
amount of labour needed on the average to produce it; (*ii*) theoretically we assume that normally commodities are bought and sold at
their values; and (*iii*) labour-power is a commodity subject to the same
laws and conditions of value and exchange as other commodities. He
aims his attack specifically on theses (*i*) and (*iii*).

Against thesis (*i*), Wicksteed argues that it was wrong of Marx to
have distilled 'abstract labour' as the only common element in an
exchange-relationship of commodities. He points out that Marx himself acknowledges that 'the labour does not count unless it is useful',
and goes on to argue that:

> Simple and obvious as this seems, it in reality surrenders the
> whole of the previous analysis, for it is only useful labour that
> counts, then in stripping the wares [commodities] of all the
> specific properties conferred upon them by specific kinds of
> useful work, we must not be supposed to have stripped them
> of the abstract utility, conferred upon them by specific kinds of

useful work, we must not be supposed to have stripped them of the abstract utility, conferred upon them by abstractly useful work. If only useful labour counts, then when the wares are reduced to mere indifferent products of such labour in the abstract, they are still *useful* in the abstract, and therefore, it is not true that 'nothing remains to them but the one attribute of being products of labour', for the attribute of being useful also remains to them. In this all wares are alike ([1884] 1938: 712).

Here we notice an apparent conflation of the idea of use-value of a commodity with the idea of utility. We find this conflation in Böhm-Bawerk's criticism of Marx as well, and we will make a few comments in this regard during our discussion of Böhm-Bawerk. Wicksteed, however, goes on to argue that the idea that 'abstract usefulness' cannot be quantitatively measured or counted is simply incorrect, as the Jevonsian revolution in theory has shown that, given the 'law of indifference' and the 'law of the variation of utility', a robust quantitative theory of value can be developed on the basis of 'abstract utility'. It is beyond the scope of this chapter to venture into a critique of Jevons's theory of value except to note that the idea of pain or disutility has never managed to get off the ground in explaining cost or supply functions. In any case, what is interesting about Wicksteed's criticism of thesis (*i*) is that though he believes that Marx's thesis is incorrect, he simply does not bother to disprove it. Instead, he provides an alternative theory of value and argues that it was illegitimate for Marx to ignore it in the first place, and second, the alternative theory of value was more general as it 'is equally applicable to things that can, and things that can not, be multiplied by labour,.' (ibid.: 722).

Wicksteed's attack on thesis (*iii*) is straightforward. If labour-power is supposed to be a commodity and its equilibrium price is supposed to be the subsistence wage, then there has to be some mechanism that increases labour supply whenever wages are higher than the subsistence wage. But since Marx had rejected the Malthusian theory of population and labourers were not produced in a capitalistic manner, Marx had no recourse to argue that the value of labour-power was equal to the labour-time needed to reproduce the labour-power:

But if there is any commodity C, to the production of which a man who has labour at his disposal can *not* direct that labour at his will, then there is no reason whatever to suppose that the value of C will stand in any relation to the amount of labour which it contains, for its value is determined by its utility at the margin of supply, and by hypothesis it is out of the power of labour to raise or lower that margin.

Now this is the case with labour-force in every country in which the labourer is not personally a slave. If I have obtained by purchase or otherwise the right to apply a certain amount of labour to any purpose I choose, I cannot direct it at my option to the production of hats (for instance) *or to the production of labour-force*, unless I live in a country where slave-breeding is possible; and, therefore, there is no economic law the action of which will bring the value of labour-force, and the value of other commodities, into the ratio of the amounts of labour respectively embodied in them (Wicksteed [1884] 1938: 723).

We have, however, argued earlier that Marx uses functional reasoning to argue that the system must maintain a 'reserve army of labour' through labour-saving technical changes. It is the structural existence of the 'reserve army of labour' that keeps the rise in real wages in check so that the existence of surplus-value itself is not threatened. Wicksteed is well aware of this argument and considers it to be 'worthy of most earnest attention', but deems it to be *logically* separate from Marx's intended 'deeper cause' of labour-power being a commodity and by the virtue of this, and this only, its value must be determined by the subsistence wages. This is the basis on which he argues that:

It appears to me, therefore, that Marx has failed to indicate any immanent law of capitalistic production by which a man who purchases labour-force at its value will extract from its consumption a surplus value. We are simply thrown back upon the fact that a man can purchase (not produce) as much labour-force as he likes at the price of bare subsistence. But this fact is the problem we are to investigate, not the solution to the problem (Wicksteed [1884] 1938: 723).

If we keep strictly to the analysis of the first chapter only, then Wicksteed's judgement has merit; but if we take the whole book into account it becomes clear that the existence of subsistence wage is not rooted in the notion of labour-power being a commodity but rather in the dynamics of the system as a whole. Elsewhere I have argued that:

Marx seems to argue that the notion that labor-power is a commodity is an *ideological*, and not the *real*, aspect of capitalism. The capital-labor relation *appears* to be a commodity exchange-relation, and this appearance is the basis of the legitimation (both ideological and juridical) of the exploitative class-relation. His analysis reveals that this appearance is deceptive and outright false (Sinha 1996: 214).

As a matter of fact, in 'Results', which was intended to be Chapter VI of *Capital*, Volume I, but for unknown reasons was left out of the final version, we find several passages where Marx explicitly denies the status of labour-power to be conceptually equivalent to a 'commodity'. For example:

> This destroys the last vestiges of the *illusion*, so typical of the relationship when considered superficially, that in the circulation process, in the market place, two equally matched *commodity owners* confront each other, and that they, like all other *commodity owners,* are distinguishable only by the material content of their goods, by the specific use-value of the goods they desire to sell each other. Or in other words, the *original* relations remain intact, but survives only as the *illusory* reflection of the capitalist relation underlying it (Marx 1977: 1062–63).
>
> However, the sale and purchase of labour-power, as the constant result of the capitalist process of production, implies that the worker must constantly *buy back* a portion of his own produce in exchange for his living labour. This *dispels* the illusion that we are concerned here merely with *relations between commodity owners* (ibid.: 1063).
>
> ... there are those who regard this superficial relation, this *essential formality*, this *deceptive appearance* of capitalist relations as its true essence. They therefore imagine that they can give a true account of those relations by classifying both workers and capitalists as *commodity owners*. They thereby gloss over the essential nature of the relationship, extinguishing its *differentia specifica* (Marx 1977: 1064).

It could very well be that these statements, which stand in such sharp contradiction to the statements in Chapter 1, were the reason why Marx decided to suppress them. But it is clear that he considered them to be the *result* of the analysis of capitalist relation and not a presupposition. Furthermore, in the *Theories of Surplus Value*, which was supposed to become the third volume of *Capital* according to his scheme and which was written during 1861–63, we find that Marx refers to exchange between capital and the labourer as a 'pseudo-exchange' (Marx [1905–10] 1971: 15).

After the publication of the third volume of *Capital* in 1894, Eugen von Böhm-Bawerk renewed his 1884 critical assessment of Marx in a long and comprehensive book-length critique entitled *Karl Marx and the Close of His System* ([1896] 1949). This famous critique of Marx is among the best and most forceful to date. In his book, Böhm-Bawerk concentrates on the reasoning Marx applied in deducing labour-values as the essence of exchange-values. He points out that Marx's reasoning that exchange of commodities represents a relation of 'equality' is not only 'very old fashioned' but also 'a wrong idea'. But he does not dwell upon it; rather he concentrates his fire on the deduction of *labour* as the 'common factor' in the equation of the commodity exchange-relation. His first line of attack is that Marx illegitimately narrows the field of exchange-values to only 'commodities', i.e., products of labour. This is a serious and legitimate criticism against Marx's procedure, which would not apply to Smith or Ricardo. Recall that Marx begins with a supposed exchange-relation such as '1 quarter of corn = x cwt of iron' and asks the question: what is the common element in the two commodities? Since the procedure is to deduce the common element from a given exchange-relation, the exchange-relations that must be taken into consideration ought to be general in nature and not particular. Böhm-Bawerk argues that:

Now it stands to reason that if exchange really means an equalisation, which assumes the existence of a 'common factor of the same amount,' this common factor must be sought and found in every species of goods which is brought into exchange, not only in products of labour but also in gifts of nature, such as the soil, wood in trees, water power, coal-beds, stone quarries, petroleum springs, mineral water, gold mines, &c. To exclude the exchangeable goods which are not products of labour in the search for the common factor which lies at the root of exchange value is, under the circumstances, a great error of method. It is just as though a natural philosopher, desiring to discover a property common to all bodies — weight, for instance — were to shift the properties of a single group of bodies — transparent bodies, for instance — and after passing review all the properties common to transparent bodies were to declare that transparency must be the cause of weight, for the sole reason that he could demonstrate that it could not be caused by ally of the other properties (Böhm-Bawerk [1896] 1949: 70–71).

The point to note here is that though it was legitimate for Marx to reduce his field of inquiry about values and price determination to only commodities to begin with, it was not legitimate for him to *deduce* labour as the common element from the exchange-relation in general. As a matter of fact, the problem lies squarely in the representation of exchange as a relation of *equality*, such as '1 quarter of corn = x cwt of iron'. If we substitute one-quarter of corn with one acre of land in the above equation, we immediately see that labour cannot be the common element in the equation and it is most likely that no common element exists in this relation.

His second line of attack is that even if we grant Marx his narrow frame of reference, it was still illegitimate for him to have drawn the conclusion that 'use-value' could be discarded as being the common element in the exchange-relation of commodities. Böhm-Bawerk argued that if the use-values of commodities are associated with the physical properties of commodities and cannot be compared quantitatively, then the same applies to the concrete labours that produce the use-values and the commodities. If labour can be 'abstracted' from its concrete manifestations, then why can't particular use-values be 'abstracted' to general *usefulness*?

> Is it possible to state more clearly or more emphatically that for an exchange relation not only any one value in use, but also any one kind of labour or product of labour is worth exactly as much as any other, if only it is present in proper proportion? Or, in other words, that exactly the same evidence on which Marx formulated his verdict of exclusion against the value in use holds good with regard to labour: Labour and value in use have a qualitative side and a quantitative side. As the value in use is different qualitatively as table, house, or yarn, so is labour as carpentry, masonry, or spinning. And just as one can compare different kinds of labour according to their quantity, so one can compare values in use of different kinds according to the same amount of the value in use. It is quite impossible to understand why the very same evidence should result in the one competitor being excluded and the other getting crown and the prize (Böhm-Bawerk [1896] 1949: 76–77).

Though there is some merit in Böhm-Bawerk's rhetoric, his basic argument that 'one can compare values in use of different kinds according to the same amount of the value in use' does not make sense. As we have seen, Marx's 'abstract labour' can be seen as simple unskilled labour of any concrete persuasion at any given historical juncture and measured on the scale of time. It is, however, hard to visualise what an 'abstract value in use' would look like and how it could be measured. For Marx, the use-value of a commodity is its physical property. For example, the use-value of a chair is that one can sit on it or at times use it to stand on, say, to hammer a nail at a high point in a wall, or put it in a room for its aesthetic appeal, etc. But none of the uses that a chair can be put to can be quantified in any way or compared in a quantitative manner with some other use-value such as a computer. The point to note is that use-value in Marx's theory (and Smith's and Ricardo's as well) does not stand for the *utility* of the commodity, which could be quantified or measured in some indirect manner. Utility, however, is a state of human subjectivity and not a property of the physical good itself. Thus, it was quite legitimate for Marx to conclude that the use-value aspect of the commodity could not explain the quantitative relations between commodities.[13]

Böhm-Bawerk, however, has further complaints against Marx's procedure. He argues that there are many other properties of commodities that could be derived as the common element in the quantitative

---

13 Pareto ([1893] 1987) understands this distinction but then chides Marx for not relating the 'use-value' of commodities to the notion of 'utility': « *La valeur d'usage* parait etre pour K. Marx, comme pour les economistes, "la propriete de satisfaire un desir ou de servir un dessein » [Stuart Mill, *Principes d'Economie Politique*] ; ce serait donc au fond l'utilite des nouvelles doctrines economiques. K. Marx tombe dans l'erreur qui a ete, et qui est celle de beaucoup d'economistes, de ne pas faire assez d'attention a ce que la *valeur d'usage* n'est pas une propriete inherente a chaque marchandise, comme serait la composition chimique, le poids specifique, etc. ; mais est au contraire un simple rapport de convenance entre une marchandise et un homme, ou des homme. » (Pareto 1987: 39). ['The use-value seems to be for K. Marx, as for economists, "the property to satisfy a desire or to serve a purpose"; it would be finally what the new doctrines of economics call "utility". K. Marx makes the mistake, which many economists have made, not to pay enough attention to the fact that the use-value is not a specific property of each good, as would be the chemical composition, the weight, etc., but is a simple relationship of convenience between a good and a man or some men.']. Faccarello (1997) has pointed out that Hegel in his *Philosophy of Rights* had also argued that exchange must represent equality. But he had resolved it in favour of *abstract need*. Marx's complete silence on the Hegelian notion of abstract need in this context suggests that he did make a conceptual distinction between the subjective notions such as needs or utility on the one hand, and use-value on the other.

relations between commodities, but Marx simply did not take them into account:

> The second step in the argument is still worse: 'If the use value of commodities be disregarded' — these are Marx's words — 'there remains in them *only one other property, that of being products of labour.*' Is it so? ... Is there only one other property? Is not the property of being scarce in proportion to demand also common to all exchangeable goods? Or that they are the subjects of demand and supply? Or that they are appropriated? Or that they are natural products? For that they are products of nature, just as they are products of labour, no one asserts more plainly than Marx himself, when he declares in one place that 'commodities are combinations of two elements, natural material and labour'. Or is not the property that they cause expense to their producers — a property to which Marx draws attention in the third volume — common to exchangeable goods? (Böhm-Bawerk [1896] 1949: 75).

Again, though there is some merit in the rhetoric, the list presented in the passage just quoted does not stand close scrutiny, except for one item in it. Is 'scarcity' a common element of commodities? Now 'scarcity' is not a property of a commodity but rather a property of the relation of human desire for a commodity and its supply. As a matter of fact, whether a commodity is 'scarce' or not can only be determined after the determination of prices and not *a priori*. Walras (1954 [1874]) had made the mistake of defining commodities as 'scarce' *a priori* and therefore, he assumed positive prices for all the commodities in his general equilibrium equations. Many years later, Wald ([1936] 1951) pointed out that the solutions of Walras's general equilibrium equations cannot rule out 'excess supply' of some and hence zero prices for those commodities. Thus the property of a commodity to be 'scarce' is an ex-post and not an ex-ante property. In other words, it is the price of a commodity that determines whether it is 'scarce' or not and not the other way round. Therefore, 'scarcity' cannot be the property that explains positive prices. As far as 'demand and supply' is concerned, it is true that all commodities are subject to the forces of demand and supply — Marx's 'law of value' amounts to admitting that. The question, however, is: what does it mean to say, 'the two commodities have equal demand and supply'? Given that the units of two commodities are usually incommensurable, and we have no means of making them commensurable as we have in the case of concrete labour, the question is absurd to begin with. Again, it is true that commodities are 'appropriated', but appropriation is not a quantifiable property; and though the role of nature in production is explicitly taken into account by Marx in the context of the production of use-value, again, it cannot be quantified. Marx's category of 'use-value' can be seen as a set of all the essential properties of commodities that cannot be quantified or compared in a quantitative manner. However, Böhm-Bawerk's last point cannot be dismissed lightly. It can be easily argued, as Marx in Volume III of *Capital* does, that in an exchange-relation the 'costs' (including the rate of profits) of producing the two commodities are equal. In this case, one will then need to investigate how cost could be measured, given that measuring cost by labour-expenditure is not necessarily the right way to measure cost. But this, of course, brings us back to the problem of transforming values to prices of production.

Böhm-Bawerk's next line of attack aims at Marx's procedure of reducing skilled labour to simple unskilled labour. He presents three fundamental criticisms in this regard. First of all, he argues that the procedure reveals the problem of incommensurability of labour. He points out that Marx conceptually confuses the idea of 'counts as' with the idea of 'to be'. For example, the idea of abstract labour implies that all kinds of labour can be reduced to a homogeneous mass in the way ice, steam and water can be reduced to H_2O molecules or all matter can be reduced to atoms (these are my examples and not Böhm-Bawerk's). In this case, the reduction implies that at a certain level they are the same thing. Such a reduction, however, is not possible with skilled and unskilled labour; for example, in the case of an exchange between a sculptor's one day of labour and a stone-breaker's five days of labour, Böhm-Bawerk argues that 'in sculpture there is no "unskilled labour" at all embodied' and thus there is no basis for equating it with unskilled labour. The idea that one day's labour of a sculptor *counts* as five days' labour of a stone-breaker is not the same thing as one day's labour of a sculptor *being* equal to five days' labour of a stone-breaker.

Second, Böhm-Bawerk points out the circularity in Marx's argument when the latter claims that the reduction of skilled labour to simple labour is made by 'a social process beyond the control of the producers':

> Under these circumstances what is the meaning of the appeal to 'value' and 'the social process' as the determining factors of the standard of reduction. Apart from everything else it simply means that Marx is arguing in a complete circle. The real subject of inquiry is the exchange relations of commodities: why, for

instance, a statuette which has cost a sculptor one day's labour should exchange for a cart of stones which has cost a stone-breaker five days' labour, and not for a larger or smaller quantity of stones, in the breaking of which ten or three days' labour have been expended. How does Marx explain this? He says the exchange relation is this, and no other — because one day of sculptor's work is reducible exactly to five days of unskilled work. And why is it reducible to exactly five days? Because experience shows that it is so reduced by a social process. And what is this social process? The same process that has to be explained, that very process by means of which the product of one day of sculptor's labour has been made equal to the value of the product of five days of common labour. But if as a matter of fact it were exchanged regularly against the product of three days of simple labour, Marx would equally bid us accept the rate of reduction of 1:3 as the one derived from experience, and would found upon it and explain by it the assertion that a statuette must be equal in exchange to the product of exactly three days of a stone-breaker's work — not more and not less. In short, it is clear that we shall never learn in this way the actual reasons why products of different kinds of work should be exchanged in this or that proportion. They exchange in this way, Marx tells us, though in slightly different words, because, according to experience, they do exchange in this way! (Böhm-Bawerk [1896] 1949: 83–84).

However, as we have argued earlier, Marx had quickly abandoned the idea of deriving the quantity of *abstract labour* from the exchange-relations of commodities and thus his attempt of reducing skilled labour to simple labour in this manner, which was built on the same principle, had to be abandoned with it. What survived in Marx's theory in this regard is the idea that skill itself could be treated as a produced commodity and its 'labour-value' could be calculated in the same manner as for any other commodity, and the multiplication factor of skilled labour could be calculated as depreciation of this commodity over the average life span of the worker. Böhm-Bawerk recognises this, but not as an alternative interpretation present in Marx's *Capital* itself; rather, he sees it as an argument advanced by Marx's successors (*epigoni*) after having realised the circularity in Marx's reasoning. He, however, rejects this argument too lightly:

'It is no fiction but a fact,' says Grabski, 'that an hour of skilled labour contains several hours of unskilled labour.' For 'in order to be consistent, we must also take into account the labour which was used in acquiring the skill.' I do not think it will need many words to show clearly the complete inadequacy also of this explanation. I have nothing to say against the view that to labour in actual operation should be added the quota due to the acquirement of the power of labour. But it is clear that the difference in value of skilled labour as opposed to unskilled labour could only then be explained by reference to this additional quota if the amount of the latter corresponded to the amount of that difference.

For instance, in the case we have given, there could only be actually five hours of unskilled labour in one hour of skilled labour, if four hours of preparatory labour went to every hour of skilled labour; or, reckoned in greater units, if out of fifty years of life which a sculptor devotes to the learning and practising of his profession, he spends forty years in educational work in order to do skilled work for ten years. But no one will maintain that such a proportion or anything approaching to it is actually found to exist (Böhm-Bawerk [1896] 1949: 84).

Although it would be interesting to check empirically the extent to which wage differentials between skilled and simple labour can be explained by the hypothesis of production of skill by labour, the argument put forward by Böhm-Bawerk is nevertheless quite weak. In calculating the labour input in producing a skill, one should not only take into account the labour-time spent by the person acquiring the skill but also the labour-time spent by the teachers, as well as the materials, etc., used up in the process of skill acquisition.

In the last section of Chapter 4, Böhm–Bawerk points out the contradiction between the first and the third volume of *Capital*. He argues that Marx's 'value' is defined as a centre of gravitation of market prices in the first volume, but in the third volume Marx defines another centre of gravitation for market prices, which by necessity is usually different from the first. This, according to him, introduces an irreconcilable contradiction in his theory:

Marx has told us himself, and we have carefully noted the passage, that commodities exchange approximately to their values only when a brisk competition exists. Thus he, at that time, appealed to competition as a factor which tends to push the prices of commodities towards their 'values'. And now we learn, on the contrary, that competition is a force which pushes the prices of commodities away from their values and on to their prices of production. These statements, moreover, are found in one and the same chapter — the tenth chapter, destined, it would seem, to an unhappy notoriety. Can they be reconciled? And, if Marx perhaps thought that he could find a reconciliation in the view that one proposition applied to primitive conditions and the other to developed modern society, must we not point out to him that in the first chapter of his work he did not deduce his theory that value was wholly labour from a *Robinsonade*, but from the conditions of society in which a 'capitalistic mode of production prevails' and the 'wealth' of which 'appears as an immense collection of commodities'? And does he not demand of us throughout his whole work that we should view the conditions of our modern society in the light of his theory of labour, and judge them by it? But when we ask where, according to his own statements, we are to seek in modern society for the region in which his law of value is in force, we ask in vain. For either there is no competition, in which case commodities do not at all exchange according to their values, says Marx; or competition exists, and precisely then, he states, they still less exchange according to their values, but according to their prices of production (Böhm-Bawerk [1896] 1949: 99).

Interestingly, Böhm-Bawerk does not notice the problem with either Marx's average rate of profits or the measure of capital investment by labour-values. Instead, he locates the technical problem with Marx's transformation procedure in the treatment of the value of variable capital. He argues, as Marx had admitted, that if the prices of production of the subsistence of the worker deviate from their value, then the variable part of capital will also deviate from its value, which is foreign to Marx's law of value (ibid.: 58ff.).[14]

In 1893 Vilfredo Pareto ([1893] 1987) wrote a long 'Introduction' to *Karl Marx Le Capital Extraits par Paul Lafargue*. He took this

14 A highly tangential response from the Marxist camp was published by Hilferding (1949) in 1904. Böhm-Bawerk, in his third edition of *Capital and Interest*, which was published in 1914, dismissed it in these terms: 'Since that time [the publication of *Zum Abschluss des Marschen Systems*] Hilferding has published an apologia by way of refutation, which appeared in Volume 1 (1904) of the *Marx-Studien*, but nothing in it has caused me to change my opinion in any respect' (Böhm-Bawerk 1959: 472).

opportunity to write a critique of Marx's *Capital*. Pareto repeats most of the points already made by Wicksteed and Böhm-Bawerk and spends a lot of time defending a 'market economy' over a 'socialist economy'. Here we will take up only one of his arguments, one that was not made by either Wicksteed or Böhm-Bawerk and which I think is original and amounts to a significant critique of Marx's dictum that the origin of profit lies solely in the exploitation of labour. Pareto argues that if commodities exchanged in proportion to their labour-values, as Marx contends, then the introduction of an efficient machine or progressive technical change would reduce the value of the commodity, leaving producers with no incentive to introduce such technical changes. He then correctly anticipates Marx's argument in Volume III that the commodities produced by new and more efficient machines must, at least for a short time, be sold above their values (or at the same value as the commodities produced by the older, 'socially necessary' techniques). Thus, in the short run, the entrepreneurs introducing new techniques would reap supernormal profits. Now, if there is continuous technical change in the system, which Marx assumes to be in the nature of capitalist competition and a requirement for the maintenance of the 'reserve army of labour', then there arises a permanent income category that cannot be accounted for by labour-time accounting:

Pourquoi un fabricant emploierait-il une machine que ne fait pas encore partie « des conditions sociales de la production » puisque cette machine « ne transfère *jamais* plus de valeur que son usure ne lui en fait perdre en moyenne » (168) (V. 148)? Les consommateurs seraient seuls intèressès à ce que des machines de plus en plus parfaites seraient seuls intèresses à ce que des machines de plus en plus parfaites Assent partie « des conditions sociales » de la production du fabricant.

Pour eviter cette difficultè, on pourrait peut-être supprimer le mot *jamais* dans la proposition de K. Marx que nous venons de citer, et entendre cette proposition dans le sens que ce n'est que quand les prix ont atteint un niveau stable d'equilibre que la machine ne transfère pas plus de valeur que son usure ne lui en fait perdre en moyenne. Mais les prix n'atteignant pas ce niveau stable immediatement après l'introduction d'une nouvelle machine, il y aurait une (*sic*) certain laps de temps pendant lequel la valeur transfèrèe serait plus grande que l'usure de la machine, c'est-à-dire pendant lequel le capital simple qu'elle represente produirait une certaine valeur, et c'est ce surplus de valeur qui servirait de prime au fabricant pour le pousser a employer la machine.

Malheureusement nous ne faisons de la sorte que sortir d'une difficulte pour tomber dans une autre; car nous ouvrons ainsi la porte aux considerations de plus-values que nous ovions ecartees pour pouvoir accepter la doctrine de Marx. Si le capital peut produire de la valeur d'echange pendant que les prix n'ont pas atteint leur point d'équilibre stable, il en peut produire toujours, car cet équilibre stable des prix est une pure abstraction, qui n'existe pas dans la nature. Ces prix, « comme l'exprime epigrammatiquement Coleridge, sont perpetuellement *trouvant* leur niveau, ce qui ressemble assez bien à une définition ironique d'une tempete [quoted from J.S. Mill]» (Pareto 1987: 54–55).[15]

Though Pareto does not clearly separate such entrepreneurial income from returns to capital in general, or from the notion of productivity of capital, it is plain that he foreshadows the idea that was later developed by Schumpeter ([1912] 1934) as an explanation for positive profits in a competitive capitalist economy. Meek, however, argues that 'Pareto's argument is academic as well as illogical' (Meek 1966: 206). According to Meek:

... an individual capitalist who introduces a new method which increases the productivity of labour in his establishment will

---

15 [Why would a manufacturer use a machine that is not yet part of 'the social conditions of production', since this machine 'never transfers more value than the average loss created by its being used'? Only the consumers would be interested in the fact that more and more perfect machines would be part of the 'social conditions' of the production of the manufacturer.

To avoid this difficulty, one could suppress the word *maybe* in Karl Marx's proposition that we have just quoted and understand that proposition in the sense that it is only when the prices have reached a stable level of equilibrium that the machine doesn't transfer more value than the average loss created by its being used. But as the prices don't reach that stable level immediately after the introduction of a new machine, there would be a certain gap of time during which the transferred value would be bigger than the cost of using the machine, that means during which the simple capital that it represents would produce a certain value and it is that surplus of value that would be an incentive for the manufacturer to use the machine.

Unfortunately we have just got out of one problem to fall in another one; we then give space to the considerations about surplus values that we had rejected to be able to accept Marx's doctrine. If the capital can produce some exchange value while the prices have not yet reached their stable point of equilibrium, then it can always produce some, because this stable equilibrium of prices is a pure abstraction that doesn't exist in nature. These prices, 'as Coleridge expresses it epigrammatically, perpetually *find* their level that is quite close to an ironic definition of a tempest' (J. Stuart Mill, *Logique*)].

be able, for a time, to sell his commodity above its individual value, thereby obtaining an extra surplus value. 'The exceptionally productive labour,' Marx writes, 'operates as intensified labour; it creates in equal periods of time greater value than average social labour of the same kind.' Eventually, however, when the new method of production has been generally applied in the industry, 'the difference between the individual value of the cheapened commodity and its social value' will disappear, and the extra surplus value received by the original innovator will be squeezed out (Meek 1996: 206–07).

Meek apparently fails to notice that he has made the same mistake as Pareto. Pareto had no legitimate reason to equate machine with 'capital'; similarly, there is no legitimate reason for Meek (and, for that matter, Marx) to equate the same simple labour working with new machines as other labour in the industry working with old machines with 'intensified' labour. The labours in both cases are exactly the same, are paid the same wages and are equally exploited. To describe the labour working with new machines as 'intensified' labour is nothing but a subterfuge. If the introduction of new and more efficient machines does not immediately reduce the 'socially necessary labour-time' in the industry, then it creates an income category that is not captured by labour-value accounting, and so long as we can maintain that such introduction of machines is almost continuous in one industry or the other in the system, we cannot deny that there is a permanent income category in the system that is not accounted for by labour-value accounting.

In 1942, Joan Robinson published a sympathetic essay on Marx's economics. The main thrust of her argument was that the concept of labour-value is devoid of operational meaning. In the 'Preface' to the second edition of the essay, she wrote:

Therefore, in spite of the offence which it has given, I cannot withdraw the remark at the end of Chapter III. The concept of *value* seems to me to be a remarkable example of how a metaphysical notion can inspire original thought, though in itself it is quite devoid of operational meaning (Robinson [1942] 1966: xi).

Now we know that at least in late 1927 Sraffa (PSP: D3/12/4/15) had also maintained that Marx's notion of labour-value is 'metaphysical': 'The typical case of Marx's metaphysics is his statement that "only human labour produces (causes) values", "values are embodied human energy (crystallised)". There is no doubt that he attached to it some metaphysical meaning' (quoted in Sinha 2006b: 84). It should, however, be noted that Sraffa does not use the word 'metaphysics' in either a Logical Positivist or Popperian sense, to which Joan Robinson's usage of the word appears to be close. In Sraffa's sense, metaphysics is 'what is absolutely necessary to make the theory living (*lebendig*), capable of assimilation and at all intelligible' (ibid.). Schumpeter also maintained that Marx's concept of value is metaphysical: 'But for Marx, the most metaphysical of theorists, the labor-quantity theory was no mere hypothesis about relative prices. The quantity of labor embodied in products did not merely "regulate" their value. It *was* (the "essence" or "substance" of) their value' (Schumpeter 1954: 596).

Amartya Sen, on the other hand, in response to Joan Robinson and in defence of Maurice Dobb, claims that it would be incorrect to characterise Marx's labour-values as 'metaphysical'.[16] He argues that 'there are at least three distinct non-metaphysical interpretations of the labour theory of value, viz., (i) descriptive, (ii) predictive and (iii) normative' (Sen 1978: 175). He agrees that Marx's labour theory of value does not do a good job with respect to the latter two interpretations; nevertheless, it can be defended from the perspective of a 'descriptive' interpretation, which is far from being metaphysical. Though Sen's paper has gone largely unnoticed by the scholars of Marx's theory of value, it is perhaps the most challenging and profound defence of the idea of labour-values that has been put forward in modern times. Sen argues that:

> Any description relies on factual statements. But it also involves a selection from the set of factual statements that

16 Though Sen interprets Dobb's interpretation of Marx in descriptive terms, it appears that Dobb (1973) himself saw his interpretation of Marx in the light of Sraffa's 'Introduction' to Ricardo (1951), which he had collaborated in writing, and Sraffa's (1960) *Production of Commodities*. In this context Dobb emphasises the inverse wage-profit relation and their determination independently of prices as in a one-good 'corn model' or Sraffa's (1960) Standard system: 'But in addition to its simplicity and appropriateness for his purpose, there was a formal reason why he [Marx] should have concentrated upon Values in terms of Labour, and hence trodden closely in Ricardo's footsteps. This is something that nearly all commentators on Marx seem to have missed, at any rate until quite recently. It will be clear from what has been said that the nature of his approach required him to start from the postulation of a certain rate of exploitation or of surplus value (or profit-wage ratio in Ricardo's terms); since this was prior to the formation of exchange-values or prices and was not derived from them. In other words, this needed to be expressed in terms of production, before bringing in circulation or exchange' (Dobb 1973: 147–48). Garegnani takes a similar position, which we deal with in more detail.

can be made pertaining to the phenomenon in question: some facts are chosen and others ignored. The selection process is part of the exercise of description, and not a 'metaphysical' exercise. ... In examining the labour theory of value, we have to ask: (*i*) What is being described? (*ii*) What are the selection criteria? (ibid.: 176).

From Sen's point of view (and, according to him, Dobb's point of view as well) Marx's object of description is the *human activity* of production and the *relations between humans* that it engenders. Thus, labour is selected not because it is the only *productive* factor in the process of production, but rather because it is the only *human* factor in the process of production. He illustrates the point by taking an example of such descriptive statements as: 'Michelangelo made this statue of David.' A statement of this nature, of course, ignores several facts such as the tools and equipments utilised in sculpting, the ownership of the block of marble and the patronage that Michelangelo received. There is thus an obvious loss of information in the statement; but on the other hand there is a clear gain of focus. According to Sen: 'The purely descriptive interpretation of the labour theory of value has much to do with such a deliberate choice of focus' (ibid.: 177).

Unfortunately, Sen does not go on to flesh out the descriptive nature of Marx's labour theory of value. But it is clear that Marx's description of the fight over the length of the working day between the capitalists and the working class, or the role of labour-saving technical changes, can be put in its proper perspective, following Sen. Though it is true that the competitive mechanism puts pressure on individual capitalists to economise or reduce their cost of production to the minimum, economising and cheapening of the material means of production do not have the same social consequences as do the economising and cheapening of labour or labour-power in the production process. Thus, if the aim of the theory is to describe the social consequences of competition and the pursuit of profits in capitalism, then it might make sense to select labour as the unit of account to describe the social process. Furthermore, this perspective would help us better understand Marx's distinction between labour and labour-power. Marx had criticised the classical economists for not making this conceptual distinction, which according to him was a serious scientific error on their part. As we have seen in the first two chapters, both Adam Smith and David Ricardo had understood that wages are not determined on the basis of per hour of labour supplied by the labourer, but rather on the basis of the social requirements of the reproduction of the worker's capacity to work on a daily basis and the requirements of the reproduction of the class of workers in the long run. The hourly wages for determining the cost of production of commodities are derived by dividing the given social requirements for the reproduction of the workers and the working class by the total hours of work performed in a 'day' or a 'year'. The classical economists took the length of the working day as given and unproblematic. But Marx describes it as a site of class struggle. Of course, the capitalists' attempt to increase or maximise the length of the working day amounts to reducing the hourly real wage, given the subsistence requirements, in a mathematical sense; but the description of the historical struggle over the length of the working day is not the same as the historical struggle over wages. While the struggle over wages is about the share in national income, the struggle over the length of the working day or week is more about control over one's life. Marx could bring this descriptive richness to his analysis through his theory of value and surplus-value.

This does not mean that Marx was only concerned with the descriptive aspect of his labour theory of value. In our opinion, the fundamental concern of Marx's theory was to develop a *scientific* theory of exploitation of labour, which required him to establish that all non-wage incomes were derived from 'unpaid labour'. Sen argues that as far as the transformation problem is concerned, it is not so much about *prediction* of prices in the causal sense as about deriving one set of magnitudes from another set (more like Sraffa's system of prices), a proposition with which I agree. But then it must be accepted that Marx's failure to calculate total profits as total surplus-value (or unpaid labour) when the price magnitudes are derived from labour-value magnitudes implies a *logical* failure of his scientific theory of exploitation.

Pierangelo Garegnani (1983c,[17] 1991), on the other hand, argues that the purpose of the labour theory of value in Marx is to determine the rate of profits and prices in a surplus-approach framework; and Marx did this as well as he could, given that in his time the technique of simultaneous determination of the rate of profits and prices was not available to him. In other words, Marx had no better option than to start with his labour-values and surplus-values to derive an average rate of profits and *then* the prices of production. Garegnani goes on to further criticise the interpretation, which claims that the aim of Marx's labour theory of value was to provide the theoretical basis of the notion that 'the origin of profit lies in the exploitation of labour'. I, however, find both his arguments unconvincing.

---

17 Garegnani (1983c) was presented at a colloquium on Marx at Ecole des Hautes Etudes en Sciences Sociales, Paris, 6–9 December 1983. An earlier version of this paper was published in 1981 in *Marx e gli economisti classici*.

First of all, though it is true that Marx did not know matrix algebra, he had enough mathematical prowess to solve a two-equation simultaneous equation problem. The problem is not all that mathematically challenging in the context of two goods, one relative price and a rate of profits. However, nowhere in the published or unpublished manuscripts of Marx do we find any attempt by him to solve the problem in a simultaneous-equation manner. The reason for this is simple. Marx was not simply interested in determining the rate of profits and prices. His main concern was to discover the so-called *essence* of prices and the profits, as after providing the 'solution' to the determination of prices of production, Marx goes on to claim:

> This inner connection is here revealed for the first time.. all economics up till now has either violently made abstraction from the distinctions between surplus-value and profit, between rate of surplus-value and rate of profit, so that it could retain the determination of value as its basis, or else it has abandoned, along with this determination of value, any kind of solid foundation for a scientific approach, so as to be able to retain those distinctions which obtrude themselves on the phenomenal level. This confusion on the part of the theorists shows better than anything else how the practical capitalist, imprisoned in competitive struggle and in no way penetrating the phenomena it exhibits, cannot but be completely incapable of recognizing, behind the semblance, *the inner essence and the inner form of this process* (Marx 1991: 268–69, emphasis added).

For such an enterprise the method of simultaneous determination of prices and the rate of profits is of no help. It is true, as we have argued earlier, that Marx was misguided in his conviction that there is an *essence* of prices. But when it comes to interpreting his theory, it cannot be denied that it is the *essence* he was after.

On the question of the relation of the labour theory of value with surplus-value and the exploitation of labour, Garegnani conflates two issues that must be kept separate. He first argues that Marx is categorically opposed to the Ricardian socialist idea that 'if the exchange value of a product equals the labour-time contained in the product, then the exchange value of a working day is equal to the product it yields'. And therefore, '[I]t was clearly not Marx's intention to resuscitate that "formula"' (Garegnani 1983c: 20–21). He goes on to argue that Marx's notion of exploitation simply amounts to the claim that 'profits have no systematic explanation other than the fact that the existing social order does not allow workers to appropriate the entire product' (ibid.: 23–24). But this begs the question: on what grounds are workers supposed to appropriate the entire product? On the one hand, Garegnani would like to disassociate Marx's notion of exploitation from his labour theory of value and surplus-value, and for that purpose he invokes Marx who rejects the claim that wages must be equal to the value workers produce; and on the other hand, he accepts that Marx's notion of exploitation is based on the principle that the entire product must belong to the workers! The central tenet of Marx's economic theory is that capitalist system is built on exploitation of labour and through his labour theory of value and surplus-value, and the transformation of values into prices of production and surplus-values into profits, he tries to provide a theoretical proof of this proposition. This does not by any means imply that Marx endorses the proposition that all products or all values *must* belong to workers, even though he consistently refers to surplus-value and profits as 'unpaid' labour. He does not think that a critique of capitalism could be conducted at the level of distribution of income. Garegnani suggests that Marx's central position is to establish that the class interests of the workers and the capitalists were *antagonistic*, and for that purpose all one needs to prove is that there is an inverse relationship between wages and profits given a level of output. But one should note that antagonistic interests do not necessarily imply *exploitative* relations. For example, the interests of the Soviet Union and the United States were antagonistic, but that did not mean that their relationship was exploitative. Or, to put it in another way, the interests of two competitive firms may be antagonistic, but their relationship need not necessarily be exploitative. If exploitation has any meaning in Marx's theory, then it is simply not captured by Garegnani's interpretation.[18]

Controversies on the Transformation Problem

In the 'Preface' to Volume II of *Capital,* Engels (1885) threw out a challenge:

> According to the Ricardian law of value, two capitals which employ the same amount of living labour at the same rate of

18 'The fact that the labour theory of value does not explain exchange value means that the concept of exploitation as "work done for others" is not tenable and, that, if we wish to continue talking about capitalist exploitation, we cannot do so while affirming a substantial sameness between it and previous forms of exploitation' (Napoleoni 1991: 229). Also see Jossa (1991) and Cohen (1979, 1983).

pay, assuming all other circumstances to be also the same, produce in the same period of time products of the same value, and
similarly the same amount of surplus-value or profit. If they
employ unequal amounts of living labour, then they cannot
produce the same surplus-value, or profit as the Ricardians say.
However, the contrary is the case. In point of fact, equal capitals produce, on average, equal profits in the same time, irrespective of how much or how little living labour they employ.
This contradiction to the law of value was already known to
Ricardo, but neither he nor his followers were able to resolve it.
Even Rodbertus could not ignore the contradiction, but instead
of resolving it, he makes it one of the starting-points for his uto-
pia (*Zur Erkenntnis ..., p. 131*) Marx had already resolved this
contradiction in his manuscript 'Zur Kritik'; in the plan of *Capital*, the solution is to be included in Volume 3. Some months
will still pass until its publication [it took ten years!]. And so
the economists who would like to discover Marx's secret source
in Rodbertus, as well as his superior predecessor, have here an
opportunity to show what Rodbertus's economics can accomplish. If they show how an average rate of profit can and must
come about, not only without violating the law of value, but
precisely on the basis of this law, then we shall have to continue
our discussion. In the meantime, they had better hurry. When
this Volume 3 appears, little more will be heard of an economist named Rodbertus (Engels in Marx 1992: 101–02).

This challenge was, of course, thrown in response to some accusation in German academic circles that Marx had plagiarised the works
of Rodbertus. Several anticipated solutions were produced in answer
to this challenge, but they were more in the nature of an intellectual
exercise rather than an attempt to prove the accusation right. Engels
(1894) reviewed them all in his 'Preface' to Volume III of *Capital*,
though not always very fairly.[19] In the process, he foreshadowed his
interpretation of the nature and procedure of Marx's transformation
of values to prices of production. According to him:

> It should go without saying that where things and their mutual
> relations are conceived not as fixed but rather as changing,

---

19 See Howard and King (1987) for details and also Howard and King (1989) for a
good account of the earlier literature on the Transformation Problem.

their mental images, too, i.e., concepts, are also subject to change and reformulation. ... It will be clear, then, why at the beginning of Volume 1, where Marx takes simple commodity production as his historical presupposition, only later, proceeding from this basis, to come on to capital — why he proceeds precisely there from simple commodity and not from a conceptually and historically secondary form, the commodity as already modified by capitalism (Engels in Marx 1991: 103).

This point was further elaborated in the 'Supplement to *Capital*', which Engels wrote in 1895, only two months before his death:

> To sum up, Marx's law of value applies universally, as much as any economic laws do apply, for the entire period of simple commodity production, i.e. up to the time at which this undergoes a modification by the onset of the capitalist form of production. Up till then, prices gravitate to the values determined by Marx's law and oscillate around these values, so that the more completely simple commodity production develops, the more do average prices coincide with values for longer period when not interrupted by external violent disturbances, and with the insignificant variations we mentioned earlier. *Thus the Marxian law of value has a universal economic validity for an era lasting from the beginning of the exchange that transforms products into commodities down to the fifteenth century of our epoch* (ibid.: 1037, emphasis added).

Lexis (1895), who called himself a 'vulgar economist' in the Marxian sense, was among the scholars who had come up with a solution to Engels's challenge in his review of Volume II of *Capital* and to which Engels (1894) had responded that he had at least correctly posed the problem. Lexis quickly replied with his review of Volume III of *Capital*. He pointed out that Marx's procedure of deriving the prices of production was unsatisfactory because he first starts with the proposition that commodities exchange according to their values and since the organic composition of capitals in different industries is different, it results in unequal rates of profits in different industries. Following this, the forces of competition come into play to bring about an average rate of profits for all the industries. According to Lexis:

> The equality in the rate of profits (apart from accidental irregularities) is of the essence of capitalistic production. There

never has been a social condition in which capitalistic methods of production and yet inequalities in the rate of profit caused by the different composition of capital have existed side by side. The equality of profits appears *pari passu* with capitalistic methods of production and in inseparable connection with them, much as, in the embryo, the circulation of the blood develops *pari passu* with the development of shape and form (Lexis 1895: 11).

In 1956, R.L. Meek revived Engels's interpretation of the so-called 'logical-historical transformation problem'. According to him:

Broadly speaking, there are two main types of supply price to be found in the history of commodity exchange — first, that of the producer who thinks of his net receipts as a reward for his labour, and, second, that of the producer who thinks of his net receipts as a profit on his capital. It seems to me quite reasonable to assume that supply prices of the first type will tend to be proportionate to quantities of embodied labour, and that such supply prices are typical of commodity exchanges in pre-capitalist societies. Thus even if the barriers standing in the way of an automatic adaptation of market prices to supply prices in pre-capitalist societies are too important to be assumed away or classified as mere 'frictions', it can at least be said that *the supply price themselves* 'gravitate towards the values fixed by the Marxian law'. What Marx actually did, in effect, was to assume that the first type of supply price was characteristic of commodity exchanges in pre-capitalist society, and to demonstrate how the introduction of capitalism brought about the transformation of the first type of supply price into the second type. This, I think, is the historical transformation of which the logical transformation considered above must be regarded as the 'corrected mirror-image' ([1956] 1966: 199–200).

Leaving aside the question of how correct Engels's and Meek's description of history is and to what extent their interpretation finds support in Marx's writings, the crucial point to note here is that both Engels and Meek are incorrect in interpreting the transformation procedure as a transformation of simple commodity production to capitalist production. As a matter of fact, the transformation problem has nothing to do with the values prevailing in simple commodity production.

It starts with capitalism in a situation where the rates of profits are unequal in such a way that relative prices coincide with value-ratios. The transformation procedure is about moving from unequal rates of profit to equal rate of profits within a capitalist system. Lexis correctly pointed out that Marx's logic deals with two stages of capitalism and that, according to him, these two stages never existed in history. That is why Lexis could claim that: 'It [Marx's solution] is the simple and obvious solution which everyone who gives any attention to the problem first turns to, and then brushes aside because he must believe that there is something more beneath' (Lexis 1895: 10). According to Lexis, once it is accepted that competition and the tendency to equalise the rate of profits is an integral aspect of capitalism, then one has to give up any attempt to determine the prices of production of individual commodities from labour-values. However, he went on to suggest that Marx's law of value could still be valid for aggregate variables, such as the division of the net output between the workers and capitalists, in the sense that total prices of the commodities appropriated by the capitalist class is equal to the total values of those commodities and the same for the working class. But though Lexis could not provide any proof for his proposition, as we shall see later, his 'solution' was revived in the 1980s as the 'New Solution' to the transformation problem.

In 1966, in his essay 'Karl Marx's Economic Method', Meek revised his argument. Here, he argues that: 'Marx's theory of value can conveniently be considered under the three headings of Pre-capitalist Society, Early Capitalism, and Developed Capitalism' (Meek 1966, second edition: 305). The transformation procedure is now interpreted as a transition from stage two to stage three. Stage two is defined by the transition from stage one to stage two, where capitalist relations impinge upon simple commodity production to the extent of generating surplus-value but still not having any impact on the exchange ratios of commodities established in stage one. The forces of competition come in only at stage three to equalise the rate of profits in the system. The problem with this interpretation is that Marx's transformation algorithm runs over one production period and it is absurd to suggest that a historical transformation from one stage of history to another takes place within one production cycle. Thus there can be no 'historical' justification for accounting the inputs of the transformation equations at their labour-values. In other words, any historical justification of the transformation algorithm is simply absurd. On the other hand, it does seem that at times Marx's logic runs the way Meek describes it, otherwise Marx's theory of absolute ground-rent does not make sense.[20]

The beginning of the modern controversy on the 'transformation problem' can be dated back to a paper written by Bortkiewicz (1907),[21] which remained unnoticed for decades due to its abstract and mathematical treatment of the subject matter. It came to the attention of the English-speaking world only in 1942, when Sweezy presented its summary argument in his book, and later also published an English translation of it from the original in German (Sweezy 1949). In his paper Bortkiewicz points out the technical flaw in Marx's transformation algorithm. He argues that Marx needs to use transformed prices of production for the accounting of his input prices as well, and once this requirement is taken into account it turns out that Marx's system is short of one equation. This is because the rate of profits cannot *a priori* be determined from the value accounting, as Marx had done. The system could be solved for prices of production and the rate of profits by adding a normalisation equation, but the solution in general can no longer assure Marx's results that total prices of production are proportional to total value as well as total profits are proportional to total surplus-value.[22]

20 See Morishima and Catephores (1975, 1976) and Meek (1976) for a debate between the two parties on this issue. Also see Mandel's 'Introduction' to *Capital Vol 1* and Nell (1973) in favour of the 'historical' transformation problem. We have already highlighted the fact that the proposition regarding exchange of commodities in accordance with the value-ratios in the regime of simple commodity-production requires restrictive assumptions; further on this issue relating to the controversy on the 'historical' transformation problem, see Samuelson (1991). Joan Robinson's (1966) comment is also pertinent here: 'Historically, it is natural to suppose that different industries are developed with widely varying rates of exploitation, varying rates of profit, and varying ratios of capital and labour. The push and pull of competition then tends to establish a common rate of profit, so that the various rates of exploitation are forced to levels which offset differences in the ratio of capital to labour. The movement from an equal rate of exploitation towards an equal rate of profit is not a process in the development of economic analysis, from the primitive labour theory of value towards a theory of interaction between relative demands and relative costs' (Robinson 1966: 16–17).

21 For good reviews of the debate on the 'transformation problem', see Desai (1974, 1979, 1991) and Howard and King (1985, 1992).

22 Ramos cites a few passages and an example from Marx's original manuscripts that were omitted by Engels in the published text of the third volume of *Capital* and claims that such omissions 'probably contributed to the subsequent confusion regarding the transformation' (Ramos 1998–99: 55–56), particularly the interpretative line that has followed Bortkiewicz. He argues that it is clear from the omitted

Another important conclusion of Bortkiewicz's paper is that, contrary to Marx's opinion, changes in the techniques of production in the luxury good sectors will have no impact on the rate of profits. Ricardo had already argued this point and Marx had criticised Ricardo for this; and now Bortkiewicz confirmed that Ricardo was right and Marx was wrong (see Chapter 4 in this volume for a formal argument). This has a far-reaching consequence for Marx's theory of surplus-value and profits than has been hitherto appreciated in the Marxist literature. The Ricardo-Bortkiewicz position points towards the fact that the rate of profits is the rate of expansion of the inputs used in a system that is productive of surplus when real wages are accounted as inputs (see Chapter 4 in this volume). Any good that does not show up as an input either directly or indirectly in the system of production, such as a purely luxury good, cannot figure in the equations that determine the rate of profits. This clearly stands in opposition to Marx's idea that surplus-value is a *substance*, such as water or oil, which is produced in each sector and then *redistributed* amongst all the sectors according to a certain rule. For example, suppose that the weight of the luxury good sector is rising in the total system of production and there has been advancement in the technique of production of only luxury goods such that $s/(c + v)$ is rising in the luxury good sector due to a fall in its c component. The Ricardo-Bortkiewicz result shows that this will have no impact on the general rate of profits, including the rate of profit earned in the luxury goods sector. The question for Marx would be: where does the relative rise in surplus-value go? This shows that the idea that value and surplus-value are *substances* is false.

Bortkiewicz uses a three-sector model that identifies each sector with a distinct *type* of good such as capital good, wage good and luxury

---

passages that Marx defined value as 'cost price' plus 'surplus value' ($W = k + m$) and the price of production as 'cost price' plus 'profit ($P = k + p$)', where 'cost price' for both value and price of production is the same. But there is nothing new about this as Ramos himself goes on to add: 'It is important to note, however, that similar formulations are found scattered in other places of the book' (ibid.: 61). Actually, this is precisely the reason why Bortkiewicz found Marx's transformation procedure to be unsatisfactory. Ramos, however, uses this to advance an implausible thesis that the 'cost prices' in Marx's equation of value are the prices of production of the previous period. A theory of 'x' that takes 'x' as given is an oxymoron; e.g., if the economy is in equilibrium and therefore its prices remain constant from period to period, then Ramos's thesis amounts to a theory of prices of production that determines prices of production by simply observing the last period's *given* prices of production! Marx, in my opinion, is definitely a better theoretician than that.

good. He also imposes the condition of 'simple reproduction' on his system. These restrictive assumptions are apparently made for simplicity's sake, or to ward off unnecessary criticisms, such as the problem of 'realisation of value and surplus-value', etc. According to him: 'Insofar as it is a question of demonstrating Marx's errors it is quite unobjectionable to work with limiting assumptions of this kind, since what does not hold in the special case cannot claim general validity' (Bortkiewicz [1907] in Sweezy 1949: 200). This notwithstanding, Winternitz (1948) was quick to point out that Bortkiewicz's assumption of 'simple reproduction' is unnecessary for describing the transformation problem. On the heels of Winternitz, Kenneth May (1948) pointed out that the context of the division of the economy into three distinct branches is also unnecessary. And in 1949, he generalised Winternitz's equations to the n-good case.

The debate on the transformation problem reached its high point with the publication of Seton (1957), who provides a fairly comprehensive and careful mathematical description of the transformation problem. He confirms that neither the assumption of 'simple reproduction' nor the assumption that 'every physical commodity [is] not merely unequivocally identifiable as the product of one or other of these [sectors], but that its ultimate use in the economy [is] equally invariable and predetermined by its department of origin' (Seton 1957: 150) is necessary for the description of the transformation problem. He confirms all of Bortkiewicz's conclusions and shows that Marx's values can be formally transformed into prices of production by adding a normalisation equation to his procedure. Formally, it does not matter whether the normalisation equation is taken to be equality of total profits with total surplus-value or equality of total prices of production with total values. However, in general, both the conditions — of equality of the sums of values and prices of production and the sums of surplus-values and profits — cannot be guaranteed simultaneously. He analyses several candidates for the normalisation equation and concludes that 'there does not seem to be an objective basis for choosing any particular invariance postulate in preference to all the others, *and to that extent the transformation problem may be said to fall short of complete determinacy*' (ibid.: 153).[23] Though Seton

---

23 Seton also pointed out that Meek's (1956) proposition regarding the normalisation equation that one should equate the ratio of the total value of labour-power to the total value of the outputs and the ratio of total wages to total prices of outputs, 'says nothing about absolute prices; it merely imposes an additional, and supernumerary, condition on the relative prices $(p_1/p_2, p_3/p_2, ...)$ *which are already determined by the principle of equal profitability*' (Seton 1957: 153).

confirms that values can be formally transformed into prices of production, he nevertheless goes on to conclude that:

> Above all, the denial of productive factor contributions other than those of labour, on which the whole doctrine of the surplus rests, is an act of fiat rather than of genuine cognition. It is these [this] doctrinal preconceptions [preconception] which must remain the centre of any reappraisal of Marxian economics, rather than the logical superstructure which our analysis has shown to be sound enough (ibid.: 160).

By 1971, the critical impact of Sraffa (1960) on Marx's transformation problem was beginning to be felt, as Samuelson's highly controversial critique of Marx's transformation problem proclaims: 'In this age of Leontief and Sraffa there is no excuse for mystery and partisan polemics in dealing with the purely logical aspects of the problem' (Samuelson 1971: 218).[24] Samuelson is of the opinion that the fundamental problem with the 'transformation problem' is due not to the existence of capital as such, but rather to the misunderstanding of the role of 'time' in the system of production. He develops an interesting example of 'turn over' tax and 'value added' tax on a pure labour economy with different 'time-structures'. He argues that the 'turn over' tax corresponds to prices of production and profits and the 'value added' tax corresponds to the value and surplus-value models of Marx. It is clear from this example that these are two different and distinct rules of appropriating a share in the total output produced. Neither one needs to have the rule of 'value added' tax first, before the rule of 'turn over' tax can be applied. Nor can we claim that the rule of 'value added' tax reveals the *essence* of 'turn over' tax. Samuelson's point is that in competitive capitalism it is agreed by all parties that the income share of the capitalists is appropriated in accordance with the 'turn over' tax and thus the accounting based on 'value added' tax is irrelevant. As Samuelson concludes:

> For when you cut through the maze of algebra and come to understand what is going on, you discover that the 'transformation algorithm' is precisely of the following form: 'contemplate two alternatives and discordant systems. Write down one. Now transform by taking an eraser and rubbing it out.

---

24 It should, however, be noted that most of Samuelson's (1971) arguments are present in his earlier (Samuelson 1957) paper, which did not get much notice at the time.

Then fill in the other one. Voila! You have completed your transformation algorithm' (ibid.: 218).

Samuelson further argues that in the case of choice of techniques, the selection of cost-minimising techniques in use is dependent on the rate of profits, and that cost-minimisation according to labour-value accounting may lead to a wrong choice of techniques (ibid.: 249–50). This criticism, however, appears to be off-target. If we accept the position that Marx's accounting is ex-post, then the problem of choice of technique is already taken care of and all Marx needs to do is to derive his value figures from the techniques in use. As Sen (1978) argues, the 'transformation problem' is about 'deriving one set of magnitudes from another set'. On the other hand, if one thinks that there is *real* movement of the economy from the value regime to the prices of production regime, as Samuelson's argument implies, then it cannot be denied that the rates of profit of various sectors would go through alteration in the process, which in its wake might bring changes in techniques and therefore changes in the value magnitudes themselves. It should, however, be noted that Samuelson's characterisation of the 'transformation algorithm' as 'erase and replace', points to the fact that he himself understands the problem as the derivation of one set of magnitudes from another set and not as a real movement of the system from one regime to another.

Samuelson also points out some inherent problems with labour accounting and the notion of socially necessary labour; for example, if there are *natural* productivity differences between different types of labourers, then how is one supposed to arrive at the determination of 'socially necessary' labour? (ibid.: 223). On the positive side, Samuelson provides a weaker condition than the uniformity of the organic composition of capital for value-ratios and prices of production to be equal. He shows that 'when every one of the departments happens to use the various raw materials and machine services in the same proportions that society produces them in toto' (ibid.: 234), then the value-ratios will be identical to the prices of productions. He calls this condition 'equal *internal* composition of (constant) capital'. Of course, this condition, too, is quite restrictive.

In defence of Marx against Samuelson, Baumol (1974) argues that Marx's transformation analysis is not essentially about deriving prices of production from values, but rather it seeks 'to describe how *non* wage incomes are *produced* and then how this aggregate is *redistributed*, ... This is the heart of the transformation process — the conversion of surplus value into profit, interest, and rent. It takes from each according to its work force, and returns to each according to its total investment' (Baumol 1974: 373).

Though Baumol correctly describes what Marx was doing, he fails to make a claim that what Marx was doing was right. His exercise is more curatorial in nature than analytical. Samuelson was quick to point out that: 'It will be seen to be logically untenable to agree with my "erase and replace" analysis of the value-price transformation, and withhold agreement from my "erase and replace" analysis of the surplus-value-profit transformation. For these are identical' (Samuelson 1974: 389).

Harcourt rejects Samuelson's claim and sides with Baumol: 'It is wrong to give the impression that Marx thought the LTV was a literal theory of the pattern of prices of production ... ' (Harcourt 2007: 130). According to Harcourt, Marx's main objective was to answer the question: '[W]here *did* profits come from?' (ibid.: 132). And to that purpose, his analysis of the labour process and its division between *necessary* and *surplus labour-time* and its necessary linkages to surplus-value and profits is satisfactory:

> [T]he working day could conceptually be split into two parts: the hours needed with the existing stock of capital goods, methods, and conditions of production to produce wage goods (necessary labor) and the rest (surplus labor) which was the source of surplus value in the sphere of production, and profits in the sphere of distribution and exchange (ibid.: 132).

But if the surplus-value of the sphere of production is the *source* of profits in the sphere of distribution and exchange, then one should expect the profits to stay constant so long as the surplus-value remains constant. Now imagine that we redistribute the given labour in such a way that the weight of high-priced goods in the system rises; given linear methods of production, it will leave values of commodities, rate of surplus-value, total surplus-value, prices of production and the rate of profits unchanged but raise the total profits in the system. For example, let us suppose that an economic system is given by:

4000 qr. Wheat + 64 ton Iron + 4/5 Labour → 8000 qr. Wheat

2400 qr. Wheat + 192 ton Iron + 1/5 Labour → 320 ton Iron

6400 qr. Wheat + 256 ton Iron + 1 Labour → 8000 qr. Wheat + 320 ton Iron

Let us say that the real wage is given by (400 qr. of Wheat + 16 ton of Iron) per unit of labour. The reader can verify that in this system the rate of profits is 3/17 or 17.6 per cent, and if we put the price of Iron $(P_I) = 1$, then the price of wheat $(P_W) = 0.030$ per unit of iron and the total profit in the system is equal to 85.161. Now let us assume that the labour is redistributed in the following way:

3750 qr. Wheat + 60 ton Iron + ¾ Labour → 7500 qr. Wheat

3000 qr. Wheat + 240 ton Iron + ¼ Labour → 400 ton Iron

6750 qr. Wheat + 300 ton Iron + 1 Labour → 7500 qr. Wheat + 400 ton Iron

The reader can verify that in this system the rate of profits and price of wheat in terms of iron as well as values of commodities and the total surplus-value remain constant, but the total profit rises to 94.838. The question is: if the source of profit is in surplus-value, then where did this rise in profit come from? Now, the problem with Baumol's explanation lies in the fact that he inadvertently equates 'non-wage incomes' with 'surplus-value', as if it were an axiom. But the critique of the 'transformation problem' has revealed that this is not true, and it is what Samuelson's response to Baumol amounts to.[25]

The root of the problem with such Marxist explanations of profit lies in our desire for a *scientific* solution to a *normative* problem. Though production of income is a technical matter that is susceptible to scientific analysis, the distribution of income, in my opinion, is essentially a *normative* problem; hence all attempts to develop a theory of distribution based on a scientific analysis of the process of production are destined to fail. It is one thing to argue, on the grounds of social justice, that labour is the only human contribution to production and thus ought to be the sole recipient of income; but an entirely other matter to conclude from such a normative position that therefore it follows that all non-wage income must represent the surplus labour in the system. The latter part of the foregoing proposition is a

---

25 In an e-mail response, Professor Harcourt wrote: 'Remember Wildon Carr's maxim: "it is better to be vaguely right than precisely wrong". I think Marx's narrative makes good sense in explaining how profits arise and what vaguely determines their size. That is why I think a finding that positive surplus labour and value will always be accompanied by positive profits makes sense. I regard this as a qualitative intuitive statement, not a rigorous quantitative one which your example seeks to overturn.'

scientific claim and its proof requires that capital should be reducible to simple labour, which, in general, is not true and hence the proposition is false. The reader should also note that all attempts to *justify* profit income on the grounds of scientific analysis of production by imputing the source of profits in either abstinence or 'productivity of capital' have also failed.

Though Morishima concedes several shortcomings of Marx's labour theory of value and proposes 'a Marxian economics without the labour theory of value' (Morishima 1973: 181), he nevertheless makes three distinct defensive arguments in support of Marx's transformation algorithm. First of all, Morishima (1973, 1974) proposes that Marx's procedure of transforming values to prices of production in Volume III of *Capital* could be interpreted as the first step of a Markov process of solving a simultaneous equation problem. Hence Marx's procedure is not wrong but incomplete.[26] Later, Morishima and Catephores (1978) point out that the most general treatment of this issue is presented by Okishio (1972) in a Japanese publication.[27] As presented by Morishima and Catephores, Okishio's iteration equation is given by:

$$P_{t+1} = (P_t x/P_t Mx)P_t M,$$

where M is the physical input plus the real wages matrix, x is the vector of real gross outputs and Ps are the vectors of prices with time subscripts. Okishio shows that 'the sequence $\{P_t\}$ from the initial point $P_0 = \Lambda$ [labour-values] converges to the long-run equilibrium price set P and $P_t x/P_t Mx$ converges to 1 plus the long-run equilibrium rate of profit' (Morishima and Catephores 1978: 166). This procedure, however, does not provide any defence for Marx's value theory as it is simply another method of solving for the prices of production and the rate of profits given the physical input-output data. The point to note here is that the convergence to long-term prices and the rate of profits will take place starting from any arbitrary prices, which indicates that labour-values have no particular significance in determining those prices and the rate of profits.

Morishima's second line of defence is that even though total profits and total surplus-values are generally not equal, one could still prove (leaving aside the case of joint-production for the time being) that

---

26 This argument is later adopted by Shaikh (1977).
27 Howard and King (1992) have pointed out that G. von Charasoff had interpreted Marx's transformation procedure as a Markov process in as early as 1910.

positive profits are possible if, and only if, the rate of surplus-value is positive — implying that in some way it proves that the *cause* of profit is rooted in surplus-value or the exploitation of labour. Morishima christens this the *Fundamental Marxian Theorem*.[28] But the idea of *causation* in Morishima's Fundamental Marxian Theorem is extra-mathematical. On the basis of the equations one can as well 'prove' that the rate of surplus-value is positive if, and only if, the rate of profits is positive, as Samuelson (1974) correctly points out. So the question is: can we argue that values and surplus-values somehow 'appear' prior to prices of production and profits?

Shaikh (1981, 1984) argues precisely that:

> But now this physical data is itself a conceptual summary of the real expenditures of social labour-time. In the real economy, the results of production on which the so-called physical data are based are themselves given only through the actual materialization of social labour-time, and hence only because value has been actually created (Shaikh 1984: 51).

Alain Lipietz also makes a similar argument: 'First we have the commodity character of the economy. From this we develop the substance and the form of value. For a given state of the productive forces (A, l), we can derive the magnitudes of v of the vectors of values' (Lipietz 1982: 71). Both Lipietz's and Shaikh's arguments are, however, flawed for a simple reason. In determining the value of a commodity it is assumed that the value of the constant capital used up in the production process is *transferred* to the commodity produced; however the amount of value that must be transferred to the commodity can only be determined *after* the physical input-output data are available.

---

28 As a matter of fact Okishio (1963) had already made this point a decade earlier. In a detailed review of Morishima's book, von Weizsacker (1973) argues that Morishima's Fundamental Marxian Theorem may not be valid in a regime of technical change. He constructs an example of an economy with fixed labour employment and working hours with a continuous rise in labour productivity at a geometric rate and constant organic composition of capital; and argues that in such a case it could be demonstrated that the economy is growing at a positive rate with zero rate of surplus-value, implying that profits would be positive with surplus-value being zero. This, however, cannot be true, as the given nature of technical change would also continuously increase the rate of surplus-value. Morishima is quick to point out that 'the wage-profit frontier and the exploitation frontier shift right-wards if we have technological improvement. After the shift, also, the exploitation frontier is above the wage-profit frontier' (Morishima 1974: 415).

Lipietz's input matrix A and labour-time vector l are not sufficient for determining values. He needs the vector of physical outputs to do so. Even in the unlikely case where we assume that the constant capital element is zero, surplus-value can be determined *only* after the physical input-output data are available, as the value of real wages cannot be determined prior to that. Thus the attempt to assign the *cause* of profit in surplus-value does not hold up.

Morishima's third argument is that in a dynamic context it can be shown that when the economy is on von Neumann's golden growth path, i.e., a balanced growth with the rate of growth equal to the uniform rate of profits, then Marx's value rate of profits, $S/(C + V)$, turns out to be equal to the prices of production rate of profits. This apparently sent Shaikh (1981, 1984) off on a wild goose chase. He came up with an ingenious argument that the reason why Marx's rate of profits diverge from the prices of production rate of profits when the balanced rate of growth of the economy is less than the maximum rate, is that in this case the capitalists' consumption is positive, which implies that a certain amount of surplus-value produced in the system falls out of the circuit of capital and therefore does not show up in the accounts of profits of the capitalist class as a whole:

> Here too [i.e., the expenditure by capitalists on the commodities for consumption], what the sellers of commodity-capital lose in value through a price below direct price is gained by the capitalists in the form of a lower price for their articles of consumption. But now a crucial difference arises. What the capitalists in this case lose as sellers will show up in business accounts as the amount by which actual profit is below direct profit [i.e., $S/(C + V)$] (by which actual profit is below profit proportional to surplus value). But what they gain as consumers shows up only in their personal accounts, as a lower amount of money required to purchase the same article of consumption. In other words, value is transferred out of the circuit of capital into the circuit of revenue, and in the business accounts this transfer manifests itself as profits lower than direct profits [surplus-value] (Shaikh 1984: 54).

I, however, find the idea that capitalists' consumption causes a certain amount of exchange of commodities to fall out of the 'business account' to be unconvincing. When the economy is on the von Neumann golden growth path, its inputs and outputs are arranged in a certain proportion, and when the economy is not on the golden growth path, its inputs and outputs are arranged in different proportions. But in both cases all the outputs are accounted for by the prices of production. The question of something falling out of the circuit of capital does not arise, given the nature of the problem. As a matter of fact, it becomes clear that the question of why the rate of profits differs from S/(C + V) when the system is growing below the von Neumann golden rate is fruitless once we understand why the rate of profits of von Neumann's system equals Marx's rate of profits. A system on von Neumann's golden growth path (with no joint-products) basically describes Sraffa's 'Standard system', with real wages showing up on the input side on the same footing as 'the fuel for machines'.[29] Since there is no capitalist consumption, the system is made up of only 'basic goods', and since the system is growing on a balanced growth path, the aggregates of all its inputs are growing at the same rate. As we shall see in the next chapter, in this case the rate of profits could be determined by the physical ratio of the total net output divided by the total inputs. In other words, when the system is on von Neumann's golden growth path, its rate of profits is independent of prices. Any set of positive prices will result in the same rate of profits. There is thus no mystery to the fact that when we apply the value-ratios as the set of given prices to this system, its rate of profits remains the same. In other words, the average rate of profits of any positive set of prices applied to von Neumann's system will yield an average rate of profits equal to the von Neumann rate of profits. There is nothing special about values and the value rate of profits here.

It seems Shaikh inadvertently over-determined the system of equations that led him to this conceptual error. He maintains that the total 'direct prices', i.e., prices in terms of gold when all prices are proportional to values, and total prices of production after the transformation must remain constant. In other words, he invokes the condition of the sum of values equals the sum of prices of production as the normalisation equation for the transformation equations. Given this

---

29 In a letter dated 3 September 1960, John Hicks wrote to Sraffa: 'Dear Piero, ... You tell us that your work on the subject goes back a long way — you mention Frank Ramsey; is it possible that it was somehow through you and your mathematical friends that von Neumann got onto what is in so many ways a similar construction (it is understood that his paper was originally given at Princeton in 1932)? I have never been able to understand how he should have hit on it out of blue. Formally, I believe, your standard system is identical with the von Neumann equilibrium, though it arises in response to a different question. But the model, even to the treatment of fixed capital, is exactly the same' (Sraffa n.d.: D/3/12/111).

normalisation equation, in general we would find that the relationships between the three aggregates, such as the total value of constant capital and the total prices of constant capital, the total values of wage goods and the total prices of wage goods, and the total surplus-values and the total profits would diverge from each other. The conceptual error seems to creep in because even after the transformation Shaikh uses the same gold as 'money' to account for the values and prices of production. He maintains that gold is not affected by the transformation of value to prices of production and therefore still represents both values and prices as one to one. But this amounts to imposing two conditions on the transformation equations, which have room for only one. If we assume that the organic composition of capital in the gold sector is such that it remains unaffected by the transformation, then we at the same time cannot guarantee the equality between the sum of values and the sum of prices to begin with.

Shaikh also provides two further defences of Marx's labour theory of value. Again, following Morishima's Fundamental Marxian Theorem, he goes a step further and proposes that the rate of profits is nothing but a displaced mirror image of Marx's rate of profits: '[W]hen the value rate of profit rises (or falls) its reflection in the sphere of circulation, the transformed rate of profit, also rises or falls' (1984: 59). However, as a general proposition, this is not true. In his equations, from which he derives this general proposition, Shaikh assumes that both the techniques of production and the length of the working day are kept constant. Given these assumptions, a rise in Marx's rate of profit can be due to only one factor: a fall in the real wages. Now this is nothing but to say that Marx agreed with Ricardo that wages and the rate of profits are inversely related. The mistake lies in forgetting the restrictive assumptions while making the generalised statement quoted above. Let us suppose that there is choice of technique available for at least one capital or wage good. Now, as wages fall, the other technique becomes more efficient to operate because it uses relatively more labour than 'capital', i.e., it produces a higher rate of profit than the previous technique at certain given real wages, and thus the system switches to the new technique. If Shaikh's proposition were true, then the system would never switch back to the previous technique as long as the wages kept falling, since the value of the constant capital in the two techniques would remain the same as it would not be affected by the fall (or rise) in wages. However, as we shall see in the next chapter, Sraffa's (1960) reswitching proposition clearly establishes the logical possibility of the system to switch back to the first technique as the wages continue to fall. This implies that the prices of production rate of profits may rise while Marx's or the value rate of profits falls. The reason for this is simple: labour-values are not the correct aggregators for 'capital' — a technique that minimises labour-values is not necessarily the cost-minimising technique. Thus Shaikh is incorrect in making a generalisation from a result that is valid only in a highly restrictive situation.

Shaikh's other line of defence is empirical. He first uses some input-output data from Italy provided by Marzi and Varri. He takes an arbitrary rate of profits of 40 per cent (the mid-point between zero and the maximum rate of 80 per cent) and derives the prices of production for that rate of profits for 25 sectors and compares these with the prices of production calculated at zero rate of profits (since at zero rate the value-ratios are supposed to coincide with prices of production ratios). He finds that the difference between the two sets of prices for these 25 goods do not vary considerably, i.e., only to the order of 8 to 13 per cent. From this Shaikh concludes that '[t]he cross-sectional variations in the calculated prices of production are entirely dominated by the corresponding variations in relative values, with between 87% and 92% of former being explained by the latter' (1984: 73). It is, however, not clear how 'values' could '*explain*' the 'prices of production' in this exercise? What we observe here is that the rise in the rate of profits from zero to 40 per cent (given the input-output system) brings about, on an average, 8 to 13 per cent changes in the prices of production. Since values must remain constant in a cross-sectional analysis, how could they explain any change? All the changes in this case are due to the changes in the rate of profits. This result, of course, is closer to what Ricardo had anticipated. Shaikh also uses inter-temporal data from two years, 1959 and 1967, provided by the same source. Again, he finds that '92% of the changes in calculated prices of production are explained by changes in calculated values' (ibid.: 74). As we know, prices of production change for only two reasons: (*i*) changes in the techniques in use, and (*ii*) changes in distribution of income. Now Shaikh, to the best of my understanding, keeps the rate of profits at 40 per cent in calculating the prices of production in the two time periods, so it is no wonder that most of the changes in prices of production must be explained by changes in techniques, which show up in the changes in values. The question that arises here is: why do changes in calculated values explain only 92 per cent of the changes in prices of production, and not 100 per cent? The theoretical explanation would be that changes in techniques must have affected the wage rate, even though the rate of profits has been kept constant, and therefore, it is the changes in distribution of income that is explaining the remaining changes.

More recently, Shaikh has used the US input-output data given in dollar terms for the years 1947, 1958, 1963, 1967 and 1972. He reconfirms his earlier results in this case as well. He goes on to conclude that:

> [...] prices of production are important because in a competitive system they directly regulate market prices; and labour values are important because they serve both as the foundation of prices of production and as their dominant components over time. This last aspect is particularly important, because over time technical change alters relative labour values and hence relative prices of production (Shaikh 1998: 242–43).

There is, however, nothing in the empirical analysis that establishes that labour-values are 'foundations' of prices of production — one can start with positive profits and prices of production and calculate prices of production/values at zero rate of profit and conclude that a large part of the value is explained by prices of production and hence the price of production is the 'foundation' of value. Nor is there anything to establish the causal link that technical change first alters the labour-values and then it is the altered labour-values that consequently affect the relative prices of production. The intermediary causal link (in Shaikh's terms 'and hence') is unwarranted and cannot be drawn from the empirical analysis.

On the theme of empirical arguments, mention must be made of Farjoun and Machover (1983). They argue that it is unscientific to assume that in a capitalist competitive economy there will be a tendency for the market prices to settle at prices of production or long-term equilibrium prices. From the perspective of statistical mechanics, they argue that commodities in such an economy should be treated like gas molecules in a closed box. The appropriateness of this analogy for the commodities and the economy is, however, not well explained. It is not clear why jet planes produced by just a few very large firms and tomatoes produced by thousands of small farmers should both behave like gas molecules in a closed box.

In any case, in this context there will be no tendency for prices to settle at their equilibrium points and therefore no tendency for the rate of profits to equalise. From here on, they propose that labour-values with unequal rates of profits are perhaps better predictors of market prices at any given time then the Sraffian prices of production.

Following Farjoun and Machover (1983) and Shaikh (1984), Cockshott, Cottrell and Michaelson (1995), Cockshott and Cottrell

(1997, 1998) and some others have produced some empirical evidence that suggests not only that the empirical rates of profit are not uniform, but more importantly, they are negatively correlated with the sectoral organic composition of capital.[30] Thus Marx's labour-value theory should be considered as a valid theory of prices.

Leaving aside the inherent problems with empirical evidence of this sort, such as the translation of input-output data given in terms of pounds to physical input-output tables and their labour-value accountings, it should be noted at the outset that such empirical evidence does not support either Marx's or Ricardo's theory. First of all, neither Marx nor Ricardo was interested in developing a theory to predict 'market prices'. Both were of the opinion that there can be no 'theory' to predict 'market prices', as it depends on too many accidental factors. Both were convinced that forces of competition create a tendency for the rates of profit to equalise and both were convinced that, in general, equilibrium prices will deviate from labour-value-ratios and 'market prices' fluctuate around the equilibrium prices. As a matter of fact, Marx chided Ricardo for 'not understanding the adjustment of values to production prices' (Marx 1991: 305 f.n.). Having clarified that such evidence does not support Marx's or Ricardo's theory, I nevertheless think that such empirical works are not without value. In this context, I would suggest an idea that may be taken up in the future for what I consider would make a better test for the prices of production hypothesis. Let us say we take a long-term time series of 'market

---

30 In this context, it is interesting to note Bronfenbrenner's response to Samuelson (1971): 'Agreeing that Marx's transformation algorithm was technically defective, let us now attempt a thought experiment. Let us correlate, for n departments, the disequilibrium prices determined by Marx's transformation algorithm with the true equilibrium ones computed by the correct transformation algorithm. Should the correlation be negative, or should it be positive but not differ significantly from zero, Samuelson's proposition would be both correct and unexaggerated. If the correlation is positive and sufficiently close to unity, the Marxists and the neo-Marxists would be right in downgrading Samuelson's contribution to a second or third-order technical correction or hair-splitting exercise. It would be my expectation, originally inspired by none other than Samuelson himself and affected by Stigler's estimate for the Ricardian system, that the Marxists and neo-Marxists will be more nearly correct' (Bronfenbrenner 1973: 324–25). On the other hand, Duncan Foley maintains that 'if we inspect the accounts of any real system of capitalist firms, ... we will find on looking at such a system of accounts that value added is not uniformly proportional to direct labor expended across sectors. Since the deviations appear to be too large to be explained by differences in the quality of labor, it seems hopeless to try to maintain the position that in reality prices are indeed proportional to labor values' (Foley 1982: 40).

prices' of several sectors. We identify periods of four to five years when the observed relative prices of these sectors are relatively stable. We characterise those prices as surrogates for 'prices of production'. Then we first check how estimated value-rates of profits correlate with the empirical rates of profits in those years, and we do the same for the estimated prices of production. It should, however, be kept in mind that the theory of prices of production assumes that the risk associated with investment in different sectors is the same, though in reality this is perhaps not true. Therefore, we should evaluate the degree of risk for different sectors, readjust the estimated prices of production profits accordingly, and then test to what extent these correlate with the empirical prices and rates of profits for those years. If the latter gives a better estimate, then the theory of prices of production could be said to be 'validated'. Furthermore, it could also explain why, in general, the rates of profit do not equalise — it may not be due to differences in the organic composition of capital but rather due to differences in the market's assessment of risks. I would think that the assessment of risk for very large enterprises producing capital goods would be rather low compared to small enterprises producing many consumer goods: hence the empirical estimates of negative correlation of rates of profit with the sectoral organic composition of capital.

In 1977, Ian Steedman published his highly provocative and controversial book, *Marx after Sraffa*. Though the main arguments of this book were by and large made earlier by Samuelson and Morishima, as well as Steedman himself, the book brought the full weight of the Sraffian revolution to bear upon Marx's labour theory of value and the transformation problem. The major argument of the book is that as long as the determination of the uniform rate of profits and the prices of production are concerned, the information contained in the physical input- output data along with the given wage rate is sufficient. There is no need for 'the labour-value algorithm' detour; it is simply redundant for the theoretical purpose at hand. Furthermore, Steedman (1975, 1977) also highlights the complications associated with value and surplus-value accountings in the case of joint-production. He shows that in the case of joint-production, labour-values of commodities may turn out to be negative and one can have situations where the rate of profits is positive but the rate of surplus-value turns out to be negative. For example, let us suppose that, in a two-good model, process 1 uses 25 units of good 1 and 0 units of good 2 along with 5 units of labour to produce 30 units of good 1 and 5 units of good 2; similarly, process 2 uses 0 units of good 1 and 10 units of good 2 along with 1 unit of labour to produce 3 units of good 1 and 12 units of good 2. If we take real wages to be unit of good 1 plus 5/6 unit of good 2 per unit of labour, then it turns out that the value of good 1 is equal to -1 and the value of good 2 is equal to 2 and the surplus-value is equal to -1; on the other hand, its prices are positive with the rate of profits equal to 20 per cent. Thus we have a situation where the rate of surplus-value, and therefore Marx's rate of profit, is negative for a system that has a 20 per cent rate of profits and is capable of growing at the rate of 20 per cent![31] This not only directly refutes Morishima's Fundamental Marxian Theorem, it also raises serious questions about the efficacy of the concept of labour-values. Now, the labour-value algorithm is not only redundant but incapable of determining the rate of profits and the prices of production. Steedman further argues that the case of joint-production is not just a curiosum but rather the most general case, as fixed capital must be treated as a joint-product. It should, however, be noted that Morishima (1973, 1974a, 1976) was well aware of the problem with his Fundamental Marxian Theorem in the case of joint-production and had proposed a modification to his theorem in such cases. Instead of calculating values as the sum of c + v + s, given the techniques in use, Morishima proposed that value be measured by linear programming method and defined as minimum labour-time needed to produce the commodities instead of actual labour-time taken by the techniques in use. This would ensure that surplus-value would never be negative. Morishima's proposal, however, turns labour-value into a notion with no material or real foundation.[32]

Steedman also argues that where choice of techniques is concerned, it is the prices of the production rate of profits that determines the technique that is chosen for use. Thus the values and surplus-values are dependent on prices of productions and profits, as values and surplus-values are dependent on the techniques in use. This, of course, is a rhetorical argument made against a misconceived Marxist opinion that somehow values and surplus-values are either *logically* or *causally* prior to the prices of production and profits. This, however, could not have been Marx's position. Marx is quite clear that capitalists or workers (i.e., economic actors in general) do not have the knowledge of the values and surplus-values, as those data are not available, and that the economic actors act only on observable signals, which are prices and profits. His point is that the empirical economy that exists due

---

31 This example is taken from Steedman (1991).
32 Harcourt and Kerr (in Harcourt 2001) credit Morishima for appropriately specifying 'Marx's sturdy intuition' in the model. Also see Rankin (1987) for a strongly argued defence of Morishima's proposal.

to the decisions taken by the economic actors can be described by the value and surplus-value algorithm to reveal its underlying essence. The point to note here is that neither values and surplus-values nor prices and profits are logically or causally prior to one or the other. At any given time an empirical economy exists, which must be taken as given for deriving both sets of measures. The issue of choice of techniques becomes relevant only in the context of a change in some variables of a *given* empirical system — for example, if the wage rate (and consequently the rate of profits) changes, then it may happen that some techniques which were not in use earlier become more profitable and the system eventually switches to those techniques. But at any point of time one technique or the other is in use, and the prevailing rate of profits and prices of production are always associated only with the techniques in use, as are the values and surplus-values. So what Steedman's claim boils down to is that the value and surplus-value algorithm is unable to '*predict*' such changes successfully; in other words, when the rate of surplus-value changes due to changes in the wage rate, the value measures are unable to correctly predict the behaviour of the system if choice of techniques exists. The reason for this is again simple: the capital account in terms of values does not take into account the complicated influence of the rate of profits on it, as Sraffa's dated labour accounting has well exposed (see the next chapter). It should be noted that such 'predictions' are, however, logical in nature and not causal; since a change in the wage rate would most likely also bring about a change in the mix of net outputs and thus scale of operation in various sectors, which could cause unpredictable changes in the system.

Steedman's book generated a lot of heat from the Marxist camp, but little light. There was a growing awareness that the transformation problem had to be abandoned — Shaikh's valiant efforts notwithstanding. A large group took refuge in Marx's idea in Chapter 1, that 'abstract labour' is determined by the market exchange. We have already shown that Marx himself had abandoned this idea since it led to contradictions. But in the face of the intractable nature of the transformation algorithm, this old idea was revived. The following quotations illustrate the generality of this view among a large group of Marxists:

> [...] there is no way to reduce observable concrete labor to social abstract labor in advance outside the market which actually effects the reduction (Gerstein 1976: 250).
>
> The exchange transaction realizes the uniformity of products as commodities by establishing an *equivalent* in which

private labour appears simply as a fraction of the overall labour of society. This uniform character of labour, as a fraction of overall social labour is what is known as *abstract labour* (Aglietta 1979: 38).

The distinction of production and exchange in the process of socialization of private activities generates the quantitative problem of the social validation of private labours. *There is no necessary correspondence between past labour and present abstract labour* (Aglietta 1979: 45).

It is the process of exchange on the market that manifests the social character of individual labours, establishes the social connections between independent commodity producers, and thereby determines that the value realized in exchange (exchange-value) is the form of appearance of that labour, and only that labour, which is socially necessary for the production of the commodity in question. Hence value is measured not in units of embodied labour-time, but rather in units of 'socially necessary labour-time.' Thus the reduction of labour to abstract labour can be done only by the market (Himmelweit and Mohun 1981: 233).

I dislike the expression 'realization of value' precisely because it suggests that value already exists before being realized and that it is a permanent property of commodities, embodied in them. For me, on the contrary, only a pretence of value (potential) exists before exchange. Furthermore, the existence of value is an instantaneous reality confined to the movement of exchange. (De Vroey 1981: 177).

Since we have already discussed such an argument in the context of Marx's own writings, I will be brief here.[33] To get to the analytical problem with such a position, let us suppose that there are three commodities, x, y and z, with 6, 7, and 8 hours of 'embodied labour' respectively, and that their organic composition of capital is such that the equilibrium exchange ratios in the market is given by 1:1:1. This means that a commodity x with 6 hours of social labour embodied in it can command 7 or 8 hours of social labour in exchange. In other words, commodity x can at the same time cover 7/21 or 8/21 parts of the total social labour. In general, every commodity will have one 'labour-embodied' value and $n - 1$ social labour-commanded value.

---

33 Also see Sinha (2003) for a more detailed treatment of this subject.

Thus, to solve for a unique value of 'abstract labour' or command of social labour, one needs to find a commodity that represents purely 'abstract labour'. The money-commodity is supposed to play this role: 'theory of value simply cannot stand without a theory of money' (De Vroey 1981: 173). But as we have already argued, if money is a commodity then it will also have one 'embodied' labour-value and n - 1 social labour-commanded value. The idea that the labour embodied in the money-commodity could be taken to represent purely 'abstract labour' does not work as there is no way of adding the indirect labour content of the money-commodity without reducing the concept of 'abstract labour' to simple unskilled labour, which is exactly what the concept of 'embodied labour' amounts to. Aglietta appears to understand that there is a problem here. Hence he proposes to exclude money from the set of commodities:

> As the permanent and exclusive representative of abstract labour, money is expelled from the set of commodities proper. Every commodity always expresses its exchange-value in money. Money, for its part, never expresses its value relative to any other commodity, since it never faces any equivalent (Aglietta 1979: 41).

But if money is expelled from the set of commodities, then how could it be related to social labour? De Vroey proposes the ratio of the sum of prices over the sum of values as the '*monetary expression of social labour-time*' (De Vroey 1981: 190). But the idea is self-contradictory. First we are told that values cannot be determined prior to exchange, and that too, prior to exchange against money, which is supposed to represent the 'abstract social labour-time'. Then we are informed that the extent of social labour-time a unit of money is supposed to represent is determined by the total values in circulation. In other words, we need to know values to determine values! The point to note here is that the total value in circulation is equal to C + V + S, though one could claim to get V + S from the observation of direct labour expenditure, the value of C cannot be known unless we perform the mathematical exercise of determining its labour-embodied content. Once we realise that, the contradiction in such arguments becomes obvious.

In this milieu arose another group of Marxists who tried to escape the transformation problem by redefining the terms of the problem. In 1980, Dumenil published a paper in French, which was translated in English in 1984; and in the meanwhile Duncan Foley published his paper in 1982. Both Dumenil (1984) and Foley (1982) independently made similar arguments and their reformulation of the transformation problem was quickly endorsed and hailed as the 'New Solution' by a large group of Marxists, though Foley likes to call it a 'new interpretation', which is more appropriate.[34]

Dumenil and Foley make two fundamental propositions: *(i)* they determine *'value of money'* by the ratio of the total observed direct labour-time spent in production (somehow adjusted for skill differentials, etc.), over the total prices of the net output (i.e., prices of total physical output minus prices of total constant capital used up in the process of production); *(ii)* they argue that the value of labour-power or the measure of variable capital should be made by the given money wages and not by the value of the real wage. Thus, given money wages and the 'value of money' from proposition *i*, the value of variable capital is immediately determined by multiplying the money wages by the 'value of money'. And given proposition *i* and the measure of variable capital so determined, the equality of total profits and surplus-value comes out as a definitional identity. But this still does not guarantee that the sum of values would be equal to the sum of prices.

Dumenil, however, argues that Marx's condition of the sum of prices equal to the sum of values applies to only the *net* output and not the *gross* output, which he claims amounts to 'double counting'; and thus, according to him, both of Marx's conditions are fulfilled by their redefinition:

> The equality between the price and the value of social production must be established on the basis of the net product, not the gross product, of a given period. In the framework of an annual period of production, it is clear that all national accounting and economic calculation addresses the yearly net product (disregarding the problem of amortization). It would never occur to take into account the totals of the columns and rows of an input-output table. Yet this is precisely what equality between total (gross) prices and total value would mean (Dumenil 1984: 441–42).

I, however, do not find this convincing. The cost of the raw materials and machines used up in the production of a commodity does form a part of the price of the commodity and it is the commodity

---

34 Also see Lipietz (1982). Laibman (1973, 2002) also has a similar approach. See Sinha (1997) for a critique of the 'New Solution'.

that circulates and exchanges in the market and not just the 'value added' part of it. Thus the total price of the total output produced must contain the prices of all the raw materials and machines used up in the annual production cycle and similarly for the value accounting. There is no double counting involved here. The constant capital element in the system of production cannot be conjured away by the magic of rhetoric. Now, since the constant capital element is part of the price of a commodity, the question is: how do we account for its value from the perspective of the 'new interpretation'? If we derive it by multiplying the prices of constant capital goods with the value of money (as was done for money wages), then the whole exercise turns into nonsense, as it amounts to a claim that values are proportional to prices. Thus the value of all commodities must be measured by the good old 'labour-embodied' method. And given that we have used the condition of the sum of prices of net output equals the sum of direct labour-time in the system as the normalisation equation, there is no guarantee that after price-value deviation the total prices of all the inputs used up would be equal to the value of the total constant capital. So the question arises: where does the discrepancy come from? Foley claims that:

> With the proposed definition of the value of money, this value gained or lost through unequal exchange may be positive or negative for any particular commodity or group of commodities, but is zero for the system of commodity production as a whole; in this interpretation value is created in production and conserved in exchange (Foley 1982: 41).

But as we have shown earlier, this is simply not true. It would be true only if there was no constant capital in the system.

In the presence of constant capital the total values would deviate from the total prices, but not due to double counting.

The problem with the 'new interpretation' does not end here. Its definition of the 'value of money' and the redefinition of variable capital turns Marx's notion of the rate of surplus-value into a variable that depends on the composition of the net output. For example, let us take a system and determine its rate of surplus-value according to the 'new interpretation'. Now, suppose that the tastes of capitalists change and the given total labour is accordingly reallocated to meet this change in taste. This, in all likelihood, would change the total prices of the net output and thus the 'value of money'. Since the money wages are the same but the value of money has changed, the value of variable capital will undergo a change as well. On the other hand, since the total direct labour has remained the same, the rate of surplus-value must change, given the change in the value of variable capital. This is a highly un-Marxist result; even Lipietz, who was the earliest and most enthusiastic supporter of Dumenil's original paper, admitted that: 'This does not fit very well with Marxist intuition' (Lipietz 1982: 83).

As a matter of fact this problem can be taken care of by the use of Sraffa's (1960) 'Standard commodity' as the 'money-commodity'. Eatwell (1974, 1975b) had already developed a solution to the transformation problem on the same lines as the 'new solution' some years earlier, but it has somehow gone largely unacknowledged in the Marxist literature even after Sinha (1997) pointed it out.[35] Eatwell's argument is in favour of the idea of using 'money wages' as *given*. However, he does not define the rate of exploitation in terms of the given money-commodity. He suggests that we should express the given money wages in terms of Sraffa's Standard commodity. Given the 'Standard net product' derived from the given system, the wages could now be expressed as a numerical ratio of the net output. Thus the rate of exploitation would be determined independently of prices for the Standard system. Given that the scale of the Standard system is the same as the scale of the actual system, i.e., the total direct labour time spent in the two systems are the same, the ratio of wages to net output given in the Standard system would apply to any allocation of the net output of the same scale, given the wages in terms of the Standard commodity. Thus the rate of exploitation can be determined independently of the composition of the net output. Eatwell shows that in this case a direct relationship between the rate of exploitation and the general rate of profits can be established as $\alpha = R[e/(1 + e)]$, where α is the rate of profits, R is the maximum rate of profit, and e is the rate of exploitation defined as one minus the proportion of total labour 'embodied' in the 'money wage', where the Standard commodity is chosen as the money-commodity.[36]

---

35 See Sinha (2000) for a critique of Eatwell. For other Sraffa inspired solutions to the transformation problem, see Medio (1972) and Krause (1982).

36 Recently Hollander (2008) has revived the case of 'money-commodity' produced by the 'average composition of capital': 'Moreover, a constant "value" (labor input, direct and indirect) is assumed to rule in the case of the monetary commodity; ... A second condition is that the monetary commodity should require the mean organic composition of capital, ... ' (Hollander 2008: 21). It should, however, be noted that Marx was well aware that the commodity with mean organic composition would not necessarily remain invariable during the transformation: 'It is quite possible, accordingly, for the cost price to diverge from the value sum of the elements of

In all these reformulations and new interpretations, the idea of 'money wages' as given has become an accepted norm and is regarded as the correct interpretation of Marx's position on wages. This, however, is simply not true. Marx's practice of taking wages in terms of pound sterling was based on his assumption of value-price proportionality. Without going into the exegetical debate, it should be noted that if Marx took 'money wages' as given, he could not derive the value of variable capital prior to the knowledge of the prices of production, and thus value and the rate of surplus-value could not be determined prior to the knowledge of prices of production. This would simply destroy Marx's purported attempt to prove that values and surplus-values are the *essential substance* of the phenomena of prices and profits.

Apparently independently of Dumenil and Foley's attempts, Wolff et al. (1984) developed a similar 'solution' to the transformation problem. They tried to redefine the determination of value in such a way that both of Marx's conditions, namely, the equality of the sum of values with the sum of prices of gross outputs and the sum of surplus-value with the sum of profits, are satisfied. Specifically, they argue that value of a commodity should be determined by adding up the direct labour-time to the prices of production of the constant capital instead of the value of the constant capital (see equation 3 below). Their so-called solution is as follows:

$$\rho = [\rho A + \rho bL](1 + r) \tag{1}$$

$$\rho[X - AX] = LX \tag{2}$$

$$V = \rho A + L \tag{3}$$

$$r = (LX - \rho bLX)/(\rho AX + \rho bLX) \tag{4}$$

where ρ is a vector of Sraffian prices of production, A is the matrix of physical inputs per unit of outputs, b is the vector of physical real wage per unit of labour, L is the vector of direct labour per unit of output, r is the uniform rate of profits in the system, X is the vector

---

which this component of the price of production is composed, even in the case of commodities that are produced by capitals of average composition. Let us assume that the average composition is 80c + 20v. It is possible now that, for the actual individual capitals that are composed in this way, the 80c may be greater or less than the value of c, the constant capital, since this c is composed of commodities, whose prices of production are different from their values.' (Marx 1991: 309).

of gross outputs produced and V is the vector of labour-value per unit of outputs.

Now let us analyse the definition of value given in equation (3): $V = \rho A + L \rightarrow VX = \rho AX + LX$. Now substituting the value of LX from equation (2), we get $VX = \rho X$, which means that the sum of gross labour-values are equal to the sum of prices of production. And this is supposed to be the solution of the 'transformation problem'. They, however, forget that from equation (4) we get

$$(\rho AX + \rho bLX)(1 + r) = LX + \rho AX$$

$$\rightarrow (\rho A + \rho bL)(1 + r) = \rho A + L$$

$\rightarrow \rho = V$, from equations (1) and (3). In other words, values are equal to prices of production.

Thus in Wolff et al.'s case, Marx's two conditions are satisfied by simply defining values to be equal to prices of production. In other words, what their 'solution' amounts to is this: take a Sraffian physical input-output system; determine Sraffian prices and the rate of profits; then translate Sraffian relative prices into absolute labour units by equating the total direct labour-time with the total prices of production of the net output; call such translated Sraffian prices 'Marx's values'; *voilà!* you have the solution to the transformation problem.

The reader would have also noticed that in all these defences of Marx's value theory, the fundamental point of Marx's argument is completely lost. Marx argues that *values and surplus-values determine profits and prices of production*. But all the arguments in defence of Marx that we just discussed, argue that, on the contrary, it is the prices or the prices of production that *determine* values. Though there are some diehard Marxists who are still in the business of trying to 'solve' the transformation problem, most attempts to do so are rooted in a misunderstanding of the nature of the problem. Once we understand that the productivity of a system of production that uses produced means of production cannot be reduced to the productivity of labour alone and that capital cannot be measured or aggregated by labour-values, it becomes clear that the 'transformation problem' is a false problem.

In 1981, Samuel Hollander published an interesting interpretation of Marx's transformation problem, which unfortunately went largely unnoticed in the Marxist literature; however, see Pokorni (1985) and Sinha (2001a). However, Hollander has recently come up with a long and comprehensive book on Marx, which places his interpretation of the transformation problem at the heart of his highly provocative reading of Marx. Hollander (2008, Chapter 1) argues that Marx's theory of price was also (as he has argued for Smith and Ricardo) an aspect of the theory of resource allocation in a general equilibrium framework. According to Hollander, Marx's value-ratios are in fact disequilibrium market prices, and the transformation algorithm is supposed to describe a *real* movement of the system from disequilibrium to an equilibrium position — in effect, it is a description of the classical gravitation mechanism. Hollander is not much concerned with the 'correctness' of the so-called 'solution' to the transformation problem. His concern is to show how Marx's equilibrium prices are demand-dependent.

Hollander argues, and I think correctly, that Marx did not assume a uniform organic composition of capital in the first two volumes of *Capital* and therefore his prices, that are supposed to be proportional to values, are disequilibrium market prices. Since Marx subscribed to the classical gravitation mechanism, it would be logical to think that when the system adjusts to prices of production or equilibrium prices, he would expect the outputs of various sectors to change. From here on, Hollander argues that as prices adjust due to supply adjustments from disequilibrium value-ratios to equilibrium prices of production ratios, it cannot be maintained that the total demand for labour would remain constant through this process. Thus, either a rise or a fall in the total demand for labour due to supply adjustments cannot fail to have impact on the wages and the rate of profits. Hence the determination of the prices of production is dependent on the level of demand as the distribution of income cannot be taken as *given* from outside the system of market adjustments:

> Most significantly, the impression left by Marx's procedure is that given both the wage rate (implied by the rate of surplus-value) and the configuration of output, it is possible to predict the average profit and the set of equilibrium prices that assures profit-rate equality. This is a false impression, as we have explained, in that both the wage and the output levels are not data but endogenous variables of the Marxian system (Hollander 2008: 52).

Now there is no doubt that Marx subscribed to the classical gravitation mechanism and argued that in a competitive capitalist economies disequilibrium prices adjust to equilibrium prices in the manner that Hollander describes, with one important caveat that we will discuss soon. But this does not mean that Marx's transformation algorithm must be interpreted as a description of the gravitation mechanism. If that were the case, then Marx would have had to present a dynamical system of price adjustment, which he clearly does not do. As we have seen earlier, Marx sets up the problem thus:

> There is no doubt, however, that in actual fact, ignoring inessential, accidental circumstances that cancel each other out, no such variation in the average rate of profit exists between different branches of industry, and it could not exist without abolishing the entire system of capitalist production. The theory of value thus appears incompatible with the actual movement, incompatible with the actual phenomena of production, and it might seem that we must abandon all hope of understanding these phenomena (Marx 1991: 252).

In other words, according to Marx, the hypothesis that commodities exchange in proportion to their labour-values seems to contradict the fact that the commodities must exchange in such proportions that the rate of profits is equalised in all the sectors. It is this apparent contradiction that needs to be resolved and not that prices have to move from value-ratios to prices of production ratios. Furthermore, as we have noted, Marx had admitted that in his transformation algorithm he needed to use prices of production and not labour-values to measure the input costs as well:

> The development given above also involves a modification in the determination of a commodity's cost price. It was originally assumed that the cost price of a commodity equalled the value of the commodities consumed in its production. But for the buyer of a commodity, it is the price of production that constitutes its cost price and can thus enter into forming the price of another commodity. As the price of production of a commodity can diverge from its value, so the cost price of a commodity, in which the price of production of other commodities are involved, can also stand above or below the portion of its total value that is formed by the value of the means of production going into it. *It is necessary to bear in mind this modified significance of the cost price, and therefore to bear in mind too that if the cost price of a commodity is equated with the value of the means of production used up in producing it, it is always possible to go wrong* (ibid.: 264–65, emphasis added).

This ought to settle the issue. Once it is admitted that prices of production ought to appear both on the input as well as the output side, then it can no longer be argued that the problem is of moving from one set of prices to another set. The problem reduces to *determining* the set of prices that appear on both sides of the equation. Thus the transformation algorithm is not about transforming values to prices of production; rather, it is about determining the prices of production of a system which is first described in terms of labour-values — Marx would have preferred to do what Bortkiewicz or Seton were able to do many years later. There is no historical dimension to the transformation algorithm and that is why outputs do not change in Marx's examples. Furthermore, if Marx allowed the outputs to change in the transformation process, then it is not clear what meaning one could assign to his two famous results — that the sum of prices equals the sum of values and the sum of profits equals the sum of surplus-values.

One question, however, remains: are Marx's outputs equilibrium outputs? Perhaps yes; but even if they are not, one could argue that as long as we assume that the techniques in use are linear, the adjustment of the *given* outputs to the equilibrium outputs should not affect the prices of production. Hollander does not agree with this. He argues that if the quantity adjustment is in favour of the commodities produced by a lower organic composition of capital sectors, then the result would be a rise in the total demand for labour and thus a rise in wages, which in turn would affect prices of production. Here lies the fundamental difference in our understanding of the classical gravitation mechanism. Hollander begins his analysis with a given set of commodities and labour that needs to be allocated according to the utility functions expressed by the demand functions for the commodities. I argue that the classical economists and Marx begin with a given empirical system of inputs and outputs. On the assumption of linear techniques, the total labour employed in the given empirical system can be reallocated in all sorts of ways to produce various different sets of net outputs. Any one of these sets of possible net outputs can be taken as 'effectual demands', and the gravitation mechanism is a description of how the empirical system would converge on this set of 'effectual demands'. In this process, the demand for total labour employment remains fixed and therefore wages have no reason to change. As we have argued in the previous two chapters, the classical 'effectual demands' are given demand points (Hollander's demand curves *must* pass through these given demand points) and these points cannot be taken to be given unless we begin with a given size of the economy.

Controversies on the Falling Rate of Profits

There are two strands to the controversy regarding Marx's proposition on the issue of the tendency of the rate of profits to fall. The first accepts Marx's formula for the rate of profits given by $(S/V)/(C/V + 1)$ and asks: was Marx right to claim that technical change would lead to a fall in the rate of profits? Of course, increased productivity of labour due to technical change would lead to a fall in V, and given the real wages and the length of the working day, a rise in S/V. Second, a fall in V does not necessarily mean that C/V will rise, since increased productivity of labour would also lead to a fall in C and there is no reason to assume that the rate of fall in V would be always higher than the rate of fall in C. Steedman, on the other hand, argues that 'Marx's normal assumptions do entail a rising organic composition of capital, despite the cheapening of the constant capital' (Steedman 1971: 210). His mathematical result, however, crucially depends on the assumption of equal organic composition of capital in all sectors of the system. Following Morishima (1973), we know that such a system can be reduced to a one-good model. Now it is clear that if we allow technical change in a one-good 'corn model', the value of both constant and variable capital will fall proportionately, as both of them are given in the same commodity 'corn'. Since Marx assumes that the technical change entails more corn per labour employed, it directly follows that in this case the ratio C/V must rise. What Steedman does, however, not show is that this result would be true even in the normal case of a system with a differing organic composition of capital.

In his examples, Marx keeps the S/V ratio constant. This has led to the accusation that he simply disregards the mathematical relationship between the productivity of labour and the rate of surplus-value (e.g., Bortkiewicz 1952). Others, like Joan Robinson (1942), hold that Marx required S/V to be constant for his falling rate of profits hypothesis, which means that he required a proportional rise in real wages with increase in labour productivity. Such an assumption would militate against Marx's own prediction regarding the long-term trend of real wages, which was supposed to be falling towards minimum subsistence.

These were the terms of the debate during the middle of the twentieth century among Dobb (1937, 1959); Sweezy (1942); Robinson (1942); Dickinson (1957); Meek (1967), etc. Now there is no denying the fact that productivity-enhancing technical change does not necessarily ensure a fall in Marx's rate of profits and Marx was well aware of this as is evidenced in the discussion of these possibilities in his chapter on countervailing tendencies. As we have noted in footnote 11, though Marx believed that technical change *would* lead to a rise in S/V, he felt that this rise would not be large enough to offset the impact of the rise in C/V on the rate of profits (also see Hollander 2008 for overwhelming evidence on this score). On the question of the rise in C/V, Marx simply assumed that the organic composition of capital *would* reflect changes in the proportion of materials to labour in the production process. Given that normally technical change would lead to dimensional incongruity, it is clear that one cannot always measure changes in such ratios — e.g., how is one supposed to measure the changes in the material contents of a typewriter and a computer? Thus it appears that Marx simply assumed that if one unit of labour processes more raw materials (assuming that the raw materials in the production process remain the same both before and after the technical change), then it would reflect in the rise in C/V ratio; and he believed that the increase in the ratio of raw materials processed by a unit of labour would be much greater than the rise in S/V.

However, no matter how one looks at it, Marx's assertion that technical changes lead to a rise in the C/V ratio is simply an assertion of an empirical nature and is not rooted in the logic of the theory.[37] Meek (1967), however, argues that at any given time there is a maximum rate of profit which is equal to S/C, on the assumption that V = 0. Now, given that V = 0 and S is a positive constant, if C is rising then the maximum rate of profits must be continuously falling. From here, Meek concludes that as V tends to zero due to productivity growth, the real rate of profits must also fall eventually.

This brings us to the second strand of the debate, which asks the question: Why would capitalists adopt technical changes that reduce their rate of profits? In as early as 1939, Shibata had already shown that prices and the general rate of profit can be determined directly from the technical coefficients of production without any reference to values. Based on this, his argument is that:

> [C]apitalist producers normally elevate the organic composition of capital only when such elevation lowers the cost of production, i.e., only when it is of such a character that its generalisation would make the purchasing power of the goods concerned become lower than it otherwise would be. Accordingly, the elevation of the organic composition of capital by

---

37 See Hollander (1991 and 2008) for detailed discussion on the nature of technical changes that would bring about the falling trend in Marx's rate of profits. Also see Steedman (1977) for the condition that ensures a fall in the rate of profits, given equal organic composition of capital in all the sectors.

capitalists far from causing a decline in the general profit rate actually tends to raise it (1939: 52).

And further:

> This, however, by no means implies that a fall in the general profit rate may not coincide with a rise in the organic composition of capital. It simply shows that if such coincidence occurs the fall in the general profit rate must be explained not by the elevation of the organic composition of capital as was done by Marx, but by other factors, such as the simultaneous shortening of the working day and what not (ibid.: 60–61).

Unfortunately, Shibata's paper remained unknown to the English-speaking world for a long time.

In the meantime, Samuelson (1957) also demonstrated that a fall in the rate of profits due to technical change is only possible if there is a rise in real wages. From here, he concluded:

> [W]e should note a contradiction in Marx's thinking that analysts have pointed out. Along with the 'law of the falling rate of profit', Marxian economists often speak of the 'law of the falling (or constant) real wage of labor. ... But he perhaps didn't fully realize the inconsistency of his two inevitable laws. (1957: 892–93).

As we have mentioned earlier, Samuelson's 1957 paper also went largely unnoticed. In 1961, Okishio published a proof of the same proposition, which was noticed and later christened Okishio's Theorem. With the help of Perron-Frobenius theorem, Okishio showed that if a technical change is more profitable at the given prices and the wage rate prevailing in the regime of old techniques, then its introduction and general adoption would result in a higher rate of profits even in the regime of new prices (if the good in question was not a luxury good; in the case of a luxury good the rate of profits would remain constant).[38] Recall that Marx's argument is that the new technique provides a higher rate of profit than the prevailing general rate when the old prices prevail, but when the adoption of the new technique becomes universal, then all values and prices change, which brings about a fall in the general rate of profits. The Shibata-Samuelson- Okishio theorem shows that this particular hypothesis of Marx was wrong.

---

38 For a general proof of this theorem, see Roemer (1977).

Shaikh (1978), however, demurs. He makes essentially two points that are not necessarily connected. On the basis of Schefold (1976), where Schefold showed that a particular kind of labour-saving and material-enhancing technical change may lead to a rise in the rate of profit but at the same time a fall in the maximum rate of profit (recall Meek 1967), Shaikh claims that:

> The proposition that mechanization, so defined, lowers the maximum rate of profit, would appear to imply that *sooner or later* the actual rate of profit must necessarily fall. And indeed this is exactly how it has been interpreted by many Marxists. The basic logic of Marx's argument, therefore, seems to emerge unscathed (1978: 240).

I find this unconvincing. All Schefold's results show is that there is a *limit* to such technical changes in the system. Once the actual rate of profits of the system reaches a point such that any further technical change of this nature would bring the maximum rate of profit below it and therefore force the actual rate of profits to fall, will simply not be adopted by the capitalists.

Actually, if the impact of technical changes on the actual and maximum rates of profit is continuous, then the rising actual rate of profits can begin to fall only after it has first become equal to the maximum rate of profit. But the maximum rate of profit is given by the rate of profit of any system when the wage bill is equal to zero. And given that both Marx and Shaikh take a positive wage rate, the actual rate of profits will be equal to the maximum rate only when labour vanishes from the system. Thus, if this is how most Marxists interpreted the law of falling rate of profits, then it is evident that their interpretation was based on a serious misunderstanding of the notion of 'maximum rate of profit' (if I understand correctly, Roemer 1979 has also made the same point).

Shaikh's second point is that Okishio's theorem works with a model with no fixed capital. However, Marx's proposition requires the presence of fixed capital and in this case it can be shown that capitalists *may choose* to introduce technical changes that lower their rate of profits.[39] His argument rests on the distinction between *profit margin on cost and profit rate*. Profit margin on cost is defined by the ratio

---

39 Also see Fine and Harris (1976).

of total net revenue to total circulation cost, including depreciation charges on fixed capital and wage bills; whereas profit rate is defined by the ratio of total net revenue to total capital investment, including the full value of the fixed capital. He argues that a fixed capital-intensive technique may have a low circulation cost of production per unit of output, i.e., high profit margin on cost, but at the same time a low profit rate due to the large weight of fixed capital in total investment — and vice-versa for a low fixed capital technique. His argument is as follows:

> For example, suppose that method A [with no fixed capital] has a unit cost-price of $100 and a selling price of $120, so that the profit-margin on costs (and also profit rate in this case) equals 20%. Now suppose that at currently ruling prices the more mechanised technique B could produce the same commodity for $50, but that owing to the heavy capitalization involved it would only yield a rate of profit of 18%. ... Faced with the possibility of a cheaper method of production, the first capitalist to make the move will be able to lower his price to a point where the others make little or no profits (or even suffer losses) — while still making a profit himself. At a price of $99, for instance, all capitalists using the old techniques will make a loss of $1 per commodity, whereas the capitalist who switched first would be making a profit of $49 per commodity — and expanding rapidly to take over the field! (Shaikh 1978: 245–46).

I find Shaikh's definition of the 'rate of profit' highly problematic. This can be seen by considering a simple example: suppose a sector has several firms that use the same technique with fixed capital equipments, but are of different ages; if Shaikh's definition of the 'rate of profit' is applied to these firms, then it is clear that the older firms would have higher rates of profits than the newer ones since the total investment costs of the older firms would be lower due to annual depreciation of fixed capital investments and thus everybody would want to buy an old firm rather than build a new one. Roemer (1979) is quick to point out that Shaikh forgets to take into account the interest cost on fixed capital investments. He shows that Shaikh's argument fails once the amortisation of fixed capital is taken into account. Shaikh's (1980) response was that the rate of interest and the rate of profit are not the same thing, as Roemer apparently assumes from his neoclassical perspective. He argues that the rate of interest must be somewhat below the rate of profit, but concedes that: 'What is given for individual capital, however, is the interest rate, for the simple reason that this magnitude is guaranteed in advance. As such, it can and does appear as a factor in the calculations of capitalists' (Shaikh 1980: 78). Shaikh, however, does not go on to show the implication of taking a positive rate of interest for the amortisation of fixed capital. I think the issue of the difference in the rate of interest and the rate of profit in this context is a sign of confusion, because the issue disappears once we treat fixed capital as a joint-product. Roemer (1979) shows that in this context, too, Shaikh's argument does not hold. The reason for this is simple. Marx's proposition regarding the falling rate of profits is about the rate that would prevail when the system is at the centre of gravitation point and all the sectoral rates of profit have become equal. This rate of profits and all the prices are determined simultaneously for the whole system. Thus what one is dealing with here is the movement of the centre of gravitation itself, which is a systemic movement and cannot be understood by looking at what is given for an individual capitalist.[40]

Even though Shaikh's argument is not convincing within the given parameters of the problem, it still has a ring of truth about it. It seems that the point both Shaikh and Marx are driving at is a description of what Marx calls the concentration and centralisation of capital (see the section of 'Falling Rate of Profits'). But in this context we must leave the hypothesis of the gravitation mechanism and the equalisation of the rates of profit behind. Instead, we need to construct an oligopoly model where the market size is given and the competition is over the share of the market size and the amount of profits over a period of time, and not necessarily the maximisation of the rate of profit as such. Unfortunately, though, Marx maintained that the concentration and centralisation of capital is a *result* of the falling rate of profits and that the large firms and the joint-stock companies do not play a role in bringing about the fall in the rate of profits, as their rates of profit are much below the average already, and that the falling trend applies to competitive sectors only (see Hollander 2008).[41]

---

40 For other criticisms of Shaikh's paper, see Steedman (1980b), Nakatani (1980), Armstrong and Glyn (1980) and Bleaney (1980). For Shaikh's response to these criticisms and also Roemer's (1979), see Shaikh (1980).

41 Dasgupta argues that: 'There is, one would suggest, implict in the nature of accumulation, as viewed by Marx, the idea of diminishing returns — diminishing returns due to a disproportionate use of factors. Marx does not spell it out, but it must be there. Since, as the economy grows, there is increasing employment of capital per man, there is no reason why the rate at which the total output increases should not be diminishing' (Dasgupta 1985: 34). This, however, cannot be accepted as

But the story does not end here. Salvadori (1981) presents an interesting example of a joint-production case where Marx's argument turns out to be true. Let us suppose that there are two processes and two commodities 'x' and 'y', such that process (1) uses 0.5 unit of commodity 'x' and 0.5 unit of commodity 'y' along with 1 unit of labour to produce 1 unit of commodity 'x' and 2 units of commodity 'y'; whereas process (2) uses 0.5 unit of 'y' along with 1 unit of labour to produce 1 unit of commodity 'x'. Let us assume that the real wage is equal to 1 unit of 'y' per unit of labour. Then our prices of production equations are given by:

$$(0.5P_x + 0.5P_y + P_y)(1 + r) = P_x + 2P_y \tag{1}$$

$$(0.5P_y + P_y)(1 + r) = P_x \tag{2}$$

$$P_x + P_y = 1 \qquad \text{(3), the normalisation eq.}$$

The solution of the equations gives us the rate of profits $r = 31/50$ and $P_x = (6-6^{1/2})/5$ and $P_y = (6^{1/2}-1)/5$. Now suppose that a new process (3) is discovered, which uses 3 units of 'y' along with 1 unit of labour to produce 3 units of 'x'. If we apply the ruling prices P_x and P_y to the process (3), then the rate of profit earned by operating process (3) will be $5/5.7$, which is greater than $31/50$. Thus process (2) would be abandoned and process (3) taken on board. However, once process (1) and process (3) begin to dominate, the rate of profits 'r' falls to around $49/80$, which is less than $31/50$. The reader can easily check that on the given prices of 'x' and 'y', when only process (1) and process (3) are operating, the rate of profit earned by operating process (2) is lower than $49/80$. Thus process (2) will not come back. This is a refutation of Shibata-Samuelson-Okishio theorem. It shows that the theorem is valid in the limited case of single production only. In the general case of joint-production, the matter becomes much more complicated.

On Marx's Theory of 'Increasing Immiseration' of the Working Class

As we have already noted, if one argues that the rate of profits must decline over a long period of time, then it is difficult to maintain that

---

Marx's reasoning, since in Marx's case the increase in 'capital' per man comes with technological changes. The new techniques are more productive as they provide a higher rate of profits on old prices given fixed wages. The problem is: will the rate of profits remain greater than the old rate of profits when new prices are allowed to set in? This problem cannot be interpreted in terms of a single production function with diminishing returns on 'capital' per man.

real wages would also decline at the same time without introducing diminishing returns in the system.

Our position has been that Marx's explanation of the falling rate of profits is theoretically incoherent, whereas his explanation of falling real wages is coherent. Many scholars, however, would like to believe that the falling rate of profits thesis is coherent and it is simply incorrect to suggest that Marx ever maintained that real wages have a long-term tendency to fall. They argue that according to Marx real wages actually have a long-term tendency to rise over time and therefore there is no contradiction in maintaining that the rate of profits has a tendency to fall at the same time (see, e.g., Sowell 1960; Mandel 1968; Rosdolsky 1980; Ramirez 1986; Lapides 1998;[42] and Lebowitz 2003).

This position, however, flies directly in the face of overwhelming evidence. Apart from the arguments and evidence presented in the section 'On Wages' in this volume, the whole of Section V of Chapter 25 (68 pages in total) in *Capital* Volume I is devoted to documenting a declining tendency of real wages in England (for the period 1846 to 1866) and Ireland (for the period 1860 to 1865). Interestingly, Marx puts a lot of stress on the deteriorating condition of housing for all strata of workers. Since housing constitutes a fair share of the real wage basket, the case for a declining tendency of real wage in this period is very strong. Furthermore, in his 1865 lecture (*Value, Price and Profit*), when the final draft of Volume I of *Capital* was under preparation and the rough drafts of Volumes II and III were already complete, Marx clearly states that: '... the general tendency of capitalist production is not to raise, but to sink the average standard of wages, or to push the value of labour more or less to its minimum limit' (Marx [1865] 1976: 61).

On the other hand, the case for a rising trend in real wages in either *Capital* or the 1865 lecture is non-existent. Marx's statement in Volume I of *Capital* that 'in proportion as capital accumulates, the lot of the labourer, be his payment high or low, must grow worse', is regularly invoked to suggest that Marx believed that though the real wages might rise, the workers conditions compared to the capitalists would continue to worsen: hence the reference to wages being 'high or low'. It should, however, be noted that there is no reference to rising wages in Marx's statement. In the real world labourers do not get one universal wage; rather, there is always a spectrum of wages for different strata of workers — some are paid relatively 'high' and some are paid relatively 'low'. Hollander (2008), in my opinion, correctly interprets

---

42 For a critical review of Lapides (1998), see Sinha (2001b).

Marx's statement as 'Marx intended a decline in the general wage rate which affects *all* classes of labourers — those high on the wage scale as well as those at a lower level' (Hollander 2008: 86). Given that Marx maintained that the rate of profits also falls, the question is: how could he speak of labourers' conditions becoming 'worse' compared to the capitalists? The answer to this question lies in the centralisation and concentration of capital. Centralisation tends to reduce the size of the capitalist class and hence increases the total profit incomes of individual capitalists even though the rate of profits is falling. Hence the worsening conditions of the workers compared to the capitalists.[43]

Ramirez (1986) argues that in Marx's theory the real wages are determined by the productivity of labour, and since technical changes increase the productivity of labour, one can expect real wages to rise. As a matter of fact, according to Marx, Carey had just such a theory of wages, to which Marx responded thus:

In an Essay on the Rate of Wages, one of his first economic writings, H. Carey tries to prove that differences in national wage-levels are directly proportional to the degree of productivity of the working day of each nation, in order to draw from this international ratio the deduction that wages everywhere rise and fall in proportion to the productivity of labour. The whole of our analysis of the production of surplus-value shows that this deduction would be absurd. (Marx 1977: 705).

Rosdolskey, Lapides and Lebowitz add the role of trade unions to the case of the rising productivity of labour. They argue that rising productivity of labour creates an opportunity for trade unions to push for and win real wage increases. Marx's statement from the 1865 lecture, where he said:

It is evident that between the two limits of this *maximum rate of profit* an immense scale of variations is possible. The

---

43 Gottheil (1962) argues that: 'Since it [centralisation] raises the rate of profit its impact would be to increase the rate of accumulation and thus demand for labor. On the other hand it would push some capitalists to the side of the proletariat and thus increase the reserve army of labor' (Gottheil 1962: 86). Gottheil is clearly wrong in thinking that Marx expected centralisation to raise the rate of profit. Actually, Marx held that large centralised firms have much lower rates of profit than average competitive firms. Though centralisation was not supposed to raise the *rate* of profit, it was supposed to increase the *total* profit of an individual capitalist who was successful in centralising larger amounts of capital in one hand.

fixation of its actual degree is only settled by the continuous struggle between capital and labour, the capitalist constantly tending to reduce wages to their physical minimum, and to extend the working day to its physical maximum, while the working man constantly presses in the opposite direction. The question resolves itself into a question of the respective powers of the combatants (Marx [1865] 1976: 58),

is usually invoked in favour of such a thesis. But this would work only if one could show that the technical changes somehow strengthen the position of the working class vis-a-vis the capitalist class. We, however, know that according to Marx technical changes are of labour-saving and unemployment-enhancing nature. This would only weaken the relative position of the working class rather then strengthen it.

It should also be noted that Marx did not think that trade unions play any role in establishing the value of labour-power. Their role, in this context, is limited to the market fluctuation of the wages around the independently established value of labour-power. Given the peculiar nature of the labour market, where the buyers are much stronger than the individual sellers, it is the trade unions in this particular market that bring some sort of parity between the buyers and sellers. Marx's argument runs on a dynamic plane over a business cycle, where fluctuation in market wages takes place around a given value of labour-power. During a period of recession, market wages most likely fall below the value of labour-power, and thus during the boom period workers must push for higher wages to compensate for the loss during the recession. This is the only way the value of labour-power can be maintained over a business cycle. This, however, can only be accomplished by an organised workers' movement, since an individual worker would still be too weak vis-a-vis the capitalists. Trade unions thus become an essential part in the workings of the market for labour-power. As Marx said in his 1865 lecture:

> The periodical resistance on the part of the working men against a reduction of wages, and their periodical attempts at getting a rise of wages, are inseparable from the wages system, and dictated by the very fact of labour being assimilated to commodities, and therefore subject to the laws regulating the general movement of prices ([1865] 1976: 56).

Furthermore, Marx did not think that trade unions could reverse the tide of demand and supply forces — they could win wage concessions only when demand and supply forces were in their favour.

Some scholars (e.g., Baumol 1983; Lapides 1998) have incorrectly identified the 'increasing immiseration' thesis with the 'Iron Law of Wages'. An 'increasing immiseration' thesis, however, must assume that real wages for most of the historical period under consideration must be considerably above 'minimum subsistence', else how could one talk of a secular decline in real wages? The Iron Law of Wages, on the other hand, maintains that the real wages cannot be higher than 'minimum subsistence' for any considerable period of time. The two theses thus mutually exclude each other. Marx himself believed that in most countries the customary standard of life of the class that became the proletariat was much higher than the 'physical minimum'. This is what constitutes the 'historical, moral and cultural' element of real wages — the element that allows for a prolonged decline in the real wages. As Marx pointed out in his 1865 lecture:

> Besides this mere Physical element, the value of labour is in every country determined by a *traditional standard of life*. It is not mere physical life, but it is the satisfaction of certain wants springing from the social conditions in which people are placed and reared up. The English standard of life may be reduced to the *Irish* standard; the standard of life of a German peasant to that of a Livonian peasant. The important part which historical tradition and social habitude play in this respect, you may learn from Mr. Thornton's work on *Over-population*, where he shows that the average wages in different agricultural districts of England still nowadays differ more or less according to the more or less favourable circumstances under which the districts have emerged from the state of serfdom (Marx [1865] 1976: 57).

And again in *Capital* Volume I:

> On the other hand, the number and extent of his [worker's] so-called necessary requirements, as also the manner in which they are satisfied, are themselves products of history, and depend therefore to the great extent on the level of civilization attained by a country; *in particular they depend on the conditions in which the class of free workers has been formed* [f.n. Cf. W.T. Thornton, *Over-Population and Its Remedy*, London, 1846]. In contrast, therefore, with the case of other commodities, the determination of the value of labour-power contains a historical and moral element (Marx 1977: 275, emphasis added).

Hollander (1984, 1986, 2008)[44] and I (Sinha 1998) agree that Marx maintained an 'increasing immiseration of the working class' thesis. Hollander, however, argues that Marx's thesis was crucially or strategically dependent on a Malthusian-type theory of population and that Marx also depended on the classical theory of wages where the rate of population growth is a positive function of the real wages, with the 'subsistence wage' defined strictly as a rate of wage associated with *zero* rate of growth in population:

> To clarify the Marxian growth path of wages, the relation between the orthodox subsistence wage and Marx's value of labor power must be first carefully defined. ... The 'ultimate limit' to the wage corresponds therefore to the orthodox subsistence wage — defined as that wage assuring zero population growth (Hollander 1984: 140).

I disagree with this. As we have seen, in his 1865 lecture Marx distinguishes between the mere *physical* and the *socio-historical* components of given wages. Hollander identifies the 'physical' component with the orthodox 'subsistence wage'. But the evidence he provides for his interpretation is highly ambiguous. In the 1865 lecture Marx defines the physiological component thus: ' ... to maintain and reproduce itself, to perpetuate its physical existence, the working class must receive the necessaries absolutely indispensable for living and *multiplying*' (quoted in Hollander 1984: 140, emphasis added). Apparently, Hollander attributes a multiplication factor of one to this statement. This attribution, however, is quite arbitrary. Usually the term 'multiplying' means a multiplication factor greater than one. It should be noted that in Marx's statement the term 'multiplying' refers to the whole of the working class (i.e., population as such) and not just one family. In the case of one family, of course, one could think of a multiplying factor greater than one eventuating in a zero rate of population growth, given the high infant and child mortality rates at the time. However, as the quotation stands, a multiplication factor greater than one implies a positive rate of population growth.

Hollander's other evidence is from Volume I of *Capital*, where Marx writes:

> The labour-power withdrawn from the market by wear and tear, and by death, must be continually replaced by, at the

---

44 Also see Tucker (1961). For the controversy on Hollander (1984), see Ramirez (1986); Hollander (1986); Cottrell and Darity Jr. (1988); Green (1991); and Sinha (1998).

very least, an equal amount of fresh labour-power. Hence the
sum of means of subsistence necessary for the production of
labour-power must include the means necessary for the worker's replacements, i.e., his children, in order that this race of
peculiar commodity-owners may perpetuate its presence on
the market (Marx 1977: 275).

Again, a careful inspection of this statement shows that all Marx is
saying is that the real wage must be at least sufficient to enable working families to rear enough children to replace the workers withdrawn
from the market due to 'wear and tear' and death. Nowhere is he suggesting that there is actually a wage rate which would ensure a zero
population growth, no more and no less. The reader should note that
Marx adds a quotation from Torrens in a footnote to his statement;
according to Torrens:

Its (labour's) natural price ... consists in such a quantity of
necessaries and comforts of life, as, from the nature of the cli-
mate, and the habits of the country, are necessary to support
the labourer, and to enable him to rear such a family as may
preserve, in the market, an *undiminished* supply of labour
(quoted in Marx 1977: 275, emphasis added).

This quotation from Torrens is quite interesting because 'undiminished
supply of labour' is consistent with either zero or positive population
growth, whereas in Adam Smith, Malthus, and Ricardo (Hollander's
'orthodox theory') the 'natural price of labour' corresponds strictly
to zero population growth. To quote Ricardo: 'The natural price of
labour is that price which is necessary to enable the labourers, one
with another, to subsist and to perpetuate their race, *without either
increase or diminution*' (Ricardo 1951: 93, emphasis added). Thus,
Marx seems to have been very careful in selecting Torrens's quotation
so that the minimum needed for the perpetuation of 'this race of peculiar commodity-owner' is not defined strictly in correspondence to a
zero rate of population growth.

Hollander's case is even weaker when we take account of a similar
statement from *Capital* only a few passages down from the quotation
previously discussed:

The ultimate or minimum limit of the value of labour-power
is formed by the value of the commodities which have to be
supplied every day to the bearer of labour-power, the man, so

that he can renew his life process. That is to say, the limit is formed by the value of the physically indispensable means of subsistence. If the price of labour-power falls to this minimum, it *falls below its value*, since under such circumstances it can be maintained and developed only in a *crippled* state, and the value of every commodity is determined by the labour-time required to provide it in its normal quality (ibid.: 276–77, emphasis added).

Thus the minimum physical part of wages is not associated with the reproduction of the 'normal' working class at zero rate of growth, but rather with a working class in a 'crippled state'. Apparently, for Marx, the 'historical and social' element of the real wage cannot be reduced to zero in any long-term sense.[45]

But what about the classical and Malthusian hypothesis that population growth is positively related to real wages? Again, we find that Marx breaks from this hypothesis:

In fact, not only the number of births and deaths, but the absolute size of families, stands in inverse proportion to the level of wages, and therefore to the amount of the means of subsistence at the disposal of different categories of workers (Marx 1977: 796–97).

---

45 In his recent book, Hollander writes: 'Sinha objects to my interpretation of Marx's subsistence wage, on the grounds that the term "necessaries absolutely indispensible for living and multiplying" is given "a multiplication factor of one" which is arbitrary (Sinha 1998: 104–06). But my reading turns on numerous expressions in the 1865 paper all pointing in the same direction: "the necessary required for... *maintenance and reproduction*"; a sufficiency "*to maintain and reproduce itself, to perpetuate its physical existence*"; an amount "necessary for the physical perpetuation of the race". "Reproduction", "maintenance", "perpetuation" — and also "*conservation*" in [*Capital III*] — strongly suggest to me zero population growth. For all that, it probably mattered less to Marx whether at subsistence population growth is zero or positive (or even negative); than that there is a general downward trend of the real wage. And Sinha too insists on the absolute immiseration interpretation (1998: 100, 104), and agrees that the population growth rate is "naturally" positive "during normal circumstances" (110, also 115)' (Hollander 2008: 91, f.n. 8). My argument, however, was not based only on the single example of the 'multiplying factor'. Moreover, it remains intriguing why Marx never used *strict* language to associate the physical minimum with zero population growth, no more and no less, as such strict language was already in use among the classical economists. Why would he choose a vague expression by Torrens over a strict expression by Ricardo?

Here, by comparing the statistics of the individual provinces and the individual countries in each province, he [Thomas Sadler] proves that the misery there is not, as Malthus would have it, in proportion to the level of the population, but in inverse ratio to this (ibid.: 861, f.n. 24).

... by applying methods which yield relative surplus-value (introduction and improvement of machinery) it would produce a far more rapid, artificial, relative over-population, which in its turn, would be a breeding-ground for a really swift propagation of the population, since under capitalist production misery produces population (Marx 1991: 218).

Of course, the above statements refer to cross-sectional data, which illuminate how a downward secular trend in wages cannot be related, one-to-one, with a lower rate of growth in population. As a matter of fact, apart from a minor statement in Volume III of *Capital*, where Marx says:

A momentary excess of surplus-capital over the working population it has commandeered, would have a two fold effect. It would, on the one hand, by raising wages, mitigate the adverse conditions which decimate the offspring of the labourers and would make marriages easier among them, so as gradually to increase the population (1991: 218)

which is followed by his statement about 'misery produces population' that we have quoted above, we find no reference in Marx of a systematic relationship between real wages and the rate of population growth. In theory, it seems, Marx takes a positive growth in population as exogenously given — 'the natural increase of population' that is completely independent of the level of real wages. This makes sense because, as we have seen, he held that population growth would be positive regardless of either decent or miserable wages. His empirical sense, however, was that miserable wages generally produced a higher growth in population than a decent level of wages. The relationship between real wages and population growth is not continuous — a subsistence wage may be associated with a high rate of population growth, and a slightly below-subsistence wage may lead to a large negative rate of population growth due to famine, etc. Marx quoted S. Lang approvingly: 'Misery up to the extreme point of famine and pestilence, instead of checking, tends to increase population' (Marx

1977: 797, f.n. 22). Thus, it would be fair to conclude that Marx had rejected the classical wage doctrine, particularly its Malthusian aspect.

But a problem remains. Hollander points out that Marx clearly maintained that though the growth rate of demand for labour would decelerate due to labour-saving technical changes, it nevertheless would be growing in absolute terms. He quotes from Volume III of *Capital*: '[I]t is but a requirement of the capitalist mode of production that the number of wage workers should increase absolutely, in spite of its relative decrease' (Hollander's emphasis), and from Volume I of *Capital*: 'A development of productive forces which would diminish the absolute number of labourers, i.e., enable the entire nation to accomplish its total production in a shorter time span, would cause a revolution, because it would put the bulk of the population out of the running', to make his point (Hollander 2008: 96ff). This, according to Hollander (if I understand him correctly), makes the demographic variable 'strategic' to Marx's 'increasing immiseration' thesis. Now, there is no denying the fact that Marx took a positive rate of population growth as 'natural'. And again, it would be reasonable to expect that a negative rate of growth in demand for labour would create a revolutionary situation if the population growth is positive. The question, however, is: does Marx's abstract theory *need* the demographic variable to generate the 'increasing immiseration' result? I think not. As we have noted, Marx maintained that: 'Capitalist production can by no means content itself with the quantity of disposable labour-power which the natural increase of population yields' (Marx 1977: 788). Thus, the labour-saving technical change is introduced as an endogenous solution of the system to the excess demand for labour problem. A zero rate of population growth does not change the terms of the problem, it only accentuates it and its solution would simply be a relatively faster rate of technical change. This is the exact *theoretical* point Marx makes by alluding to the case of Ireland:

> What were the consequences for the Irish labourers left behind and freed from the surplus population? These: the relative surplus population is as great today as it was before 1846; wages are just as low; the oppression of the labourers has increased; misery is forcing the country towards a new crisis. The reasons are simple. *The revolution in agriculture has kept pace with emigration. The production of a relative*

surplus population has more than kept pace with the absolute depopulation (ibid.: 862, emphasis added).

The fundamental difference between us, i.e., Professor Hollander and I, lies in the fact that the Professor takes such technical changes as 'exogenous', whereas I maintain that Marx's reasoning is *functional* in nature.

4

THE THEORY OF VALUE
IN SRAFFA'S *PRODUCTION*
OF COMMODITIES

Part I

Introduction

Among the four classics discussed in this book, Sraffa's *Production of Commodities by Means of Commodities* (PCMC) is the thinnest by several times, is the least ambiguous in what it says, and perhaps the most beautiful in its construction. The precision of his writing is extraordinary. One would be hard-pressed to find a superfluous word or even a punctuation mark in the entire book: it is as if the book is a display of minimalist art in economic prose. No less a personality than Paul Samuelson, one of Sraffa's great admirers and critics, once wrote: 'His [Sraffa's] pen writes as if a lawyer were at hand to ensure that no vulnerable sentence appears' (Samuelson 2000a: 134, f.n. 7). Yet, even after about half-a-century of its publication, the book has, to a large extent, remained a closed one for both his critics and followers alike.[1] The greatest difficulty in understanding this book lies precisely in the precision of its expression. The book is composed as if it were a

---

1 In one of the earliest reviews of the book, Sir Roy Harrod wrote: 'The publication of this book is a notable event. ... A reviewer would be presumptuous if he supposed that he could give a final assessment of the value of its net product, or even single out what may prove to be its most lasting contributions. Before that result could be achieved, much prolonged consideration and reconsideration would be required.' (Harrod 1961: 783). In another review, Maurice Dobb wrote: 'It can be confidently said that never in the history of economic theory has so much fundamental and formally refined thought, and of so path-breaking a character, been packed into so slender and elegant a volume.

It is a book that will perhaps be misunderstood and remain unappreciated by many more than will understand it; few probably will wholly grasp even the major part of it, though many can and will gain illumination and inspiration from it in part' (Dobb 1961: 491).

Beethoven sonata, with silences that are perhaps more important than the scores. It is these well-thought-through silences of the book that need to be paid fuller attention and decoded if we are ever to understand the full meaning of his theoretical intervention in economics.

The 'Preface' of the book begins with a clarion declaration:

> Anyone accustomed to think in terms of the equilibrium of demand and supply may be inclined, on reading these pages, to suppose that the argument rests on a tacit assumption of constant returns in all industries. ... In fact, however, no such assumption is made. No changes in output and (at any rate in Parts I and II) no changes in the proportions in which different means of production are used by an industry are considered, so that no question arises as to the variation or constancy of returns. The investigation is concerned exclusively with such properties of an economic system as do not depend on changes in the scale of production or in the proportions of 'factors' (Sraffa 1960: v).

As we shall see later, in spite of this precise statement regarding the assumption of 'constant returns', all the leading neoclassical economists have simply ignored it since they are unable to make sense of his propositions unless a 'constant returns' assumption is invoked as implicit in them: 'In sum, if a Sraffian denies constant returns to scale, the one-hundred page 1960 classic evaporates into a few pages of vapid chit-chat' (Samuelson 2000a: 123). The reader should also take note of the first sentence in Sraffa's declaration. Many of Sraffa's followers have read it as a reference to the 'demand and supply theory' (i.e., the neoclassical theory of price). However, Sraffa does not say any such thing. The expression refers to 'the equilibrium of demand and supply', implying that his propositions do not depend on the notion of 'equilibrium of demand and supply'. Those who are accustomed to think in terms of such an 'equilibrium' might, by implication, think that his propositions implicitly assume 'constant returns'; but as a matter of fact they do not make any such assumption and therefore do not require thinking in terms of *equilibrium* of demand and supply.

Sraffa further goes on to say: 'This standpoint, which is that of the old classical economists from Adam Smith to Ricardo, has been submerged and forgotten since the advent of the "marginal" method.' (Sraffa 1960: v). Many followers of Sraffa have read this statement as an admission of taking on board what Garegnani (1984) has characterised as 'the classical theory', with Marx's name gratuitously added to the list. The reader, however, should note that Adam Smith and Ricardo, as well as Marx, believed in the notion of 'centre of gravitation', i.e., that there are forces in the market that bring supplies into equilibrium with their effectual demands. But as we have earlier noted, Sraffa declares that his propositions do not depend on the 'equilibrium of supply and demand'. His statement is thus highly enigmatic. It seems to suggest that on Sraffa's reading at least, Adam Smith and David Ricardo did not assume the 'centre of gravitation' mechanism (the equilibrium of supply and demand) in their theory of 'natural prices'; or at least they did not need to do so. However, it is one thing to agree or disagree with Sraffa's statement regarding the standpoint of the old classical economists, but quite another to interpret it as taking on board the notion of 'centre of gravitation' or the equilibrium of supply and effectual demand of classical economics. We will return to these issues later in the chapter.

Sraffa further continues:

> The reason is obvious. The marginal approach requires attention to be focused on change, for without change either in the scale of an industry or in the 'proportions of the factors of production' there can be neither marginal product nor marginal cost. In a system in which, day after day, production continued unchanged in those respects, the marginal product of a factor (or alternatively the marginal cost of a product) would not merely be hard to find — it just would not be there to be found (1960: v).

The point to note here is that Sraffa's statement refers to a shift of attention. Apparently, the classical standpoint is one of *given output,* whereas the marginal approach works on the notion of *changes in output.* Furthermore, Sraffa refers to the real as opposed to a *notional* existence of a marginal product or marginal cost. The marginal approach (or the neoclassical approach) works on given production functions. Given these functions, if they are differentiable, the marginal products are well defined at any given point of time. However, these marginal entities are notional or hypothetical entities. Sraffa's claim is that if the functions are real, then such changes should be able to produce the expected results in reality; and that can occur only if the proportions of the factors of production (or the scale of production) change and a comparison of total produced outputs is made at two points in time. Thus a system that does not admit any change in its total output simply cannot include either a notional or real marginal product or cost.

After making clear the nature of the propositions that are to follow in the book, he goes on to declare the purpose of the book:

> It is, however, a peculiar feature of the set of propositions now published that, although they do not enter into any discussion of the marginal theory of value and distribution, they have nevertheless been designed to serve as the basis for a critique of that theory (Sraffa 1960: vi).

In other words, a set of propositions built on the notion of no-change is designed to provide the basis for a critique of a theory that is fundamentally based on the notion of change. In some sense it appears that Sraffa wants to develop a sort of *geometry* (in Euclidean geometry the propositions do not admit of time or causation; they are simply relations of logical necessities) that would serve as a theoretical basis for criticising *mechanics* (which is built on the notion of causation and change).[2] Let us probe this point a little further. The propositions of the 'marginal approach' are based on functional relations, so that the theory builds itself by working out the effects of hypothetical marginal changes in the causes.[3] For example, utility is functionally related to consumption, and a hypothetical marginal change in consumption is supposed to cause a change in utility in a determinate manner. Similarly, cost is functionally related to production, and changes in the quantity of production would have a determinate effect on costs. These functional relations give rise to the notion of demand and supply functions, which together create a force-field that explains both the equilibrium of the system and the movements of the variables given any shock to the equilibrium. Sraffa's claim appears to be that the set of his logical propositions will provide the basis to challenge the legitimacy of the causal functional relations of the neoclassical theory.[4] It is a curious exercise indeed!

2 'The theory of Economy thus treated presents a close analogy to the science of Statical Mechanics, and the Laws of Exchange are found to resemble the laws of Equilibrium of a lever as determined by the principle of virtual velocities. The nature of Wealth and Value is explained by the consideration of indefinitely small amounts of pleasure and pain, just as the Theory of Statics is made to rest upon the equality of indefinitely small amounts of energy' (Jevons 1957a [1871]: vii).

3 The mathematical notation, $y = f(x)$, only represents a mapping and not a causal relation. The reading of $y = f(x)$ as y is *caused* by x is an additional theoretical statement, which lies outside of mathematics.

4 Sen has also argued that '[t]he temptation to see Sraffa's contribution as a causal theory of price determination... must be resisted. ... The sense of "determination" invoked by Sraffa concerns the mathematical determination of one set of facts from another set' (Sen 2003: 1253).

The Major Propositions of the PCMC

Single Product Industries and Circulating Capital

Chapter 1 begins with a system of 'Production for Subsistence'. This chapter deals with a simple subsistence economy with specialisation. Thus the production process requires distribution of commodities given by the requirements of the technology (for a subsistence economy consumption is part of the technical requirements), whereas commodities are concentrated in the hands of separate industries after the production process is over (Sraffa assumes an annual market after the harvest). In this case Sraffa finds that there is a set of exchange ratios or prices of commodities that 'spring directly from the methods of production' and which can restore the original distribution of the commodities and make it possible for the system to repeat itself at the same scale. This result is due to the fact that in a subsistence economy there are, in general, n - 1 independent equations to determine n - 1 unknown prices.

Chapter 2 complicates matters by considering the case of a system that produces more than its minimum requirements.

(A system that produces less than its minimum requirements is not considered by Sraffa, since such a system cannot have historical viability.) Once a 'surplus' is admitted in the system, it becomes, in Sraffa's words, 'self-contradictory', i.e., the system becomes over-determined as it has n independent equations to solve for only n - 1 unknown prices. Apparently, the required distribution of the commodities after production is no longer entirely determined by the methods of production. The problem of distribution of the 'surplus' must therefore be solved. He argues that the surplus cannot be distributed prior to the determination of prices because

> [t]he surplus (or profit) must be distributed in proportion to the means of production (or capital) advanced in each industry; and such a proportion between two aggregates of heterogeneous goods (in other words, the rate of profits) cannot be determined before we know the prices of the goods (Sraffa 1960: 6).

The upshot of the argument is that both the prices and the rate of profits need to be determined simultaneously by the same mechanism. Accordingly, he adds a rate of profits, which he claims *must* be uniform, to his system of equations as an unknown, which gives him a system of n independent equations with n unknowns (n - 1 prices and one rate of profits) that has an economically meaningful solution. But on what grounds does Sraffa claim that the rates of profit across the sectors 'must' be uniform? We shall return to this important question later.

One effect of the emergence of surplus is that commodities can now be divided into two categories. There can be some commodities that appear in the system only as outputs and do not enter the system as inputs. Such commodities can be characterised as *non-basics*. Commodities that enter the system both as inputs and outputs can be characterised as basics.[5] Any change in the conditions of production of the basics would have an impact on the prices of all commodities through its influence as an input in the system. But any such change in the conditions of production of non-basics can affect only their own price or the prices of limited goods of which they may be an input.[6]

Sraffa further complicates the system by arguing that workers' remuneration may contain a part of the 'surplus', thus adding another unknown to the system as *wages*. With this the system acquires one more unknown than the number of equations, and thus the system can move with one degree of freedom. Sraffa's attempt to break from the classical position of treating wages as part of capital is a clear move away from taking a particular class position in viewing the 'surplus', to taking a purely technical position where the technically given net output is viewed as the 'surplus' of the system. In this context a physically given subsistence for workers could be incorporated as part of the technical inputs and only the wages over and above subsistence could be reckoned as taking part in the distribution of the net output. Sraffa, however, refrains from 'tampering with the traditional wage concept'. Joan Robinson correctly points out that 'we could hardly imagine that, when the workers had a surplus to spend on beef, their physical need for wheat was unchanged' (Robinson 1961: 54).

Chapters 3–6 are devoted to analysing the nature of the relation of prices to the distribution of income, given the system of inputs and outputs, in the case of single-product industries with only circulating capital. Sraffa finds that changes in wages would have no impact on prices if the proportions of the means of production to labour were the same for all industries. This is because a change in wages will have a proportionately equal impact on the costs of all industries and thus a

---

5 A non-basic can appear as an input in the production of non-basics but is not directly or indirectly an input in the production of all the commodities in the system.

6 Harcourt and Massaro (1964) describe basic goods as 'price determining' and non-basics as 'price determined'.

proportionate change in the rate of profits in all industries will leave prices unaffected. In the general case where the proportions are not the same, however, a change in wages (or the rate of profits) would affect all prices in a highly complicated way.[7] This is because as wages take on a higher (or lower) value, the cost of production is affected more in one sector than in another, thus affecting the rates of profit disproportionately. In this case prices must change to bring the rates of profit to equality across industries. The relation between changes in wages (or rate of profits) and prices is thus highly complicated. As Sraffa puts it:

> The relative price of two products may move, with the fall of wages, in the opposite direction to what we might have expected on the basis of their respective 'proportions'; besides, the prices of their respective means of production may move in such a way as to reverse the order of the two products as to higher or lower proportions; and further complications arise. (Sraffa 1960: 15).

This is because the impact of a change in wages on the cost of a product does not depend only on the input configuration of the industry in question, but also on the input configurations of the industries that produce its inputs and the input configurations of the industries that produce *those* inputs, and so on. It should be noted that throughout this analysis Sraffa allows no role for time or relations of causation. When he argues that prices must change to redress the divergence in the rates of profit arising due to changes in wages, he does not resort to the classical long-period argument that price movements are brought about by capital mobility and changes in supply. In his analysis the size and the composition of the net output do not change. These relations are purely mathematical, or logically necessary. It would be a mistake to think that Sraffa expects the real world to solve his equations. In fact, the word 'change' is not appropriate for describing the nature of Sraffa's proposition. Rather, it should be understood as various price solutions for different levels of wages or a uniform rate of profits given the input-output data; and therefore, given the level of wages or the rate of profits, only one real solution exists. No change on a real-time

---

7 The determination of equality or inequality of proportions can be made by measuring means of production by taking their values at any wage, since when proportions are the same then changes in wages have no impact on the prices and thus on the proportions so measured. From this it follows that if the proportions are not equal at one wage, they will not be equal at any wage.

dimension is contemplated here, as there is no guarantee that at any other level of wages or rate of profits the real input-output data would not emerge as different. Sraffa's solutions are not designed to *predict* the changes in variables in the real world but are only a *description* of the mathematical properties of the given set of data.

As we have seen, a change in wages has a very complicated relation with prices. However, at this stage one can argue that wages and the rate of profits are inversely related. This is because no price can fall (or rise) at a rate higher than the fall (or rise) of wages measured by any arbitrary *numéraire*. For, if it were possible for a product to do so, it would only be due to some of its means of production falling (or rising) at a still higher rate. But this could not be applied to the product that fell (or rose) at the highest rate, which would be less than the rate of fall (or rise) of the wage rate. Thus no price can fall (or rise) at a rate higher than the wages and so the rate of profits and wages must be inversely related. In general, however, this relation would be non-linear. This is because a change in wages affects all prices, including the commodity chosen as the *numéraire*. Thus the relation between the rate of profits and wages is contaminated by the changes in the size of the measuring rod itself. In other words, a change in the size of a piece of a pie apparently changes the size of the pie itself. This was a problem that Sraffa (1951) thought engaged Ricardo to the end of his life.

Sraffa's solution to this problem is to construct a composite commodity that is unaffected by changes in wages or the rate of profits. He calls this commodity the *Standard commodity*, which, in a way, is embedded in any given system. Any given system can be mathematically rearranged in such a way that the proportions of its outputs are the same as the proportions of its aggregate inputs. This he called the *Standard system*. The Standard commodity is made up of all the basic commodities of the system combined in such proportions.[8] In the Standard system a physical ratio of net output (or the *Standard net product*) to the aggregate means of production can be ascertained, since the ratio is made up of the same commodities arranged in the same proportions. This ratio, which is independent of prices, Sraffa calls the *Standard ratio*. The Standard ratio is, of course, equal to the maximum rate of profits of the given system, i.e., it is equal to the

---

8 No non-basic commodity can feature in the composition of the Standard commodity because non-basics do not appear as inputs in the system. S. Baldone (2006) has confirmed that Sraffa's Standard commodity makes the *numéraire* effect null. Also see Bellino (2004) on this issue.

rate of profits in the system when the wage is equal to zero. In any given Standard system the rate of profits can always be ascertained without any recourse to prices by deducting any positive proportion of the Standard net product as the wage-share and taking the ratio of the residual Standard net product and the aggregate inputs, since the proportion of a fraction of the Standard net product must be the same as the Standard net product. Thus, in a Standard system the wage rate, expressed in terms of the Standard commodity, and the rate of profits must be inversely and proportionately related to each other. Now if the Standard commodity is taken as the *numéraire* for the given system and it measures the wages, then the rate of profits in the real system must be the same as the rate of profits in the Standard system since the Standard system is made up of the same equations of production — only arranged in different proportions — as the real system. Thus for any given system the relationship $r = R(1 - w)$ must hold, where r is the rate of profits, R is the maximum rate of profits (i.e., the rate of profit of the system when w is equal to zero), and w is the wage rate expressed in terms of the Standard commodity.[9] This equation gives the structural relationship between the methods

9 Burmeister (1975, 1977) argues that 'Sraffa's measure of the "real wage" is economically flawed. Sraffa's unique consumption basket weights $c_1, ..., c_n$ are determined from the technology alone; they are weights derived from the right hand characteristic vector associated with Frobenius root of the production technique matrix. These weights are not related in any way to human needs or preferences, and there is absolutely no economic reason why they should be relevant for defining any "real wage". (Thus, for example, Sraffa's Standard Commodity may be such that he must assign a relatively large weight in his consumption basket to a commodity such as pig iron which is never consumed by humans!)' (Burmeister 1977: 68, f.n. 1). This is clearly a misinterpretation. The Standard commodity, as Sraffa states, is only a 'medium in which wages are estimated' (Sraffa 1960: 22). Workers are not expected or required to consume the Standard commodity or a fraction of the Standard Net Product. The Standard commodity is used as the normalisation equation for the system. Since wages are paid post factum, any given real wage can be estimated by the Standard commodity on the basis of the prices so derived. Thus the wage in terms of the Standard commodity in Sraffa's system is not the 'real wage' but rather the 'nominal wage'. That is why, as we shall see, Sraffa drops the explicit use of the Standard commodity in his system by taking the rate of profits as given from outside. In this case wages can be derived in terms of any commodity (see ibid.: 32ff.). Burmeister, however, is right in stating that higher values of wages in terms of the Standard commodity 'do not, in general, imply anything about economic welfare' (Burmeister 1975: 456). This is because an ambiguous change in the real wage basket could result in a definite rise or fall in its estimate in terms of the Standard commodity but it would, of course, remain ambiguous in terms of its welfare connotation. Sraffa's use of the measure of wages in terms of the Standard commodity, however, has no such welfare connotation.

of production (represented by R) and the two distributional variables, r and w. Prices must adjust in such a way that these relations hold. Furthermore, Sraffa proves that the Standard system and the Standard commodity so derived from any given system are unique to the system.

Thus, any change in the method of production of a basic commodity would result in a change not only in the value of R, but also in the rod that measures the wages and relative prices. The upshot of the analysis is that there is in general no basis for comparing the values in the two systems.[10] Given the relation $r = R(1 - w)$, we could insert this equation instead of taking the Standard commodity or the Standard net product equal to 1 as the normalisation equation for the determination of n prices. This indirectly ensures that the Standard commodity is used as the *numéraire*, since the relationship $r = R(1 - w)$ will hold only if the Standard commodity is used as the *numéraire*, apart from the trivial cases of either a one-commodity world or an economy with an equal organic composition of capital in all sectors. Furthermore, the relationship $r = R(1 - w)$ can be also written as: $1/w = R/(R - r)$. If we take the ratio $1/w$ as the unit of prices for a given rate of profits r, then we no longer need to express wages in terms of the Standard commodity: they could be expressed in terms of any commodity by taking the reciprocal of the price of that commodity. This leads Sraffa to reverse the practice of taking the wages rather than the rate of profits as 'given'. He argues that once the notion of wages is liberated from some kind of subsistence notion and when analysis needs to vary wages and the rate of profits, then the rationale for taking wages as 'given' loses most of its force. Furthermore, when wages are regarded as 'given' in terms of 'a more or less abstract standard' (say, money), then it does not acquire a definite meaning until commodity prices are determined. On the other hand, he argues:

> The rate of profits, as a ratio, has a significance which is independent of any prices, and can well be 'given' before prices are fixed. It is accordingly susceptible of being determined from outside of the system of production, in particular by the level of the money rates of interest (Sraffa 1960: 33).

---

10 See Cockshott and Sinha (2008), where we have argued that the direction of changes in prices of commodities is contingent on the choice of the *numéraire*. Thus such comparison of prices in two systems turns out to be meaningless. This result points to the arbitrary nature of the neoclassical supply functions, as they inevitably compare prices across several Sraffa systems on the basis of an arbitrarily chosen *numéraire*.

On the Uniform Rate of Profits

Now we are ready to come back to our earlier question about the grounds on which Sraffa could claim that the rate of profits *must* be uniform. As a matter of fact, during the early period of his theoretical breakthrough, i.e., from late 1927 to 1931 (see Garegnani 2005), we find that Sraffa was worried about how to 'justify or explain the equal percentage added to initial stock of each industry'. And after arguing that capital might not be reinvested in sectors having a lower rate of profits and thus not being able to reproduce themselves in the long run, he goes on to add: 'In this way *we are allowing to come back through the window the [notion of cost as] "inducement" we had excluded from the door*' [Piero Srafa Papers (PSP) n.d., D3/12/6, emphasis added; also cited in Garegnani 2005: 475]. During the same period, we find him writing in another note: 'I must find a "force" capable of obliging those people in the market to actuate my equations' (Sraffa n.d.: D3/12/7/107–14).[11] It should be noted that Sraffa had taken the philosophical or methodological position that theoretical understanding must be built on only things that are, at least ideally, *observable* and thus no subjective element (such as 'inducement') could be allowed to enter his equations.

During the same period, in an attempt to explain the meaning of his equations Sraffa wrote:

> The significance of the equations is simply this: that if a man fell from the moon on the earth, and noted the amount of things consumed in each factory [...] during a year he could deduce at which values the commodities must be sold, if the rate of interest must be uniform and the process of production repeated. In short, the equations show that the conditions of exchange are entirely determined by the conditions of production (Sraffa n.d.: D3/12/7).

The reader should take note of the qualifier: '*if* the rate of interest must be uniform'. Interestingly, the qualifier 'if' disappears from the relevant passage in the book and its place is taken by 'must'. So the question is: what could have happened between the early period of the breakthrough and the publication of the book in 1960?

---

11 I am obliged to Nerio Naldi for the English translation of the original in Italian, 'devo trovare una <forza > che costringa quella brava gente sul mercato a realizzare le mie equazioni'.

To the best of my knowledge, Sraffa has not left any clear account of how he came to resolve the problem of how to 'justify or explain the equal percentage added to initial stock of each industry'. However, in his response to Harrod's review of his book, Sraffa does hint that his prices are not necessarily the equilibrium prices when he writes: 'Now this is clearly a misunderstanding, since the exchange ratios are, of course, determined by the equations of production and not by the ratios between the excess productions of the commodities' (Sraffa 1962: 477). It is, I think, safe to conjecture that it was his discovery of the Standard system and the Standard commodity in the early 1940s that probably convinced Sraffa that the uniformity of the rate of profits is a logical necessity of any given system of production that determines prices internally, irrespective of the equilibrium of demand and supply.

To prove the foregoing proposition, let us take Sraffa's example of a three-sector economy included in his book (Sraffa 1960: 19):

90t. iron + 120t. coal + 60qr. wheat + 3/16 labour → 180t. iron

50t. iron + 125t. coal + 150qr. wheat + 5/16 labour → 450t. coal I

40t. iron + 40t. coal ɪ 200qr. wheat + 8/16 labour → 480qr. wheat

(For simplicity's sake, we will assume wages of labour to be equal to zero.) It is clear that Sraffa's statement regarding the rate of profits being 'a proportion between two aggregates of heterogeneous goods' relates to the net physical output divided by the aggregate of physical inputs of the system, as such a statement will be meaningless at the industry or sector level since at these levels the physical surplus remains undefined. So what we have here is that the aggregate or the *global* rate of profit of the empirical or the real system of production is given in terms of a ratio of heterogeneous goods. Since it is a ratio of heterogeneous goods, its value is unknown.

In the foregoing example, if the aggregate or the global rate of profit of the system is given by R, then the value of $(1 + R) = (180t.$ iron $+ 450t.$ coal $+ 480t.$ wheat$)/(180t.$ iron $+ 265t.$ coal $+ 410t.$ wheat$)$. Now, if we multiply the physical amounts of iron, coal and wheat by taking several arbitrary prices of iron, coal and wheat, we would find that the value of the above-given ratio will change with changes in prices. However, since the physical ratio remains the same, it immediately tells us that prices can create a 'nominal' effect on R (a sort of optical illusion), which is completely independent of its physical value. Nevertheless, at this level one can at least establish that the physical ratio of (R) gives us the rate of expansion of this economy, as by multiplying the aggregate of inputs with the physical ratio of (1 + R) we get exactly the aggregate of gross output of the system.

Now imagine a system equivalent to the given empirical system, which is constructed by reallocating the total labour used in the empirical system in such a way that the proportions of its aggregate inputs and aggregate outputs are equal for all the basic goods in the system. This is nothing but Sraffa's Standard system, which produces Standard net income:

120t. iron + 160t. coal + 80qr. wheat + 1/4 labour → 240t. iron

40t. iron + 100t. coal + 120qr. wheat + 1/4 labour → 360t. coal II

40t. iron + 40t. coal + 200qr. wheat + 2/4 labour → 480qr. wheat

In this imagined equivalent system the *global* rate of profit or the ratio of the aggregate physical net output to the physical aggregate inputs can be known without the knowledge of prices since it is a ratio of heterogeneous goods made up in the same proportion. This ratio is completely independent of prices — no matter what prices prevail, they will not affect the global rate of profit of the Standard system. Let us say that this ratio is equal to a number R*; in our example it is equal to 20 per cent. Thus, we come to our first conclusion that as far as the Standard system is concerned, its global rate of profit is the physical property of the system of production and its value is known independently of prices. But since the real system is nothing but an *equivalent* of the *Standard system*, the physical rate of profits in the two systems must be equal, i.e., R* = R; as the real system is nothing but a rescaled Standard system.

Suppose we start with the Standard system and an arbitrary set of prices that gives different rates of profit for different sectors: its global rate of profits would nevertheless be equal to R*. Now, keeping those prices constant, we convert the system back to its real state. Since we have kept all the prices constant, it implies that the individual or sectoral rates of profits would remain constant as well. However, since the weights of the sectors have changed in the move from the Standard to the real system, the unequal rates of sectoral profit would most likely result in deviating the global rate of profit R of the real system from R*. This contradicts the property of equivalent systems. Thus the sectoral rates of profit must be equal to ensure that R = R*. Let us suppose that in a highly unlikely but mathematically possible scenario the prices are such that for the real system R = R*, but still the sectoral rates of profit are not equal. However, the fact that the property R = R* must hold for all possible imaginary reallocations of the total labour of the real system, ensures that the sectoral rates of profit must also be equal, as even a slight change in the allocation of labour would ensure that R would diverge from R* for that given set of prices (see the mathematical appendix in Sinha and Dupertuis 2009a for a formal proof). In other words, as long as equations remain the same, the global rates must remain equal for all the input-output configurations, and this is possible if, and only if, all the sectoral rates of profits are equal. A positive real wage will not affect the analysis as long as the wages are measured by the Standard commodity, which is a composite commodity made up of all the basic goods put together in the Standard proportion.

In *PCMC*, Sraffa seems to be arguing in a similar manner when he declares that the mathematical property of the rate of profit of the Standard system commutes to the real system:

> But the actual system consists of the same basic equations as the Standard system, only in different proportions; so that, once the wage is given, the rate of profits is determined for both systems regardless of the proportions of the equations in either of them. Particular proportions, such as the Standard ones, may give transparency to a system and render visible what was hidden, but they cannot alter its mathematical properties (Sraffa 1960: 23).

The reader should note that Sraffa could not implicitly assume that supplies were equal to their effectual demands for both the real and the Standard systems — it would be bizarre to assume that the effectual demands were in Standard proportion. Thus Sraffa could not impose the condition of a uniform rate of profits on his Standard system on the basis of the so-called implicit assumption that the system is at its centre of gravitation. Hence the rate of profit of the Standard system that Sraffa is referring to is the *global rate of profit* of the Standard system and the claim is that the two *global rates* must always be equal as long as the wages are measured by the Standard commodity. It is the proposition regarding the equality of the global rates of profit of the rescaled systems that allows Sraffa to directly deduce that all the sectoral or industrial rates of profits *must* also be uniform in the two systems. This point becomes absolutely clear in the paragraph immediately following the passage we have just quoted:

> The straight-line relation between the wage and the rate of profits will therefore hold in all cases, provided only that the

wage is expressed in terms of the Standard product. The same rate of profits, which in the Standard system is obtained as a ratio between *quantities* of commodities, will in the actual system result from the ratio of aggregate *values* (ibid.: 23).

The reader should note that the ratios of 'quantities of commodities' and of 'aggregate values' are both well defined only at the *global* level and have no meaning at the local or industrial level.

Further on, in his unpublished notes written in 1955, we find that Sraffa invokes a similar reasoning behind the possibility of an existence of a Standard commodity:

With changes in w —

The impulse towards price change is an internal one to each industry. It arises from its own internal conditions — not from those conditions *compared* with those of other industries. Hence the possibility of an *invariable* commodity (Sraffa n.d.: D3/12/6, emphasis in original).

The reader should yet again note that here Sraffa specifically and with emphasis denies the cause of changes in prices due to conditions *compared* with other industries, which is the sole *cause* of the gravitation mechanism — it is the comparison of the rates of profits across sectors that give rise to the gravitation mechanism. Let us suppose that with the rise in wages, prices did not change and thus the rates of profits across sectors become unequal. In this case when we raise wages from zero towards its maximum value we find that before wages reach their maximum value some profits would become negative, a possibility not allowed in the system. This is evidence that there is some outside constraint on the prices. Therefore, in a system that is free from outside constraint on its prices 'the impulse towards price change is an internal one to each industry.'

The intuitive reasoning behind Sraffa's result comes from the property of the Standard system. One can clearly see in the Standard system that its *global* rate of profit is a 'non-price phenomenon' — it is apparently embedded in the physical system of production of commodities by means of commodities. As Sraffa says in another note he wrote in 1955:

..., the rate of profits at the various individual levels of $\underline{w}$ will be $r = R(1 - w)$. Individual prices will move in all directions with the variation of w, but here again prices will make no difference: r is a ratio between two quantities of the same composite commodity and can actually be discovered before knowing what those prices are. The rate of profit is embedded 'in the things' and no manipulation of prices could ever affect it. [There could be no more tangible evidence of the rate of profits [being, as] a non-price phenomenon (effect)] (Sraffa n.d.: D3/12/53, all parentheses and brackets are in original).

This finding shows that the uniformity of the rate of profits in the system has nothing to do with the equalisation of the supplies with their effectual demands.[12] As a matter of fact, relative prices cannot go anywhere they like — they are completely constrained by the system of production and the condition of its reproduction. In a sense, Sraffa's result points to a break in economics that is similar to the break from classical mechanics to quantum mechanics.[13] Classical and neoclassical economics treat individual industries as independent entities, which through their interaction generate centres of gravitation that bring a system into being. Sraffa's result shows that the system is not made up of independent industries but is an interconnected whole, and that the properties of the whole determine the properties of its parts.

12 Joan Robinson (1961) comes closest to understanding this as she claims that the 'clue' to understanding the *PCMC* could be found in the 'corn model' of Sraffa's (1951) 'Introduction' to Ricardo's *Principles*. In the 'corn model', e.g., 1 ton of corn produces 1.5 tons of corn; the rate of profit is 50 per cent no matter what the final demand for corn is. This physical relationship between inputs and outputs that is palpably evident in a single basic good model is obscured in an n-basic goods model. But Sraffa's analysis with the help of the Standard system reveals that the insight of the corn model remains valid in a more general case as well.

13 It may be noted that Sraffa was well aware of the developments in quantum mechanics. As early as 1928, he had noted down a passage from H.S. Allen's paper on 'The Quantum Theory' published in Nature, where Allen writes: 'Heisenberg put forward the demand that only such quantities as are observable should be represented in the mathematical formulation of atomic theory. ... This led to the development of the matrix mechanics, every term in a matrix corresponding to something which is, at least ideally, observable' (Allen 1928). Of course, Sraffa makes the same demand for economic theory. Furthermore, Professor Heinz Kurz has informed me that 'There are several books devoted to (what was then) modern physics in Sraffa's library. And in some of that there are annotations. Not many, but apparently Sraffa had read or at least skimmed through the books. In his papers he also refers to books that are not in his library, e.g., Bridgman.'

Dated Labour Approach to Price Determination

Chapter VI of the book is devoted to showing that all attempts at measuring 'capital' as a homogeneous entity independently of the given rate of interest or profits, are doomed to failure for a logical reason. The reason is simple, but not apparent. To bring this logic out into the open, Sraffa constructs a description of the price of a commodity in terms of 'reduction to dated quantities of labour'. The idea is to reduce the price of a commodity to only its wage and profit components — recall Adam Smith's attempt to reduce prices to wages, profits and rents only. Take any equation from Sraffa's system of price equations, as for instance:

$$(A_a p_a + B_a p_b + \ldots + K_a p_k)(1 + r) + L_a w = A p_a,$$

where the symbols are self-explanatory. Now collect $L_a w$ from the equation and replace the means of production of A with their own means of production and labour with profits accounted at a compound rate. Repeat the process for their means of production and so on and on and at every stage collect the wage content augmented by the rate of profits earned on the value added by the wage content in the previous period. One can carry on with this exercise until the residue means of production becomes negligible. Through this process one can reduce the total value of any commodity to its components in terms of only wages and profits with a great deal of precision. The resulting equation can be represented as:

$$L_a w + L_{a1} w(1 + r) + \ldots + L_{an} w(1 + r)^n + \ldots = A p_a,$$

where 1 to n represent the successive period of time the means of productions are replaced by their own means of production and labour. If wages and prices are measured in terms of the Standard commodity, then any nth term of the resulting equation can be represented by:

$$L_{an}(1 - r/R)(1 + r)^n, \text{ given } w = 1 - r/R.$$

It is clear that when $r = 0$, the system reduces to accounting value in terms of a simple labour theory of value, and when $r = R$, then the left-hand side of the equation becomes zero, implying that the commodity residue becomes all-important in determining value. However, in the region where both w and r are positive, the reduction could always be carried out to the extent that the influence of the commodity residue on value becomes negligible. It is also clear from the expression of the nth term that any increase (or decrease) in wages (or rate of profits) would have a very complicated influence on value. A rise in the rate of profits would lead to a decline in the contribution of the labour term of the recent past; however, the terms more remote in the past would have a tendency to rise first, reach a maximum, and then decline to zero as r approaches R. By solving the nth term for its maximum point with respect to the rate of profits, we can derive that:

$$n = (1 + r)/(R - r) \text{ and conversely, } r = R - (1 + R)/(n + 1).$$

Thus for all n less than or equal to 1/R, the value of the labour term reaches its maximum at $r = 0$, and therefore they continually fall and constitute the 'recent' past. Such complicated movements of the values of the various labour terms make it quite clear that the price movements of any commodity due to changes in the rate of profits (or wages) would be highly complicated.[14]

To highlight the complicated nature of price movements with respect to changes in the rate of profits, Sraffa takes the example of the proverbial wine aged in the cellar and one old oak made into a chest. He assumes that both goods have identical labour terms except for three terms: 'One of them, "a", has excess of 20 units of labour applied 8 years before, whereas the excess of the other, "b", consists of 19 units employed in the current year and 1 unit bestowed 25 years earlier' (Sraffa 1960: 37). The difference between their prices in terms of the Standard commodity is given by:

$$p_a - p_b = 20w(1 + r)^8 - \{19w + w(1 + r)^{25}\}$$

On the assumption of R = 25 per cent, Sraffa shows that the price of 'a' or the old wine rises relative to 'b' or the oak chest as the rate of profits rises from 0 to 9 per cent, then it falls between 9 per cent to 22 per cent, to rise again from 22 per cent to 25 per cent. This proves that any attempt to measure capital independently of the rate of profits is doomed to failure. Sraffa parenthetically remarks that: 'But the case just considered seems conclusive in showing the impossibility of aggregating the "periods" belonging to the several quantities of labour into a single magnitude which could be regarded as representing the

---

14 It should be noted that the method of 'reduction' cannot be applied in the case of joint-production, as this would lead to negative quantities of labour for some of the terms, which cannot be properly interpreted.

quantity of capital' (ibid.: 38) — a remark apparently aimed at the Austrian attempts to measure capital. However, the same argument lies behind the possibility of 'reswitching' in the presence of choice of techniques (we will take up this issue later). It also proves conclusively not only that the simple labour theory of value would be an incorrect theory of prices, but also that any prediction of the direction of price changes based on the comparison of the organic compositions of capitals would give incorrect results. All this due to one simple fact — *profits must be reckoned at a compounded rate!*

All these complications notwithstanding, it can be unambiguously stated that if the price of a commodity falls due to a rise in the rate of profits, its fall can never be greater than the fall in wages. To see this, take the reduction equation for 'a' given above:

$$L_a w + L_{a1} w(1 + r) + \ldots + L_{an} w(1 + r)^n + \ldots = A p_a.$$

It is obvious that a rise in r cannot lead to a greater fall in p_a than the fall in w.

Joint-Production, Fixed Capital and Rent

Further on, in 'Part II' of his book, Sraffa yet again complicates the system by introducing joint-production. The case of joint-production was specifically introduced not for the sake of generality but rather to develop an explanation of depreciation of fixed capital and rent of land in a system that does not allow for any change or passage of time. In general, if a production process produces more than one output, then we have more commodities than equations and the system therefore becomes under-determined. Thus, in a case of joint-production, the solution to the relative prices and rate of profits requires that we have as many number of processes of production as the number of commodities; for example, if one process produces mutton and wool, then there must exist another process that also produces mutton and wool but in different proportions. Sraffa assumes that the requirements of the goods within the system of production (i.e., the input requirements) are generally in different proportions than any one single process of producing joint-products produces. [15] Given this assumption,

15 Sraffa's use of the term 'required for use' (Sraffa 1960: 43, f.n. 2), is usually interpreted as total final demand rigidly fixed in terms of quantity of commodities. This, I think, is a misinterpretation, as it does violence to common English expression. There could be final demand for diamond rings but it would be bizarre to say that

the requirement of reproducing the system guarantees that there must be as many processes of production as the number of commodities in the system.

Before we take up the case of fixed capital and rent of land, it is important to note that Adam Smith, Ricardo and Marx had developed their 'labour theory of value' in the context of single-product industries only; and there was a long-standing criticism from Jevons (1957a) [1871] that the cost-based labour theory of value is incapable of developing a theory of prices in the case of joint-production or by-products. It is clear that in the case of joint-production it is not possible to assign labour-values to individual commodities either through the use of the 'dated labour approach' or by solving the simultaneous equations of given input-output data. Sraffa argues that one, and possibly the only, way to assign labour-values to individual commodities in the joint-production case would be to readjust or rescale the processes such that the total output in the system remains exactly the same except for one additional unit of the commodity under consideration. The change in the total labour input of the system as a whole should give the labour-value or the labour content of the commodity. This labour content need not always turn out to be positive, however; the reason being that in the readjustment or rescaling process one might have to contract processes that use relatively more labour rather than processes that use relatively more materials. Thus a rise in the output by one unit of a commodity may be associated with a total fall in the labour input used by the system as a whole. This may lead to the possibility of negative labour-values, but such negative labour-values have a clear explanation.

Furthermore, in the case of joint-production, the proposition regarding the inverse relationship between wages and the rate of profits cannot be maintained if the unit of measure is taken to be any arbitrary *numéraire*. For, what could be a fall of the wage in terms of one *numéraire* may turn out to be a rise in terms of some other *numéraire*. This is because in the case of joint-products a fall in wages may lead to an even higher rate of fall in the price of a commodity as long as its joint-product is either rising or not falling sufficiently such that the rate of fall of the joint-product in aggregate is less than the rate of fall of wages. However,

---

the use of diamond rings is 'required'! In my opinion, 'required for use' only refers to the required use of goods as inputs at the given scale of production. The usual misinterpretation is again due to the false insistence that Sraffa's system must be in a state of equilibrium of demand and supply.

once this possibility is introduced for joint-products, it cannot be denied for a singly produced commodity either, provided it employs one of such joint-products as its means of production. This implies that a 10 per cent fall in wages measured by a *numéraire* commodity 'x' may lead to a 15 per cent fall in the price of 'y'. Therefore, if 'y' were used as the *numéraire*, then the same fall in wages measured by 'x' would amount to a 5 per cent rise in wages measured by 'y'. That is, as Sraffa puts it, 'the rule that the fall of the wage in *any* standard involves a rise in the rate of profits must now admit of an exception' (Sraffa 1960: 61). Thus the role of the Standard commodity in the theory becomes essential as the fundamental proposition that wages and the rate of profits are inversely related cannot be sustained unless the Standard commodity is chosen as the unit of measure or the *numéraire*.[16] Sraffa goes on to show that even in the case of joint-production there exists a unique Standard system and a Standard commodity for any given system of production. This also shows why Sraffa has to break from the classical tradition of treating real wages as part of capital and transferring it from the left-hand side of the equations to the right-hand side. If wages were taken as a basket of commodities on the left-hand side of the equations, then a change in the wage basket would *ipso facto* imply a change in the Standard system and the Standard commodity; and thus the proposition that wages and the rate of profits are inversely related could no longer be established in the general case of joint-production.

Carlo F. Manara [1968] (1980), however, argues that in the general case of Sraffa's multiple-production system a Standard system may not exist in the realm of real space. This has stood as a serious technical roadblock on the path of generalisations and development of Sraffa's economic theory. In Dupertuis and Sinha (2009b), however, we argue that in a generalised multiple-production case, the definition and identification of 'basic goods' and the techniques or processes of production associated with a system of only basic goods are more complex than hitherto understood. And further, that the Manara problem arises because the 'basic goods' of the system are misidentified, leading to self-reproducing sub-systems hiding inside the system of only the so-called basic goods.

16 To minimise the theoretical importance of the Standard commodity, Hahn claims that: 'A *numéraire* is a *numéraire*. The price of the *numéraire* can be set equal to one. Sraffa has chosen Standard net product as *numéraire* and there's an end to it' (Hahn 1982: 358). However, had Hahn considered the case of joint-production, which is the most general case for Sraffa, he would have noticed that he could not derive an inverse profit-wage frontier with any arbitrary *numéraire*.

In a single-production system, a good is clearly identified by the sector or the technique that produces it. Since each good is produced by only one technique and each technique produces only one good, the system is always square and the techniques cannot be combined to form other techniques. In this case, the identification of goods that do not directly or indirectly appear in the production of all goods (i.e., 'non-basics') can be made in a straightforward manner through observation. Since each non-basic good is associated with one independent technique, by suppressing all techniques that produce non-basic goods we end up with a square system of only basic goods. If the system of basic goods has more than one good, then a technique cannot use just the good it is producing (otherwise, the system would turn into a one-good 'corn' economy). In other words, there can be no self-reproducing sub-system within a system of only basic goods. It is well known that for such a system an associated Standard system must exist.

This property, however, does not necessarily hold in a generalised multiple-production case. For one could think of a process or a technique using n goods and producing the same n goods. If the quantities of all the n goods used are less than or equal to their outputs, then this system of one technique is self-sufficient. This is a one-good 'corn' economy in disguise. Since by observation we find that all the n goods are basics as they are all required for the production of the n goods, the usual way to solve such a system is to add n - 1 linearly independent processes that also use and produce n goods in different proportions. This gives us a square system to solve for n - 1 prices and the rate of profits of the system. The problem with such a procedure is obvious: it combines a self-reproducing sub-system with a system that is supposed to be made up of only 'basics', implying that there is no self-reproducing sub-system within it. In a generalised multiple-production system, self-reproducing sub-systems may hide in a complicated manner within what is only *apparently* a system of basic goods.

Sraffa was well aware of the fact that in the case of a multiple-production system the definition of the 'basic goods' is not so straightforward as in the case of single-production system (Sraffa 1960: § 57–59, 49–51). He, however, seemed to be interested in multiple-production systems only to the extent that they took into account the by-products — such as aging machines — as by-products of a process or technique of production.[17] In general, the case of *by-products* may be defined as a

---

17   In a recent paper Schefold reports: 'When he [Sraffa] was confronted with the difficulties of joint-production systems, which had surfaced in the 1960s and early 1970s, he told me that, if he had known, he should have written much less about

system of production in which each technique is allowed to produce at most one good that it uses as input and that all other inputs used by the technique are not produced and all other outputs are not used as inputs by the same process. In Dupertuis and Sinha (2009b), we show that in such a restricted system of multiple products, no hidden self-reproducing subsystem could exist within a system of only basic goods as defined by Sraffa, i.e., in a multiple-product system of only by-products a Standard system always exists; and thus there is no possibility of a Manara problem to occur.

However, in a general case when a process or technique is allowed to produce as many goods as it uses as its input, then the Manara problem must be confronted (see Bidard 1997). As we have stated earlier, the root of this problem lies in the misidentification of basic goods or what we define as 'atomic goods'. In a single-product case, when we define a 'good' from the perspective of an *observer*, it coincides with the perspective of the *system* as well. A system is defined by the exchanges the various sectors or techniques *must* make amongst themselves to be able to reproduce themselves; and since in a single-product system a sector is defined by the observed goods it produces, there is a one-to-one relationship between the goods observed and the goods exchanged amongst the sectors of the system. Such one-to-one relationship between the identification of a 'good' by an observer and the system as such does not necessarily exist in a multiple-production case. For example, let us suppose that all the techniques use two goods 'x' and 'y' in the same proportion as 1:1. For an outside observer the system is using and producing two distinct goods, 'x' and 'y', but in reality the system is always exchanging the bundle $(x + y)$ as one good against other goods within itself. Thus, from the system's perspective there are not two goods, 'x' and 'y', out there but only one good: 'z'$(= x \oplus y)$.

What we need to do, therefore, is to find out how goods are defined from the perspective of the internal structure of the system itself. In

---

general joint-production systems and more about fixed capital and land, and that he would have liked to treat only part of the problematic of joint-production and, finally, that it might have been better to begin the exposition with the analysis of fixed capital, followed only by some thoughts on joint-production in general' (Schefold 2005: 545). See also Schefold (1978a), where he shows that no Manara problem could exist in the case of fixed capital as the only joint-product; also see Baldone (1980) and Varri (1980). All the above, however, take only one machine for each process of production; whereas Salvadori (1988) generalises the result for jointly utilised machines.

Dupertuis and Sinha (2009b) we have presented a method for doing precisely this. We show that once commodities are properly identified, the Manara problem disappears.

Fixed Capital as Joint-Product and Land

Leaving aside technicalities, it is enough for our purposes to note that Sraffa reduces the problem of fixed capital and depreciation to a general joint-production schema, where buildings, machines and equipments that last for more than one production cycle are treated as 'one-year-old' joint-products, with their prices to be determined within the system of production. He shows that if the productivity of the fixed capital remains the same throughout its whole life, then the joint-production and the usual straight-line depreciation methods would give the same results for the measure of depreciation.[18] However, if the productivity of the fixed capital varies over time, then it is the joint-production method that would give a better measure. The point to note here, however, is that the usual measure of depreciation introduces an unobservable in the system, whereas Sraffa's method turns it into an observable.

Natural resources such as land, which provide rent to their owners, are obviously not free goods and their position in the system is similar to but the reverse of the position non-basic commodities occupy in the system. These resources appear on the input side of the equations, not on the output side. Thus, they cannot appear in the Standard system or the Standard commodity. In the case of lands of various fertilities in use for the production of one commodity, the logic of the Standard system requires that at least one kind of land, identified as marginal land, must not pay any rent. Only in this case the product, if it is a basic good, could enter the equations of the Standard system, with land treated as a free good and eliminated from the side of inputs. Thus, in such cases, the existence of marginal land which pays no rent is a logical requirement of the theory. The rents of lands of various fertilities can be determined by substituting n + 1 equations for one equation in the system, for a commodity produced by lands of n different fertilities, such as:

$$(A_{c1}p_a + \dots + C_{c1}p_c + \dots + K_{c1}p_k)\,(1 + r) + L_{c1}w + \Lambda_1\rho_1 = C_{(1)}p_c$$

$$(A_{c2}p_a + \dots + C_{c2}p_c + \dots + K_{c2}p_k)\,(1 + r) + L_{c2}w + \Lambda_2\rho_2 = C(2)p_c$$

18　See Harcourt (1965) for an understanding of the practical complications associated with the measurement of depreciation, particularly the difference between an accountant's measure and a theoretician's measure.

.....

$$(A_{cn}p_a + \ldots + C_{cn}p_c + \ldots + K_{cn}p_k)(1 + r) + L_{cn}w + \Lambda_n\rho_n = C_{(n)}p_c$$

And

$$\rho_1\,\rho_2\ldots\,\rho_n = 0$$

where c stands for the commodity corn, ρ_1, ρ_2, ..., ρ_n stand for rents on land of varying fertilities 1, 2, ... n, and Λ_1 Λ_2, ..., Λ_n represent the different types of lands in use. The last equation ensures that one of the ρ's is equal to zero, i.e., one type of land among the n types is marginal.

Where there is only one type of land, the land will not pay any rent so long as it is not 'scarce'. But the evidence of its scarcity can be found only in the presence of two methods of production existing side by side at the same time for the production of a single commodity. Suppose there is an abundance of land that is uniformly fertile. As long as some of the land is freely available, its use will not incur any rent. However, once all the land is under cultivation, any increase in output can be obtained only by introducing another method, which is more expensive (the cost is calculated on the basis of the ruling rates of profits, wages and prices) but produces more of the good (say, corn) per unit of land. Once the new technique is introduced, all the land will pay a uniform rent — this is a case of 'intensive rent'. In this case two equations are introduced for one commodity with one price and a uniform rate of rent as unknowns in the system. Both equations would also enter the Standard system, but with coefficients of opposite signs with such values as to eliminate the land in aggregate from the production equations.

Switch in Methods of Production

In the last chapter (Chapter XII), Sraffa returns to a fundamental proposition of his book: *wages and profits are inversely related*. After proving this proposition in the case of both single-product and multiple-product industries, he asks what would happen if the techniques of production change as profits or wages take on higher or lower values. In the case of single-product industries it is assumed that only one technique of producing a commodity exists. If, however, there is also another technique, then as the rate of profits rises from zero to its maximum values, the second technique at some level of the rate of profits could become the more efficient or cheaper technique to produce the commodity; and at that level of profit the system would switch to the new technique.

On the basis of his analysis of the old wine and the oak chest, Sraffa shows that with the rise (or fall) in the rate of profits, it would be possible for the system to switch back to the old technique and that such switching and re-switching could happen several times. The logical possibility of re-switching can be proved by a simple example. Let us assume a two-commodity world, with both being basic commodities. Suppose that there exist two techniques to produce commodity 'a' and one technique to produce commodity 'b', such as:

$$(A_a p_a + B_a p_b) (1 + r) + L_a w = A p_a$$
$$(A'_a p_a + B'_a p_b) (1 + r) + L'_a w = A p_a$$
$$(A_b p_a + B_b p_b) (1 + r) + L_b w = B p_b$$

Of the two techniques to produce commodity 'a', the one whose left-hand side is smaller would be chosen by the system since that technique would be cheaper. If one of the techniques is cheaper for all the possible values of r from zero to its maximum, then the other technique is simply inefficient and will never be chosen by the system. However, with changes in the value of r, the left-hand side of the two equations would change and the techniques could be such that at some values of r one technique would be cheaper whereas at some other values of r the other technique would become cheaper. Thus, if we raise r from zero to its maximum, a time would come when the system would switch from one technique to the other. At the switching point, i.e., the rate of profits when the other technique becomes viable, the two techniques would be equally cheap and the system would be indifferent about which technique it chooses. Now, let us suppose that the rate of profits is r^* at the switching point. At this rate, three techniques could be in use to produce two commodities. This is possible because the introduction of a third technique in the system would exhaust the one degree of freedom it had, since in this case neither the rate of profits nor the wages would have any freedom to move. Now by substituting r^* for r in the above three equations, we can find a solution for r^*. The reader can verify that the solution of r^* is not unique — it can have two positive values implying that the first technique could be preferred when r is between zero and r_1^* and the second technique could be chosen when r is between r_1^* and r_2^*, but then the first technique might become preferable when the rate of profits is greater than r_2^*. In the general case of n commodities such re-switching can happen several times.[19] This result destroys the possibility of aggregating capital as a homogeneous entity independently of the rate of profits. It also proves that techniques cannot be classified as capital- or labour-intensive independently of the rate of profits — in other words, the concepts of 'isoquants' and 'aggregate production function' are illogical. Again, it should be noted that the switching and re-switching of techniques does not happen in real time. To use the word 'choice' (of technique) is inappropriate in this context. What we have here is a set of given gross outputs and various input configurations that could produce the same set of outputs. Sraffa analyses the relationship between various levels of wages or the rate of profits and the most efficient or cheapest input configuration that results due to differing price solutions.

Both Sraffians and their detractors have taken this to be Sraffa's main critique of the neoclassical or marginal theory of value and distribution and have interpreted this result as the grand finale towards which the book was driving.[20] But a close reading of the chapter does not support this position. Sraffa introduces the possibility of re-switching rather matter-of-factly at the beginning of the chapter, as a consequence of the analysis in the chapter on 'dated labour'. If re-switching is the climax towards which Sraffa was driving, then the book could have ended with Chapter VI. Sraffa's real concern in the last chapter is not 're-switching' but 'switching', and the chapter is appropriately entitled 'Switch in the Methods of Production', not 'Re-switch in the Methods of Production'. The main contention of the chapter is that if there is a switch from one method to another during the movement of profits from zero to its maximum when the commodity under question is a basic good (i.e., the system turns into another system), then it loses the Standard commodity which could be used to measure the movement in wages as a consequence of the movements in the rate of profits. The problem is: can one still at least claim that there is an inverse relationship between the rate of profits and wages when there is no single Standard commodity to measure wages throughout its movements? Sraffa's answer to this question is: yes. The intuitive reason for this is simple. It is already established that within a given system there is an inverse relationship between rate of profits and wages. The

19 See Bharadwaj (1989, Ch. 11) on the question of maximum number of switches.
20 For an early controversy over the re-switching proposition, see symposium on re-switching in 'Paradoxes in Capital Theory: A Symposium', *Quarterly Journal of Economics* LXXX, November (1966) and Harcourt (1969, 1972) for a celebrated survey of the controversy.

movements in the rate of profits and wages always happen within a given system. At the switching point from one system to another there is no change in the rate of profits and wages — the switch takes place at a *given* level of wages and rate of profits. After establishing the proposition that wages and profits are inversely related even when there are switches in the methods of production in most general cases of multiple-product systems, the book ends as abruptly as it began.

Some Remarks on the Nature of Sraffa's Propositions

Before we take up other interpretations and criticisms of Sraffa's propositions, let us briefly recall their peculiar nature and the method of analysis he employs.[21] Sraffa's theoretical propositions are built on *objective* data of the economy as it stands. It is a *post factum* description of an economy after a production cycle is over. There is no *agent* in the system as no decision is being taken — the question of why the data are what they are is not asked. By freezing the data of the given economy, Sraffa effectively shuts the door to *psychology* and all the *subjective* variables that percolate in economics. As we have seen in the previous chapters, though classical economists, particularly Ricardo and Marx, emphasised the objective cost (labour being a surrogate for homogenising such costs) aspect of price, their theory of price was dependent on the solution to the problem of 'equilibrium', which entailed the psychological or subjective notion of demand and 'profit motive' of the capitalists to be taken on board. It was the solution to this specific problem that led them to impose an implicit assumption of constant returns on the given techniques in use — a point about which Sraffa warned his readers in the very first sentence of his 'Preface'. Given the position of classical economists, it was easy for the alternative theory that sought to root the theory of price in psychology (as a calculus of pleasure and pain) to argue that an 'objective' theory of price is untenable when variable returns to scale or even constant returns prevail, but there are alternative techniques available. Interestingly, Sraffa neither raises nor solves the problem of 'equilibrium' — he simply dissolves the problem. He shows that a robust 'objective' theory of price exists independently of any consideration of

---

21 Elsewhere (Sinha 2009) I have drawn a close parallel between Sraffa's method and the later Wittgenstein's philosophy of language and meaning.

'equilibrium' of the system and thus firmly shuts the door that was left open for human psychology by the classical economists.[22]

Furthermore, classical economists, particularly Marx (and to some extent Ricardo), argued that the 'cause' of price is the labour or human energy spent in the process of production. Again, it was easy for the alternative theory that sought to root economics in psychology to argue that there are goods that have a price but no labour is spent in their production, and that in the case of joint-production the value of commodities cannot be reduced to labour; however, the price of such goods could be explained by their 'scarcity'. Thus, generally speaking, the 'essence' or 'cause' of price lies in the subjective notion of 'utility' that determines the degree of 'scarcity' of any commodity. Yet again, instead of solving the problem of 'essence' or 'cause' of price, Sraffa dissolves the problem itself. The question of 'where does a commodity get its price from' is not asked. Instead of any particular commodity, a whole system of production is taken into account and it is shown that prices play a certain role in the scheme of the reproduction of the system as a whole. It has a functional explanation within a system of production and distribution but no 'essence'. But what about goods that are not part of the system of production and distribution but still have prices — such as paintings by the great masters? Sraffa remains silent. The reason for this silence is simple. He did not take on the question of 'why a good has a price'. His concern was to describe the logical relations that must exist between variables of a given system of production and distribution. Within this frame, the prices of commodities must take certain values independently of any psychological factors of agents. It may very well be true that the prices of paintings by the great masters can be explained only on the basis of psychological factors, but they have nothing in common with the commodities

---

22 Recently Kurz and Salvadori (2005a, b) have also emphasised Sraffa's 'objectivism'. However, following Garegnani, they also subscribe to the idea that Sraffa's outputs are the 'equilibrium' centre of gravitation outputs and that Sraffa does not assume constant returns. This introduces a serious contradiction in their position. If Sraffa's outputs are the objective empirical outputs, then there is no reason to think that they would necessarily be at the centre of gravitation or the equilibrium. Thus one is forced to take on board subjective elements, such as the notion of final demand and the entrepreneurs' motive to maximise the rate of profits in order to introduce the notion of the gravitation mechanism in Sraffa's framework along with the assumption of constant returns, since one needs to maintain that the adjustment mechanism leaves the production equations unchanged. See section entitled 'Does Sraffa Implicitly Assume the Centre of Gravitation Mechanism' later in this chapter for a detailed criticism of Garegnani's position.

that are part of the system of production and distribution, and bringing the psychological aspect of price to these commodities can only create confusion.

But why do people produce in the first place? Where does the economy come from? The usual answer to such questions is that human beings have material needs and since nature does not provide all those materials spontaneously and in unlimited quantity, human beings must sacrifice their leisure and take on the pain of work to produce those things to satisfy their needs. This is a linear narrative where the origin of the economy or the cause of production is explained by the end-result of fulfilment of needs; and the whole enterprise of economics is explained based on the rationale of a human agent. Economists find the story of Robinson Crusoe to be highly illustrative of the fundamental economic problem — Crusoe has to make the economic calculation of how to allocate his limited resources (mainly labour) to best satisfy his various needs, which includes the problem of sacrificing some consumption today to be able to consume more in the future. Yet again, Sraffa dissolves the problem. The question of the origin of the economy or the cause of production is not raised. A system of production is taken as a circular process — its end-result is to repeat itself. Agents are perpetually caught in some system of production and distribution, just as they are born in one language or another.

Part II
Some Major Controversies

Since Sraffa's book is still contemporary, we will break from our previous practice of taking up controversial interpretations more or less chronologically. Here we will discuss the major controversial issues relating to Sraffa's book to develop a coherent interpretation of our own. The issues that we will discuss are:

1. Does Sraffa implicitly assume constant returns to scale?
2. Does Sraffa implicitly assume the notion of centre of gravitation?
3. Is Sraffa's system a special case of inter-temporal general equilibrium?

Does Sraffa Implicitly Assume Constant Returns to Scale?

In one of the earliest reviews of the book, Roy Harrod argued that Sraffa apparently derives the relative prices of commodities in his two-good subsistence model by the ratio of the respective excess productions of the two sectors; and in the case of more than two sectors, 'we have a system of simultaneous equations, in which the exchange values of the commodities in terms of one another are determined by the same principle' (Harrod 1961: 783–84). Further on, he argues:

Then we pass to a state of affairs in which more commodities are produced than are required for their own reproduction (and labour can have more than a subsistence wage). Before proceeding to Mr. Sraffa's theories concerning wages and profit, we may note at the outset that Mr. Sraffa does not seem to be interested in the commodity-mix in which wage- and profit-earners choose to take out their income. In an early passage (p. 7), where he is still dealing with a two-commodity world of wheat and iron, he assumes that the whole net income is taken out in wheat. That may seem sensible, as consumers do not presumably desire iron as such. But there is nothing in this passage to require that the second commodity, iron, is specifically a capital good. On the contrary, it is supposed to be setting the matter out in a perfectly general way. This is a difficulty arising, at the very outset, from the neglect of the composition of consumer demand. If consumers did happen to wish to have some iron, that would at once, in accordance with Mr. Sraffa's own equations, affect the price ratios, which his system purports to be determining without reference to consumer demand. I believe that this objection runs through all the complications of his subsequent treatment (Harrod 1961: 784).

Sraffa responded to Roy Harrod thus:

[This] concerns Sir Roy's belief that the system presented must be indeterminate because it fails to take into account the composition of consumer demand. He starts from the example, in [§ 1] of the book, of a system consisting of two industries which produce respectively commodities a and b, and from this he concludes: 'the rate of exchange of a for b is *determined*, quite simply, by the ratio of the excess production of a to the excess production of b' (p. 783, italics mine). He then proceeds to consider 'a greater number of industries and commodities,' and here again he finds that the exchange values 'are determined by the same principle' (p. 784), namely by the ratios between the excess production of the various commodities.

Now this is clearly a misunderstanding, since the exchange ratios are, of course, determined by the equations of production and not by the ratios between the excess productions of the commodities. Sir Roy has been misled by the fact that the two ratios *happen* to be equal in the first example given (a no-surplus two-commodity system which is in a self-replacing state). Even in this simple case, however, if, with the same equations, the two commodities were produced in different proportions (so that the system ceased to be in self-replacing state) the exchange ratio would remain the same but the ratio between the excess productions of the two commodities would be changed, so that the two would no longer be equal. In the case of a system of more than two commodities the ratios of the excess productions would not in general be equal to the values *even* in the self-replacing state.

Sir Roy, however, having adopted the notion that the exchange values are always equal to, and determined by, the ratio between the excess productions of the commodities, is led to the conclusion that a change in the composition of consumer demand 'would at once, in accordance with Mr. Sraffa's own equations, affect the price ratios' (p. 784); and this even though the words that I have italicised necessarily imply that the methods of production would be unchanged. This misunderstanding, if I may adopt Sir Roy's own words, 'runs through all the complications of his subsequent treatment' (Sraffa 1962: 477–78).

This highly interesting response, written in Sraffa's typical style, has gone largely unnoticed in the literature. Sraffa corrects the 'technical' mistake of Harrod's but remains *silent* on the problem raised by him. Sraffa makes it clear that taking into account of the composition of demand is not required to make his prices *determinate*. This confirms our point that the uniformity of the rate of profits in Sraffa's system (which is required for the determination of his prices) is not contingent on the assumption that supplies are equal to effectual demands. Once this point is understood, Harrod's problem of the relation of prices with the changes in the composition of demand does not require any solution — it is simply dissolved. Hence Sraffa's silence.

In the literature, however, there have been mainly two ways of interpreting Sraffa's silence and in our opinion both of them are incorrect: one is to attribute constant returns to scale (CRS) to Sraffa's production equations, and the second is to attribute Sraffa's outputs to be *already* in equilibrium position. In this section we deal with the first proposition; the second is dealt with in the next section. The neoclassicists, in spite of Sraffa's explicit declaration that he does not assume CRS, claim that Sraffa's propositions do not make sense without it. Samuelson has gone so far as to claim that:

> In cautioning (p. v) against readers 'mistaking' spurious "margins" for the genuine article', the author [Sraffa] seems to overlook that much of his first 78 pages themselves do involve

shifts in the 'scale of an industry' — as, for example, in working with specified *standard* market baskets of productions, or in supposing that demand and taste shifts do not alter real prices in a no-joint-production world, and as, for example, in Chapter I's crucial sole footnote (Samuelson 2000a: 116).

The same points are made in a more formal way by Samuelson and Etula (2006). In Sinha (2007), all three arguments of Samuelson and Etula (2006) are refuted. Here I provide refutations of Samuelson's three examples very briefly.

Let us first take the example of Sraffa's footnote in Chapter I. I reproduce the complete footnote below and show how Samuelson's interpretation is incorrect.

> This formulation presupposes the system's being in a self-replacing state; but every system of the type under consideration is capable of being brought to such a state merely by changing the proportions in which the individual equations enter it. (Systems which do so with a surplus are discussed in §4ff. Systems which are incapable of doing so under any proportions and show a deficit in the production of some commodities over their consumption even if none has a surplus do not represent viable economic systems and are not considered.) (Sraffa 1960: 5, f.n.1).

Now, let us take Sraffa's simple example of the two-goods subsistence economy.

280 qr. wheat + 12 t. iron → 400 qr. wheat   (I)

120 qr. wheat + 8 t. iron → 20 t. iron

It is clear that this system is in a self-replacing state and the exchange ratio between iron and wheat must be 10 qr. of wheat for 1 t. of iron. Now suppose there is a system that is not in a self-replacing state. For example:

280 qr. wheat + 12 t. iron → 400 qr. wheat

      (I')

240 qr. wheat + 16 t. iron → 40 t. iron

Obviously system I' is not producing enough wheat to reproduce itself at the same scale. The reader can verify that the exchange ratio between iron and wheat in this case is also 10 units of wheat for 1 unit of iron. Thus the wheat sector will exchange 120 qr. of wheat (its surplus wheat) for 12 t. of iron and reproduce itself at the same scale. On the other hand, given a single technique, the iron sector can now combine 120 qr. of wheat with only 8 t. of iron (the remaining 20 t. of iron in this time period goes to waste). Now when the iron sector's scale is reduced by half, there can be only three possibilities: (*i*) if the sector displays decreasing returns, then its output will be > 20 t. of iron; (*ii*) if the sector displays increasing returns, then its output will be < 20 t. of iron; and (*iii*) if the sector displays constant returns, then its output will be = 20 t. of iron. As Sraffa's remark in the parenthesis explains, if case (*i*) happens to be true, then this system is of a type that always produces surplus and is dealt with in §4ff. of the book; if case (*ii*) happens to be true, then this system is of a type that always produces a deficit and is not viable and not considered; and if case (*iii*) happens to be true, then it is of the *type* depicting a system of 'production for subsistence'. Therefore, any system of production, if it is of the *type* that depicts production for subsistence, 'is capable of being brought to such a state [self-replacing state] merely by changing the proportions in which individual equations enter it'. Clearly the remark in the footnote is about the *logical necessity* of a system of a particular *type* and not about any given empirical system. No 'returns to scale' assumption is implied in the remark. Sraffa's book is full of riddles for the reader. Here the word 'type' contains the secret of the riddle, and the answer to it, in Sraffa's own code, is provided in the parenthesis.

Samuelson's second point is that Sraffa's construction of his Standard system implicitly assumes constant returns, as he multiplies both the left- and the right-hand sides of the equations with the same constants to construct his Standard system. Yet again, the mistake in interpretation is a simple one — that is, of mistaking a mathematical proposition for an empirical one. Nowhere does Sraffa maintain that a Standard system must exist in the real world. All he means is that *if* we can imagine a system that represents a Standard system (which logically we can), then certain properties of this system can be made clearly visible. And since its equations of the methods of production and the total labour used are common with the given empirical system, it is possible for another mathematical proposition to be deduced: that those relations would also hold for the real empirical system if the Standard commodity were used as the *numéraire*: 'Such a relation is of interest only if it can be shown that its application is not limited to the imaginary Standard system but is capable of being extended to the actual economic system of observation' (ibid.: 22, emphasis added).

Thus there is no requirement for the Standard system to exist empirically and therefore no need for any returns to scale assumption. It is a theoretical construct that was devised to make visible certain mathematical relationship that exists between certain variables of a given empirical system; as Sraffa points out: 'The *Standard system* is a purely auxiliary construction. It should therefore be possible to present the essential elements of the mechanism under consideration without having recourse to it' (ibid.: 31).

Samuelson's third example is a non-existent one. He simply assumes that Sraffa maintains that changes in demand will have no affect on his prices, and this could happen only if Sraffa implicitly assumed constant returns. He appears not to have read Sraffa's response to Harrod closely. There, as we have noted, Sraffa says that prices are determined by the production equations and will remain the same if changes in demand do not affect the production equations; he, however, did not go on to say that changes in demand cannot have *any* affect on production equations. The fundamental reason behind Samuelson's incorrect interpretation of Sraffa — and, for that matter, of most of the neoclassical authors who have dealt with Sraffa's book (see, for example, Burmeister 1968, 1975, 1977; Hahn 1982; Samuelson 1990, 2000a, b)— is the conviction that Sraffa's prices are 'equilibrium prices' and thus must have demand lurking behind them; and since his prices are supposed to be independent of the composition of the demand, his system must implicitly assume 'constant returns', given the single technique of production.[23] In other words, demand plays a passive role in the story. A change in demand causes supplies to readjust; however, given constant returns, it does not affect the production equations and thus prices. This is how Arun Bose had also interpreted Sraffa, who had responded to Bose in a letter dated 9 December 1964:

I am sorry to have kept your MS so long — and with so little result.

23 Among the neoclassicists, Hicks was one who categorically rejected the centre of gravitation thesis for Sraffa's prices: 'Sraffa leaves us to find out what his prices are, but I doubt if they are equilibrium prices. They seem to be prices which are set upon products, by their producers, according to some rule. Now it is perfectly true that we are nowadays familiar with that method of price-fixing, by "mark-up"; but when that method is used, the rate of profit that is used to establish the mark-up is conventional. Now it may be that Sraffa wants us to think of his rate of profit as being conventional; and that the uniformity of the rate of profit throughout his system, of which he makes so much, is just a uniformity of convention' (Hicks 1985: 306).

The fact is that your opening sentence is for me an obstacle which I am unable to get over. You write: 'It is a basic proposition of the Sraffa theory that prices are determined exclusively by the physical requirements of production and the social wage-profit division with consumers demand playing a purely passive role.'

Never have I said this: certainly not in the two places to which you refer in your note 2. Nothing, in my view, could be more suicidal than to make such a statement. You are asking me to put my head on the block so that the first fool who comes along can cut it off neatly.

Whatever you do, <u>please</u> do not represent me as saying such a thing (Sraffa n.d.: C32, emphasis in original).

Evidently Sraffa was well aware of the fact that a proposition regarding demand playing a passive role in the determination of prices would amount to assuming constant returns to scale, and that would mean putting his head on the block for any fool to cut it off. The main motivation for treating Sraffa's prices as 'equilibrium prices' comes from Sraffa's use of equal rate of profits for all sectors. However, as we have already shown, the uniformity of the rate of profits in Sraffa's system does not require the notion of 'equilibrium' of demand and supply.

The other motivation for invoking constant returns in Sraffa's system comes from the belief that any meaningful economic theory must be a *predictive* one (i.e., a causal theory); otherwise it is mere chit-chat. As we have argued earlier, Sraffa's 'prelude to a critique of economic theory' is not supposed to be an alternative theory that comes up with different predictions from the orthodoxy. Rather, it is a *description* of the given system, which is designed to show that the *basis* on which the predictive theories of the orthodoxy stand is simply non-existent. Burmeister makes this point amply clear when he writes:

Now consider a new situation with a different size and composition of output denoted by subscripts two. We may again calculate Sraffa's Standard Commodity in this new situation and his corresponding 'real wages,' [*sic*] w_2^s, as well as the new maximum profit rate r_2^*. It remains true, by virtue of (1), that

$$r_2 = r_2^* \, (1 - w_2^s).$$

But in general *nothing* more can be said unless the two different situations are generated from a constant returns to scale technology! Thus if Sraffa's 'real wages' [*sic*] remain constant in both situations with $w_1^s = w_2^s = 50\%$, the equilibrium profit rate in the second situation may change in *any* direction (Burmeister 1975: 69).

But isn't this precisely what Sraffa's point is? In the real world a change in the composition of real output leaves the theoretician devoid of any basis for prediction, unless CRS is invoked. But the assumption of CRS is simply *arbitrary*. In the light of his Chapter XI on Land, it is most unlikely that Sraffa could implicitly assume CRS for his propositions since, in the presence of a non-produced fixed input such as land, a continuous increase in the scale of production would imply a periodic change in the methods of production and thus the Standard system.[24] The absence of demand in Sraffa's system is due neither to an implicit assumption of CRS, nor to the opinion that demand plays a 'purely passive role'. Sraffa's system shows that, given a rate of profits or wages, prices are determined by the methods of production in use. The role of demand can only be determined by analysing the effects on prices of changes in demand. But demand can affect prices only via affecting the methods of production. In a general equilibrium framework, a rise in demand for a commodity will relatively raise the demand for that factor of production which the commodity uses relatively more intensively and thus the price of that factor, e.g., a rise in the demand for a relatively 'labour-intensive' good would raise the wages of labour, which in turn would lead to a general shift in the choice of production techniques in favour of more 'capital-intensive' techniques. It is this change in techniques brought about by a change in demand that explains the effect of demand on prices. Sraffa's analysis shows that once the methods of production (of basic goods) change, the system loses its Standard commodity and thus all scientific grounds for comparing the two sets of prices: '[A]s a consequence a comparison of the prices by the two methods becomes meaningless since its result appears to depend on which commodity is chosen as standard of prices' (Sraffa 1960: 82).

---

24 As a matter of fact, in relation to his early critique of Marshall's theory of prices, Sraffa explained to Keynes that 'he had focused on the horizontal supply curve, not because he held that case to be most realistic but because it was almost the only case of importance which could be analysed rigorously within Marshall's framework' (Schefold 1997: 3).

Thus the impact of demand on prices is not passive but rather *unpredictable. Hence no causal functional relationship between quantity supplied and prices, or demand and prices, can be established.*[25] Cockshott and Sinha (2008) have shown that in the absence of a Standard commodity even the direction of the changes in prices due to changes in methods of productions become contingent on the arbitrary selection of a *numéraire*. In Sinha (2009) some parallels have been drawn between Sraffa's propositions and those made by Wittgenstein in his later writings. In *Philosophical Investigations*, Wittgenstein (1978) argues that meaning of a word is its use in a particular 'language game'.

Any attempt to drag a word from its proper language game to another language game creates non-sense. Similarly, Sraffa apparently suggests that the value or price of a commodity is well defined within a given system of production; but once the system of production changes, it becomes meaningless to compare changes in the values or prices of a commodity in one system with another.

But Sraffians themselves have to take some responsibility for adding to confusion on this score. For example, after vehemently denying the existence of CRS in Sraffa's book, Harcourt and Massaro go on to state that: 'The inclusion of joint-production in the analysis explains why Sraffa did not use the more familiar input per unit of output notation in the single commodity system. This notation has no meaning once there is joint-production; ...' (Harcourt and Massaro 1964: 48). Though Harcourt and Massaro are correct in pointing out that in the presence of joint-production the input per unit of output notation is meaningless, this cannot be the only reason for Sraffa's rejection of this notation. This is because the use of 'input per unit of output notation' in effect implies an assumption of CRS, unless the unit of account is so adjusted that the total gross output of every sector is counted as one unit.[26] Similarly, Levine writes:

That is, commodity prices in the model [i.e. Sraffa's] are determined entirely independently of those relative weights or

---

25 The reason why Samuelson was confident that Sraffa implicitly assumes constant returns on his production equations in spite of warning against it in his 'Preface' was his belief that Sraffa consistently confused the concept of constant returns in a general equilibrium setting with the Marshallian notion of 'constant cost'. The unpublished Sraffa papers, however, have now revealed that Samuelson's hypothesis in this regard was false and that Sraffa was well aware of the difference between the Marshallian notion of 'constant cost' and the concept of constant returns in general at least as early as 1928. See Sinha (2007) for details.
26 Professor Harcourt has pointed out to me that Sraffa had read the draft of their paper cited above and had 'approved' it.

scalars, of the equations of production, that display the mix of total demand. These relative weights may change without changing the commodity-price set, provided, of course, that neither the techniques of production nor distributive share change (Levine 1974: 879).

This cannot be true either, since a change in the composition of real outputs will not leave Sraffa's techniques unchanged unless CRS is implied.

Finally, Ian Steedman argues that:

> ... [R]eturns questions are unambiguously irrelevant to Parts I and II of Sraffa's book. ... [However,] [i]t may be concluded that Sraffa's analysis of switches of production methods for a non-basic implicitly assumes that every basic industry has *either* a constant gross output or constant returns to scale: the only non-arbitrary interpretation of this implicit assumption is that every basic industry exhibits constant returns (Steedman 1980a: 5, 10).

Steedman's argument is that the presence of choice of techniques makes the system over-determined. For the system to have a unique solution, either all the gross outputs of the basic industries must be assumed constant, *which is what Sraffa does throughout his book*, or assume CRS for all basic industries. He further argues that assuming fixed gross outputs implies that there is no reason why net outputs of many industries may not have to become *negative* for the switch in technique to take place. This, for him, is why a 'non-arbitrary interpretation' of the reswitching proposition must assume constant returns.

Steedman, in this context, is making the same mistake as Samuelson and the other neoclassical scholars who read Sraffa's propositions as 'predictive' have made. To avoid the negative net outputs, Steedman believes that many sectors will have to expand their outputs, and that could happen without changes in techniques only if constant returns are assumed. The problem with such thinking is that the expansion of the sectors will require more labour, but there is no indication in Sraffa's given system that more labour, over and above what is being used by the system, is available — the system is defined by the total labour in use. Again, Sraffa's proposition regarding re-switching is logical and not empirical in nature. He takes a system of production as given. At the ruling rate of profits the system has already made a choice of techniques to be used and those techniques are being used.

Then a hypothetical question is raised: what if the rate of profits were different? Sraffa argues that, in general, different rates of profits would have given a different set of prices for the given system. The next question is: what if the new set of prices makes some alternative techniques more efficient? In that case, Sraffa's answer is that *if* such a rate of profits prevailed, then the system would be defined by a different set of techniques. The possibility of re-switching techniques is built on such hypothetical reasoning only to show that techniques cannot be characterised as capital- or labour-intensive independently of the knowledge of the rate of profits, and to draw a functional relationship between choice of techniques and the rate of profits is illogical. In Steedman's example, if the re-switching of techniques required (given the gross outputs of the basic goods and the total labour of the system constant) that net outputs of several basic goods must become negative, then such re-switching is not viable, as the condition on the system is that it should be able to reproduce itself.

Does Sraffa Implicitly Assume the Notion of Centre of Gravitation?

The Sraffians have tried to deal with Sraffa's silence on this question differently. They accept that Sraffa's system is of *given outputs* and therefore admits no assumption regarding returns to scale. They, however, interpret Sraffa's *given outputs* as long-term 'equilibrium' outputs.[27] Garegnani (1976, 1984, 1990a, 1990b, 1990c, 1990d, 1998, 2000) has been in the forefront of providing the Sraffian reading of the classical economists that apparently squares with Sraffa's claim of the 'classical standpoint' of a 'given output' with the notion of the 'centre of gravitation' without the assumption of constant returns. There are two aspects to his main argument. First, in his opinion, the notion of centre of gravitation is fundamental to both classical and the early neoclassical theories of value. However, according to Garegnani, the move away from such a notion within the neoclassical tradition with Hicks's temporary equilibrium and Arrow-Debreu's inter-temporal

---

27 Among the Sraffians, Roncaglia appreciates that 'there is no reason to believe that Sraffa's prices of production should equate quantity demanded and quantity supplied' (Roncaglia 1978: 16); however, he does not manage to show how Sraffa could then take the rate of profits to be uniform and thus succumbs to holding the contradictory position that Sraffa's system is a snapshot of the market-place, and at the same time believes that his system is assumed to be at the centre of gravitation (also see Roncaglia 2000).

general equilibrium is nothing but an attempt to escape from the problem of aggregation of capital, which could not be avoided within the context of the early neoclassical theories.

> The study of the permanent effects of changes by means of comparisons between positions of the economic system characterized by a uniform rate of profits was in fact the method used by Ricardo and the English classical economists, when they explained profits in terms of the surplus product left after paying wages at the rate determined by independent economic or social circumstances. But fundamentally the same method was preserved after Ricardo, across the deep change which the theory underwent in favour of a symmetric explanation of profits and wages in terms of the equilibrium between the forces of demand and supply for labour and capital. ... It was only in the last few decades that this method, which was centred on 'long-period positions' of the system ... was increasingly challenged: ... this departure from tradition has not been due to weaknesses of the method as such, but rather to weaknesses of the dominant theory of distribution and, in particular, of the conception of capital it relies on (Garegnani 1976: 25–26).

Second, classical economics takes 'effectual demand' as given data of the theory, and the given quantity is taken as equal to the given 'effectual demand'. Thus the theory of value deals only with the long-term equilibrium point and since the equilibrium quantity is already a known datum, the theory does not need any assumption about changes in quantity and returns to scale:

> In his Preface Sraffa writes that he assumes outputs to be given, 'so that no question arises as to the variation or constancy of returns' (Sraffa 1960: v). This passage has induced Professor Hahn, for example, to write that the claim reduces Sraffa's analysis to 'just a fancy way of presenting accounts ex post'. However, Hahn would be correct only if the modern *simultaneous* determination of prices and outputs by 'demand and supply' were the only conceivable way to determine outputs. Only then would taking outputs as data when determining prices be equivalent to 'presenting accounts ex post'. However, as we shall see, a *separate determination of outputs* is possible and was in fact associated with the different classical theory of distribution considered above — and this is precisely what

underlies Sraffa's assumption of given outputs and the independence of his analysis from constant returns to scale.

In fact, let us consider, one by one, the circumstances on which it will be generally agreed the output of each commodity will depend. These will be, to begin with: (1) the level of aggregate income and activity; (2) the technical conditions of production (governing, among other things, the outputs of means of production);

(3) the distribution of the social product among the social classes (and therefore, in terms of the classical theories, the level of the independent distributive variables), since different classes generally spend their income on different commodities. Now, we have seen that classical authors take all three circumstances as given when approaching the determination of relative prices and dependent distributive variables (§19, above). The outputs can therefore, also be taken as given in that determination, in so far as they depend on those same circumstances (Garegnani 1990a: 129).[28]

Let us begin with the first point. If Garegnani's contention that the method of long-term equilibrium or the notion of centre of gravitation is common and fundamental to both the classical as well as neoclassical theories of value prior to the development of temporary and inter-temporal equilibrium, then this aspect of classical economics cannot be the 'classical standpoint' that Sraffa is alluding to, since his allusion refers to a standpoint that has been 'submerged and forgotten since the advent of the "marginal" method'. As a matter of fact, Sraffa's analysis, as we have shown in the context of 'dated labour', multiple-production and re-switching, brought to fore the highly complex nature of the interconnectedness of the system of a large number of basic goods, which reveals that the idea of the 'centre of gravitation' is not all that self-evident. Steedman (1984) raises some pertinent questions and Dupertuis and Sinha (2009a)

---

28 Recently, Garegnani has reluctantly accepted that the classical authors did implicitly assume constant returns in the context of allocation of resources: 'However, Ricardo treated decreasing returns from land, just as Smith had treated the increasing returns from division of labour: as relevant, that is, only for the comparatively large output changes involved in capital accumulation and growth. Unlike what happens in neoclassical theory, Smith and *Ricardo could therefore* [it is not clear what is the significance of "therefore" in this context] *leave physical returns to scale quite naturally aside* [this is a strange way of admitting "taking CRS on board"] *when dealing with relative prices in a given position of the economy, with the kind of comparatively small output changes generally involved in that specific analysis*' (Garegnani 2007: 188, emphasis added).

comprehensively show that the 'centre of gravitation' is not an attractive point — something that would have been obvious to Sraffa.

Now we come to Garegnani's second point that Sraffa and the classical economists take 'effectual demand' as given data of the theory and the given quantity is taken as equal to the given 'effectual demand'. It is, however, universally accepted, even by Professor Garegnani himself, that the classical economists did not believe that the *actual supplies* of any given system at any given point were equal to the given effectual demands. Thus we have two sets of given data available at any point of time: one is the 'effectual demand' data and the other is the actual data of inputs and outputs. If the two sets are not equal, then equalising the supplies with the 'effectual demands' while keeping the proportions of the given input-output data constant would amount to assuming constant returns, which is what the classical economists do. Since there are no production functions available in the context of classical economics or Sraffa's book, there is no way of avoiding CRS if one wants to assume that the given supply quantities will equal the given 'effectual demand' quantities. And this is the reason why Sraffa at the very outset proclaims that his system does not require thinking in terms of equilibrium of demand and supply.

To avoid such pitfalls Garegnani maintains that Sraffa's given outputs are *ex-ante* and not *ex-post*, as he writes: 'The outputs he [Sraffa] takes as given are *ex ante normal* outputs just like the neoclassical "equilibrium" outputs...' (Garegnani 1990a: 132). In his 'Comments' on Asimakopulos's paper in the same volume, Garegnani gives us a glimpse of what he could mean by taking the 'social physical product' as given. He believes that the *ex ante* outputs that the theoretician takes as given is some sort of average of several years of actual outputs: '... (the actual magnitude corresponding to it [Sraffa's system], would, if anything, be a moving average calculated over *several* years)' (Garegnani 1990c: 350). The question is: if Sraffa's outputs are the averages of several past years of outputs, then what are his inputs? They must also be the averages of the inputs of the same past years. Thus Sraffa's representative technique turns out to be a simple average of the input-output data of past several years. But a representation of such an average technique is possible only if constant returns are assumed.

Furthermore, an attribution of such a procedure to Sraffa contradicts his two fundamental methodological principles. First of all, the averages (or the average technique) are unobservable — they may not exist in reality. Sraffa's principle, however, was to build his theoretical propositions only on things that are, at least ideally, observable. Second, Sraffa's prices and the rate of profits are precise and not some kind of statistical averages. In a note after the publication of the *PCMC*, Sraffa wrote: 'The wage and the aggregate profit of reality are, at best, rough approximations of the standard wage and profit. But the rate of profit of reality is identical to that of the standard' (n.d.: D3/12/111/139, the English translation from the original in Italian is quoted in Gehrke 2007). Of course, such a statement would be incorrect if his input-output data were not the data of the real system in *use* but rather a representative average of past several years. Sraffa's statement further reinforces our interpretation that the uniformity of the rate of profits in Sraffa's system is not contingent on the system being at the centre of gravitation.

Moreover, in Chapter III of the *PCMC* Sraffa works out complicated changes in prices due to changes in the distribution of the net output, all the while keeping the gross as well as the net output constant. Unless it is assumed that both the capitalists and the workers receive their incomes in exactly the same commodities and in the same proportion, it simply cannot be maintained that all those price solutions would be the equilibrium prices or the given output would conform to the effectual demands for the various income distributions. No such assumption, however, is made in the book![29] The reader should also recall that we have already noted in Section III that Sraffa requires a uniform rate of profits for his Standard system and it would be hard to argue that Sraffa could assume that the effectual demands are equal to the supplies in this case too. Furthermore, in Appendix B (Sraffa 1960: 90–91) Sraffa deals with a curious case of a non-basic commodity which uses itself at a very high proportion in its own production: for example, say 100 units of 'beans' are needed to produce 110 units of 'beans'. In this case, the rate of profits in the 'beans' sector cannot be more than 10 per cent, but if the rate of profits in the basic goods sectors happens to be more than 10 per cent then there cannot be an equal rate of profits in all sectors with all prices being positive. This case would simply not arise if one assumes that Sraffa's system deals only with long-term equilibrium situations since, given the long-term equilibrating mechanism of the market, the 'beans'-producing capitalists would simply move out of 'beans' production and start producing

---

29 In a recent paper Garegnani (2005) argues that a fundamental shift in Sraffa's theoretical approach took place in late 1927, and he goes on to show that it is only afterwards Sraffa tried to relate his new position with the classical economists. In this context, Garegnani emphasises the given output approach of Sraffa and the classical economists without bringing up the notion of centre of gravitation. This might be an indication that Garegnani's position itself might be shifting on his interpretation of Sraffa's position on the notion of centre of gravitation.

some basic goods resulting in the disappearance of 'beans' from the system. Thus Sraffa's 'beans' would be produced only when the system is not in long-term equilibrium, which is evidence to the effect that his system is not necessarily in long-term equilibrium.

Finally, Garegnani's or the 'Sraffian' position rests on the conviction that Sraffa made several 'implicit assumptions' of an empirical nature in his system of equations. But a careful reading of the book reveals this claim to be untenable. In the book we find that Sraffa is extremely particular about stating his empirical assumptions even when they are of an unproblematic nature. For example, there is no *logical* reason for any good in Sraffa's system to be 'basic'; therefore, Sraffa explicitly writes: 'We shall assume throughout that any system contains at least one basic product' (Sraffa 1960: 8). Further on we find Sraffa explicitly stating: 'We retain however [from classical economists] the supposition of an annual cycle of production with an annual market' (ibid.: 10). Again, in the context of joint-production there is no *logical* necessity that the number of processes and the number of goods be equal. In Sraffa's context it depends upon the assumption that the proportions in which commodities are produced by any one method are different from the proportions in which they are required for use. This is a mild assumption for any given empirical system but it is explicitly made, and it is on the basis on this assumption that Sraffa goes on to state: '(The assumption previously made of the existence of "a second process" can now be replaced by the more general assumption that the number of processes should be equal to the number of commodities)' (Sraffa 1960: 44). And finally: 'We have been assuming that in a system of single-product industries only one way of producing each commodity is available, with the result that changes in distribution can have no effect on the methods of production employed' (ibid.: 81). The question is: if Sraffa assumes that his system of equations is based on a particular empirical assumption that its outputs correspond to *given* effectual demands, then why does he not make this assumption explicitly in this case? Why does he begin the book by telling the reader not to think in terms of equilibrium of demand and supply and then go on to implicitly assume it himself?

Before closing this section, let us look critically at the evidence provided in support of the received interpretation that Sraffa's outputs are at the centre of gravitation. We may be asked: if what we have said thus far is true, then what could Sraffa mean by his statement in the 'Preface' that: 'This standpoint [i.e., of given output], which is that of the old classical economists from Adam Smith to Ricardo, has been submerged and forgotten since the advent of the "marginal" method' (ibid.: v), as the gravitation mechanism was clearly part of Adam Smith's and Ricardo's systems. The answer to this question can be found in one of Sraffa's notes written during the early period of his breakthrough:

> When A. Smith etc. said '*natural*' he did not in the least mean the 'normal' or the 'average' nor the 'long run' value. He meant that physical, truly natural relations between commodities, that is determined by the equations, and that is not disturbed by the process of securing a greater share in the product. ... (n.d.: D3/12/11, quoted in Garegnani 2005: 474).

Clearly, from the beginning of his new theoretical adventure, Sraffa had completely discounted the notion of 'centre of gravitation' as part of the 'classical standpoint'. The reader should note that we are here not concerned with the 'correctness' of Sraffa's reading of Adam Smith. The evidence shows that when Sraffa uses the term 'natural price', unlike the classical economists, he is not using it as the long-term equilibrium or centre of gravitation price. It should also be noted that in his lecture notes of 1928, Sraffa spends a lot of time on the classical theory of value. However, it is the *objective* aspect of this theory that he emphasises, while completely ignoring the notion of the centre of gravitation.

The second bit of evidence that is cited in support of the received interpretation is that Sraffa refers to the approach of his book as being 'reminiscent to certain points of view taken by the old classical economists from Adam Smith to Ricardo...'. They are all listed in Appendix D of the book: (1) Quesnay's *Tableau Economique* is credited for the circular point of view; (2) The notion of basic goods can be discerned in Ricardo's 'corn model'; (3) The idea of the Standard commodity can also be discerned in Ricardo; (4) the notion of maximum rate of profits is found in Marx; and (5) the treatment of fixed capital as a kind of joint-product can be found in Torrens. Interestingly, there is no reference to the notion of 'natural prices' or the 'centre of gravitation' in the list. If Sraffa had accepted the notion of the centre of gravitation in his book, then the question is: why did he not acknowledge Adam Smith for this idea?

Anyway, the most important evidence that is invoked in favour of the received interpretation is Sraffa's statement in the book that 'such classical terms as "necessary price", "natural price" or "price of production" would meet the case, but value and price have been preferred as being shorter and in the present context (which contains no reference to market prices) no more ambiguous' (Sraffa 1960: 9). A closer reading of this passage, however, confirms our interpretation and rejects the received interpretation. As we have shown, quantitatively Sraffa's price is the same as Smith's and Ricardo's 'natural price' and Marx's 'price of production'; however, Sraffa's price is not defined to hold only at the centre of gravitation. Thus it does not need any reference to 'market prices'. Sraffa's caveat that his context 'contains no reference to market prices', takes away the essential element of the gravitational mechanism. It is the 'market prices' that gravitate toward the centre in the classical system. What meaning can be assigned to a concept whose essential complement is deliberately left out of the theoretical context? Can we imagine a centre of gravitation in a space without matter?

Finally, as we have noted above, Sraffa argues that '[t]he rate of profits, as a ratio, has a significance which is independent of any prices, and can well be "given" before prices are fixed. It is accordingly susceptible of being determined from outside of the system of production, in particular by the level of the money rates of interest' (Sraffa 1960: 33). This clearly points to the fact that no gravitation mechanism is postulated in his theory, as the equalisation of the rate of profits is precisely the result of the gravitation mechanism in the classical theory, and taking a uniform rate of profits from outside the system *ipso facto* rules out the market mechanism of supply adjustments and market price changes that brings about this result.

We may be asked: if what we have just said is true, then how does the system react if there are excess demands and excess supplies in the system? The logic of the gravitational mechanism suggests that when the quantity supplied of a commodity is below the quantity demanded, then the demanders will raise its price; and in the case of the quantity supplied being higher than the quantity demanded, the suppliers will lower the price. But one can *raise* or *lower* prices only from some *given* prices. As a matter of fact, if the quantity demanded of a commodity depends on its price, then the price must be given before the excess demand or excess supply of a commodity can be determined. In the neoclassical general equilibrium theory these *given* prices are announced by an auctioneer. But neither the classical economists nor Sraffa have the instrument of the auctioneer. Sraffa's solution to prices, which is the internal solution of the system of production as a whole, is the solution of the 'offer' prices that suppliers would make. Let us suppose that there are excess demands and excess supplies on those 'offer' prices that lead to a rise and fall of the prices in the market; and that this is taken as a signal for rescaling the sectors during the next time period. But in the next time period, if the equations have remained the same, the suppliers will offer new quantities at exactly the same 'offer' prices. Thus 'market prices' may guide the system towards equilibrium but cannot change the 'offer' prices as the system moves from disequilibrium to equilibrium. Here we should note that once we allow the real system to adjust its output, we must bring in the returns to scale assumption. As a mater of fact, it is on the assumption of CRS that Dupertuis and Sinha (2009a) show that such fixed-price quantity adjustments are the only adjustment mechanisms that are compatible with the centre of gravitation. Of course, Sraffa does not consider any supply adjustment mechanism and therefore has no reason to impose any kind of CRS assumption on his equations.

Is Sraffa's System a Special Case of Inter-temporal General Equilibrium?

In his influential defence of neoclassical economics against the Sraffian or the neo-Ricardian attacks, Hahn (1982) argues that Sraffa's system is a special and a highly restrictive case of the inter-temporal general equilibrium. Here we analyse Hahn's critique in the light of our interpretation of Sraffa.[30] Following Hahn, let us consider a case of two commodities and a two time-period model. We will refer to the two commodities as 'x' and 'y' and the two time-periods as 0 and 1. Production takes one time-period (a harvest cycle). It begins at the beginning of the time-period 0 and the world ends at the end of period 1. Thus there is no production at the beginning of time-period 1. We have four prices: P^0_x, P^0_y, P^1_x, P^1_y and to these we add a wage rate w, which is paid to the workers at the beginning of period 1. On the assumption of CRS, the equilibrium condition for the producers is:

$$P^1_j = \Sigma_i a_{ij} P^0_i + a_{0j}w, \ i, j = x, y \tag{1}$$

where a_{ij} are the fixed input coefficients given technology and a_{0j} is the amount of labour used in the production of 1 unit of j. Let us define a normalisation equation as:

$$P^0_x + P^0_y + P^1_x + P^1_y + w = 1 \tag{2}$$

---

30 This section is based on Sinha and Dupertuis (2009b).

Let us also define:

$$P^0_i/P^1_i = (1 + R^0_i), i = x,y \tag{3}$$

Substituting (3) in (1), we get

$$P^1_j = \Sigma a_{ij}P^1_i (1 + R^0_i) + a_{0j}w, i, j = x, y \tag{4}$$

Hahn claims that equations (4) have the exact Sraffa form except that (4) assume CRS and thus are written in terms of per unit of outputs, whereas Sraffa's equations would be for the real amount of outputs produced. On the basis of this Hahn goes on to claim that: 'It will now be clear that Sraffa is considering a very special state of the economy where ... the relative prices of 1976 wheat and barley are the same as those of 1977 wheat and barley. The neoclassical economist is quite happy with a more general situation' (Hahn 1982: 363–64).

Hahn, however, is clearly mistaken. If we write the equations (4) for 'x' and 'y' separately, we get:

$$P^1_x = a_{xx}P^1_x (1 + R^0_x) + a_{yx}P^1_y (1 + R^0_y) + a_{0x}w \tag{5}$$

$$P^1_y = a_{xy}P^1_x (1 + R^0_x) + a_{yy}P^1_y (1 + R^0_y) + a_{0y}w \tag{6}$$

These equations are not according to sectors as the rates of profit applied to the inputs are not the sectoral rates of profit but rather the discount rates on commodities (or their 'own rates of profit'). They will take a Sraffian form if we *assume* that $R^0_x = R^0_y$, which also *ipso facto* implies that all sectoral rates of profit in Sraffa's system *must* be equal. Thus it is not Sraffa's assumption, but rather a condition that must apply when the inter-temporal price equations are translated into Sraffian form.

The problem with Hahn's interpretation of Sraffa's equations is clearly revealed when we take a look at Sraffa's Standard system. Let us recall Sraffa's Standard system given by:

120t. iron + 160t. coal + 80qr. wheat + 1/4 labour → 240t. iron

40t. iron + 100t. coal + 120qr. wheat + 1/4 labour → 360t. coal

40t. iron + 40t. coal + 200qr. wheat + 2/4 labour → 480qr. wheat

Clearly, the global rate of profit or the ratio of aggregate net outputs to aggregate inputs in this system is equal to 20 per cent or 1/5, on the assumption that the wage rate is zero. This maximum rate of profit or the standard ratio is a *physical property* of the system and is derived independently of the knowledge of the prices. Now, if we apply *any* positive set of prices on both sides of the equations, we find that it leaves the Standard ratio untouched. However, if we apply a different set of prices on the inputs and a different set of prices on the outputs, then the Standard ratio in general will no longer be equal to 1/5, which is in conflict with the *physical property* of the system. This shows that there is something fundamentally wrong in interpreting Sraffa's equations in the inter-temporal fashion.

Now, since $R°_x$ need not be equal to $R°_y$ in the inter-temporal general equilibrium, Hahn, on the basis of his misinterpretation of Sraffa's equations, goes on to claim that the condition that $R°_x = R°_y$ is highly restrictive and is possible only for a restricted set of initial endowments: 'If Mr. Sraffa lands on an island whose history does not belong to this set, he will be out of luck' (Hahn 1982: 336). However, since the $R°_x$ and $R°_y$ of Hahn's equations are not the same thing as Sraffa's sectoral rates of profit, the general result of the general equilibrium theory that $R°_x$ need not be equal to $R°_y$ does not contradict Sraffa's logical result. Let us suppose that the utility functions were such that the equilibrium result turns out to be $R°_x = R°_y$. In that case, Sraffa's R_x will be equal to R_y. Now suppose that utility functions change in such a way that techniques and total final output remain the same, but $R°_x$ is not equal to $R°_y$. But this would still be compatible with P^1_x/P^1_y [previous case] $= P^1_x/P^1_y$ [new case] by appropriately modifying P^0_x/P^0_y [new case]. In other words, all sorts of $R°_x$ and $R°_y$ are compatible with the claim that given a system of production, all Sraffa's rates of profits *must* be equal.

5

CONCLUSION: ON THE 'CLASSICAL STANDPOINT'

Let us return to where we began. In the Preface we alluded to Sraffa's claim that the investigation in the *Production of Commodities* was concerned exclusively with the properties of a system that did not admit change and this, according to him, was the standpoint of the old classical economists from Adam Smith to Ricardo. Now, our reading of the *Production of Commodities* has led me to the conclusion that Sraffa's own standpoint was that a set of prices or values of commodities plays only a *functional* role in an economic system. In a subsistence economy, a set of prices springs directly from the given equations of production, if the system is to reproduce itself. In the case of economies that produce 'surplus', the situation remains essentially the same — given the equations of production, the role of the set of prices is to ensure that for any *given* physical system of production the *given* distribution of income is properly accounted for. For example, if the given physical system is in the 'Standard' proportion, then *any* set of positive prices would be compatible with the *given* proportion in which the 'Standard net product' is distributed between the wage labourers and the capitalists; however, if the physical system is not in the 'Standard' proportion, then there is one, and only, one set of positive prices that *must* prevail for the *given* physical system such that it is compatible with the *given* distribution of the net income. In other words, there is only one set of prices that makes the aggregate or the average rate of profit and wages, expressed in the Standard commodity, of the Standard system equal to its given real system. This is a purely logical proposition requiring no causal inferences or any notion of change.

I find that both Adam Smith and Ricardo, who were highly concerned with the dynamics of the system as a whole, and Ricardo who was particularly concerned with the notion of causation, fall, nevertheless, within the frame of Sraffa's 'standpoint' when it comes to their theories of value.

Adam Smith's theory of value is also situated in the context of a given empirical system with a well-defined physical surplus, which, in his case, is given by the natural productivity of *land that produces food* over and above the given cost of used up means of production, wages and profits. It is the 'resolution' of the physical surplus as 'rent' on food-producing land that defines the *problematique* of value in Adam Smith. His idea of 'effectual demand' as *given* demand *points*, requires him to begin his analysis with a *given* empirical system.

For Ricardo the physical surplus must not only be resolved as rent but also as profit. He simplified his system by getting rid of rent by hypothesising that the rent is zero for marginal land and that the equations for determining values take account of the technique used on the marginal land only. Thus the *problematique* of value reduces to resolving the physical surplus into the rate of profit by taking only the marginal or no-rent land into account. Ricardo, however, did not succeed in resolving the physical surplus into a particular rate of profit and so he went about establishing his proposition in a roundabout manner. He tried to show that a change in physical surplus (due to production moving on to inferior land or due to diminishing returns on the extra 'dose' of labour and capital on the same land) leads to a change in the rate of profits and this change does not have any impact on the values of commodities and thus the measure of the surplus itself. However, he, failed to establish the second proposition, which was crucial to his proof, but his search for an 'invariable measure of value', with which he was busy till the end of his life was essentially concerned with establishing that the change in the rate of profits has no impact on the measure of commodity-values.

It is quite intriguing that Marx is excluded from Sraffa's list even though he appears to be explicitly more concerned with the notion of 'surplus' and its resolution into profits and rent than either Adam Smith or Ricardo. My reading shows that though Marx's reasoning was *functional* in nature when it came to the dynamics of the system as a whole, he, however, maintained that prices and profits are the appearances of a deeper *essence*. It was Marx's explanation of price on the basis of the metaphysical notion of *essence* that must have, in my opinion, persuaded Sraffa to exclude Marx from his list. Furthermore, instead of taking distribution as *given*, Marx seems to *derive* the law of distribution from his general theory of value — this, too, did not fit well with Sraffa's 'classical standpoint'.

Hollander and Samuelson have been leading the charge that Sraffa's claim of a paradigm shift in the history of economics is false: as Samuelson famously put it: 'So to speak, within every classical economist

307

there is to be discerned a modern economist trying to be born' (Samuelson 1978: 1415). Samuelson highlights the role of marginal land in classical theory.[1] He argues that a change in demand pattern would affect the total demand for land if commodities were not produced by a uniform ratio of land to a 'dose' of capital and labour:

> The point is obvious that any classicist who thinks he can separate 'value' from 'distribution' commits a logical blunder. He also blunders if he thinks that he can 'get rid of land and rent as a complication for pricing' by concentrating on the external margin of no-rent land: where that external margin falls is an *endogenous* variable that shifts with tastes and demand changes so as to vitiate a hoped-for labor theory of value or a wage-cum-profit-rate theory of value (ibid.: 1420).

Hollander (1992), on the other hand, highlights the classical gravitation mechanism as the precursor to the general equilibrium price mechanism of resource allocation. He argues that the classical economists assumed 'constant cost' during the market adjustment or the gravitation mechanism only for simplicity's sake, as they were well aware that 'constant cost' is a restrictive assumption. In the general case, Hollander argues that there is no reason to think that the classical economists would not admit that the process of resource allocation would lead to a rise and fall in the demands for resources and therefore affect their prices. In other words, the classical economists could not separate income distribution from the problem of price determination, as both income distribution and prices are determined by one and the same process described by the classical gravitation mechanism.

My reading suggests that though Professors Hollander's and Samuelson's critiques may be effective against Sraffian[2] and other

---

1 Hollander (1995: Ch. 20) has criticised Samuelson for imputing to Adam Smith a theory similar to Ricardo's based on 'diminishing returns on land'. But Samuelson's argument has force at least against Ricardo and the classical tradition that follows Ricardo's theory of rent. Even if we assume that the demand for food is determined by the size of the population as Ricardo does, it cannot be denied that supply adjustments of industrial goods may lead to changes in the demand for agricultural raw materials and hence total land under cultivation. Once land is recognised as an indirect input in the production of industrial goods, then the margin of land may be affected by the gravitation mechanism itself.

2 See Garegnani (1984) for a canonical Sraffian interpretation of the 'classical standpoint'. Most Sraffians have followed Garegnani's lead; e.g., see Kurz and Salvadori

post-Keynesian interpretations of Sraffa's claim of the 'classical stand-point', they, in fact, largely miss the real target. Now, it cannot be denied that the gravitation mechanism plays an important role in the classical theory of value, since the legitimacy of the notion of natural-prices, which are determined by *objective* data alone, rests on the fact that it turns out to be the equilibrium market-prices, which are determined solely by the forces of demand and supply that are driven by the *subjective* motives of the agents. Clearly this aspect of the classical theory did not fit with Sraffa's 'standpoint'. Sraffa's proof (as interpreted in this book) that the uniformity of the rate of profits in the system does not require any hypothesis about the equilibrium of the quantities supplied with their effectual demands succeeds in severing the gravitation mechanism from the 'classical standpoint'. Sraffa's emphatic statement in the 'Preface' of his book that his propositions do not assume constant returns is evidence to the fact that the gravitation mechanism is not a part of what he considers the 'classical standpoint', since the classical gravitation mechanism must implicitly assume constant returns. Furthermore, Hollander's argument fails to recognise a subtle difference between the classical gravitation mechanism and the market mechanism of the general equilibrium analysis. The concept of *effectual demand* is crucial to the classical gravitation mechanism. And, as has been mentioned, the 'effectual demands' are demand points and not demand schedules. Such demand points can only be defined on the basis of the *given* employment of labour and linear techniques. The question of changes in the demand for labour during the adjustment mechanism therefore does not arise and therefore its impact on wages.

(1995). In my opinion, Garegnani's position is too restrictive. It more or less generalises Ricardo's alleged 'corn model' as the 'core' of all the classical economic theory including Marx. Also see Blaug (1999) for a critique.

AFTERWORD
A Response to My Critics

I take this opportunity to first of all thank all my colleagues who wrote reviews of my book. The ones that were in languages other than English, I unfortunately could not read. Among those that I have read, some were largely positive but many, particularly coming from the 'Sraffian' quarters, were highly critical. Below I have tried to take up some of those critical issues to further clarify my position in the hope of adding to the understanding of the underlying theoretical problems. Since most of reviews that I have come across were written by either 'Sraffians' or 'Marxists', the chapters on Sraffa and Marx received disproportionate attention, so I have decided to arrange my response in the opposite order of the book, i.e. take up the Sraffa chapter first, Marx second, Ricardo third and Adam Smith at the end.

The Chapter on Sraffa

There are mainly three issues raised by my critics on Sraffa: (i) I'm wrong in suggesting that Sraffa eschews the notion of Classical equilibrium of effectual demand and quantity supplied; (ii) the idea of 'commodity residue' that I highlight has no theoretical significance; and (iii) I am incorrect in suggesting that the condition of 'uniform rate of profits' in Sraffa's system of equations is a structural property of his economic system. Below I take up these criticisms one by one.

Point (i): On the question of equilibrium

Typical examples of criticisms on point (i) can be found in the reviews by Tony Aspromourgos (2012), Levrero (2012) and Reati (2012, 2014):

> In the Sraffa chapter, Sinha immediately confronts a difficulty (278–9). On the one hand, he wants to read Sraffa's (1960: v)

prefatory statement, concerning those readers who are 'accustomed to think in terms of the equilibrium of demand and
supply', as referring not merely to marginalist theory, but to
any theory in which supplies and demands, in some sense of
those terms, exhibit an equality. On the other, Sraffa himself
(ibid.) immediately describes his standpoint as 'that of the
old classical economists from Adam Smith to Ricardo'. But
the classical economists clearly were theorising situations in
which commodity demands and supplies (in some sense) were
balanced, while not having recourse to demand and supply
functions along the lines of latter-day marginalist theory. Isn't
it then obvious that Sraffa must intend by 'the equilibrium
of demand and supply', to denote just the latter-day theory?
(Aspromourgos 2012, p. 492–3).

While it is true that in *Production of Commodities by Means of Commodities*, Sraffa says nothing about the process that equalizes the different rates of profits in the long period, he explicitly identifies his
analysis with "that of the old classical economists from Adam Smith
to Ricardo," who certainly did adopt the gravitation mechanism I have
just described (see Sraffa 1960: v). It is therefore reasonable to suppose
that Sraffa was thinking along those same lines. (Reati 2014, p. 403)

In Chapter IV, Sinha interprets Sraffa's (1960, p. v) statement
that his prices do not depend on 'the equilibrium of supply and
demand' as if this implies the rejection of any consideration of
those prices as 'centres of gravitation' for actual prices—and
not simply the rejection, as seems obvious, of the marginalist
theory versus that of the 'old classical economists'. (Levrero,
2011, p. 530).

Unfortunately none of my critics bother to tell their reader that I
anticipate their argument in the book (see pp. 300–2) and answer
them in advance to which they prefer to close their eyes. However,
before coming to the arguments and evidence produced in the book,
which, I repeat, my critics have not cared to engage with, let me point
out that in 1960 when Sraffa's book was published, Garegnani was
a non-entity in the intellectual world and the whole idea of Classical gravitation mechanism being radically different from the so-called
Neoclassical idea of market mechanism did not even exist. No established historian of economic thought, who Sraffa would have taken
seriously such as Cannan, Stigler, Schumpeter, etc., had made this

argument and, of course, no pioneer of Neoclassical economics such as Jevons, Walras or Marshall had made Adam Smith's and Ricardo's argument in relation to free competition and the tendency for the industrial rate of profits to equalize to be an issue between them. So, on what grounds Sraffa could have naturally assumed that his readers would distinguish his general statement about 'equilibrium of demand and supply' as 'obviously' applying specifically to the intersections of Neoclassical demand and supply functions and not equilibrium of supplies and effectual demand points?[1] Furthermore, in his Cambridge PhD dissertation submitted in 1959, Garegnani explicitly accepts that 'Smith and Ricardo's theory of price is founded on the assumption of constant returns to scale for manufactures' (Garegnani 1959, p. 29, f.n. 2). It was only after reading Sraffa's (1960) 'Preface', in which Sraffa explicitly states that in his book 'there is, however, no such assumption made', Garegnani realized that he had a problem to solve, i.e., how to reconcile his understanding of Classical economics, which rested on the assumption of constant returns, with the standpoint of Sraffa's book, which claimed to represent the classical standpoint? Garegnani's tentative solution was to put Classical equilibrium into Sraffa's book and remove constant returns to scale from Classical economics. Not only do I show in the book that Garegnani did not succeed in this attempt but there is enough evidence in his own writings that show that his followers have no reason to believe in the 'obviousness' of this distinction that Sraffa could have naturally assumed that his readers would 'obviously' understand.

For example, Garegnani in 1976 writes:

> The study of the permanent effects of changes by means of comparisons between positions of the economic system characterized by a uniform rate of profits was in fact the method used by Ricardo and the English classical economists, when they explained profits in terms of the surplus product left after paying wages at the rate determined by independent economic or social circumstances. *But fundamentally the same method was preserved after Ricardo, across the deep change which the theory underwent in favour of a symmetric explanation of profits and wages in terms of the equilibrium between the forces of demand and supply for labour and capital. ...*

---

1 I leave aside the question of the 'correctness' of Garegnani's interpretation of Classical gravitation mechanism and the question of to what extent Sraffa would have ever accepted it.

It was only in the last few decades that this method, which was centred on 'long-period positions' of the system ... was increasingly challenged: ... this departure from tradition has not been due to weaknesses of the method as such, but rather to weaknesses of the dominant theory of distribution and, in particular, of the conception of capital it relies on. (Garegnani, 1976, pp. 25–26, emphasis added).

So if Garegnani himself believed in 1976 that the idea of 'long-term' equilibrium was common to both the traditions then obviously this could not be the point Sraffa was referring to in his 'Preface' as the 'classical standpoint'; since, according to Sraffa, the reference is to the standpoint that 'has been submerged and forgotten since the advent of the marginal method' (Sraffa 1960, p. v). Surely, Sraffa's reference to 'since the advent of the marginal method' does not relate to Hick's (1939) 'temporary' equilibrium or Arrow-Debreu's (1954) 'intertemporal' equilibrium. So, on what grounds do Garegnani's followers keep claiming that Sraffa had naturally assumed that not only a deep divide on this score existed but everybody must be so aware of it that they would 'obviously' interpret his reference to be pointing to one 'equilibrium' and not the 'other'?

Now, let me come to the question of constant returns to scale, which is intricately linked with the question of equilibrium in Classical economics. We have already noted that in 1959 Garegnani had maintained that Classical economics was 'founded on the assumption of constant returns to scale'. After the publication of Sraffa's book (Sraffa 1960) Garegnani dropped this position and developed a *vague* idea that the Classical centre of gravitation was just an attractive point for 'market prices' and it did not need any assumption of constant returns to scale. Elsewhere (see Sinha 2015, also reprinted in Sinha 2018) I have discussed this issue in great details and given the space constraint here, I refer the reader to that publication. Here I would only mention that when push came to shove, Garegnani accepted that the classical centre of gravitation does assume constant returns to scale:

However, Ricardo treated decreasing returns from land, just as Smith had treated the increasing returns from division of labour: as relevant, that is, only for the comparatively large output changes involved in capital accumulation and growth. Unlike what happens in neoclassical theory, Smith and Ricardo *could therefore leave physical returns to scale quite naturally aside when dealing with relative prices in a given position of the economy, with the kind of comparatively small output changes generally involved in that specific analysis.* (Garegnani 2007, p. 188, emphasis added).

The reader should have noticed that in 1976 Garegnani distinguished the Classical centre of gravitation from the notion of equilibrium of the Moderns on the basis of time allowed to elapse — Classical was 'long-period', i.e., allowed a long period of time for the adjustment to work itself out whereas the Moderns allowed very little time or no time. Now it appears that he thinks the Classical quantity adjustments allow for very small adjustments whereas the Moderns allow large adjustments. One wonders, if Classicists allow for only very small adjustments then why do they need long-period? All this shows that there is something amiss. In any case, the 'comparatively small output changes' that Garegnani refers to above are the precise conditions for which the Neoclassical supply functions are well defined — i.e., they are well defined only in the neighbourhood of the equilibrium point, e.g., any large change in output would clearly break the Marshallian assumption of *ceteris paribus*. Thus to suggest that returns to scale are irrelevant to 'small output changes' is a red herring. What Garegnani is doing above is accepting, albeit very reluctantly, that the Classical adjustment of 'market prices' to 'natural prices' needs constant returns to scale assumption. Now it is a problem for Garegnani's followers to square it with Sraffa's claim that he makes no such assumption.

The importance of the *absence* of the assumption of returns to scale was crucial to Sraffa because on it depended the *novelty* of his theory. After stating in the first paragraph of the 'Preface' that 'no question arises as to the variation or constancy of returns' (Sraffa 1960, p. v), he revisits this issue on the next page:

> The temptation to presuppose constant returns is not entirely fanciful. It was experienced by the author himself when he started on these studies many years ago—and it led him in 1925 into an attempt to argue that only the case of constant returns was generally consistent with the premises of economic theory. And what is more, when in 1928 Lord Keynes read a draft of the opening propositions of this paper, he recommended that, if constant returns were *not* to be assumed, an emphatic warning to that effect should be given. (Sraffa 1960, p. vi).

Here the 'premises of economic theory' stands for Marshall's theory. And in Sraffa's 1925 paper we read, 'The case of constant costs, rather than those of increasing or decreasing costs, should be regarded as normal. This must have been Ricardo's opinion, since he states that commodities which can be produced at constant costs constitute "by far the greatest part of the goods that are daily exchanged on the market" ' (Sraffa [1925] 1998, p. 354). And before this, we were told in the same paper that "It can be said that all classical writers accept implicitly, as an obvious fact, that cost is independent of quantity, and they do not bother to discuss the contrary hypothesis' (*ibid*, p. 325). Thus Sraffa was quite explicit in 1925 that the Classicists assume constant returns and therefore it becomes a curious problem as to what is the nature of the *emphatic absence* of this assumption in Sraffa's book in 1960, and how does it relate to what he refers to as the 'classical standpoint'? I shall presently return to this question — a question my critics never ask.

However before that, let me first reregister some evidence from Sraffa's book to show that it would be incorrect to assume that the output quantities in Sraffa's equations are assumed to be in the Classical centre of gravitation. First of all, as already mentioned several times, the 'Preface' of Sraffa's book begins with a clarion declaration:

> Anyone accustomed to think in terms of the equilibrium of demand and supply may be inclined, on reading these pages, to suppose that the argument rests on a tacit assumption of constant returns in all industries. If such a supposition is found helpful, there is no harm in the reader's adopting it as a temporary working hypothesis. In fact, however, no such assumption is made. No changes in output and (at any rate in Parts I and II) no changes in the proportions in which different means of production are used by an industry are considered, so that no question arises as to the variation or constancy of returns. The investigation is concerned exclusively with such properties of an economic system as do not depend on changes in the scale of production or in the proportions of 'factors' (Sraffa 1960, v).

Let us unpack the arguments made in this paragraph. (i) Those readers who are accustomed to think of 'price theory' in terms of 'equilibrium of demand and supply' would think that the propositions published in the book are based on an *implicit assumption* that constant returns prevail in all the industries. But why would Sraffa think so? It is because bringing in the idea of 'equilibrium of demand and supply' to his propositions would *logically* imply the assumption of constant returns, as we have already discussed above (and for more exhaustive discussion see Sinha 2015). (ii) However, his propositions do not rest on the assumption of constant returns. Therefore, thinking in terms of 'equilibrium of demand and supply' is not the correct way of approaching his book. (iii) This approach, which is not to think in terms of 'equilibrium of demand and supply', is so revolutionary or novel that the first reading of the book may not make any sense to the reader if she does not bring in the *illegitimate* point of view that constant returns and therefore the equilibrium of demand and supply are tacitly assumed. Hence, the reader may assume them as 'a temporary working hypothesis'. However, a correct understanding of the book must finally enable the reader to jettison this working hypothesis. (iv) The idea of 'returns to scale', constant or otherwise, has meaning only in situations when changes in the output are contemplated. His propositions are, however, built on the idea that no such changes take place — neither in the outputs nor in the inputs for Parts I and II, i.e., Chapters 1–11, and only in the inputs in the last Chapter 12.

Secondly, on the very first page of Chapter 1, Sraffa refers to the data of his equations as 'A year's operations can be *tabulated* as follows' (Sraffa 1960, p. 3, emphasis added). Then again he refers to his system of equations on page 22 of the book as the 'actual economic system of observation':

> Such a relation is of interest only if it can be shown that its application is not limited to the *imaginary Standard system* but is capable of being extended to the *actual economic system of observation*. (Sraffa 1960, p. 22, emphasis added).

The expression 'the actual economic system of observation' should not leave any room for speculation or spin, it definitely does not refer to an *ideal* situation that would prevail in the Classical equilibrium. Even Garegnani accepts that it is most unlikely to be ever observed, '... no economist had previously supposed the economy to ever actually *be* in equilibrium position, or more generally in a position of rest, except by fluke' (Garegnani, 2012, p.1429). But even this could not deter Fratini (2012), a student of Garegnani, to spin the evidence as:

> [Sinha] interprets the expression 'real system' that sometimes appears in Production of Commodities as an 'empirical system of production' (p. 290) or 'post factum description of an economy after a production cycle is over' (p. 307). In other words, in this particular view, the given outputs in Sraffa's equations are not equal to the quantities in the effectual

demand, as is commonly understood, but 'actual supplies' (p. 324). The prices that solve the equations are therefore not Smith's natural prices because they are not and cannot be at the centre of a process of gravitation. ...First, on reading Sraffa's book, it is easy to see that he uses the expression 'real system' as the opposite of the 'Standard system'. It is not therefore to be understood as an actually observed input–output table, as Sinha claims, but rather and quite simply as the system in which the quantities are given magnitudes, unlike the 'Standard system', where the proportions among sectors are instead endogenously determined. (Fratini 2012, p. 103).

I leave the reader to come to his/her own conclusion.

Thirdly, In Appendix B of the book, Sraffa discusses a case of a non-basic good, 'beans', which uses a very large proportion of itself in its production, implying that its rate of profit cannot exceed the ratio of its own net output to its input. Sraffa discusses the problem with the assumption of positive prices for all goods in this case when the rate of profits of the basic goods industries is higher than the one the 'beans' can admit. This problem, however, cannot arise if the system was assumed to be at the centre of gravitation, as the gravitation mechanism would ensure that the 'beans' industry disappears in the process. So, how could Sraffa find it to be a technical problem significant enough to be assigned a full appendix? Though I have raised this question repeatedly in publications and conferences but to the best of my knowledge no 'Sraffian' has ever responded to this.

Furthermore, I point out all the explicit assumptions made by Sraffa in his book, which shows that he is very particular about stating his assumptions even when they are not significant in nature. I also list all the ideas Sraffa thinks he has borrowed from the Classical economics (listed in Appendix D of Sraffa 1960) and show that here again there is no mention of Adam Smith and the idea of centre of gravitation. So the question arises: why does such a careful author as Sraffa tell his readers at the outset not to bring the baggage of 'equilibrium of demand and supply' to his book and then go on to *implicitly* assume it throughout the book — an assumption on which all his propositions would depend?

Now, when we move from Sraffa's book to his unpublished notes, we find more evidence that he did not consider his equations to be in any sort of equilibrium. During the period 1942–44, when Sraffa was working on his 'Hypothesis', which was to show that the ratio of net output to aggregate inputs (i.e., output-capital ratio) remains constant when the actual rate of profits takes values from zero to its maximum. Sraffa for a few months worked on the hypothesis that the statistics of the aggregate of the inputs and outputs of any empirical system could be taken to be in the Standard proportion; and he thought he could defend this hypothesis on the basis of the 'law of large numbers'. Now it is highly unlikely that Sraffa implicitly assumed that people's tastes must also be such that effectual demands would also turn out to be in the Standard proportion. But more importantly, once Sraffa realized that rescaling of an equation system does not affect the mathematical properties of it, he abandoned his previous hypothesis and went on to search for the appropriate rescaling of any empirical system to a Standard system. One great advantage of this procedure, Sraffa thought, was that now he could take account of even 'non-repetitive' systems. By 'non-repetitive' system Sraffa means a system that has some industries with more aggregate inputs used than outputs produced and hence in this case a pure physical net output or surplus is not defined. Such situations are typical of industries that are being phased out due to emergence of new technologies etcetera and are important consideration in the context of accumulation:

> The importance of this question is not its applicability to the arbitrarily transformed system. But the possibility of <u>extending</u> it (Hypo) from a strictly repetitive to a <u>non-repetitive system</u> (e.g. accumulating) where (as in transformed system) not all l.h.{left hand} commodities reappear on r.h.s.{right hand side} (Sraffa ND, D3/12/35: 42).

Clearly, this is not a case of any kind of 'equilibrium'. Again, during the early period (1927-31) of his theoretical breakthrough, Sraffa referred to his object of analysis as: 'Its object is, as it were, the photograph of a market place' (D3/12/7: 116); and as late as 1968, eight years after the publication of the book, Sraffa, in his response to a letter from a German student, Soltwedel, wrote: 'As regards your own interpretation, I must say frankly that you have gone astray the moment you speak of "equilibrium" or of "elasticity of factor supply": all the quantities considered are what can be observed by taking a photograph, there are no rates of change, etc.' (C 294: 3, dated 1.3.68). Clearly, no one would use the metaphor of a 'photograph' for something that does not physically exist, as the idea of the 'centre of gravitation'. Furthermore, as late as 1957, Sraffa had thought of starting the 'Preface' to his book in this manner:

> This is not proposed as a complete system of equilibrium. The data assumed are not sufficient to determine either

distribution or values. Only the effects of hypothetical, arbitrarily assumed extra data (such as wages, or the rate of profits) are discussed. {...} It is offered as a preliminary and there is no a priori reason why, on the basis of it, an equilibrium system should be built: there is some room left for it, as this is confessedly indeterminate; but the question is whether there is room enough for the marginal system. (Sraffa ND, D3/12/46: 20, dated 2.4.1957).

As a matter of fact, the beginning of the original sentence was 'This is no system of equilibrium' then the 'no' was crossed out and in its place was inserted 'not proposed as a complete'. All this is yet not an exhaustive list of evidence in support of my position, but I hope it is more than sufficient to rebut my critics on this crucial point.

Now, let us look at the evidence my critics repeatedly present against my position as the trump card that overrides all evidence on the other side. It turns out to be a singular quotation that appears on page 9 of Sraffa's book and at the first sight appears to support my critics' position. Here is an example from Levrero:

Indeed Sraffa (1960, p. 9) indicates that his prices are identical to classical long-period prices when he remarks that 'Such classical terms as "necessary price", "natural price" or "price of production" would [serve my purpose], but value and price have been preferred as being shorter and in the present context (which contains no reference to market prices) no more ambiguous.' What Sraffa rejects is only the determination of those prices in terms of the neoclassical forces of demand and supply. (Levrero, 2012, p. 533).

The reader should however note that nowhere in the quotation Sraffa says that his prices are *identical* to long-period prices'. Neither Sraffa has anywhere endorsed the 'long-period price' interpretation of those terms. As we shall see, he actually has a very different interpretation. It is also highly curious that Levrero felt the need to expunge three words from Sraffa's original quotation, which said 'meet the case' and replace it with three words of his own 'serve my purpose'. What does removing of Sraffa's own words and putting Levrero's words in his mouth do? Well, 'meet the case' obviously refers to 'the case', i.e., the context in which the statement appears but the expression 'serve my purpose', on the other hand, refers to a 'purpose to which those words could be put to serve'. The design is to remove the statement from its immediate context and place it in a general context of the 'purpose of the book'. Very *cleaver*, indeed! Now that the murder is out, let us get down to the post-mortem of the body.

This quotation from Sraffa appears in the second chapter of his book. In the first chapter Sraffa establishes the fact that the production equations contain sufficient information to uniquely determine prices in a subsistence economy — no information from human psychology such as effectual demand etcetera are needed. In the second chapter Sraffa allows those equations to produce surplus output and the question is: can prices be still determined without bringing in additional information from the side of demand? At this stage Sraffa argues that on the condition that the rate of profits 'must be uniform', prices are yet again uniquely determined by the information contained in the equations of production. This brings him to the conceptual distinction between basic and non-basic goods. In this context Sraffa writes:

> It is desirable at this stage to explain why *the ratios which satisfy the conditions of production* have been called 'values' or 'prices' rather than, as might be thought more appropriate, 'costs of production'.
>
> The latter description would be adequate so far as *non-*basic products are concerned, since, as follows from what we have seen in the preceding section, their exchange ratio is merely a reflection of what must be paid for means of production, labour and profits in order to produce them — there is no mutual dependence.
>
> But for a basic product there is another aspect to be considered. Its exchange-ratio depends as much on *use* that is made of it in the production of other basic commodities as on the extent to which those commodities enter into its production. (One might be tempted, but it would be misleading, to say that 'it depends as much on the Demand side as on the Supply side'). (pp. 8–9, first emphasis added).

Here Sraffa claims that the exchange ratios derived from the 'surplus' equation system by adding a *uniform* rate of profits as an unknown 'satisfy the *condition* of production'. And the fact that the price of a basic commodity enters as cost in the production of all other commodities whereas other basic commodities' prices enter as cost in its price renders the idea of determining 'price' of a commodity by its 'cost of production' meaningless, since there is no one-way avenue of

determining cost prior to and independent of prices. Then in a parenthetical remark he adds that '[o]ne might be tempted, but it would be
misleading, to say that "it depends as much on the Demand side as on
the Supply side" '. The point to note is that Sraffa says that the price
of a *basic* commodity 'depends as much on *use* that is made of it in
the production of other basic commodities as on the extent to which
those commodities enter into its production'. Here it is clearly stated
that the price of a basic commodity *depends* on the internal structure
of the system of production, i.e., how much of it is *used* by the system
and how much of other commodities it *uses* in its production — the
'profit' elements of the left hand side of the equations are completely
left out of the description. Hence the demand emanating from the use
of the surplus output is completely left out of the consideration. This
is what 'the condition of production' represents and it is claimed that
the prices determined on the basis of a *uniform* rate of profits are the
prices that satisfy the 'condition of production'. In other words, these
prices can be derived from the objective data of the method of production alone without bringing any additional information, as was the
case with the 'subsistence system'. The parenthetical remark is a clue
to warn the reader that how the profits are disposed of has no impact
on prices and that is why it would be misleading to think of his solution of prices as an equilibrium of demand and supply.

It is immediately after this para that Sraffa goes on to add the para
under consideration:

> A less one-sided description than cost of production seems
> therefore required. Such classical terms as 'necessary price',
> 'natural price' or 'price of production' would meet the case,
> but value and price have been preferred as being shorter and
> in the present context (which contains no reference to market
> prices) no more ambiguous. (p. 9).

Now it is clearly inconceivable that after giving the clue that his prices
were derived directly from only objective data of inputs and outputs
and that they should not be interpreted as an equilibrium solution of
demands and supplies, Sraffa would go on to suggest that his prices
crucially rest on the additional information contained in the data on
effectual demands. It appears that Sraffa interprets such Classical terms
as 'necessary price', 'natural price' or 'price of production' differently
than 'long-period equilibrium prices'. A clue to this could be found in
an early brief note written sometime in Winter 1928 soon after he had

written down his subsistence economy and surplus equations, which he refers to in the 'Preface' as 'the opening propositions of this paper':

> When A. Smith etc. said 'natural' he did not in the least mean the 'normal' or the 'average' nor the 'long run' value. He meant that physical, truly natural relations between commodities, that is determined by the equations, and that is not disturbed by the process of securing a greater share in the product. (Sraffa ND, D3/12/11: 83).

Clearly, he maintains that 'natural prices' of Classical economics were determined by physical data of production alone and were not affected by the competitive process — the exact point he is trying to make for his prices, as I have explained above. The interested readers are encouraged to consult Sinha (2016) in which I have documented a detailed story based on archival evidence of how Sraffa struggled over the years to 'justify' the condition of uniform rate of profits in his equations without bringing any outside information from the side of demand.

Aspromourgos (2012), however, further argues:

> But quite apart from the status of the uniform rate of profit in Sraffa's equations, the uniformity of the prices of distinct commodities, and of the wages of homogeneous labour, which are features as well of Sraffa's equations, also requires justification. The justification, at core, is the same as that for the uniform profit rate: the operation of competition causing the elimination of abnormal returns, for given magnitudes of the parameters governing 'fundamental' (Quesnay), or 'natural' (Smith, Ricardo), or 'production' (Marx), or 'normal' (Garegnani), or 'equilibrium' prices. Sraffa's recourse to these uniformities as much implies recourse to 'subjective' motivations 'to maximise' (308n), as does the uniform net rate of profit. (Aspromourgos 2012, p. 493).

Kurz (2012) also makes this point (see Sinha 2013 for a specific rebuttal of Kurz 2012). There is clearly a confusion here between the notion of 'arbitrage' and 'competitive mechanism' that brings unequal rates of profits to uniformity. If Kurz and Aspromourgos were right then one should expect a spectrum of 'market prices' for one commodity to exist while the rate of profits are not uniform — but no Classical economist assumes that. Market for each commodity clears at *one* 'market price', they simply happen to be either above or below the 'natural price' thus giving rise to a spectrum of rates of profits in different industries.

A market by definition assumes one price for homogeneous goods. That is why the general models of Monopoly, Duopoly, Oligopoly, etc., which are by definition not competitive markets, also assume 'one price' for homogeneous goods. An existence of a possibility of arbitrage by definition means existence of more than one market such that someone can take advantage of buying in low price market and selling in high price market. In one market, where by definition there is no space, time and information constraint for a buyer, no reason exists for the buyer to buy from a high price seller when low price is available.

Now, let us take the case of 'uniform wage' for one unit of labour. Sraffa writes:

> We suppose labour to be uniform in quality or, what amounts to the same thing, we assume any differences in quality to have been previously reduced to equivalent differences in quantity so that each unit of labour receives the same wage. (Sraffa 1960, p. 10).

So what Sraffa does is to take empirical wage differentials as data and uses those differentials as multiplication factor (taking one given wage rate as unit) to reduce quality into quantity. After which he normalises the total homogenous labour units to 1 and assigns every industry its aliquot proportion of total labour used in the system, which is equal to their proportion of wages in total wage bill in the system. It is a simple mathematical exercise conducted on given data and there is no implicit 'competitive mechanism' working behind it.

Point (ii): 'Commodity Residue' has no theoretical significance

Angelo Reati's largely sympathetic review (2012) criticized me on a couple of technical points. He was kind enough to share the draft with me before the publication. I felt that he had made a couple of logical errors (at least in understanding my points) and with the kind consent of the editor, I pointed them out in the same issue (Sinha 2012b). To which Reati (2014) reacted rather harshly with doubling down on those points.[2] I present his second point first:

> Another point of disagreement arose from Sinha's contention that "it is no longer possible to hold that *only labour*

---

2 Sadly Angelo died in a bicycle accident soon after writing those comments—he was a good friend. I mourn his death and regret that I did not get a chance of changing his mind.

is productive... What *is* productive is *the system of production as a whole"* (Sinha 2010: 187; emphasis in the original). In my review I presented, as a counterargument, a simple parable to show that "Labour alone can make all the capital goods [while] Capital goods alone can make nothing" (Pasinetti 1981: 199–200). Then I added that Sraffa's logical exercise of reduction of prices to dated quantities of labor does not undermine this conclusion because the "commodity residue" that in any case exists could eventually be reduced to the products of nature that could be exploited directly by human activity.

In response Sinha (2012: 401) writes: "What Reati forgets is that when [the] commodity residue becomes negligible then the labor content going along with the residual commodity also becomes negligible, and if and when [the] commodity residue becomes zero then the labor content *must* also become zero along with it." This astonishing assertion must lead us to wonder whether Sinha has understood Sraffa's discussion of the reduction of prices to dated quantities of labor. If Sinha had considered the reduction equation found near the top of page 35 of Sraffa (1960), he would have seen that the labor content is not determined solely by the term referring to the most remote period of time but by an entire series of quantities of labor, weighted by the rate of profit. Thus, contrary to what is argued by Sinha, labor remains the sole true factor of production. (Reati 2014, p. 404).

The logical error I had pointed out in my response is contained in Reati's statement: 'Then I added that Sraffa's logical exercise of reduction of prices to dated quantities of labor does not undermine this conclusion because the "commodity residue" that in any case exists could eventually be reduced to the products of nature that could be exploited directly by human activity'. This expresses a profound misunderstanding of Sraffa's theoretical project. First of all, the statement that 'commodity residue' could be 'eventually reduced to products of nature' is a logical impossibility — as Sraffa had immediately realized once he had written his physical equations. He had realized that once a produced 'commodity' enters as input in the production equation of any industry, i.e., a produced input that is acquired by an industry through exchange from some other industry, then the reduction process will never reach a stage where all commodities will disappear. In other words, the reduction chain becomes infinite — the path to the primordial state that Reati and Pasinetti are so fond of is blocked forever! One immediate consequence of this revelation was that the attempts by Jevons, Böhm-Bawerk and Wicksell to measure capital by 'round-about way of production' or 'period of production' were flawed — since there always will exist some 'commodity residue', there exists no absolute measure of the 'period of production' and therefore one will have to be satisfied with reducing the commodity residue to an extent that it could be ignored. However, at what stage in the reduction chain the 'commodity residue' becomes negligible depends on the wage rate — if wage is high then commodity residue will become negligible at an earlier stage than when wage is low and when wage is zero then 'commodity residue' will never become negligible. This gave Sraffa an insight that a measure of capital independent of wages or the rate of profits is not possible: 'The length of the period of production is not a purely physical (objective) fact, which can be measured by a clock; and which is independent from the way in which, after it is completed, the product is going to be divided between workers and capitalists' (Sraffa ND, D3/12/7: 90, dated 8.7.28, quoted in Sinha 2016, p. 113). It also gave Sraffa the insight that the relationship between wages and the rate of profits turns out to be radically different — if the 'commodity residue' could be reduced to zero then all the capital could be reduced to a long chain of advanced wages and in this case if wages are reduced to zero then the rate of profits must rise to infinity. However, Sraffa reckoned that since there must be a positive 'commodity residue', when wages are reduced to zero then the rate of profits must reach a finite maximum and not infinity. This is the foundation of the notion of 'maximum rate of profits' in Sraffa's system. Then came the problem of proving that the 'maximum rate of profits' is a physical property of the production system and therefore independent of wages and the rate of profits. This led Sraffa to search for the Standard system and the Standard commodity associated with any given empirical system to prove that the 'maximum rate of profits' is a physical property of the production system. On the basis of which he could derive his main equation $r = R(1 - w)$, where R, the maximum rate of profits (or the net output-capital ratio), is constant with respect to changes in r (the rate of profits) and w (the wage rate). Only if R could be proven to be constant with respect to changes in r or w that it could be argued that if w is given from outside the equation system then r is also determined independently of prices, i.e., both the distributional variables are determined independently of prices as was the case with Marx. Prices can then be determined by plugging in the value of r in the equations, which turns it into a system of linear equations — just like the equations for the subsistence economic system. The idea of 'commodity residue' was so central to Sraffa's theoretical project that he titled his book emphasizing this very point — *Production of Commodities by Means of Commodities* highlights the circular nature of the problem. Once commodities enter the production equations then there is no way of getting rid of them — there is no primordial or 'originary' anchor to which productive activity could be reduced to, there is no such thing as, what Reati calls, 'sole true factor of production'.[3] All this is now carefully documented in Sinha 2016. Here I present just one excerpt from Sraffa's unpublished notes that conveys the message:

> The error of Jevons-BB (omitting Commodity residue term) has much more far reaching consequences than the trifling ones that are made to appear above.
>
> For in the above, the relation of w and r in the Reduction equation is still as determined in the original equation. But since the original equation included (implicitly) the Residue Term, the latter has not been effectively eliminated.
>
> But J-BB start from a <u>finite</u> series similar to the Reduction series, and know nothing of an original equation. Therefore they have no "given" relation between $\underline{w}$ and $\underline{r}$: they must deduce this from their finite series of pure labour terms, But the relation thus deduced must be very different for the one obtained from the original equation – in particular: a) there can be no maximum for $\underline{r}$, and b) r <u>throughout its movement</u> (as w falls) cannot behave as if it approached a maximum.
>
> Therefore the effects of omitting Residue term are not shown only for values of r very near the maximum (as is implied in the previous pages) but throughout. (Sraffa ND, D3/12/26: 13; dated 29.11.42, quoted in Sinha 2016, p. 116).

---

3 In his book, Sraffa gives credit to Marx for bringing this theoretical point to fore: '... but more generally owing to his [Marx's] emphatic rejection of the claim of Adam Smith and of others after him that the price of every commodity 'either immediately or ultimately' resolves itself entirely (that is to say, without leaving any commodity residue) into wages, profits and rent — a claim which necessarily presupposed the existence of 'ultimate' commodities produced by pure labour without means of production except land, and which therefore was incompatible with a fixed limit to the rise in the rate of profits.' (Sraffa 1960, Appendix D, p. 94).

Point (iii): Uniform Rate of Profits is not a Structural Property of the System

The second point Reati makes is:

> In his book Sinha maintains that for Sraffa the uniform rate of profit is not the result of a gravitation process of the different industries' rates of profit resulting from competition among capitals but, rather, that it is "a logical necessity of any ... system of production that determines prices internally, irrespective of the equilibrium of demand and supply" (Sinha 2010: 289). He substantiates this argument in a confusing chapter "On the Uniform Rate of Profits" where, instead of referring to the actual rate of profits – *i.e.* the rate of profits that results when the wage rate is fixed at some positive level – he bases his reasoning on the *maximum* rate of profit, that is the rate of profit that could be theoretically charged on costs when the wage rate is zero (workers live on air!). Then Sinha develops a lengthy argument to show that this maximum rate of profits should be the same in the real and the standard system (R for the real system and R* for the standard system). From this he deduces that the maximum rates of profits (which *are not* the actual rate of profits) of the different industries must be uniform, otherwise the equality R = R* would not hold. Thus, one cannot invoke the gravitation process for the uniformity of the actual rates of profits. Thus, Sinha contends, the gravitation process is not what underpins Sraffa's uniform rate of profits assumption: the sectoral rates must be equal as a matter of logical necessity. As we shall see in a moment, Sinha's reasoning is hopelessly confused.
>
> To support his argument that Sraffa did not rely upon any gravitation mechanism, Sinha (2010: 293) misrepresents a passage from Sraffa's manuscripts, dated 1955, in which Sraffa notes that "With changes in w [the wage rate]... The impulse towards price change is an internal one to each industry ... not from those conditions *compared* with those of other industries." Sinha does not discuss the context in which Sraffa made this remark, but its meaning is quite obvious, and not at all what Sinha takes it to be: Sraffa is saying that if *w* changes, all prices will change simply because production costs will change *within each sector*. Sraffa's observation has got nothing to do with gravitation, and therefore has no bearing on Sinha's argument. (Reati 2014, pp. 402–3).

If Reati's argument were to be true then a rise in wages should change all the prices even when the direct to indirect labour ratios (or the organic composition of capital) of all the industries were equal too, since 'production costs *within each sector*' would still change. But it is well known that in this case wages would move from zero to its maximum value without affecting the prices—it only affects the rate of profits and since its effect on profits is proportional to their capital investments it has no effect on the prices.

Reati, however, further goes on to argue:

> This confusion between the maximum rate of profit and the actual rate of profits is reiterated in Sinha (2012) when he states that "R is the weighted average of the industrial rates of profits," which would imply that, to ensure that $R = R^*$, the industrial rates of profits must be equal. ...
>
> Comparing the actual and the maximum rates of profits we see that they are different in nature. While the actual rate of profits reflects a market mechanism, the maximum rate of profits is the value which guarantees the *compatibility* of the different industries at the level of the economic system. More precisely, R is univocally associated with a positive vector of prices (see below). This also means that, taking into consideration the complex network of industrial relations, no industry could *theoretically* charge a price on which the rate of profits is higher than R.
>
> Concerning the equality of the maximum rate of profit of the real system (R) with the maximum rate of profits of the standard system (R^*), in my review I noted that this is simply due to the fact that both depend on the maximum eigenvalue of the input matrix, which is the same for both systems. It is perhaps worth recalling the details here (see Pasinetti 1977: 76–78). If we assume the wage rate is zero, the price system may be written as:

$$p = pA(1 + R) \qquad (1)$$

> where p is the vector of prices and **A** the irreducible non-negative input matrix (I assume for the sake of simplicity that all capital is circulating capital). Equation (1) can be written

$$p[I - (1 + R)A] = 0 \qquad (2)$$

Writing

$$1/(1 + R) = \lambda \tag{3}$$

equation (2) becomes

$$p(\lambda I - A) = 0 \tag{4}$$

This homogeneous system has solutions different from zero if the determinant of the expression within the parentheses is zero, and the roots of the characteristic equation

det $(\lambda I - A) = 0$ are the eigenvalues of matrix **A**.

From the Perron-Frobenius theorems we know that only one eigenvalue – the maximum one λ_m – is certainly associated with all prices being positive. Thus, making use of equation (3), we can see that the highest profit rate compatible with the viability of the system is:

$$R = (1/ \lambda_m) - 1$$

The relation between R and the actual rates of profits is clear: R represents the upper limit for the rates of profits of the individual industries (*ri*). Thus, Sinha (2012) is quite wrong, and thoroughly confused, when he asserts that R is a weighted average of the sectoral maximum profit rates. Also, R cannot be identified with the average of the surpluses of the various industries. (Reati 2014, pp. 403–4).

So let us take a simple example:[4]

$$x \rightarrow 2y$$
$$\tfrac{1}{2} y \rightarrow x$$

We can write the price equations for this economy as:

<u>System 1</u>

$$p_x(1 + r_1) = 2p_y \tag{i}$$
$$\tfrac{1}{2} p_y(1 + r_2) = p_x \tag{ii},$$

4 I am indebted to Professor Bertram Schefold for coming up with this simple example in an e-mail exchange.

where p's and r's are industrial prices and rates of profits. We take x as the *numéraire*. Therefore, $p_x = 1$. If we assume $r_1 = r_2 = R$, then we derive $R = 1$ and $p_y = 1$. Now suppose r_1 is not equal to r_2. Suppose the so-called 'market price' of y, $p_y = 3/2$. This gives us $r_1 = 2$ and $r_2 = 1/3$. Since $r_1 = 2$ is greater than $R = 1$ and p_x, p_y and r_2 are positive, we have proved that, from Reati's own perspective, his statement, 'no industry could *theoretically* charge a price on which the rate of profits is higher than R', is false.

The question of positive or zero wages is irrelevant to the issue. If one lives in the 'market-prices-natural prices' world, which is Reati's world, then in disequilibrium situation 'market-prices' (or $(n-1)$ rates of profits) could be arbitrarily taken from outside and n remaining unknowns can be solved, as we have done in our example. This would generate an average 'R' ($= 9/7$ in our example) and some r's must be higher than 'R' by definition, if all r's are not equal. My argument, however, denies this *crucial assumption* that under disequilibrium condition one can take sufficient numbers of 'market prices' or rates of profits arbitrarily to solve the system of basic equations as I now explain below.

Let us multiply the first equation of system 1 with ½, we get our two equations as:

System 2

$$½\, p_x(1 + r_1) = p_y \qquad \text{(i)}$$
$$½\, p_y(1 + r_2) = p_x \qquad \text{(ii)}$$

$$(½\, p_x + ½\, p_y)\,(1 + R^*) = p_x + p_y$$

This is our Standard system. The aggregate of our equations (i) and (ii) of System 2 gives us the average rate of profits of the system $R^* = 1$, independently of our knowledge of p_x and p_y. Sraffa (1960) has proved that there always exists one and only one Standard system that is associated with any given system such as system-1. Sraffa's argument turns out to be that *the properties of the whole of the system determine the properties of its parts*—just as in quantum theory in physics.

So let us go back to our original equations (i) and (ii) of system 1 with the additional aggregate equation:

System 3

$$p_x(1 + r_1) = 2p_y \qquad \text{(i)}$$
$$½\, p_y(1 + r_2) = p_x \qquad \text{(ii)}$$

$$(p_x + ½\, p_y)\,(1 + R) = p_x + 2p_y$$

Here R is the average rate of profits of the whole system, which is an unknown. If $r_1 = r_2$ then $r_1 = r_2 = R$. If r_1 is not equal to r_2 then they must be either above or below R and if one is above then the other must be below. Let us hypothesize that r_1 is not equal to r_2 and they deviate from R by d_1 and d_2. In other words, $r_1 = R + d_1$ and $r_2 = R + d_2$. Without loss of generality, we assume $d_1 < 0$ and $d_2 > 0$. Now we can write our equation system as:

System 4

$$p_x(1 + R + d_1) = 2p_y \qquad \text{(i)}$$
$$\tfrac{1}{2} p_y(1 + R + d_2) = p_x \qquad \text{(ii)}$$

$$(p_x + \tfrac{1}{2} p_y)(1 + R) = p_x + 2p_y$$

By definition $(p_x d_1 + \tfrac{1}{2} p_y d_2) = 0$. Now we multiply equation (i) by 1/2 and transform the system to:

System 5

$$\tfrac{1}{2} p_x(1 + R + d_1) = p_y \qquad \text{(i)}$$
$$\tfrac{1}{2} p_y(1 + R + d_2) = p_x \qquad \text{(ii)}$$

$$(\tfrac{1}{2} p_x + \tfrac{1}{2} p_y)(1 + R') = p_x + p_y$$

Here R' is the unknown average rate of profits and could be different from R as we have rescaled equation (i). Given that we have assumed $d_1 < 0$ and shrunk the size of the 1-industry by half while leaving the 2-industry undisturbed, we should expect the average rate of profits of the system to rise, i.e., we should expect R' > R. However, by inspection we can see that R' = 1, independently of p_x and p_y, as it is the Standard system. Thus R' = R* and we have already established that R = R* = 1 (in our example). Therefore, R' = R. Now, this could happen only if $(\tfrac{1}{2} p_x d_1 + \tfrac{1}{2} p_y d_2) = 0$—condition 1. But we have already (from System 4) stablished that, by definition, $(p_x d_1 + \tfrac{1}{2} p_y d_2) = 0$—condition 2. Since both p_x and p_y are positive, conditions 1 and 2 would simultaneously hold if and only if $d_1 = d_2 = 0$, QED. The crucial point to note in this argument is that condition 1 could be derived only because System 5 happens to be a Standard system and so the value of R' can be derived independently of the knowledge of prices. It was Sraffa's discovery of the Standard system and his proof of its uniqueness that provide us with the crucial argument in the proof of the proposition that the 'rate of profits must be uniform'.

Now, a positive wage does not change the terms of the problem. Take System 2 and add 1 unit of labour to the whole system with wages equal to ($\frac{1}{4}$ x + $\frac{1}{4}$ y) per unit of labour, the half of the Standard net output. This will change R^* to $\frac{1}{2}$, independently of what prices prevail. Rescale this system back to System 1 with total labour used in the whole system equal to 1 unit. Apply the wages equal to ($\frac{1}{4}$ p_x + $\frac{1}{4}$ p_y) and change the *numéraire* equation from p_x = 1 to ($\frac{1}{2}$ p_x + $\frac{1}{2}$ p_y) = 1. Apply r_1 = r_2 = R. We find R = $\frac{1}{2}$ in this case as well. This is why the Standard commodity as the *numéraire* and wages measured in terms of the Standard commodity becomes crucial in linking the properties of the Standard system, which shows the physical nature of these properties, to the empirical system. From here on, the argument goes one-one as above.

So what have we done here that is different from Reati's understanding? Following the traditional Sraffian mathematical tradition (hence his reference to Pasinetti), Reati takes average of n-independent equations as the 'statistical average'. Once you assume that empirical prices are 'market prices', i.e., determined by demand and supply conditions in the market and independently of Sraffa's system of equations, then the statistical average rate of profits need not be constrained by Sraffa's equations. That is what I did when I arbitrarily chose p_y = 3/2 in system 1 to show that r_1 could theoretically go above R and the statistical average rate of profits 'R' (= 9/7) would be different from R, if either the rates of profits or prices are taken arbitrarily. This is why it is important to claim that *all* prices must be determined by the system of equations, and Sraffa showed that there is sufficient information in his equation system of basic goods to do so. Sraffa from early on works with a notion of 'algebraic average'. For him, it is by definition that an average can be distributed equally over the population. That is why, by assuming equal rate of profits in his equations he was simply deriving the average, i.e., the 'algebraic average' rate of profits of his equation system. For example, if we put our 'statistical average' rate of profits 'R' = 9/7 = r_1 = r_2 in our System 1 then the equation system becomes contradictory. During the Winter 1927–28 while writing his 2nd equation, that is the equation of a system producing surplus, Sraffa put it this way: 'But since we have (in the no-surplus system) a spare equation, we can use it to determine, simultaneously with value, *the ratio that total surplus bears to total initial stocks of the community.*' (Sraffa ND, D3/12/6: 17, emphasis added, quoted in Sinha 2016, p. 57). Then he goes on to put equal rate of profits for all industries to solve for it. Clearly, the solution for equal rate of profits for him was designed to solve for the ratio of the aggregate equation, which is the average rate of profits of the system. And in 1942–43, when he was struggling to work out the Standard system he explicitly wrote: 'Yet the aggregate is *not a statistical* result but an algebraic one' (D3/12/36: 79, emphasis in original, quoted in Sinha 2016, p. 134). Above we have alluded to quantum physics in relation to the properties of the whole determining properties of the parts, we could also invoke another analogy from physics to bring our point to sharp relief: in the Newtonian world, space and time are separate but Einstein showed that that was incorrect, one cannot separate space and time—the universe is a fabric of space-time. Similarly, for Sraffa industrial equations cannot be separated from the aggregate equation of the system—they together constitute the whole.

Fred Moseley (2012), who wrote a comparatively sympathetic review, raises two questions. Both of them related to wages and the Standard commodity. Moseley argues:

> However, this necessary assumption [that wages are measured in Standard commodity] invalidates the argument. If, instead, the wage share in the actual system is measured in terms of the actual product, as it should be in the determination of the rate of profit in the actual system, then the actual rate of profit will not in general be equal to the rate of profit in the standard system, and thus there is no logical necessity on this basis for the [*sic*] all the industry rates of profit to be equal. (p. 525).

There is a widespread confusion that Sraffa's system requires workers to receive/consume wages in terms of the Standard commodity. But this is not true. Wages expressed in terms of the 'Standard commodity' as the money-commodity is equivalent to wages expressed in any commodity such as gold. That does not mean that workers are assumed to consume gold—it is simply a unit of account. As Sraffa has shown in his book (Sraffa 1960, pp. 31–33), once the mathematical property of the system, which is given by $r = R(1 - w)$ is discovered, the Standard commodity can be removed from the system even as a measuring rod by taking r as given from outside. In this case, whatever w turns out to be would be by definition in terms of the Standard commodity without having to know what the Standard commodity consists of. The Standard system is like a scaffolding that was essential for building the building but once the building is built, it can be taken off—it does not change the property of the building, it only helps show it.

Moseley's second point happens to be:

> Finally, I am left wondering what is the relation between the prices in Sraffa's theory and prices in the capitalist economy? According to Sinha, the prices in Sraffa's theory do not represent long-run 'center of gravity' prices in the real economy; at the same time, Sraffian prices are not actual prices, because market prices do not have equal rates of profit. So what are Sraffian prices? (p. 526).

On my interpretation, there is no distinction between 'market' and 'natural' prices in Sraffa's system. His prices are the actual prices that would hold if the input-output data are complete with well-defined industries and wages or rate of profits is given from outside and when there is no outside interference on prices, such as taxes or subsidies on goods etcetera.

The Chapter on Marx

Most of the 'Sraffians' liked the chapter on Marx and they do not have any substantial criticism of the book on this score, apart from Levrero's minor criticism, which we shall come to presently. Fred Moseley (2012), however, engages with the Marx chapter, particularly with my treatment of the 'transformation problem'. Moseley argues:

> The usual interpretation of Volume 1 (including Sinha's) in terms of labor-values alone loses sight of the monetary nature of Marx's theory of surplus-value.
>
> The general formula for capital, augmented to include production (M-C...P...C'-M+ΔM), is the *logical framework* for the rest of Marx's theory; it is the symbolic expression of the *process* that is the *subject* of Marx's theory—money becoming more money. ... That is why Marx did not 'fail to transform the inputs' of constant capital and variable capital from values to prices of production—because no such transformation is necessary or appropriate in Marx's theory. The inputs of constant capital and variable capital in Marx's theory of prices of production in Volume 3 are the *same* quantities of money capital advanced in the real capitalist economy that are inputs in Marx's theory of total surplus-value in Volume 1. (p. 523).

Moseley nowhere explains what he means by 'money'. Is money a commodity such as gold, which is produced in the system, or is it fiat money, or high powered bank deposits? An investment of money capital M could grow into (M+ΔM) simply on account of inflation during the period of production. Would that also be considered profit earnings and realization of surplus value? If not, then isn't the general formula not so general? How does the system ensure that total supply of 'money' increases from M to (M+ΔM) after a period of production? Let us suppose that at the beginning of the production cycle all the capitalists begin with their money capital M_i's, since all the capitalists own nothing but their money capital at this stage who do they buy their means of production from? It is one thing to think of a new capitalist (or a fresh capital) entering the system with credit money but an entirely different matter to generalize it for the whole system—a productive system as a whole cannot begin with 'money capital', it's an impossible scenario.

Moseley's main contention is that constant and variable capital is measured by money spent in buying means of production and wage payments. Hence prices at which the means of production are bought are known data. In that case, those prices must be the 'market prices' prevailing at the beginning of the production cycle. So we take the money value of all the means of production and wage advances as the cost price for every industry as given data, which are M_i's, $\Sigma M_i = M$. Then we take the money value of all the final goods produced (this again has to be taken at 'market prices'), $(M_i + \Delta M_i)$, $\Sigma(M_i + \Delta M_i) = (M + \Delta M)$. At this stage, Moseley defines the average rate of profits of the system, say $r = \Delta M/M$ and prices of production $p_i = M_i(1 + \Delta M/M)$.

Now, here comes the problem. As I have pointed out above, after the sale of the fresh batch of outputs the resultant $(M_i + \Delta M_i)$ and $(M + \Delta M)$ may result due to inflation. So to remove this possibility one has to make a *theoretical assumption* that for every commodity their input prices and the output prices remain the same. This immediately takes us out of the empirical world to a theoretical world. In the empirical scenario of Marx, commodities exchange at 'market prices' and 'market prices' are continuously changing as long as industrial rates of profits are unequal. Thus at the rest point, where input prices are equal to output prices, the industrial rates of profits are equal and such prices are called 'prices of production'. This explains the contradiction in Moseley's presentation. After stating, '[t]he cost price in Marx's theory is not an unknown, but is instead taken as given, as a quantity of money capital advanced, as an empirical fact', Moseley goes on to state, '[t]he initial capital (M) does depend on the rate of profit, because

M is equal to the *prices of production of the inputs*, and prices of production depend on the rate of profit' (p. 553, emphasis added). But 'prices of production' are not known data, they are theoretical prices derived from some other known data. Once we are in this theoretical world of the prices of production, where input prices are equal to output prices, we face the problem of how to explain ΔM? This problem takes us to the production equations, i.e., in Marx's expanded 'general formula for capital $(M-C...P...C'-M+\Delta M)$' 'P' must be opened up and written in full. But Sraffa's equations are nothing but that—the full expression of 'P' in Marx's circuit. So there is no escape from Sraffa's equations—they are fundamental.

Now, let us unpack Moseley's 'the general formula for capital'. According to Moseley, the initial aggregate M is divided into industrial M_i's in the production equations and all these M_i's are augmented by a uniform rate of profit r in the equations of prices of production. Let me write down Moseley's production equations, as I understand it.

$$M_i = A_{1i}p_1 + A_{2i}p_2 ...+ A_{ni}p_n + L_iw$$

$$M_i + \Delta M_i = (A_{1i}p_1 + A_{2i}p_2 ...+ A_{ni}p_n + L_iw)(1 + r) = A_ip_i$$

Thus, we have n independent equations and (n+1) unknowns (n prices and one rate of profits with given wages). Moseley claims that the value of total capital, i.e.,

$$\Sigma M_i = \Sigma(A_{1i}p_1 + A_{2i}p_2 ...+ A_{ni}p_n + L_iw) = M = (C + V) \text{ is given.}$$

So we use this as the normalisation equation to solve for n prices and one rate of profits. Thus the difference between my interpretation of Marx's transformation (see Sinha 2010, pp. 181–88) and Moseley's turns out to be simply this: I argue that after admitting that his solution of the prices of production was flawed because he had not converted his inputs from labour-values to prices of production (see Marx 1991, p. 264), Marx uses $\Sigma A_ip_i = (C + V + S)$ as the normalisation equation and Moseley argues that it should be $\Sigma(A_{1i}p_1 + A_{2i}p_2 ...+ A_{ni}p_n + L_iw) = M = (C + V)$. But then what is the fuss about? As we all know, the normalisation equation does not change the terms of the problem. The only difference is that my normalisation equation guarantees at least one of Marx's two invariance conditions by definition whereas Moseley's does not do it for either of the two. Now, if Moseley is arguing that $\Sigma(M_i + \Delta M_i)$ must also be equal to $(C + V + S)$, then he is simply over-determining the system, i.e., there is no room for this equation in the system. The criticism of the transformation problem, however, is not about the appropriate normalisation equation but rather the fact that both the labour-value accounting as well as the prices of production accounting can be independently derived from the same set of physical (i.e., C...P...C') data, and therefore there is no *causation* that runs from either labour-values to prices of production or prices of production to labour-values. Moseley's criticism does not touch this basic problem.

In the Chapter on Marx, I argue that, contrary to the popular opinion, Marx did entertain a thesis that a consequence of capitalist development is an absolute immiseration of the working class. Levrero (2012) criticises me for this:

> Sinha attributes to Marx a claim of absolute rather than relative immiseration. Sinha bases his interpretation on Section V of Chapter 25 in *Capital* Volume 1 and on Marx's *Value Price and Profit* (1865). But the first of these refers to the declining tendency of real wages in England and Ireland for short period of time, while Marx's remark in his 1865 lectures that there exists a tendency for capitalist production to 'push the value of labour more or less to its minimum limit' does not negate the many passages in *Capital* that refer to the possibility of a relative, and not absolute, immiseration of the working class. (p. 530, f.n. 4).

Actually, the data quoted by Marx for England is for the 20-year period from 1846 to 1866. Twenty years is a period of two full business cycles in Marx's reckoning; but it is a 'short period' for Levrero, who reckons that the Classical supply-demand adjustments for commodities take 'long-period'! The reader would have noticed that not a single reference to the 'many passages in *Capital*' that is supposed to invalidate my thesis is provided. His readers are also not told that the below given passage appears in my book:

> Marx's statement in volume one of *Capital* that "in proportion as capital accumulates, the lot of the labourer, be his payment high or low, must grow worse" is regularly invoked to suggest that Marx maintained that the real wages would rise but still the workers conditions compared to the capitalists would worsen, hence the reference to wages being "high or low". It should, however, be noted that there is no reference to rising wages in the above statement. In the real world "the lot of the

labourer" does not get one universal wage but rather there is always a spectrum of wages for different strata of workers, some are paid relatively "high" and some are paid relatively "low". Hollander (2008), in my opinion, correctly interprets the above statement as "Marx intended a decline in the general wage rate which affects *all* classes of labourers—those high on the wage scale as well as those at a lower level" (p. 86). Given that Marx maintained that the rate of profits also falls, the question is: how could he speak of labourers' conditions becoming "worse" compared to the capitalists? The answer to this question lies in the centralization and concentration of capital. The tendency of centralization reduces the size of the capitalist class and hence increases the total profit incomes of the individual capitalists even though the rate of profits is falling. Hence the worsening conditions of the workers compared to the capitalists. (Sinha 2010, pp. 246–47).

The Chapter on Ricardo

Let us continue with Levrero's review. On Ricardo, I argue that Ricardo did not try to develop a theory to determine the rate of profits at any given time; instead, he was only interested in establishing the proposition that a rise in the difficulty of producing the wage basket or a rise in the labour-time needed to produce the given wage basket must lead to a fall in the rate of profits. Levrero retorts: 'But, contrary to what Sinha suggests, there is no evidence that Ricardo ever abandoned the project of explaining the rate of profit' (p. 528). As a matter of fact, I never maintained that Ricardo ever had the project of 'explaining the rate of profit', so the question of abandoning it does not arise. What I suggested was that Ricardo abandoned the project of determining the long-term relative prices in favour of determining the *cause* of variations in those prices. Levrero, however, goes on to quote Sraffa's well known passage from his 'Introduction' (Sraffa 1951) on Ricardo's problem of the 'invariable measure of value' as evidence to settle the matter. Since I have strongly argued against Sraffa's interpretation of Ricardo's problem of the 'invariable measure of value' where this passage from Sraffa is extensively discussed (see Sinha 2010, pp. 96–106), it is not clear to me how this passage from Sraffa could settle the matter under dispute about Ricardo?

Now, on the question of wages in Ricardo, Levrero writes: 'With respect to wages, Sinha surprisingly rejects Garegnani's interpretation of the Classical wage theories in terms of the "relative strength of the competing parties"' and then goes on to add '...Ricardo often speaks of the market wage rate as an average or normal price that can be above subsistence if "*the state of the market for labour*" is such that the workers "will be able to demand and obtain a great quantity of necessaries" due to "the advantageous position in which the labourers found himself placed" (Ricardo, 1951–73, IV, pp. 366, 369 emphasis added)' (pp. 529–30).

First of all, it is not clear why Levrero should be 'surprised' to see a scholar of Classical economics reject Garegnani's thesis on wages, as there aren't more than a handful of scholars who hold such an opinion anyway. In any case, Lavrero says that Ricardo 'often speaks ...'. He, however, could not find one reference from Ricardo's book. So he goes to Ricardo's 'Draft' on 'Absolute and Exchangeable Value of 1823' and patches together a statement from bits that run over four pages; and on top of it, out of the statement of 52 words, 23 words turn out to be his own! But why Levrero had to put his words in Ricardo's mouth? It is because otherwise the reader would have come to know that Ricardo endorses my position; since the true quotation reads: '... but it [profit] depends also on the state of the market for labour (or on the quantity of necessaries which competition obliges the master to give for these necessaries), *for if labour be scarce the workman will be able to demand and obtain a great quantity of necessaries*' (emphasis added). Levrero had to cut the phrase 'for if labour be scarce' out to give an impression that the phrase 'the state of the market for labour' implies a bargaining theory of wages! Now, if we follow Levrero, then, of course, the demand and supply theory of prices of commodities must be interpreted as bargaining theory of prices! The fact of the matter is that in the book I take pains to explain that Ricardo does not have a subsistence theory of wages and that whenever the rate of growth of the demand for labour is positive the real wage must be higher than the subsistence wage, as positive rate of growth of population is required to meet those demands and whenever the rate of growth of the demand for labour is higher than the population growth wages must rise to bring forth a higher rate of growth of population. But this is no bargaining theory of wages.

Here I might add that on the question of introduction of machinery and unemployment, I have given evidence from Ricardo's *Principles* to show that Ricardo treated introduction of machineries mostly as a consequence of rise in wages (i.e., as an effect of excess demand for labour) and that he rejected Barton's claim by stating that "It is not easy, I think, to conceive that under any circumstances, an increase in capital should not be followed by an increased demand for labour;

the most that can be said is, that the demand will be in a diminishing ratio' (Ricardo 1951–52, *Works I*, p. 396, f.n.). But Levrero does not let any of this known to his readers when he says that 'it is difficult to deny that ... the classical economists viewed permanent labour unemployment as normal for a given stage of accumulation (cf. for instance Smith, 1776, Bk I, pp. 80, 87 and Ricardo, 1821, p. 393; 1951–73, II, p. 241; IV, p. 346, 368)' (p. 529). So I went and checked all the references; and I can report that *not a single* reference cited by Levrero contains an *iota* of evidence to support his claim that 'the classical economists viewed permanent labour unemployment as normal for a given stage of accumulation'.

The Chapter on Adam Smith

The same pattern follows on Adam Smith. In my chapter on Smith, I argue that rent is the only surplus category in Adam Smith's theory and both the natural wages and the natural profits are taken as necessity for production. On this, Levrero writes:

> ... by denying that Smith includes profits in the surplus, Sinha falls into contradiction when he considers Smith's treatment of interest as a *component part* of the rate of profit (see for instance Smith, 1776, Bk. 2, p.59). The contradiction is particularly glaring if we recall Sinha's definition of surplus as that part of social product that is freely taxable without hindering the reproduction of the economy on an unchanged scale, for Sinha (pp. 43–44) recognises that, according to Smith, interest can usually be taxed with no effect on that reproduction. (p. 528).

So the impression is given that I unwittingly fall into a contradiction since I had not seen my mistake. Levrero, however, yet again fails to tell his reader that actually I raise this problem and devote six pages to a discussion on it with the conclusion that in Smith's theory interest is rather a 'derivative' and not an 'original' income category. Since it is a transferred income, a tax on it therefore has no effect on production. Now, one may not be convinced by my argument but to suggest that my position is simply contradictory is to not read what I write. And by the way, I do not define surplus 'as that part of the product that is freely taxable' (Fratini (2012) also makes this argument). My definition of surplus follows Sraffa's discussion on 'Surplus' in his unpublished notes (see Sinha 2016, pp. 82–89) closely and I take one full paragraph in the book (see Sinha 2010, pp. 32–33) to explain it. Moreover, the idea of a 'tax *test*' to test the status of a theoretical category also came to me from Sraffa. In his response to Peter Newman's review of his book, Sraffa wrote:

> You find a further ground for attacking the distinction between basics and non-basics in the supposition of its being 'partly a matter of the degree of aggregation in the system' (p. 67). Now aggregation is the act of the observer, whilst the distinction is based on a difference in objective properties. I have argued, for instance, that a tax on the price of basics will lower the general rate of profits for a given wage, whereas a similar tax on non-basics will leave the rate of profits unchanged. Surely, to answer this, one must prove the alleged consequence does not follow, instead of drowning the distinction through an appropriate degree of aggregation. (Sraffa, quoted in Bharadwaj 1989, p. 268).

On the question of the relationship between the rate of profits and the wage rate in the dynamic context of capital accumulation in Smith's theory, Tony Aspromourgos (2012) argues that:

> [M]ost astonishingly, Sinha seeks to demonstrate that Smith had a conception of an inverse functional relation between the rates of real wages and profit rates (26–31, 35). The argument is not convincing. Sinha offers a couple of Smith quotations which might seem to endorse a direct causal connection from higher wages to lower profit rates (27, 29; Smith 1776 [1976]: 105, 107). But Smith's use twice elsewhere of the phrase, 'at both ends', when speaking of how the pace of capital accumulation can simultaneously raise (lower) real wages and lower (raise) profit rates, points to the truth that two separate causal processes are involved. (p. 492).

To begin with, I never argued that there is 'an inverse functional relation between the rates of real wages and profit rate'. Apparently Aspromourgos incorrectly identifies 'functional relation' with 'causal relation'. My position, however, does not even endorse an unqualified or mechanical causation. My argument is that under certain condition, which I identify as the context of Adam Smith's famous statement about the fall in the rate of profits due to accumulation of capital, a case can be made that it is due to the rise of wages. However, before

I explain my case, let me point out that it is clear from Aspromour-gos's quotation that he does not deny my claim that Adam Smith does endorse an inverse relation between rise in wages and the rate of profits. All he is suggesting is that given Smith's use of a phrase, 'at both ends', he may be referring to two separate causes for this phenomenon and not just one. So it is not clear to me what is it in my claim that he found 'most astounding'?

In the book, I argue that there are two distinct contexts in which Adam Smith deals with the phenomenon of falling rate of profits. One is the context of a ripe economy, i.e., an economy that has reached its natural historical potential of maturity or growth and from where there is a natural tendency of all such economies to stagnate in a stationary state. In this case, both the rate of profits and wages fall to zero and subsistence wage respectively. The other context is of growing economy. Actually the specific context is not only of a growing economy but an economy that is growing at an accelerating pace, i.e., its rate of growth is rising. This gives rise to the phenomenon of rising real wages and the question is: does this also lead to a fall in the rate of profits? The reason for this to be a problem is that given the Ricardo-inspired accepted interpretation of Smith's theory of value as the 'adding up' theory of value, one should expect a general rise in prices and not necessarily a fall in either the rate of profits or rent. This is the context in dispute. I argue in the book (Sinha 2010, pp. 25–27) that Smith's answer to the question is: yes. And the argument works this way: on the assumption that real wages are expressed in 'corn' a rise in corn wages (or money wages with fixed corn price) would immediately reduce the rate of profits in the 'corn' or agricultural sector, given rent. Now, if manufacturing sector could increase their prices to compensate for a rise in wages then there would be a tendency for the agricultural capital to move to manufacturing sector, which would put pressure against the favourable terms of trade for the manufacturing sector and bring about a lower rate of profits in the manufacturing sector as well. The question is: why the flight of agricultural capital does not put enough pressure on rent to absorb the rise in wages? The answer to this question, I argue, is that the economy is growing ever faster, which creates power or bargaining imbalance between the capitalist class and the landlords—since capital is growing so fast that some movement of agricultural capital to manufacturing capital will not reduce the demand for agricultural land and hence the burden of rising wages must be borne by the capitalists. This case can be contrasted with the static case of tax on wages, where a movement of agricultural capital to manufacturing sector would reduce the total demand for land and therefore put pressure on the landlord to absorb the rise in wages due to the tax. Now the question is: how would this scenario work out in the market? Let us suppose all the capitalists raise the prices (in terms of money commodity) proportionately to compensate for the rise in wages, as the 'adding up' theory would suggest. If they could sell all they bring to the market at those prices then in effect it negates the initial assumption that real wages have risen. Thus clearly, given the initial assumption of rise in real wages, capitalists would find that they are unable to sell their commodities at prices that maintains their old rate of profits. So they will be forced to reduce their prices that result in a fall in their rate of profits. Their inability to sell at a price that would ensure their old rate of profits appears as overcrowding of capital in the market. Actually, Adam Smith argues that the fall in the rate of profits has a much larger effect on the 'natural price' of a commodity than the rise in wages, thus there would be a tendency for commodity prices to fall below their original prices: 'In countries which are fast advancing to riches, the low rate of profit may, in the price of many commodities, compensate the high wages of labour, and enable those countries to sell as cheap as their less thriving neighbours, among whom the wages of labour may be lower. In reality high profits tend much more to raise the price of work than high wages. ...In raising the price of commodities the rise of wages operates in the same manner as simple interest does in the accumulation of debt. The rise of profit operates like compound interest.' (Smith 1981, I.ix, pp. 114–5). Clearly, Smith considers the rate of profits to be a determinant of prices and not the other way around.

Now let us take the case of 'of both ends' that Aspromourgos has raised. This quotation appears on page 110–11, in para I.ix.13, about two to three pages before the quotations presented above appear (and a similar one on pp. 352–3). In section para I.ix.12, Adam Smith discusses the case of 'acquisition of new territory, or new branches of trade' and argues that this 'may sometimes raise the profits of stock, and with them the interest of money, even in a country which is fast advancing in the acquisition of riches' (p. 110). The reason for this is that high profit opportunity in the new territories or new branches would lead to withdrawal of some capital from old established industries to new ones—reducing the supply of goods in the old branches thereby increasing the prices and also rate of profits along with it. This is the usual case of rise in 'market prices' leading to higher rate of profits. This is followed by the observation in I.ix.13:

The diminution of the capital stock of the society, or of the funds destined for the maintenance of industry, however, as it lowers the wages of labour, so it raises the profits of stock, and consequently the interest of money. By the wages of labour being lowered, the owners of what stock remains in the society can bring their goods at less expence to market than before, and less stock being employed in supplying the market than before, they can sell them dearer. Their goods cost them less, and they get more for them. Their profits, therefore, being augmented at both ends, can well afford a large interest. (pp. 110–11).

Clearly the phrase, 'and less stock being employed in supplying the market than before, they can sell them dearer', refers to fall in the supply of goods meeting the fixed downward sloping demand curve at a higher price—a typical case of 'market prices' rising above the 'natural prices'. So there is no logical problem in Smith's apparent contradictory statements. When he appears to suggest 'competition' or changes in supply having independent effect on the rate of profits, i.e., independently of changes in wages, he is simply referring to 'market prices' and not the 'natural prices'. The 'natural prices' are affected by changes in wages alone.

References

Arrow, K.J. and G. Debreu. 1954. 'Existence of an Equilibrium for a Competitive Economy', *Econometrica*, 22(3), pp. 265–290.

Aspromourgos, Tony. 2012. Review of 'Ajit Sinha, *Theories of Value from Adam Smith to Piero Sraffa*', *European Journal of the History of Economic Thought*, 19(3): 490–95.

Bharadwaj, K. 1989. *Themes in Value and Distribution Classical Theory Reappraised*, London: Unwin Hyman.

Fratini, S.M. 2012. Review of 'Ajit Sinha, *Theories of Value from Adam Smith to Piero Sraffa*', *Contributions to Political Economy*, 31: 102–5.

Garegnani, P. 1976. 'On a change in the Notion of Equilibrium in Recent Work on Value and Distribution: A Comment on Samuelson', in Murray Brown, Kazuo Sato and Paul Zarembka (eds.), *Essays in Modern Capital Theory*, Amsterdam: North Holland, pp. 25–45.

Garegnani, P. 2007. 'Professor Samuelson on Sraffa and the Classical economics', *European Journal of the History of Economic Thought*, vol. 14(2), pp. 181–242.

Hicks, J.R. 1939. *Value and Capital*, Oxford: Clarendon Press.

Hollander, S. 2008. *Economics of Karl Marx Analysis and Application*, New York: Cambridge University Press.

Kurz, H.D. 2012. 'Don't treat too ill my Piero! Interpreting Sraffa's papers', *Cambridge Journal of Economics*, 36(6), 1535–1569.

Levrero, E.S. 2012. 'Review of *Theories of Value from Adam Smith to Piero Sraffa*', *Review of Political Economy*, 24(3): 527–35.

Marx, Karl. 1976 [1865]. *Value, Price, and Profit*, New York: International Publishers.

Marx, Karl. 1977 [1867]. *Capital vol. I*, New York: Vintage.

Marx, Karl. 1991 [1894]. *Capital vol. III*, London: Penguin Classics.

Moseley, Fred. 2012. 'Review of *Theories of Value from Adam Smith to Piero Sraffa*', *Review of Political Economy*, 24(3): 519–27.

Reati, Angelo. 2012. Review of *Theories of value from Adam Smith to Piero Sraffa. Review of Radical Political Economics* 44 (3) (Summer): 395–400.

Reati, Angelo. 2014. 'A Note on Some Misunderstanding of Sraffa's System', *Review of Radical Political Economics*, 46(3), pp. 402–5.

Ricardo, David. [1821] 1951. *On The Principles Of Political Economy And Taxation*, 3rd edition, Cambridge University Press.

Ricardo, David. 1951–52. *The Works and Correspondence of David Ricardo*, (ed.) Piero Sraffa, vols. I, II, IV, Cambridge: Cambridge University Press.

Sinha, Ajit. 2010. *Theories of Value from Adam Smith to Piero Sraffa*, London: Routledge.

Sinha, Ajit. 2012a. 'Listen to Sraffa's Silences: A New Interpretation of *Production of Commodities*, *Cambridge Journal of Economics*, 36(6), 2012, pp. 1323–1339.

Sinha, Ajit. 2012b. 'A Response to Angelo Reati', *Review of Radical Political Economics*, 44(3), pp. 401–402.

Sinha, Ajit. 2013. 'The New Interpretation of Sraffa's Prices: A Response to Heinz Kurz', *Cambridge Journal of Economics*, 37(6), pp. 1449–1453.

Sinha, Ajit. 2015. 'A Reflection on the Samuelson-Garegnani Debate', *Economic Thought*, 4(2), pp. 48–67.

Sinha, Ajit. 2016. *A Revolution in Economic Theory: The Economics of Piero Sraffa*, Cham: Palgrave Macmillan.

Sinha, Ajit. 2018. *Essays on Theories of Value in the Classical Tradition*, Cham: Palgrave Macmillan, 2018 (Forthcoming).

Smith, Adam. [1776] 1981. *An Inquiry Into The Nature And Causes Of The Wealth Of Nations Volumes I*, Indianapolis: Library Fund.

Sraffa, P. [1925] 1998. 'On the Relation between Costs and Quantity Produced', in L. Pasinetti (ed.), *Italian Economic Papers*, translated from Italian, Volume III: Il Mulino and Oxford: Oxford University Press.

Sraffa, P. 1951. 'Introduction', in *Works and Correspondence of David Ricardo*, vol. I, Cambridge: Cambridge University Press.

Sraffa, P. (1960). *Production of Commodities by Means of Commodities*, Cambridge, Cambridge University Press.

Sraffa, P., ND. *Piero Sraffa Papers*. Wren Library, Trinity College, Cambridge.

REFERENCES

Aglietta, M. 1979. *The Theory of Capitalist Regulation, The US Experience*. London: New Left Books.

Allen, H.S. 1928. 'The Quantum Theory', Supplement to *Nature*, No. 3084, pp. 887–95.

Armstrong, P. and A. Glyn. 1980. 'The Law of the Falling Rate of Profit and Oligopoly: A Comment on Shaikh', *Cambridge Journal of Economics*, 4: 69–70.

Arrow, K.J. 1991. 'Ricardo's Work as Viewed by Later Economists', *Journal of History of Economic Thought*, 13(1): 70–77.

Ashley, W.J. 1891. 'The Rehabilitation of Ricardo', *Economic Journal*, 1(3): 474–89.

Bailey, Samuel. 1825. *A Critical Dissertation on the Nature, Measure, and Causes of Value Chiefly in Response to the Writings of Mr. Ricardo and his Followers*. London: Printed for R. Hunter, St. Paul's Churchyard.

_____. 1826. *A Letter to a Political Economist; Occasioned by an Article in the Westminster Review on the Subject of Value*. London: Printed for R. Hunter, St. Paul's Churchyard.

Baldone, S. 1980. 'Fixed Capital in Sraffa's Theoretical Scheme', in L.L. Pasinetti (ed.), *Essays on the Theory of Joint Production*. London: Macmillan.

_____. 'On Sraffa's Standard Commodity: Is It Price Invariant with Respect to Changes in Income Distribution?', *Cambridge Journal of Economics*, 30(2): 313–19.

Barkai, H. 1959. 'Ricardo on Factor Prices and Income Distribution in a Growing Economy', *Economica*, 26: 240–50.

_____. 1965. 'Ricardo's Static Equilibrium', *Economica*, 32: 15–31.

_____. 1967. 'The Empirical Assumptions of Ricardo's 93 Per Cent: Labour Theory of Value', *Economica*, 34: 418–23.

_____. 1970. 'The Labour Theory of Value as an Operational Proposition', *Economica*, 37: 187–90.

Barton, John. 1817. *Observations on the Circumstances which Influence the Condition of the Labouring Classes of Society*. London: John and Arthur Arch.

Baumol, W. J. 1974. 'The Transformation of Values: What Marx "Really" Meant (An Interpretation)', *Journal of Economic Literature*, 12(1): 51–62.

————. 1983. 'Marx and the Iron Law of Wages', *American Economic Review*, 73(2): 303–08.

Bellino, E. 2004. 'On Sraffa's Standard Commodity', *Cambridge Journal of Economics*, 28: 121–32.

Bharadwaj, K. 1989. *Themes in Value and Distribution Classical Theory Reappraised*. London: Unwin Hyman.

Bidard, C. 1997. 'Pure Joint-Production', *Cambridge Journal of Economics*, 21: 685–701.

————. 2004. *Price, Production, Scarcity*. Cambridge: Cambridge University Press.

Bladen, W.W. 1975. 'Command over Labour: A Study in Misinterpretation', *Canadian Journal of Economics*, 8(4): 504–19.

Blaug, Mark. 1958. *Ricardian Economics: A Historical Study*. New Haven: Yale University Press.

————. 1962. *Economic Theory in Retrospect*. London: Heinemann.

————. 1982. 'Another Look at the Labour Reduction Problem in Marx', in I. Bradley and M. Howard (eds), *Classical and Marxian Political Economy: Essays in Honour of Ronald L. Meek*. London: Macmillan.

————. 1999. 'Misunderstanding Classical Economics: The Sraffian Interpretation of the Surplus Approach', *History of Political Economy*, 31(2): 213–36.

Bleaney, M. 1980. 'Maurice Dobb's Theory of Crisis: A Comment', *Cambridge Journal of Economics*, 4: 71–73.

Boggio, L. 1992. 'Production Prices and Dynamic Stability: Results and Open Questions', *The Manchester School*, 60(3): 264–94.

Böhm-Bawerk, Eugen von.[1896] 1949. *Karl Marx and the Close of His System* in *Karl Marx and the Close of His System by Eugen von Böhm- Bawerk & Böhm-Bawerk's Criticism of Marx by Rudolf Hilferding Together with an Appendix consisting of an article by Ladislaus von Bortkiewicz on the Transformation of Values into Prices of Production in the Marxian System Edited with an Introduction by Paul Sweezy*, New York: Agustus M. Kelley.

————. [1884]1959. *Capital and Interest*, Vol. I. Trs. George D. Huncke and Hans F. Sennholz. Illinois: Liberation Press.

Bortkiewicz, Ladislaus von. [1907] 1949. 'On the Correction of Marx's Fundamental Theoretical Construction in the Third Volume of *Capital*' in Paul M. Sweezy (ed.), *Karl Marx and the Close of his System*. Trs. Paul M. Sweezy.

————. [1907] 1952. 'Value and Price in the Marxian System', *International Economic Papers*, 2.

Bose, A. 1965. 'Consumers' Demand, Distributive Shares and Prices', *The Economic Journal*, LXXV: 771–86.

Bowles, S. and H. Gintis. 1977. 'The Marxian Theory of Value and Heterogeneous Labour: A Critique and Reformulation', *Cambridge Journal of Economics*, 1(2): 173–92.

Brens, H. 1960. 'An Attempt at a Rigorous Restatement of Ricardo's Long Run Equilibrium', *Canadian Journal of Economics and Political Science*, February, pp. 74–86.

Bronfenbrenner, M. 1973. 'Samuelson, Marx, and Latest Critics', *Journal of Economic Literature*, 11(1): 58–63.

Brown, V. 1994. *Adam Smith's Discourse Canonicity, Commerce and Conscience*. London: Routledge.

Buchanan, D. [1817] 2000. *Observations on the Subjects Treated of in Dr. Smith's Inquiry into the Nature and Causes of the Wealth of Nations*. Edinburgh. Reprinted in H. Mizuta (ed.), *Adam Smith: Critical Responses*, Vol. II. London: Routledge, 2000.

Buchanan, D.H. 1929. 'The Historical Approach to Rent and Price Theory', *Economica*, IX: 123–55.

Burmeister, E. 1968. 'On a Theorem of Sraffa', *Economica*, February, pp. 83–87.

_____. 1975. 'Comment: This Age of Leontief ... and Who?', *Journal of Economic Literature*, 13(2): 454–57.

_____. 1977. 'The Irrelevance of Sraffa's Analysis without Constant Returns to Scale', *Journal of Economic Literature*, 15(1): 68–70.

Cannan, Edwin. 1929. *A Review of Economic Theory*. London: P. S. King and Son, Limited.

_____. [1893] 1997. *A History of the Theories of Production and Distribution in English Political Economy 1776 to 1848*. London: Routledge/ Thoemmes Press.

Caravale, Giovanni A. 1985. 'Diminishing Returns and Accumulation in Ricardo', in G.A. Caravale (ed.), *The Legacy of Ricardo*. New York: Basil Blackwell.

Caravale, G.A. and D.A. Tosato. 1980. *Ricardo and the Theory of Value, Distribution and Growth*. London: Routledge and Kegan Paul.

Casarosa, Carlo. 1978. 'A New Formulation of the Ricardian System', *Oxford Economic Papers*, 30: 38–63.

_____. 1985. 'The "New View" of the Ricardian Theory of Distribution and Economic Growth', in G.A. Caravale (ed.), *The Legacy of Ricardo*. New York: Basil Blackwell.

Cassels, J.M. 1935. 'A Re-Interpretation of Ricardo on Value', *Quarterly Journal of Economics*, 49, 518–32.

Cockshott, P. and A. Sinha. 2008. 'Can We Meaningfully Speak of Changes in Price under the Regime of Changes in Techniques?', *Review of Political Economy*, 20(3): 393–403.

Cockshott, W.P. and A. Cottrell. 1997. 'Labour Time versus Alternative Value Bases: A Research Note', *Cambridge Journal of Economics*, 21: 545–49.

_____. 1998. 'Does Marx Need to Transform?', in R. Bellofiore (ed.), *Marxian Economics: A Reappraisal*, Vol. 2. London/New York: Macmillan/ St. Martin Press.

Cockshott, W.P., Cottrell, A. and G. Michaelson. 1995. 'Testing Marx: Some New Results from UK Data', *Capital and Class*, 55: 103–29.

Cohen, G.A. 1979. 'The Labour Theory of Value and the Concept of Exploitation', *Philosophy and Public Affairs*, VIII (4): 338–60.

————. 1983. 'More on Exploitation and Labour Theory of Value', *Inquiry*, XXVI: 309–31.

Cottrell, A. and W.A. Darity Jr. 1988. 'Marx, Malthus, and Wages', *History of Political Economy*, 20(2): 173–90.

Dasgupta, A.K. 1960. 'Adam Smith on Value', *Indian Economic Review*, 5(2): 105–15. Also reprinted in J.C. Wood (ed.), *Adam Smith: Critical Assessments*, Vol. IIII. London, New York: Routledge,1984.

————. 1985. *Epochs of Economic Theory*. Oxford: Basil Blackwell.

Davidson, Paul. 1959. 'A Clarification of the Ricardian Rent Share', *Canadian Journal of Economics and Political Science*, 25: 190–95.

De Vivo, Giancarlo. 1985. 'Robert Torrens and Ricardo's "Corn-Ratio" Theory of Profits', *Cambridge Journal of Economics*, 9(1): 89–92.

————. 1996. 'Ricardo Torrens, and Sraffa: A Summing Up', *Cambridge Journal of Economics*, 20(3): 387–91.

————. 2003. 'Sraffa's Path to Production of Commodities by Means of Commodities: An Interpretation', *Contributions to Political Economy*, 22: 1–25.

De Vroey, Michael. 1981. 'Value, Production, and Exchange', in Steedman (ed.), *The Value Controversy*, London: New Left Books.

Desai, M. 1974. *Marxian Economic Theory*, London: Gray-Mills.

————. 1979. *Marxian Economics*, Oxford: Blackwell.

————. 1991. 'The Transformation Problem', in G.A. Caravale (ed.), *Marx and Modern Economic Analysis*, Vol. I, Aldershot: Edward Elgar.

Dickinson, H.D. 1957. 'The Falling Rate of Profit in Marxian Economics', *The Review of Economic Studies*, 24(2), No. 64: 120–30.

Dmitriev, V.K. [1904] 1974. *Economic Essays on Value, Competition and Utility*. Edited by D.M. Nuti. Cambridge: Cambridge University Press.

Dobb, M. 1961. 'An Epoch-Making Book', *Labour Monthly*, 40 (October), pp. 487–91.

————. 1937. *Political Economy and Capitalism*. London: Routledge.

————. 1959. 'The Falling Rate of Profit', *Science and Society*, 23: 97–103.

————. 1973. *Theories of Value and Distribution since Adam Smith: Ideology and Economic Theory*. Cambridge: Cambridge University Press.

Douglas, P.H. 1928. 'Smith's Theory of Value and Distribution', in J.M. Clark, Paul H. Douglas, Jacob H. Hollander, Glenn R. Morrow, Melchior Palyi, Jacob Viner (eds), *Adam Smith, 1776–1926 Lectures to Commemorate the Sesquicentennial of the Publication of "The Wealth of Nations"*. Chicago: Chicago University Press.

Dumenil, G. 1984. 'Beyond the Transformation Riddle: A Labor Theory of Value', *Science and Society*, 47(4): 427–50.

Dumenil, G. and D. Levy. 1985. 'The Classicals and the Neoclassicals: A Rejoinder to Frank Hahn', *Cambridge Journal of Economics*, 9: 327–45.

————. 1987. 'The Dynamics of Competition: A Restoration of the Classical Analysis', *Cambridge Journal of Economics*, 11(2): 133–64.

Dupertuis, M.-S. and A. Sinha. 2009a. 'A Sraffian Critique of the Classical Notion of Centre of Gravitation', *Cambridge Journal of Economics*, 33(6): 1065–87.

Dupertuis, M.-S. and A. Sinha. 2009b. 'Existence of the *Standard System* in the Multiple Production Case: A Solution to the Manara Problem', *Metroeconomica*, 60(3): 432–54.

Eatwell, John. 1974. 'Controversies in the Theory of Surplus Value: Old and New', *Science and Society*, 38(3): 281–303.

_____. 1975a. 'The Interpretation of Ricardo's *Essay on Profits*', *Economica*, 42: 182–87.

_____. 1975b. 'Mr. Sraffa's Standard Commodity and the Rate of Exploitation', *Quarterly Journal of Economics*, 89(4): 543–55.

_____. 1977. 'The Irrelevance of Returns to Scale in Sraffa's Analysis', *Journal of Economic Literature*, 15(1): 61–68.

Edelberg, V. 1933. 'The Ricardian Theory of Profits', *Economica*, 13: 51–74.

Elster, John. 1978. 'The Labor Theory of Value: A Reinterpretation of Marx's Economics', *Marxist Perspectives*, 1(3): 70–101.

Eltis, Walter. 1984. *The Classical Theory of Economic Growth*. London: Macmillan.

_____. 1985. 'Ricardo on Machinery and Technological Unemployment', in G.A. Caravale (ed.), *The Legacy of Ricardo*. New York: Basil Blackwell.

Engels, F. 1937. 'Supplement to *Capital*, in *Capital* Vol. III by Karl Marx.

Faccarello, G. 1982. 'Sraffa versus Ricardo: The Historical Irrelevance of the "Corn-Profit" Model', *Economy and Society*, 11: 122–37.

_____. 1983. *Travail, Valeur et Prix. Une Critique de la Valeur*. Paris: Anthropos.

_____. 1997. 'Some Reflections on Marx's Theory of Value', in R. Bellofiore (ed.), *Marx's Economics Rivisited Volume I*, pp. 29–47. London: Macmillan.

Farjoun, E. and M. Machover. 1983. *Laws of Chaos*. London: Verso.

Fine, B. 1979. 'On Marx's Theory of Agricultural Rent', *Economy and Society*, 8: 241–78.

Fine, B. and Harris, L. 1976. 'Controversial Issues in Marxist Economic Theory', *The Socialist Register*.

Flaschel, P. and W. Semmler. 1987. 'Classical and Neoclassical Competitive Adjustment Processes', *The Manchester School*, 55(1): 13–37.

Foley, Duncan. 1982. 'The Value of Money, the Value of Labor Power and the Marxian Transformation Problem', *Review of Radical Political Economics*, 14(2): 37–47.

Fonteyraud, Alcide. 1847. *Oeuvres Completes de David Ricardo traduites en Frangais par MM. Constancio et Alc. Fonteyraud, Augmentees Des Notes De Jean-Baptiste Say, de nouvelles notes et de commen- taires par Maltus, Sismondi, MM. Rossi, Blanqui, Etc*. Paris: Chez Guillaumin et CIE Libraires.

Foucault, M. 1973. *The Order of Things: An Archaeology of the Human Sciences*. New York: Vintage Books.

Franke, R. 2000. 'Optimal Utilization of Capital and a Financial Sector in a Classical Gravitation Process', *Metroeconomica*, 51(1): 40–66.

Ganguli, P. 1997. 'Differential Profit Rates and Convergence to the Natural State', *The Manchester School*, 65(5): 534–67.

Ganssmann, Heiner. 1988. 'Abstract Labour as a Metaphor? A Comment on Steedman', *History of Political Economy*, 20(3): 461–70.

Garegnani, P. 1976. 'On a Change in the Notion of Equilibrium in Recent Work on Value and Distribution: A Comment of Samuelson', in Murray Brown, Kazuo Sato and Paul Zarembka (eds), *Essays in Modern Capital Theory*. Amsterdam: North Holland.

_____. 1982. 'On Hollander's Interpretation of Ricardo's Early Theory of Profits', *Cambridge Journal of Economics*, 6: 65–77.

_____. 1983a. 'Ricardo's Early Theory of Profits and its Rational Foundation: A Reply to Professor Hollander', *Cambridge Journal of Economics*, 7: 75–78.

_____. 1983b. 'The Classical Theory of Wages and the Role of Demand Schedule in the Determination of Relative Prices', *American Economic Review*, Papers and Proceedings, 63: 309–13.

_____. 1983c. The labour theory of value in Marx and in the Marxist tradition. Paper presented at a colloquium on Marx at Ecole des Hautes Etudes en Sciences Sociales, Paris, 6–9 December 1983.

_____. 1984. 'Value and Distribution in the Classical Economists and Marx', *Oxford Economic Papers*, 36(2): 291–325.

_____. 1985. 'On Hollander's Interpretation of Ricardo's Early Theory of Profits', in G.A. Caravale (ed.), *The Legacy of Ricardo*. New York: Basil Blackwell.

_____. 1990a. 'Sraffa: Classical versus Marginalist Analysis', in K. Bharadwaj and B. Schefold (eds), *Essays on Piero Sraffa: Critical Perspectives on the Revival of Classical Theory*, Delhi: Oxford University Press.

_____. 1990b. 'Reply', in K. Bharadwaj and B. Schefold (eds), *Essays on Piero Sraffa: Critical Perspectives on the Revival of Classical Theory*. Delhi: Oxford University Press.

Garegnani, P. 1990c. 'Comment', in K. Bharadwaj and B. Schefold (eds), *Essays on Piero Sraffa: Critical Perspectives on the Revival of Classical Theory*. Delhi: Oxford University Press.

_____. 1990d. 'Quantity of Capital', in J. Eatwell, M. Milgate and P. Newman (eds), *The New Palgrave Series: Capital Theory*. London: Macmillan.

_____. 1991. 'The Labour Theory of Value: "Detour or Technical Advance"', in G.A. Caravale (ed.), *Marx and Modern Economic Analysis*, Vol. I. Aldershot: Edward Elgar.

_____. 1997. 'On Some Supposed Obstacles to the Tendency of Market Prices towards Natural Prices', in G.A. Caravale (ed.), *Equilibrium and Economic Theory*. London and New York: Routledge.

_____. 1998. 'Sraffa: The Theoretical World of the "Old Classical Economists"', *The European Journal of the History of Economic Thought*, 5(3): 415–29.

_____. 2000. 'Savings, Investment and the Quantity of Capital in General Intertemporal Equilibrium', in H. Kurz (ed.), *Critical Essays on Piero Sraffa's Legacy in Economics*. Cambridge: Cambridge University Press.

Garegnani, P. 2005. 'On a Turning Point in Sraffa's Theoretical and Interpretative Position in the Late 1920s', *The European Journal of the History of Economic Thought*, 12(3): 453–92.

_____. 2007. 'Professor Samuelson on Sraffa and the Classical Economics', *European Journal of the History of Economic Thought*, 14(2): 181–242.

Gee, J.M.A. 1981. 'The Origin of Rent in Adam Smith's *Wealth of Nations*: An Anti-Neoclassical View', *History of Political Economy*, 13(1): 1–18.

Gehrke, C. 2007. Sraffa's correspondence relating to the publication of *Production of Commodities by Means of Commodities*: Some selected material. Paper presented at the annual meetings of the European Society for the History of Economic Thought, Strasbourg, France.

Gerstein, I. 1976. 'Production, Circulation and Value', *Economy and Society*, 3: 243–91.

Gorden, D.F. 1968. 'Labour Theory of Value', in *International Encyclopedia of Social Sciences*, Vol. 15. New York: The Macmillan Co. & The Free Press.

Gordon, S. 1968. 'Why Does Marxian Exploitation Theory Require a Labor Theory of Value', *Journal of Political Economy*, 76, Jan-Feb.: 137–40.

Gottheil, F. M. 1962. 'Increasing Misery of the Proletariat: An Analysis of Marx's Wage and Employment Theory', *Canadian Journal of Economics*, 28: 103–13.

Green, F. 1991. 'Marx, Malthus, and Wages: A Comment on Cottrell and Darity', *History of Political Economy*, 23(1): 95–99.

Groenewegen, P.D. 1972. 'Three Notes on Ricardo's Theory of Value and Distribution', *Australian Economic Papers*, 11: 53–64.

_____. 1982. 'History and Political Economy: Smith, Marx and Marshall', *Australian Economic Papers*, June.

Hahn, F. 1982. 'The Neo-Ricardians', *Cambridge Journal of Economics*, 6: 353–74.

Harcourt, G.C. 1965. 'The Accountant in a Golden Age', *Oxford Economic Papers*, 17(1): 66–80.

_____. 1969. 'Some Cambridge Controversies in the Theory of Capital', *Journal of Economic Literature*, 7: 369–405.

_____. 1972. *Some Cambridge Controversies in the Theory of Capital*. Cambridge: Cambridge University Press.

_____. 2001. *50 Years a Keynesian and Other Essays*. UK: Palgrave.

_____. 2007. 'Paul Samuelson on Karl Marx: Were the Sacrificed Games of Tennis Worth It?', in M. Szenberg, L. Ramrattan and A. Gottesman (eds), *Samuelsonian Economics and the Twenty-First Century. USA: Oxford University Press*.

Harcourt, G. C. and V. G. Massaro. 1964. 'Mr. Sraffa's Production of Commodities', *The Economic Record*, September: 442–54.

Harrod, R.F. 1961. 'Review of *Production of Commodities by Means of Commodites: Prelude to a Critique of Economic Theory*', *The Economic Journal*, LXXI: 783–87.

Hicks, John. 1972. 'Ricardo's Theory of Distribution', in M. Peston and B.A. Corry (eds), *Essays in Honour of Lord Robbins*. London: Weidenfeld and Nicolson.

_____. 1985. 'Sraffa and Ricardo: A Critical View', in G.A. Caravale (ed.), *The Legacy of Ricardo*. New York: Basil Blackwell.

Hicks, John and S. Hollander. 1977. 'Mr. Ricardo and the Moderns', *Quarterly Journal of Economics*, 91: 351–69.

Hilferding, R. [1904] 1949. 'Böhm-Bawerk's Criticism of Marx', in *Karl Marx and the Close of His System* in *Karl Marx and the Close of His System by Eugen von Böhm-Bawerk & Böhm-Bawerk's Criticism of Marx by Rudolf Hilferding Together with an Appendix Consisting of an Article by Ladislaus von Bortkiewicz on the Transformation of Values into Prices of Production in the Marxian System Edited with an Introduction by Paul Sweezy*. New York: Agustus M. Kelley.

Himmelweit, S. and S. Mohun. 1981. 'Real Abstraction and Anomalous Assumptions', in Ian Steedman (ed.), *The Value Controversy*. London: New Left Books.

Hodges, D.C. 1965. 'The Value Judgement in *Capital*', *Science and Society*, 29(3): 296–311.

Hollander, J. H. 1904. 'The Development of Ricardo's Theory of Value', *Quarterly Journal of Economics*, 18: 455–91.

Hollander, S. 1973a. *The Economics of Adam Smith*. Toronto: University of Toronto Press.

_____. 1973b. 'Ricardo's Analysis of the Profit Rate', *Economica*, 40: 260–82.

_____. 1975. 'Ricardo and the Corn Profit Model: A Reply to Eatwell', *Economica*, 42: 188–202.

_____. 1979. *The Economics of David Ricardo*. Toronto: University of Toronto Press.

_____. 1981. 'Marxian Economics as "General Equilibrium" Theory', *History of Political Economy*, 13: 121–54.

_____. 1983. 'On the Interpretation of Ricardian Economics: The Assumption Regarding Wages', *American Economic Review*, Papers and Proceedings, 73: 314–18.

_____. 1984. 'Marx and Malthusianism: Marx's Secular Path of Wages', *The American Economic Review*, 74: 139–51.

_____. 1986. 'Marx and Malthusianism: A Reply to Miguel Ramirez', *The American Economic Review*, 76: 548–50.

_____. 1989. 'On Composition of Demand and Income Distribution in Classical Economics', *History of Economic Society Bulletin*, Fall: 216–21; also reprinted in S. Hollander, *Ricardo — The New View*, London: Routledge, 1995.

_____. 1991. 'Marx and the Falling Rate of Profit', in G. A. Caravale (ed.), *Marx and Modern Economic Analysis*, Vol. 2. Aldershot: Edward Elgar.

_____. 1992. *Classical Economics*. Toronto: University of Toronto Press.

_____. 1995. *Ricardo — The New View*. London: Routledge.

Hollander, S. 2008. *Economics of Karl Marx: Analysis and Application.* New York: Cambridge University Press.

Howard, M.C. and J.E. King. 1985. *The Political Economy of Marx.* Second edition. London and New York: Longman.

_____. 1987. 'Friedrich Engels and the Prize Essay Competition in the Marxian Theory of Value', *History of Political Economy,* Winter: 571–90.

_____. 1989. *A History of Marxian Economics, Vol. I, 1883–1929.* Princeton: Princeton University Press.

_____. 1992. *A History of Marxian Economics, Vol. II, 1929–1990.* Princeton: Princeton University Press.

Jevons, H.S. [1871] 1957a. *The Theory of Political Economy.* New York: Kelly & Millman, Inc.

_____. [1879] 1957b. 'Preface to the Second Edition', in *The Theory of Political Economy.* New York: Kelly & Millman, Inc.

Jossa, Bruno. 1991. 'The Theory of Exploitation in Marx', in G.A. Caravale (ed.), *Marx and Modern Economic Analysis,* Vol. 1. Aldershot: Edward Elgar.

Kauder, E. 1953. 'Genesis of the Marginal Utility Theory', *Economic Journal,* 63(251): 638–50.

Kaushil, S. 1973. 'The Case of Adam Smith's Value Analysis', *Oxford Economic Papers,* 25(1): 60–71.

Knight, F.H. 1935. 'The Ricardian Theory of Production and Distribution, Parts I-II', *Canadian Journal of Economics and Political Science,* 1: 3–25 and 171–96.

Konus, A.A. 1970. 'Empirical Assumptions of Ricardo's 93% Labour Theory of Value: A Comment', *Economica,* 37: 185–86.

Krause, Ulrich. 1981. 'Heterogeneous Labour and the Fundamental Marxian Theorem', *Review of Economic Studies,* XLVIII: 173–78.

_____. 1982. *Money and Abstract Labour.* London: New Left Books.

Kurz, H. and N. Salvadori. 1995. *Theory of Production: A Long-period Analysis.* New York: Cambridge University Press.

_____. 2005a. 'Representing the Production and Circulation of Commodities in Material Terms: On Sraffa's Objectivism', *Review of Political Economy,* 17(3): 413–41.

_____. 2005b. 'Removing an "Insuperable Obstacle" in the Way of an Objectivist Analysis: Sraffa's Attempts at Fixed Capital', *The European Journal of the History of Economic Thought,* 12(3): 493–524.

Laibman, David. 1973. 'Values and Prices of Production: The Political Economy of the Transformation Problem', *Science and Society,* 37, 404–36.

_____. 2002. 'Value and the Quest for the Core of Capitalism', *Review of Radical Political Economics,* 34(2): 159–78.

Lapides, K. 1998. *Marx's Wage Theory in Historical Perspective: Its Origin, Developments and Interpretation.* Westport, CT: Praeger.

Larsen, R.M. 1977. 'Adam Smith's Theory of Market Prices', *Indian Economic Journal,* 24(3): 219–35.

Lebowitz, M. 2003. *Beyond 'Capital': Marx's Political Economy of the Working Class*. Basingstoke: Palgrave-Macmillan.

Levine, A.L. 1974. 'This Age of Leontief … and Who? An Interpretation', *Journal of Economic Literature*, 12(3): 872–81.

_____. 1975. 'This Age of Leontief … and Who? A Reply', *Journal of Economic Literature*, 13(2): 457–61.

_____. 1977. 'The Irrelevance of Returns to Scale in Sraffa's Analysis: A Comment', *Journal of Economic Literature*, 15(1): 70–72.

Levy, D. 1976. 'Ricardo and the Iron Law: A Correction of the Record', *History of Political Economy*, 8(2): 235–51.

Lexis, W. 1895. 'The Concluding Volume of Marx's *Capital*', *Quarterly Journal of Economics*, 10: 1–33: also reprinted in J.C. Wood (ed.), *Karl Marx's Economics: Critical Assessments, Vol. I*. London and New York: Routledge (1987).

Lipietz, A. 1982. 'The So-Called "Transformation Problem" Revisited', *Journal of Economic Theory*, 26: 59–88.

Malthus, T.R. 1815. *Observations on the Effects of the Corn Laws*, London: John Murray.

Manara, C.F. [1968] 1980. 'Sraffa's Model for the Joint-production of Commodities by Means of Commodities', in L.L. Pasinetti (ed.), *Essays on the Theory of Joint Production*. London: Macmillan.

Mandel, E. 1968. *Marxist Economic Theory, Vol. I*. New York: Monthly Review Press.

_____. 1976. 'Introduction' to *Capital, Vol. I*. New York: Vintage.

Marshall, A. [1890] 1949. *Principles of Economics: An Introductory Volume*, eighth edition. London: Macmillan and Co. Limited.

Marx, Karl. [1859]. *A Contribution to the Critique of Political Economy*, with an Introduction by Maurice Dobb. New York: International Publishers.

_____. [1905–10] 1963. *Theories of Surplus Value, Part I*. Moscow: Progress Publishers.

_____. [1905–10] 1968. *Theories of Surplus Value, Part II*. Moscow: Progress Publishers.

_____. [1905–10] 1971. *Theories of Surplus Value, Part III*. Moscow: Progress Publishers.

_____. [1865] 1976. *Value, Price, and Profit*. New York: International Publishers.

_____. [1867] 1977. *Capital, Vol. I*. New York: Vintage.

_____. [1894] 1991. *Capital, Vol. III*. London: Penguin Classics.

_____. [1885] 1992. *Capital, Vol. II*. London: Penguin Classics.

May, K. 1948. 'Value and Price of Production: A Note on Winternitz Solution', *Economic Journal*, 58: 596–99.

_____. 1949. 'The Structure of Classical Value Theories', *Review of Economic Studies*, 17(1): 60–69.

McCulloch, J.R. 1838. 'Introductory Discourse', in J.R. McCulloch (ed.), *An Inquiry into the Nature and Causes of the Wealth of Nations*. Edinburgh:

also reprinted in H. Mizuta (ed.), *Adam Smith: Critical Responses Vol. III.* London: Routledge, 2000.

Medio, A. 1972. 'Profits and Surplus-Value. Appearance and Reality in Capitalist Production', in E.K. Hunt and J.G. Schwartz (eds), *A Critique of Economic Theory.* Harmondsworth: Penguin Books.

Meek, R.L. 1956. 'Some Notes on the "Transformation Problem"', *Economic Journal,* 66: 94–107.

_____. [1956] 1966. *Studies in Labour Theory of Value.* Second Edition. New York and London: Monthly Review Press.

_____. 1967. *Economics and Ideology and Other Essays: Studies in the Development of Economic Thought.* London: Chapman and Hall Ltd.

_____. 1976. 'Is There an "Historical Transformation Problem"?: A Comment', *Economic Journal,* 86(2): 342–47.

Mill, J.S. 1848. *Principles of Political Economy with Some of Their Applications to Social Philosophy.* London: John W. Parker, West Strand.

Mizuta, H. (ed.) 2000. *Adam Smith: Critical Responses, Vol. III.* London: Routledge.

Morishima, M. 1973. *Marx's Economics: A Dual Theory of Value and Growth.* Cambridge: Cambridge University Press.

_____. 1974a. 'Marx in the Light of Modern Economic Theory', *Econometrica:* 611–32.

_____. 1974b. 'Marx's Economics: A Comment on C.C. von Weizsacker's Article', *Economic Journal,* 84(334): 387–91.

_____. 1976. 'Positive Profits with Negative Surplus Value — A Comment', *Economic Journal,* 86: 599–603.

_____. 1978. 'S. Bowles and H. Gintis on the Marxian Theory of Value and Heterogeneous Labour', *Cambridge Journal of Economics,* 2(3): 305–09.

_____. 1989. *Ricardo's Economics: A General Equilibrium Theory of Distribution and Growth.* Cambridge: Cambridge University Press.

Morishima, M. and G. Catephores. 1975. 'The "Historical Transformation Problem": A Reply', *Economic Journal,* 86(2): 348–52.

_____. 1976. 'Is There an "Historical Transformation Problem"?', *Economic Journal,* 85(2): 309–28.

_____. 1978. *Value Exploitation and Growth.* London: McGraw Hill Ltd.

Mossner, E.C. and I.S. Ross (eds). 1987. *The Correspondence of Adam Smith.* Second edition. Oxford: Oxford University Press.

Myers, M.L. 1976. 'Adam Smith's Concept of Equilibrium', *Journal of Economic Issues,* 10(3): 560–75. Also reprinted in J.C. Wood (ed.), *Adam Smith: Critical Assessment, Vol. III.* London, New York: Routledge, 1984.

Nakatani, Takeshi. 1980. 'The Law of Falling Rate of Profit and the Competitive Battle: Comment on Shaikh', *Cambridge Journal of Economics,* 4: 65–68.

Napoleoni, C. 1991. 'Value and Exploitation: Marx's Economic Theory and Beyond', in G.A. Caravale (ed.), *Marx and Modern Economic Analysis, Vol. 1.* Aldershot: Edward Elgar.

Nell, E.J. 1973. 'Review of *Marx's Economics: A Dual Theory of Value and Growth* by M. Morishima', *Journal of Economic Literature*, 9: 1369–71.

Nikaido, H. 1983. 'Marx on Competition', *Journal of Economics*, 43(4): 337–62.

O'Brian, D.P. 1975. *The Classical Economists Revisited*. Princeton and Oxford: Princeton University Press.

———. 1981. 'Ricardian Economics and the Economics of David Ricardo', *Oxford Economic Papers*, 33: 352–85.

———. [1975] 2004. *The Classical Economists Revisited*. Oxford: Oxford University Press.

O'Donnell, R. 1990. *Adam Smith's Theory of Value and Distribution: A Reappraisal*. New York: St. Martin's Press.

Okishio, N. 1961. 'Technical Changes and the Rate of Profit', *Kobe University Economic Review*, 7: 85–99.

———. 1963. 'A Mathematical Note on Marxian Theorems', *Waltwirtschaftliches Archiv*, 91(2): 287–99.

———. 1972. 'On Marx's Production Prices' (in Japanese), *Keizaigaku Kenkyu*, 19.

Ong, Nai-Pew. 1983. 'Ricardo's Invariable Measure of Value and Sraffa's "Standard Commodity"', *History of Political Economy*, 15(2): 207–27.

Pareto, Vilfredo. [1893] 1987. *Pareto Oeuvres Completes publiees sous la direction de Giovanni Bugino Tome IX, Marxisme et Economie Pure*, Librairie Droz S.A. Geneve.

Pasinetti, L. 1960. 'A Mathematical Formulation of the Ricardian System', *Review of Economic Studies*, 27: 78–98.

Peach, Terry. 1993. *Interpreting Ricardo*. Cambridge: Cambridge University Press.

Piel, J. 1999. *Adam Smith and Economic Science: A Methodological Reinterpretation*. Cheltenham: Edward Elgar.

Pokorni, D. 1985. 'Karl Marx and General Equilibrium', *History of Political Economy*, 17: 109–32.

Quesnay, F. 1972. *Quesnay's Tableau Economique*. Edited by M. Kuczynski and R. Meek. London: Macmillan.

Ramirez, M.D. 1986. 'Marx and Malthusianism: Comment', *The American Economic Review*, 76: 543–47.

Ramos, A.M. 1998–99. 'Value and Price of Production: New Evidence on Marx's Transformation Procedure', *International Journal of Political Economy*, 28(4): 55–81.

Rankin, S. 1980. 'Supply and Demand in Ricardian Price Theory: A Re-Interpretation', *Oxford Economic Papers*, 32(2): 241–62.

———. 1987. 'Exploitation and the Labour Theory of Value: A Neo-Marxian Reply', *Capital and Class*, 32: 104–16.

Ricardo, David. [1821] 1951. *On the Principles of Political Economy and Taxation*. Third edition. Cambridge: Cambridge University Press.

———. 1951–52. *The Works and Correspondence of David Ricardo*, Vols. I-II, IV, VI-IX, Edited by Piero Sraffa. Cambridge: Cambridge University Press.

Robertson, H.M. and W.L. Taylor. 1957. 'Adam Smith's Approach to the Theory of Value', *Economic Journal*, 67: 181–98. Also reprinted in J.C. Wood (ed.), *Adam Smith: Critical Assessment, Vol. III*. London and New York: Routledge.

Robinson, Joan. 1961. 'Prelude to a Critique of Economic Theory', *Oxford Economic Papers*, 13: 53–58.

_____. [1942] 1966. *An Essay on Marxian Economics*. Second edition. Philadelphia: Orion Edition.

Roemer, J.E. 1977. 'Technical Change and the "Tendency of the Rate of Profit to Fall" ', *Journal of Economic Theory*, 16: 403–24.

_____. 1979. 'Continuing Controversy on the Falling Rate of Profit: Fixed Capital and Other Issues', *Cambridge Journal of Economics*, 3: 379–98.

_____. 1986. *Value, Exploitation and Class*. Chur: Harwood Academic Publishers.

Roncaglia, A. 1978. *Sraffa and the Theory of Prices*. Chichester: John Wiley & Sons.

_____. 2000. *Piero Sraffa: His Life, Thought and Cultural Heritage*. London: Routledge.

Rosdolsky, R. 1980. *The Making of Marx's 'Capital'*. London: Pluto Press.

Rosenbluth, G. 1969. 'A Note on Labour, Wages, and Rent in Smith's Theory of Vale', *Canadian Journal of Economics*, 2(2): 308–14.

Rosselli, Annalisa. 1985. 'The Theory of the Natural Wage', in G.A. Caravale (ed.), *The Legacy of Ricardo*. New York: Basil Blackwell.

Rothschild, E. 2001. *Economic Sentiments: Adam Smith, Condorcet and the Enlightenment*. Cambridge, Massachusetts: Harvard University Press.

Rowthorn, Bob. 1974. 'Skilled Labour in the Marxist System', *BSEB*, September, pp. 25–45.

_____. 1980. *Capitalism, Conflict and Inflation: Essays in Political Economy*. London. Lawrence and Wishart.

Salvadori, Neri. 1981. 'Falling Rate of Profit with a Constant Real Wage: An Example', *Cambridge Journal of Economics*, 5(1): 59–66.

_____. 1988. 'Fixed Capital within the Sraffa Framework', *Journal of Economics*, 48(1): 1–17.

Samuelson, P.A. 1957. 'Wages and Interest: A Modern Dissection of Marxian Economic Model', *The American Economic Review*, 47(6): 884–912.

_____. 1959. 'A Modern Treatment of the Ricardian Economy: I & II', *Quarterly Journal of Economics*, 73(1): 1–35 and 79(2): 217–31.

_____. 1971. 'Understanding the Marxian Notion of Exploitation: A Summary of the So-Called Transformation Problem between Marxian Values and Competitive Prices', *Journal of Economic Literature*, 9(2): 399–431.

_____. 1974. 'Insight and Detour in the Theory of Exploitation: A Reply to Baumol', *Journal of Economic Literature*, 12(1): 62–70.

Samuelson, P.A. 1977. 'A Modern Theorist's Vindication of Adam Smith', *American Economic Review*, 67(1): 42–49.

_____. 1978. 'The Canonical Classical Model of Political Economy', *Journal of Economic Literature*, 16: 1415–34.

_____. 1990. 'Revisionist Findings on Sraffa', in K. Bharadwaj and A *Schefold (eds)*, Essays on Piero Sraffa: Critical Perspectives on the Revival of Classical Theory. *Delhi: Oxford University Press*.

_____. 1991. 'Logic of the Historical Transformation Problem: Exchange Ratio under Simple Commodity Production', in G.A. Caravale (ed.), *Marx and Modern Economic Analysis, Vol. 1*. Aldershot: Edward Elgar.

_____. (2000a). 'Sraffa's Hits and Misses', in H.D. Kurz (ed.), *Critical Essays on Piero Sraffa's Legacy in Economics*. Cambridge: Cambridge University Press.

———. (2000b). 'Reply', in H.D. Kurz (ed.), *Critical Essays on Piero Sraffa's Legacy in Economics*. Cambridge: Cambridge University Press.

Samuelson, P.A. and E.M. Etula. 2006. 'Testing to Confirm that Leontief-Sraffa Matrix Equations for Input/Output Must Obey Constancy of Returns to Scale', *Economic Letters*, 90(2): 183–88.

Say, J.-B. [1803] 1818. *Traite D'Economie Politique, Ou Simple Exposition*. Fourth edition. A Paris, Chez Rapilly, Libraire Passsage Des Panoroma, No. 43.

Schefold, B. 1978a. 'Fixed Capital as a Joint-Product', *Jharbucher fur Nationalokonomie und Statistik*, 192: 415–39.

_____. 1978b. 'Multiple Product Techniques with Properties of Single Product Systems', *Journal of Economics*, 38: 29–53.

_____. 1989. *Mr. Sraffa on Joint Production and Other Essays*. London: Unwin Hyman.

_____. 1997. *Normal Prices, Technical Change and Accumulation*. London and New York: Macmillan and St. Martin's Press.

_____. 2005. 'Joint-Production: Triumph of Economic over Mathematical Logic?', *The European Journal of the History of Economic Thought*, 12(3): 525–52.

Schumpeter, J.A. [1912] 1934. *The Theory of Economic Development: An Inquiry into Profits, Capital, Credit, Interest, and Business Cycle*. Cambridge, MA: Harvard University Press.

_____. 1954. *History of Economic Analysis*. New York: Oxford University Press.

Sen, Amartya. 1978. 'On the Labour Theory of Value: Some Methodological Issues', *Cambridge Journal of Economics*, 2: 175–90.

_____. 2003. 'Sraffa, Wittgenstein, and Gramsci', *Journal of Economic Literature*, 41: 1240–255.

Seton, F. 1957. ' The "Transformation Problem" ', *The Review of Economic Studies*, 65: 149–60.

Shaikh, A. 1977. 'Marx's Theory of Value and the "Transformation Problem" ', in J. Schwartz (ed.), *The Subtle Anatomy of Capitalism*. Santa Monica: Goodyear Publishing Co.

_____. 1978. 'Political Economy and Capitalism: Notes on Dobb's Theory of Crisis', *Cambridge Journal of Economics*, 2: 233–51.

Shaikh, A. 1980. 'Marxian Competition versus Perfect Competition: Further Comments on the So-called Choice of Technique', *Cambridge Journal of Economics*, 4: 75–83.

_____. 1981. 'The Poverty of Algebra', in I. Steedman (ed.), *The Value Controversy*. London: Verso.

_____. 1984. 'The Transformation from Marx to Sraffa', in A. Freeman and E. Mandel (eds), *Ricardo, Marx, Sraffa*. London: Verso.

_____. 1998. 'The Empirical Strength of the Labour Theory of Value', in R. Bellofiore (ed.), *Marxian Economics: A Reappraisal, Vol. 2*. London: Macmillan.

Shibata, K. 1939. 'On the General Profit Rate', *Kyoto University Economic Review*, 14(1): 40–66.

Sinha, Ajit. 1996. 'A Critique of Part One of *Capital* Volume One: The Value Controversy Revisited', in P. Zarembka and A. Sinha (eds), *Research in Political Economy*, (15): 195–222.

_____. 1997. 'The Transformation Problem: A Critique of the "New Solution"', *Review of Radical Political Economics*, 29: 51–58.

_____. 1998. 'Hollander's Marx and Malthusianism: A Critique', *The History of Economic Review*, 29: 104–12.

_____. 2000. 'The Transformation Problem: Is the Standard Commodity a Solution', *Review of Radical Political Economics*, 32(2): 265–81.

_____. 2001a. 'Transformation Problem', *Readers Guide to Social Sciences*, ed., Jonathan Michie. London: Fitzroy Dearborn Publishers.

_____. 2001b. 'Review', *Review of Radical Political Economics*, 33: 241–44.

_____. 2003. 'Some Critical Reflections on Marx's Theory of Value', in R. Westra and A. Zuege (eds), *Value and the World Economy Today*. London: Palgrave.

_____. 2006a. 'A Comment on Sen's "Sraffa, Wittgenstein, and Gramsci"', *Journal of Economics Behavior and Organization*, 61(3): 504–12.

_____. 2006b. 'Some Critical Comments on de Vivo's Interpretation of Sraffa's Path to *Production of Commodities*', *Contributions to Political Economy*, 25: 83–89.

_____. 2007. 'Sraffa and the Assumption of Constant Returns to Scale: A Critique of Samuelson and Etula', *Contributions to Political Economy*, 26: 61–70.

_____. 2009. 'Sraffa and the Later Wittgenstein', *Contribution to Political Economy*, 28(1): 47–69.

_____. 'In Defence of Adam Smith's Theory of Value', *European Journal of the History of Economic Thought*, 17(1) (forthcoming).

_____. 'A Note on Ricardo's Invariable Measure of Value', *Cahiers d'economie politique*, 58 (forthcoming).

Sinha, Ajit. and M-S. Dupertuis. 2009a. 'Sraffa's System: Equal Rate of Profits and the Notion of Centre of Gravitation', *Journal of Economic Behavior and Organization*, 71(2): 495–501.

_____. 2009b. 'Sraffa and the Question of Equilibrium', *Cahiers d'economie politique*, 56(3): 91–100.

Smith, Adam. [1759] 1976. *The Theory of Moral Sentiments*, Sixth edition (1790) ed. D.D. Raphael and A.L. Macfie. Oxford: Oxford University Press.

_____. [1766] 1978. *Lectures on Jurisprudence*, ed. R.L. Meek, D.D. Raphael and P.G. Stein. Oxford: Oxford University Press.

_____. [1776] 1981. *An Inquiry into the Nature and Causes of the Wealth of Nations, Volumes I and II.* Indianapolis: Library Fund.

Sowell, T. 1960. 'Marx's "Increasing Misery" Doctrine', *American Economic Review*, 50(1): 111–20.

Sraffa, P. 1925. 'Sulle relazioni tra costo e quantita prodotta, *Annali di Economia*, Vol. 2: 277–328, trans. John Eatwell and A. Roncaglia, 'On the Relations between Cost and Quantity Produced', in L.L. Pasinetti (ed.), *Italian Economic Papers, Vol. 3*. Oxford: Oxford University Press.

_____. 1926. 'The Laws of Returns under Competitive Conditions', *The Economic Journal*, 36: 535–50.

_____. 1951. 'Introduction', in *Works and Correspondence of David Ricardo, Vol. I*. Cambridge: Cambridge University Press.

———. (1960). *Production of Commodities by Means of Commodities*. Cambridge: Cambridge University Press.

_____. 1962. 'Production of Commodities. A Comment', *The Economic Journal*, LXXII: 477–79.

_____. n.d. *Piero Sraffa Papers*. Wren Library, Trinity College, Cambridge.

St. Clair, O. 1953. 'David Ricardo: A Review Article', *South African Journal of Economics*, 21: 251–60.

Steedman, Ian. 1971. 'Marx on the Falling Rate of Profit', *Australian Economic Papers*, 10(6): 61–66.

_____. 1975. 'Positive Profits with Negative Surplus Value', *The Economic Journal*, 85: 114–23.

———. 1977. *Marx after Sraffa*. London: New Left Books.

———. 1980a. 'Returns to Scale and the Switch in Methods of Production', *Studi Economici*, 35: 5–13.

Steedman, Ian. 1980b. 'A Note on "Choice of Technique" under Capitalism', *Cambridge Journal of Economics*, 4: 61–64.

_____. 1982. ' Marx on Ricardo', in Ian Bradley and Michael Howard (eds), *Classical and Marxian Political Economy Essays in Honour of Ronald L. Meek*. London: MacMillan.

_____. 1984. 'Natural Prices, Differential Profit Rates and the Classical Competitive Process', *The Manchester School*, 52 (2): 123–40.

_____. 1985. 'Heterogeneous Labour, Money Wages, and Marx's Theory', *History of Political Economy*, 17(4): 551–74.

_____. 1991. 'The Irrelevance of Marxian Values', in G. A. Caravale (ed.), *Marx and Modern Economic Analysis, Vol. 1*. Aldershot: Edward Elgar.

Stigler, G.J. 1952. 'The Ricardian Theory of Value and Distribution', *Journal of Political Economy*, 60: 187–207.

_____. 1958. 'Ricardo and the 93% Labour Theory of Value', *American Economic Review*, 48: 357–67.

Stigler, G.J. 1976. 'The Successes and Failures of Professor Smith', *Journal of Political Economy*, 84(6): 1199–213.

Sweezy, Paul. [1942] 1949. *The Theory of Capitalist Development*. London: Dennis Dobson Limited.

Sylos-Labini, P. 1976. 'Competition: The Product Market', in T. Wilson and A.S. Skinner (eds), *The Market and the State: Essays in Honour of Adam Smith*. Oxford: Clarendon Press.

'Symposium 1966 on Reswitching of Methods', in *Quarterly Journal of Economics, 81*.

Torrens, Robert. 1818. 'Stricture on Mr. Ricardo's Doctrine Respecting Exchangeable Value', *Edinburgh Magazine* (October): 335–38.

_____. 1821. *An Essay on the Production of Wealth; with an Appendix, in which the Principles of Political Economy are applied to the Actual Circumstances of the Country*. London: Longman, Hurst, Rees, Orme, and Brown, Paternoster Row.

_____. 1827. *An Essay on the External Corn Trade*. Fourth edition. London: Longman, Rees, Orme, Brown, and Green.

Tucker, G.S.L. 1961. 'Ricardo and Marx', *Economica* 28: 252–69.

Varri, P. 1980. 'Prices, Rate of Profit and Life of Machines in Sraffa's Fixed Capital Model', in L.L. Pasinetti (ed.), *Essays on the Theory of Joint Production*. London: Macmillan.

Wakefield, E.G. 1843. 'Introduction', in E.G. Wakefield (ed.), *An Inquiry into the Nature and Causes of the Wealth of Nations*. London: Charles Knight & Co.

Wald, Abraham. [1936] 1951. 'On Some Systems of Equations of Mathematical Economics', *Econometrica*, 19: 368–403.

Walras, L. 1954. *Elements of Pure Economics*. Fourth edition. Edited by W. Jaffe. London: George Allen and Unwin Ltd.

Weizsacker, C. C. von. 1973. 'Morishima on Marx', *Economic Journal*, 83(332):1245–254.

Whewell, William. 1831. *Political Economy and Miscellaneous Writings* in *Collected Works of William Whewell, Vol. 14*. Edited by Richard Yeo. Bristol: Thoemmes Press, 2001.

Whitaker, A.C. 1904. *History and Criticism of the Labor Theory of Value in English Political Economy*. New York: Columbia University Press.

Wicksell, Knut. 1934. *Lectures on Political Economy, Vol. I: General Theory*. London: George Routledge and Sons, Ltd.

Wicksteed, P.H. [1884] 1938. 'The Marxian Theory of Value: *Das Kapital: A Critique*', *To-day*, October: also reprinted in *The Common Sense of Political Economy*, Vol. II, pp. 705–24. London: Routledge.

Wilson, G.W. and J.L. Pate. 1968. 'Ricardo's 93 Per Cent Labour Theory of Value: A Final Comment', *Journal of Political Economy*, 76: 128–36.

Winternitz, J. 1948. 'Values and Prices: A Solution of the So-called Transformation Problem', *Economic Journal*, 58: 276–80.

Wittgenstein, L. [1953] 1978. *Philosophical Investigations*. Oxford: Basil Blackwell.

Wolff, R.D., A. Callari and B. Roberts. 1984. 'A Marxian Alternative to the Traditional "Transformation Problem"', *Review of Radical Political Economics*, 16(2/3): 115–35.

Woods, J.C. (ed.). 1984. *Adam Smith: Critical Assessments, Vol. III*. London, New York: Routledge.

_____. 1985. *David Ricardo: Critical Assessments*, Vols. I-IV. London: Routledge.

Young, G. 1976. 'A Note on Marx's Terminology', *Science and Society*, 40(1): 72–78.

INDEX

Printed in the United States
by Baker & Taylor Publisher Services